D1599923

Keep Up Good Courage

A Yankee Family and the Civil War

For Cindy,
Alan

Fourteenth NHV Regimental Battle Flag. Courtesy of New Hampshire Historical Society

KEEP UP GOOD COURAGE

A Yankee Family and the Civil War

The Correspondence of Cpl. Lewis Q. Smith,
of Sandwich, New Hampshire,
Fourteenth Regiment New Hampshire Volunteers
1862–1865

ALAN FRASER HOUSTON

PETER E. RANDALL
PUBLISHER LLC
Portsmouth, New Hampshire
2006

Additional copies available from:
Sandwich Historical Society
P.O. Box 244, Center Sandwich, NH 03227

ISBN: 1-931807-49-3
ISBN13: 9781931807494

Library of Congress Control Number: 2006904284

Published by:
Peter E. Randall Publisher LLC
P. O. Box 4726
Portsmouth NH 03802
www.perpublisher.com

Book design: Grace Peirce

Contents

Preface . . . vii

Acknowledgments . . . xiii

1. Prologue to War . . . 1
2. Duty in Maryland: Guarding the Potomac and the Northwestern Approaches to Washington City, October 30 to December 31, 1862 . . . 13
3. Death and Darkness at Home, January 1 to January 31, 1863 . . . 39
4. Gloom Continues: Duty on the Potomac and Winter Camp at Poolesville, Maryland, February 1 to February 28, 1863 . . . 59
5. Politics, Smallpox, Sapping, and Spring, March 1 to April 21, 1863 . . . 77
6. Washington City: Duty in the Union Capital, April 22 to June 30, 1863 . . . 95
7. Rebel Invasion of New Hampshire and Union Successes, July 1 to July 31, 1863 . . . 117
8. More Guard Duty in the Capital, August 1 to October 31, 1863 . . . 131
9. The Holidays and Year's End, November 1 to December 31, 1863 . . . 151
10. Washington and Harpers Ferry, January 1 to February 28, 1864 . . . 167
11. Battle with Ballots and Duty at the Crescent City, March 1 to June 6, 1864 . . . 181
12. Searching for the Enemy, Affair at Bayou Grossetête, and Return to Washington, June 7 to July 31, 1864 . . . 201
13. Battles of Third Winchester (or Opequon Creek) and Fisher's Hill, August 1 to October 17, 1864 . . . 215
14. Battle of Cedar Creek: Eve of Near Defeat and Final Victory, October 18 to December 31, 1864 . . . 241
15. The New Year 1865: Ordered to Georgia and War's End, January 1 to July 27, 1865 . . . 265

Epilogue: Lewis Q. Smith, Post–Civil War . . . 283

Endnotes . . . 293

Bibliography . . . 317

Index . . . 323

About the Author . . . 337

John J. Weed, Leslie Weed, & Lucy M. (Smith) Weed, about 1907. Author's Family

Preface

The impetus for the publication of the Civil War letters and diary of Lewis Quimby Smith lies in a fortuitous chain of events in 2002 that began with the *Eighty-Third Annual Excursion of the Sandwich Historical Society,* known as the "Bulletin." Tom Okie's article in the Bulletin, titled "Coming Back to the Land: 240 Years of Human Activity at Mead Base," documented the history of Mead Base, the site where the Smith family lived and farmed, at the foot of Mount Israel in Sandwich, New Hampshire. In his article, Okie cited a number of Lewis Smith's Civil War letters in the collection of the Sandwich Historical Society—letters that increased in significance with the discovery of Lewis's Civil War diary.

In the fall of 2002, my mother, Miriam Taylor Houston, and her sister, Martha Taylor Lea, visited their ninety-eight-year-old cousin by marriage, Alice Weed. Alice, who at this writing lives in Needham, Massachusetts, is the widow of Leslie Weed (1906–1990), son of John J. Weed (1884–1957) and Lucy M. Smith (Lewis's granddaughter), of North Sandwich.[1] At some point, Alice indicated that she had an item that might be of interest—it was Lewis's 1864 pocket diary. Lewis, a three-year volunteer of Company K, Fourteenth Regiment of New Hampshire Volunteers, fought in Gen. Phil Sheridan's important 1864 Shenandoah Valley campaign.

Lewis married Mary Elizabeth "Libby" Paine of Moultonborough, and they named their fourth child (of nine) Lucy M., born about 1860. Lucy M. (Smith) Hutchins died in childbirth and her daughter, also Lucy M., was adopted and reared by Lewis and Libby and given the Smith name. John J. Weed, "Uncle John," my great-uncle, married Lucy M. Smith in 1905. Thus,

1. Larkin D. Weed (1855–1937), the builder of Sandwich's Wentworth Library and the town hall, was Miriam and Martha's grandfather. John J. Weed was Larkin Weed's second son. John's siblings were Chester A. Weed, Hortense (Weed) Taylor, and Cleveland Weed.

Lewis's diary passed to his daughter Lucy M.; to granddaughter Lucy M. ("Aunt Lucy," wife of Uncle John); to Leslie and Alice Weed; and thence by donation to the Sandwich Historical Society.

Recognizing an opportunity for an article focusing on the diary, I contacted the Sandwich Historical Society for access to Lewis Q. Smith's correspondence. I was pleasantly surprised by the number of letters: ultimately about 125 of them. It was obvious that the letters should be published, and the scope of the project became much broader than just the 1864 diary. More important, the collection includes many letters not only from Lewis to home, but also from Libby and other family members to Lewis. Under conditions of rain, sleet, snow, and mud—camp life—it is remarkable that the correspondence from home survived. The letters are generally not the writings of sophisticated correspondents and, in that sense, they do not stand alone. Moreover, most are devoid of context, which I have attempted to provide without losing focus on the collection or attempting to write a history of the war.

Because some of the letters are undated, fortunately just a handful, and a larger number only partially dated, the first task was to establish a chronological order. The letters that are undated, or incompletely dated, can usually be placed in sequence from the context of events. Where dates are erroneous and corrected, the change is added in brackets. In the absence of a date, the best estimate is similarly placed. I have tried to identify most events, people, and places that the correspondents refer to whenever possible. Where identification is tenuous, it has been relegated to a footnote or omitted altogether. Comment on single or isolated references has been limited to avoid a mere catalog of names. In the same vein, a definitive elaboration of all the Smith relations—there were *many* Smith households in Sandwich—is beyond the scope of this effort.

The letters are transcribed as they were written, without altering spellings (or misspellings) and punctuation (or lack thereof). Realistically, to add "sic" after every idiosyncratic spelling would render the correspondence unreadable. In situations of obvious repetitions of words or phrases, the repetition has been deleted. Occasional undecipherable words are replaced with dashes that about equal the words and their characters (--- ----- --). Areas of ink blotting that obscure are indicated (blot).

I have taken the liberty of placing a double space between unterminated sentences to sustain readability. With the same goal in mind, I have attempted to minimize insertions and footnotes except for occasional omitted letters or words that present stumbling blocks in reading or in meaning. Finally, writing paper and postage were not to be wasted during the war: the result was run-on sentences without paragraphs or indentations. These writers used every square inch of space.

To avoid secondary sources as much as possible and to focus on primary ones, I have used fragments from the letters of some of Lewis's contemporaries in the Fourteenth (and occasionally from outside the Fourteenth) to develop context. I have also relied on newspapers of the period—the *Winnipesaukee Gazette;* the *Belknap Gazette and Carroll County Advertiser;* the *New Hampshire Democrat,* which became the *Laconia Democrat* in 1861; the *Boston Daily Evening Transcript;* the *New York Times;* and others—for background material. In addition, the published (in 1882) history of the Fourteenth, written by Francis H. Buffum (Company F), of Winchester, New Hampshire, has been useful.

The Sandwich Historical Society's Lewis Q. Smith collection of correspondence follows his experiences as a soldier and his exposure to disease, privation, and, later, battle. The letters provide a rare, if not unique, view of Civil War life at home, on the farm, in New Hampshire. The situation of the home folks was often not much better than Lewis's. They, too, faced disease, epidemics, financial straits, uncertain politics, rumors, and, at times, unreliable war news. They anxiously awaited an end to the conflict, an end that always lay just over the horizon.

Both Lewis and his family continually exhorted each other to "keep up good courage," and perhaps these exhortations kept these New Hampshire farm folk from despairing, though at times they came close. As some of Lewis's family lived elsewhere than Sandwich—in Moultonborough, Meredith Village, Lake Village (Lakeport), and Manchester—the news from home is therefore broader than just one town. Throughout the reading and transcribing of these letters, I pondered why Lewis and his friends, about eighty Sandwich men, enlisted and fought. To do other than join would have meant forgoing some incentives (bounties) and facing uncertain prospects with the draft. Thus, the number of conscripts from the draft(s) in the Civil War was actually quite small.

Having contemplated the same choices (the draft or enlistment) myself in 1969, I volunteered, together with a handful of friends. The draft offered fewer or no options. Fighting is another question altogether, and there is no simple answer as to why soldiers and sailors fight. For them, the opposite of "being there" is desertion, fostered by hunger, privation, poor pay, incompetent leaders, lack of support from home, and failure of political will on the national level. Although the North had all of these problems in varying degrees and at various times, it continued the contest and succeeded because its soldiers and sailors persevered. Lewis wrote that he would stay and see "the thing" through, but in the end, it is the political process, or its failure, that places the soldier or sailor in the position of killing or being killed. That is the real choice—or, perhaps, no choice at all.

It is likely that few of the Sandwich volunteers had ever been south of the Mason-Dixon line or seen a black face. Lewis Q. Smith was probably typical of his peers in that he had no strong abolitionist sentiments. His concerns were home, family, and, perhaps reluctantly, preservation of the Union. Smith's preoccupation can be seen as health, both his and his family's, often precarious and threatened, followed by news from home, and, last, the progress of the war. Lewis's anxiety, usually mitigated by frequent letters from his wife and family, is palpable and by no means unusual. Several wars later, his reality is reflected in a vignette from *All Quiet on the Western Front:* "He is worried. His wife has to look after the farm. They've already taken away two of his horses. Every day he reads the papers that come, to see whether it is raining in his little corner . . . They haven't brought in the hay yet."[2] In Lewis and Libby Smith's rural New Hampshire, success on the farm was survival itself.

Nor is it a surprise that Lewis's letters have few sentiments or even descriptions of the later battles that he experiences. Again his situation is not unique: "They [front-line days] are too serious for us to be able to reflect on them at once. If we did that, we should have been destroyed long ago. I soon found out this much:—terror can be endured so long as a man simply ducks;—but it kills, if a man thinks about it . . . We want to live at any price; so we cannot burden ourselves with feelings which, though they might be

---

2. Erich Maria Remarque, translated from the German by A. W. Wheen, *All Quiet on the Western Front* (Boston: Little, Brown and Company, 1958), 80–81.

ornamental enough in peace time, would be out of place here."[3] No "ornamental" prose or sentiments are found in Lewis's simple correspondence, but they do reside in Civil War regimental histories—including that of the Fourteenth written years after the smoke of battle had cleared and the dead were buried.

3. Ibid., 139–40.

Acknowledgments

In some jest, my wife, mentor, and partner, Jourdan, and I classify people into gatekeepers and facilitators. Fortunately, the latter are far, far more numerous than the gatekeepers. First and foremost among the facilitators are the staff and officers of the Sandwich Historical Society, of Sandwich, New Hampshire, who have opened their collection for my use. Without their participation and assistance, this project would not have even had a start. Former curator Craig Evans, of Brookfield, New Hampshire, past presidents Bruce Montgomery and Peter Booty, and now-president Caroline Snyder have lent me help and encouragement.

Local historian Geoff Burrows has kept me straight on local geography, burial locations, and place names. Dottie Burrows sent images of Lewis Smith and the farm from the collection of her late husband, Robert Burrows (1933-2003). My cousin, Jonathan Taylor, also of Sandwich and a Weed descendant, provided a number of images in higher resolution than I previously had had. Jon has been my Sandwich anchor and has been most generous with his time. At the beginning, another relative, uncle Frederick Lea, a World War II army veteran, first copied Lewis Smith's diary and sent me his typescript transcription.

Other facilitators are scattered about the state of New Hampshire and beyond. In Concord, Bill Copeley and David Smolen of the New Hampshire Historical Society have generously copied and sent me material, as well as assisting in their library. Similarly, a small city block away, the staff of the New Hampshire State Library have maintained their humor and helped me with their considerable resources, in summer, when the "air conditioning" is a fan by the open door. Russell Bastedo, curator of artifacts at the statehouse, facilitated my pursuit of the Fourteenth Regiment's tattered battle flags.

Farther from central New Hampshire, the staff at Milne Special Collections and Archives Division at the University of New Hampshire, especially Rebecca Earnest and director Bill Ross, have patiently taken phone calls, answered inquiries, photocopied what could be copied, and helped me in their reading room. In the southwest corner of the state, Alan Rumrill, of the Cheshire County Historical Society in Keene, generously searched that society's collections and sent copies of more soldiers' correspondence.

Barbara Krieger of the Rauner Special Collections Library of the Dartmouth College Library also answered my inquiries, found more writers of the Fourteenth, and even sent me page copies of a diary without my asking. Peter Collins of Dartmouth's Baker–Berry Library helped me locate mid-nineteenth century newspapers that would have been read by Carroll and Belknap County (N.H.) citizens. When these papers were not available through interlibrary loan, he directed me to a microfilm reproduction service that had them.

Outside of the Granite State, I found Ben Ritter at the visitor center in Winchester, Virginia, who kindly provided directions to the national cemetery there. Fortunately, I kept his card. As a former facilitator librarian and active in local history, Ben kept me clear of geographical confusion, town name changes, and even the pronunciation of "Opequon." He was willing to read the Shenandoah Valley chapters and sent me some valuable sources that I had not uncovered. High school classmate Bobbi Jackson and her husband Bruce, also of Winchester, kindly photographed monuments at the cemetery and sent images of superior quality to my own.

Farther south, the staffs of the New Orleans Public Library, the Williams Research Center of the Historic New Orleans Collection, and the Special Collections Department of Tulane University were generous with their time as I rushed in during lunch hours and before closings to maximize my research during a week-long emergency medicine review course. In Savannah, thanks go to the Savannah Public Library (where there were usually more children than adults awaiting the door's opening) and the Georgia Historical Society, both excellent facilities with helpful, energetic staffs.

Back home in Durango, Fort Lewis College's Reed Library was a tremendous resource. In particular, Phyllis Kroupa processed numerous interlibrary loan requests, and no submission, not even one tied in Gordian knots, ever went to the bottom of the pile. Her energy and commitment are commendable.

Closing the gate on this project leaves one with the fun of discovery—not only of letters, diaries, and images—but also of places, good will, and people, along the way. I am indebted to all.

~ One ~

PROLOGUE TO WAR

I have decided to call into service an additional force of 300,000 men.
—Abraham Lincoln, July 1, 1862

BY NEW YEAR'S DAY OF 1862, the armies of North and South were in their winter camps; other than skirmishing and small engagements, there was, in general, little military activity. With the new year, New Hampshire's citizens experienced severe cold and high winds. Many people in "exposed localities feared to retire at all" and others "passed many wakeful hours" as chimneys were blown off buildings.[1] Near Sewell's Falls, in Concord, a three-hundred-foot span of bridge was "lifted bodily from its supporters and tossed with a tremendous crash upon the ice of the river." In Nashua, "the car house of the Concord Railroad" was "completely demolished."[2] The same wind "at the [Franconia] Notch moved a barn at the Profile House, 30 by 100 feet, three inches, through its entire length."[3]

Amid the cold, William M. Weed's store burned in Sandwich, a typical New Hampshire farming community, lying at the foot of the White Mountains to the north and at the head of the Lakes Region to the south. The fire, in Sandwich's "Lower Corner," destroyed not only the building but also the records and files of the Carroll County Court—Weed was clerk of courts.[4] There were also outbreaks of smallpox, both in the nation's capital and in Laconia, New Hampshire, said to have been introduced into the latter community by a visitor from New York, or possibly from Sandwich itself. In Sandwich, smallpox ran for several weeks but was predominantly "a mild form." The family of Albert Tilton was an exception, losing "two lovely children," one four years old, a second, five months.[5] Quarantines, "prompt and efficient measures to confine it," were quickly established.[6]

In New Hampshire's manufacturing localities, textile mills were finally slowing down due to both war-related shortages and the rising cost of cotton. Many converted to wool: "The woolen mills are all making money

Map of Sandwich, New Hampshire, 1860. Sandwich Historical Society.

rapidly from the army demand for their fabrics."[7] There was also a resurgence of the "old fashioned spinning wheel and the hand loom."[8] In a matter of months, the price of wool, reflecting increased demand, rose to levels not seen in decades. If the state's residents needed woolens, it was undoubtedly the result of continuing cold weather.

Joseph E. Smith, of Sandwich, was discovered frozen on the morning of February 25. "Bewildered," probably from cold, he had wandered from the road leading home and was found sitting in a pasture against a stone wall—"up to his knees in snow."[9] In Bellows Falls, Vermont, just across the Connecticut River about fifty miles west of Concord, a man and a woman also died from cold: "Three empty rum jugs found near them furnished their epitaph."[10]

As winter gave way to spring on the Smith farm, which lay at the foot of Mount Israel on the Sandwich Notch Road, sapping began, preceding the anxieties and hopes over planting. The first Smiths to farm there, hailing from England, initially lived on the New Hampshire seacoast. Jacob Smith (1739–1816), of Exeter, who served in the Continental Army during the Revolutionary War, moved to Sandwich with his wife, Dorothy. Their son, Eliphalet Smith (1741–1824), worked the land and was active in town affairs in the latter decades of the eighteenth century.

Eliphalet, Lewis Quimby Smith's grandfather, who also served in the Revolution, fathered seven children. One of them, John Smith (1793–1869), married Elizabeth "Eliza" Webster (the daughter of Sandwich's Dr. Jacob Webster) and raised eight (or possibly nine) children on the farm—Lewis was next to last in order of birth. As the Civil War unfolded, John and Eliza farmed jointly with Lewis; his wife, Libby; and Lewis and Libby's children. On the Smith homestead, the hard work and simple joy of sapping were annual, as were the uncertainties of spring

Lewis Quimby Smith (1832–1913) Courtesy Dottie Burrows. Collection of Robert Burrows

weather, breaking the ground, and planting. Added were mounting anxieties related to the war, which began in April 1861 with the Confederate shelling of Fort Sumter at Charleston, South Carolina.

By the spring of 1862, after a number of Union embarrassments in the field and a full year of war, the Lincoln administration recognized that the struggle would be prolonged. The enthusiastic ninety-day volunteers of 1861 had long been mustered out and the country again needed men—many more. On June 30, 1862, President Abraham Lincoln wrote "To the Governors of the several States":

> The capture of New Orleans, Norfolk, and Corinth by the national forces has enabled the insurgents to concentrate a large force at and about Richmond, which place we must take with the least possible delay; in fact, there will soon be no formidable insurgent force except at Richmond. With so large an army there, the enemy can threaten us on the Potomac and elsewhere. Until we have reestablished the national authority, all these places must be held, and we must keep a respectable force in front of Washington. But this, from the diminished strength of our army by sickness and casualties, renders an addition to it necessary . . . To accomplish the object stated we require without delay 150,000 men, including those [50,000 on May 30, 1862] recently called for by the Secretary of War.[11]

New Hampshire Gov. Nathaniel S. Berry (1796–1894), of Bristol, was a former Democrat who became an abolitionist and an early advocate of emancipation. Elected as a Republican in 1861, he was considered a strong "war governor."[12] On June 28, 1862, Governor Berry and seventeen other governors submitted a joint letter to President Lincoln. Their message concluded with the sentence: "All believe that the decisive moment is near at hand, and to that end the people of the United States are desirous to aid promptly in furnishing all reenforcements that you may deem needful to sustain our Government."[13] The president's response was issued from the Executive Mansion in Washington City, as the nation's capital was then known, on July 1, 1862:

> Gentlemen: Fully concurring in the wisdom of the views expressed to me in so patriotic a manner by you in the communication of the 28th day of June, I have decided to call into service an additional force of 300,000 men. I suggest and recommend that the troops should be chiefly of infantry. The quota of your State would be____. I trust that they may be

> enrolled without delay, so as to bring this unnecessary and injurious civil war to a speedy and satisfactory conclusion. An order fixing the quotas of the respective States will be issued by the War Department to-morrow.
>
> Abraham Lincoln[14]

Lewis was one of about eighty-five men from Sandwich who answered the call to arms. On July 30, 1862, farmer John M. Prescott was the first to enlist. Lewis volunteered with the majority of enlistees—amid a veritable rush—on August 14. There was a good reason for the mid-August scramble: a presidential order prohibited bounties for volunteers to new regiments after August 15. Following that date, bounties could be paid only to fill regiments already in the field or for other specific conditions, stipulations that expired on September 1. If Uncle Sam's incentives to enlist by August 15 were insufficient and the three hundred thousand were not raised, the deficiency in any state would "be made up by special draft from the militia."[15]

Furthermore, Secretary of War Edwin M. Stanton issued an order on August 8, 1862, prohibiting those subject to the draft (generally men ages eighteen to forty-five) from leaving the country.[16] Stanton also ordered the arrest of anyone eligible who *left* his "county or State before such draft is made . . ."[17] There was a bounty of a different sort for an arresting officer—five dollars deducted from the apprehended soldier's pay as well as the cost of both the arrest and transportation to the nearest military post. Additionally, the writ of habeas corpus was "suspended in respect to all persons so arrested and detained . . . "[18] Provision was made for legitimate travel: "The Governors of the respective States are authorized to give passes and permits to their own citizens desiring to leave the State without intent to evade military duty."[19] There was nothing equivocal about Lincoln's call to arms.

"Rigid enforcement" of Stanton's order and arrests of "skeedaddlers" began almost immediately in New York, Baltimore, Chicago, and Detroit.[20] Three such fugitives from Plymouth, New Hampshire, boarded the cars of the Boston, Concord, and Montreal Railroad at nearby Rumney, New Hampshire, headed for Canada. An alert agent spotted the trio, read them the War Department's order, and threatened them with arrest. The men disembarked at West Rumney and walked the eight or nine miles home. As of August 8, passports were no longer granted to anyone eligible for the draft. The rather sudden imposition of these constraints may have had an impact on tourism in the Granite State:

> Conjugal Dilemmas. Gentlemen whose better halves are ruralizing in the pleasant places of New Hampshire . . . have been sadly puzzled by the order . . . for the arrest of persons leaving the county or State . . . His honor the Mayor, to his other multitudinous duties has superadded the service of affixing the broad seal of the city to passes securing to disconsolate husbands and lovers immunity from arrest while in the amiable pursuit of wives and sweethearts . . . [*Chelsea Telegraph*][21]

The War Department order also dealt with the suppression of "disloyal practices." Governor Berry had Dr. Nathaniel Batchelder, of Epping, detained for "discouraging enlistments." A newspaper account noted that "Dr. Batchelder, who is an old line Democrat, and has been known lately as the 'Epping secessionist,' is now in Portsmouth jail."[22] The order of August 8 also suspended habeas corpus "in respect to all persons" incarcerated "for disloyal practices."[23] At that time, baseball, a little more than two decades old, was poised for a mercurial rise in popularity. "Hardball," as politically descriptive, lay more than a century over the horizon; nonetheless, it characterizes the action taken by a government whose very survival was at stake.

Given these terms, it is not a great surprise that about seventy of the Sandwich volunteers enlisted from August 13 to August 15. The recruiting officers, paid a commission for each enlistee, were Oliver H. Marston and William M. Weed, both of Sandwich, who, it would appear, must have had an easy task. The men signed up at Town Hall, located at the time in North Sandwich. Sandwich supported the enlistees with a one-hundred-dollar bounty for each. However, federal bounties were no longer paid "up front." Too many bounty jumpers simply pocketed the money and deserted—some to enlist repeatedly and gain more bounties, often federal, state, and local. The government had learned to defer payments, to the detriment of honest enlistees and their families.

New Hampshire's men filled the state's quota of about forty-five hundred by August 21: a draft would not be necessary. Sandwich's Company K volunteers had an average age of just under twenty-eight years, with the youngest seventeen and the oldest forty-four. Of the sixty-two privates, corporals, and sergeants, forty-eight were farmers, five were shoemakers, and nine represented other trades: student, blacksmith, teamster, boatman, carpenter, tinman, laborer, furniture dealer, and tailor—a fair cross-section of the town itself.

Sandwich's 1860 population, like that of the state, was intensely homogeneous: white, Anglo-Saxon, and mostly Protestant. Ninety-five percent of the town's residents (2,116 of 2,227) had been born in New Hampshire. Those foreign born were rare: two Irishmen and five Canadians.[24] There was some value derived from Sandwich's homogeneity: Mutual backgrounds and interdependent lives in a small community (or communities) translated to unity and strength under arms. The Fourteenth Regiment of New Hampshire Volunteers and the Sandwich men who constituted most of Company K were no exception.

This cohesiveness diminished later, however, especially after the institution of a federal draft by the Enrollment Act of March 3, 1863. As "recruits" (draftees and substitutes) reached the lines that summer, there were no such community bonds. Sgt. John Henry Jenks, of Keene, New Hampshire, and a member of the Fourteenth's Company C, reflected on the impact of recruits in a letter home from Washington on July 30, 1863:

> There are but few Regt's but what is filled up with foreigners and all those York and Western Dutch are good for nothing for duty in the city. Some days half of the Regt. will get in the guard house for getting drunk. While very few of our Regt. have been picked up in the city drunk, and we have but very few who are not New England born.[25]

Beginning on August 14, 1862, the Sandwich volunteers drilled several times per week. On September 19, after traveling to Concord "without much drunkenness," the regiment assembled and seventeen of the eighty-five men from Sandwich (plus one from Moultonborough) were rejected by the examining surgeon.[26] Stripped, the enlistees were examined for free use of all four limbs (mobility was essential); ample chest; perfect hearing, vision, and speech; no visible tumors; no evidence of old head or leg wounds; no ruptures (hernias); and not subject to seizures or insobriety. On the afternoon of September 22, any man lacking a vaccination scar was vaccinated against smallpox. Medical officers could provide certificates of disability (exemptions), but had to maintain a wary eye for candidates feigning such. On the other hand, they had to be equally alert for those men who attempted to conceal chronic problems. To say that medical examinations were subject to abuse in either direction would be an understatement.

Finally, as a result of medical exemptions and in order to fill out their company of one hundred men, the Sandwich volunteers agreed to combine

Capt. Oliver H. Marston, of Company K and Sandwich, Author's Collection

Lt. Moulton S. Webster, of Company K and Sandwich, Author's Collection

ranks with two dozen volunteers from Pembroke, New Hampshire. As part of the agreement, Jason D. Snell, of Pembroke, became 1st lieutenant while Oliver H. Marston and Moulton S. Webster, both of Sandwich, served as captain and 2nd lieutenant, respectively. Prior to their arrival at Concord, the Sandwich men had elected fifty-two-year-old Calvin Hoit as company captain and Marston and Webster as 1st and 2nd lieutenants. Hoit, who had served in New Hampshire's militia and had been captain of the Nineteenth Regiment from 1841 to 1846, for reasons unknown, failed to arrive with Company K.[27]

Although the officers were elected by the soldiers, they were commissioned by the governor and his council. Sandwich's Oliver H. Marston, who at age twenty-four was in charge of the company in Hoit's absence, wrote:

> We are having considerable of a time about the Capt. They are trying to shove him out & I don't know but what they will. They have a petition signed by over 40 of the company to give to the Gove[r]nor.[28]

One week later, Marston was commissioned as Company K's captain: "as it is decided that I shall have it."[29] Marston would go on to survive both illness and a gunshot wound to his left arm. At the battle of Cedar Creek, where he "acted with great coolness," he assumed command of the Fourteenth after Capt. Theodore Ripley was captured by the enemy.[30] Marston would be promoted to lieutenant colonel on March 24, 1865.

Company K, thus constituted, was the last formed of the ten companies comprising the Fourteenth Regiment of New Hampshire Volunteers (NHV), and would serve for the next three years. Four of the Fourteenth's companies were from Cheshire County; the other six were from Carroll, Coos, Grafton, Hillsborough, Merrimack, and Sullivan Counties. Of course, the men of Company K were not the only ones from Sandwich to serve in the war; a fair number served in the Eighteenth Regiment and others were scattered about the remaining seventeen infantry regiments, cavalry and artillery units, and sharpshooters.

The regiment camped in Concord and drilled daily. On October 9, the men were issued rubber blankets, for use as ground cloths, and haversacks, and each was paid his fifty-dollar state bounty on the following day. After receiving muskets on October 15, the regiment formed before the statehouse for inspection on October 16 and received its colors. Spirits were high. Reflecting a common misperception, Company C's Sgt. J. Henry Jenks wrote: "most of the folks think the war is most over."[31] With departure from Concord imminent, many of the men attended to last-minute items amid a "continual swarm of hawkers & pedlars of every mix . . ." Because marked clothes and "equipments" reduced the "probability of losing them . . . stencil men [were] doing a lively business marking & cutting plates."[32]

Some men bought bulletproof vests, a different sort of plates fabricated of heavy iron that hung over the torso and were inevitably discarded on the first hot, overloaded march along the Potomac River. Even Jenks had been interested in the armor. On October 3, he wrote to his wife: "I went down to town yesterday and examined one of the bullet proof vests. I shall buy one I think. Shut [should] I?"[33] It is not known that he did, but in the end, it wouldn't really matter.

On October 18, the regiment's ten companies, totaling about one thousand men, marched a mile and a half to the railroad station and embarked for Worcester, Massachusetts. After passing through Norwich, Connecticut, they transferred at Allyn's Point, near New London, to a steamer taking them to Jersey City, New Jersey. Passenger cars of the Camden and Amboy Railroad bore them to Camden, New Jersey, after which the regiment crossed the Delaware River. After a march across Philadelphia, another train conveyed them to Baltimore.

On April 19, 1861, a violent mob had killed a handful of Sixth Regiment Massachusetts Volunteers as they arrived in Baltimore, the first Union soldiers to die in the war. Northerners were shocked. The deaths brought the war to their door. Consequently, the Fourteenth's men were issued two rounds of ammunition for their "Old Harper Ferry musketts of the pattern of 1852."[34] Any defense, perhaps, was better than none, although the proposition is debatable, as no caps were provided with the ammunition. Rolling into Baltimore at four in the morning, there "were more Hectors and Nestors in the smoky cars on that dark morning than ever rallied on the plains of Troy." Upon pulling "into the dreadful Baltimore station," the men discovered they were surrounded—"three negroes, two drunken sailors, a policeman, and two newsboys prematurely out of bed."[35]

Arriving in Washington without incident, the regiment camped about a mile east of the Capitol. They had just missed the Confederates' bold foray into Maryland, which culminated in the battle of Antietam. With winter imminent, the campaigning season was about over and the Fourteenth would soon be in winter quarters—their assignment, picket duty on the upper Potomac. Serving with regiments from Maine, Massachusetts, and Vermont and a detachment of New York cavalry, the Fourteenth belonged to Col. A. B. Jewett's brigade, one of four brigades ordered to the "Defenses North of the Potomac" at Offutt's Cross-Roads, Maryland.

At the end of March 1863, Jewett's brigade would be designated Corps of Observation at White's Ford and Edward's Ferry, both Potomac crossings, and at nearby Poolesville, Maryland.[36] On October 24, 1862, with the band playing and colors streaming, the regiment, including Lewis Smith and many of his neighbors, marched down Pennsylvania Avenue past the White House and followed the Chesapeake and Ohio Canal from Georgetown upriver along the northern bank of the Potomac.

Lincoln's summons to arms on July 1, 1862, had defined not only the numbers needed but also the mission: the protection of Washington and the Potomac River and the capture of Richmond. After another two years of war, the Union Army's mission would change. No longer would protection of fixed positions or the capture of Richmond alone suffice. The Lincoln administration and its newer, more aggressive generals would seek to destroy both the enemy's force in the field and his sources of supply.

A blockade of the entire southern coastline by the federal navy and control of the Mississippi River by navy and army efforts validated the Anaconda Plan, originally advocated by Gen. Winfield Scott (1786–1866), to encircle and strangle the Confederacy. For two long years, reflecting President Lincoln's June 30 policy, the Fourteenth guarded the approaches to Washington and served provost (military police) duty in the capital. In their third year, led by Gen. Philip Henry Sheridan (1831–1888) in the Shenandoah Valley, they would destroy Gen. Jubal Early's (1816–1894) army and lay waste to the granary of the rebellion.

When Lewis Quimby Smith departed for war, he left behind family and friends, although seven other Sandwich Smiths went with him.[37] Remaining behind were his parents, John and Eliza (Webster) Smith; his wife, Libby; and five children: sons John B., Frank B., and Hiram G. and daughters Lucy M. and Hepsa A., ages, approximately, six, five, four, two and a half, and one year old, respectively. A sixth child, Lewis E., from all appearances, was born very shortly after his father's departure.

One of Lewis and Libby's best friends was Asa Magoon. Asa, a neighbor, was like family, and in fact was married to Mary Eliza Smith, the daughter of nearby Levi Smith. Asa also farmed and was one of Sandwich's few foreign born: from "Canada East," Stanstead County, Quebec, just over the border from Newport, Vermont.[38] Another Smith family intimate was Moulton S. Webster, a machinist, born in Sutton, Vermont, on October 9, 1823, who moved with his parents to Sandwich at an early age. His father, Samuel W. Webster, was a brother of Eliza Webster Smith, Lewis's mother—Lewis and Moulton were first cousins. Moulton had spent a few years in Massachusetts, where he served as a sergeant in the Sixth Massachusetts Militia. Moulton subsequently enlisted from Sandwich with the mid-August rush. Asa served as a private and Moulton as Company K's second lieutenant.[39] Both are mentioned frequently in the Smiths' correspondence.

Lewis's encouragement to the folks back home to "keep up good courage," reciprocated by his family, was essential for coping with the trials of the next three years. As Lewis, his Sandwich cohorts, and the other New Hampshire men of the Fourteenth marched by the White House toward duty on the upper Potomac, the transition to soldiering was now under way, albeit slowly.

~ *Two* ~

Duty in Maryland:

Guarding the Potomac and the Northwestern Approaches to Washington City October 30 to December 31, 1862

> *I think of a dear brother sick in a land of strangers with[out] the comforts of life and a dear niece one that seems to us more like a sister suffering the agonies of death and all I can do is to sit here alone and weep over them not being able to lend a helping hand in this time of greatest need.*
>
> —Lucy Jane (Smith) Wiggin, December 26, 1862

THE WAR'S FIRST CHALLENGE WAS DEATH NOT FROM battle, but instead from illness—bacilli, not bullets. As Lewis settled in camp, he became ill and, incapacitated for months, experienced a very close brush with death. He quite likely had typhoid fever, a severe illness often contracted from bacteria-laden water or food contaminated by typhoid carriers. Typhoid is characterized by persistent fever, often as long as four to eight weeks in duration, with profound loss of appetite, weight loss, and, at times, change in mental state or confusion. Death was not uncommon: in the Fourteenth's camp, typhoid claimed twenty-two lives by the third week of January 1863.[1] It was said that "typhoid fever revels in every camp on the [Potomac] river."[2] Prevention, not clearly recognized at the time, was an issue of basic sanitation.

Company K lost seventeen of its soldiers to disease by the time of its mustering out in the summer of 1865—more than were killed or mortally wounded in battle. Nor was Company K's experience unusual; most of the other companies lost almost twice the number to disease than from battle. At year's end, Lewis's family would be equally devastated by the serious illness, perhaps typhoid, of a young niece over the Christmas holidays.

Col. Jacob Smith (1739–1816) & Dorothy Smith

↓

Eliphalet Smith (1762–1848) & Mercy Smith

↓

John Smith (1793–1869) & Elizabeth "Eliza" (Webster) Smith

↓

Lewis Quimby Smith and Siblings
Birth Dates from Census/Death Records

Mary W., b. 1817, d. 1848, married Jonathan P. Chase

Sally M., b. 1818, married Jonathan P. Chase

Sarah, b. 1819

Benjamin Burleigh, b. 1820, married Dorcas Folsom

Susan A., b. 1822, married Albert F. Hackett

Jacob, b. 1826

Lucy Jane, b. 1831, married Joseph "Frank" Wiggin

Lewis Quimby, b. January 20, 1832, m. Mary Elizabeth Paine

Lizzie Ann, b. 1843, married Charles E. "Ned" Moulton

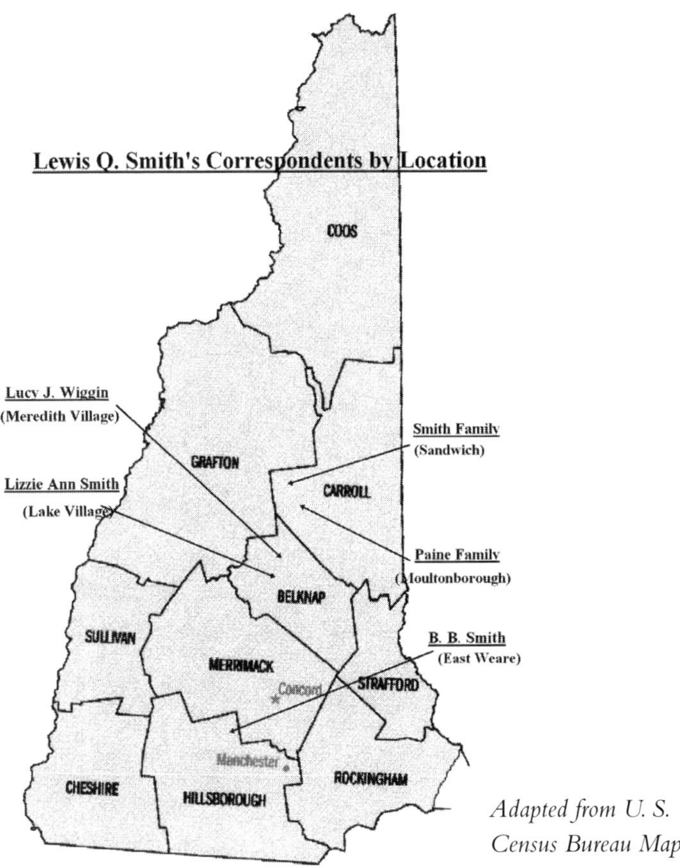

Adapted from U. S. Census Bureau Map

Lewis had six older living siblings, but to his great irritation, only two corresponded. Sisters Sally M. (Smith) Chase and Sarah were fourteen and thirteen years his senior, respectively, and brother Benjamin Burleigh, "B. B." or occasionally "B," twelve years. Susan A. (Smith) Hackett and brother Jacob followed B. B. and were born ten and six years before Lewis. Sister Lucy Jane, to whom Lewis was quite close, preceded Lewis by one year. The much younger Lizzie Ann Smith followed. Other than to and from his wife, most of Lewis's correspondence was with B. B., Lucy Jane, and Lizzie Ann. Lucy, who was married to harnessmaker J. (Joseph) Frank Wiggin, of Meredith Village, New Hampshire, was a dedicated and sanguine writer. Lewis also corresponded with several in-laws, often addressed as "brother" or "sister," a common practice at the time.

The earliest surviving letter of the Civil War period, dated only August 25, is from Lizzie Ann Smith, from Lake Village, now Lakeport, New Hampshire. Given the familiarity she expresses, it is difficult to not conclude that she is a sister to Lewis and Lucy. On January 23, 1863, at age nineteen, in Meredith, she married Charles E. "Ned" Moulton, a twenty-seven-year-old foundry worker from Gilford.[3] However, born about 1843, she would have been a rather late child of Eliza W. Smith, at about age forty-eight.

> *Dearest Brother I have waited long and patiently for a letter from you but never have received any as yet. I often think that I am forgotten in Sandwich. Let me assure you that if you all have forgotten me I often think of you and think how kind you have been to me. It has been nearly a year since I was at home and in all that time I have not received but one letter from home and that was from Mother. I feel to night as if I was alone in this world no one to love me nor no one to care for me. I heard that you had enlisted and I feel very sorry for when I am at home I shall miss you very much I know that some one has got to go but I do not want you to go but as you have enlisted I hope that you will be one of the number that will return in safety to their homes. I can not bear the thought of your going off and my not seeing you if you will write to me and let me know what night or day you will be at Lucy's I will come up there and see you or you write to me when you will come down here and I will stay out of the hill. How does little johnnie get along has he forgotten all about Lib Ann kiss all of the children for me and tell them that when I come home I will bring them something give my love to Lib and tell her that I want to see her very much tell her to write to me tell Father and Mother I want to see them very much give my love to them also to Burleigh and Dorcas and Mariett tell them all that I want them to write to me Edwin carried Sue and I up to Lucy's last Saturday and brought us back last night we expected to have seen you there but as it is getting late I must close give my love to all and write just as soon as you get this write so I can get it Wednesday if you can and come and see us. Oh Lewis wont you have your picture taken for me if you will I will pay for it be sure and write from your Sister Lizzie A Smith If you have your picture taken for me I will pay for it and write right back and let me know when you are going to leave Sandwich wont you Lizzie*

The first surviving letter from "Libby," Mary Elizabeth (Paine) Smith, to Lewis followed on October 27. She refers to a little one who grows like a piglet. Once again, Lewis and Libby's younger children are Hepsa A. Smith, about three and a half years old; Lucy M. Smith, about two and a half; and a son, Lewis E. Smith, who is a newborn.

Sandwich Oct 27 [1862] Dear Lewis

I received to letters from you Saturday night I was glad to hear from you we are all wel and I hope this will find you the same Frank [Wiggin] was up hear saturday to bring Burleigh up Lucy [Wiggin] want very wel the rest is all wel Sal[l]y was up hear Sunday and old Chase

Farther has paid for the Colts we can have a place to ride now Rachel is hear now with me She wil stay a day or to John Clark is better the children is all wel and send a ciss to you the little one groes lik a little pig she says that her par is [gone] to the war I hope it will soo[n] be over so that you can come home again to see her and all the rest it is very lonsome hear without you I get along very wel and hope you wil I have paid Irene Chase [a niece] She has gone home and I am glad of it I must close by biding you good nite your wife Mary E Smith

After enlisting in August, Lewis remained in Concord for about a month and departed from there with the regiment on October 18, 1862. He would pass through Concord on returning home to vote in March 1864 and again very briefly in midsummer of 1865, when he was mustered out—his only other known visits to Concord during his Civil War service.

Sandwich Nov [1862] Dear Lewis

I received your letter to night I was very glad to hear from you glad th[a]t you wont fare eny woes [worse] then what be you fare hard I no I hope for better days but I no not when we are all wel and in good hea[l]th the childrin is all gone to bed the boys has bin diging potatoes with farther to day Burleigh and Mother has ben to the north [North Sandwich] to day thire are all wel she aunt Ruth she was well Susan was up hear yesterday Jacob went down to concord to see you but you was gone Burleigh is agoing to have your coalt we have paid for

> *parstring them they look wel I wil send you some letters s[t]amps if you want eny thing els let us no and we will send if we can give love to Asa and tel him I want to no if his road aint a hard one to travel Mother sendes her love to you ses that you must keep up good courage we get along wel I [can't] think of eny thing els to rite now I will bid you good night I wish that you could be hear with me my little boy groes finly he has got so he can laf when he se me a coming to him Hipsy goes to the window and cals her par good night Lew I hope the war wil have an end soon this is from your wife Mary E Smith*

After nine years of absence, brother Benjamin Burleigh Smith and family had returned to the Granite State in 1861. Born on March 17, 1820, B. B. was a schoolteacher, "regarded by his pupils with a feeling akin to reverence."[4] B. B., from 1848 a member of the Second Freewill Baptist Church of Sandwich, studied at the Biblical School in Whitestown, not far from Utica in central New York, in 1849 and 1850, and became a Freewill Baptist minister. He married Dorcas Folsom on January 1, 1852, and they became frequent travelers.

By 1867, the Freewill Baptists, whose northern branch was organized in New Durham, New Hampshire, in 1780, had 1,252 churches and more than one thousand ordained ministers. These churches were all in the northern states due to "their denominational opposition to slavery."[5] B. B., thoroughly a Christian gentleman, spent many years, both pre– and post–Civil War, as a missionary in eastern India, dying there at Balasore, 130 miles southwest of Calcutta, on November 22, 1872.[6] Mention of their son Eddie (or Eddy), Edwin Augustus Smith, appears occasionally in the correspondence.

> *Sandwich Nov. 6/62 My dear Bro. Lewis*
>
> *Your dear wife's letter came to hand last evening, and we were truly glad to hear from you again. We thank you a thousand times, for your promptness in writing, and hope you will continue to write as often as you can. We know that it must often be difficult for you to write, but if you can write only a few lines, you cannot tell how glad we shall be to get them. Lizzie [Lewis's wife, Libby] seems to be getting on quite as well as could be expected. I went down to Mr. [William M.] Weed's with her on the 1st inst. to get her bounty, and he paid over the 12 dollars very willingly. She laid out a part of the money for cloth to*

make the children winter clothes, and has kept the rest. I think that she intends to get on with just as little expense as she comfortably can. She is very prudent, and you may be assured that we shall do all that we can to assist her. I shall try to do by her, as I should wish to have you do by my dear wife were our circumstances reversed.

I am to travel about here in New England, for our Mission Society this winter; but shall be coming home pretty often, and you never need be affraid to ask me to do anything for yourself or family; for, as I told you before you left home, I shall be glad to assist you any way I can have it in my power. Dorcas has not been to Sandwich since we came from General Conference. Her sister Hannah was confined with a young daughter the day that we returned as far as Weare [New Hampshire], and has been very sick ever since. Dorcas wrote me yesterday that she feared that Hannah would never be well again. I have concluded to take Eddie, who has been here with his grand-parents ever since you left, and go down to Weare tomorrow, as his mama cannot come up here. I believe that I told you in my last that Dorcas Sister Ann was dead. She died while we were at Conference. We heard of her death when we got into N. York city, and the news very nearly overcame Dorcas. She felt her death more particularly as we had not been to see them since our arrival in this country. So it is. There are troubled hearts every where, these days. But he, who has said "Call upon me in the day of trouble, and I will answer thee," will comfort and sustain every aching heart, if they will only trust in Him. He is my only hope, and may God grant that he may be yours also! O Lewis, do not fail to give your heart to the Saviour! He will comfort and sustain you, and prepare you for all the hardships you may be call[ed] to endure if you will seek Him, and put your trust in Him. God will surely be the soldier God if they will only look upward to Him.

If He is with you, you need not fear the dark night's picket duty, or the battle's stormy field. The balls of the enemy may fall thick and fast around you, and you will be safe if God is your friend and protector.

He will not suffer you to fall as long as it shall be for your own good, even, to remain.

Be faithful, dear Bro. in the discharge of your duties as a soldier, in the defence of your country; but above all, be faithful in the discharge of the duties you owe to yourself and to your God! I know you will pardon me for plainess; for you know that I am your friend and brother.

Mother sends much love and will write you soon. Father and all the rest of the family unite with me with much love and kind wishes.

Give my love to Mr. Magoon and tell him that we saw his wife yesterday and she said that they were all well.

Keep up good courage and write as often as you can.

In Haste From your brother B. B. Smith

Lucy Jane (Smith) Wiggin's first letter mentions the already apparent abuses of exemptions. The confusion she refers to in the Twelfth Regiment New Hampshire Volunteers (NHV) is likely a crisis of leadership as the result of Governor Berry's refusal to appoint Thomas J. Whipple, elected by the regiment, as colonel. The governor's action created "a strong feeling of dissatisfaction which, with many, soon ripened into bitter resentment." The issue did not disappear for, weeks later, as the men of the Twelfth were boarding the train from Concord, "Governor Berry, on his way home from Washington, made his appearance, and was greeted with cries for Whipple, instead of cheers for himself."[7]

Johnny and Frank are Lewis's oldest children and are now about six and five years old. Frank Wiggin's (Lucy's husband's) inability to hire help to dig his potatoes may already indicate war-related labor shortages.

Meredith Ville Nov 9 [1862] My Dear Brother

It affords me a great deal of pleasure to have a chance to write you. I have been waiting to hear from you so that I might know where to write to you, but I have not heard one word from you only by the paper that you were in camp near Washington till father came down last night, and Lizzie [Libby Smith] sent me an envelope. You can better immagine than I can describe what my feelings are for you those cold stormy nights friday night I could not sleep for thinking of the lonely vigil of the poor soldier on such stormy night. our hearts would die in us were it not for the hopes this thing could not last long. by this time you are well aware what a soldier's life is, and all I can say to you is keep good courage and pray that the time may soon come when you may again return to your home and friends. you are there and who will be called for next God only knows. I have not been up to Sandwich since you left but I am going in a week or two sometimes it seems as though I never go up there again, but duty bids me go and I must. Frank says he shall not know what to do with himself up there. I expect to take Johnny home with me this winter when I go up. Father thinks he can get along better with Frank alone than with both of them. he says they are very good boys gets along well with them. Burleigh say[s] Lizzie is getting along bravely, he likes her very much better than Mary. by the way Burleigh said Jacob had met with an accident a shave had fallen upon the back of his hand and cut off some of the cords so the[y] thought he would loose the use of some of his fingers. to be honest is the way to prosper. I began to think the reason you had not written was because you felt hurt because I did not go to Concord Susan [Hackett] said you felt bad about it. the whole reason I did not come was I was so excited and nerved up that I had no power to control my feelings and I knew we should both feel better if I kept away I knew if I went there I should come home sick upon it if I had gone and seen where you were draging yourself out it would make me heart sick and be constantly before my eyes for I have never been in such an excitable condition in all my life as this fall. this was the only reason that I had not gone with Father dont think for a moment it was because I had forgotten you Oh no no could you witness my evenings here when all alone after Lizzie [Lucy and Frank's daughter] is asleep you would never say she has forgotten me. We have all been sick this fall I have had a diarhea most all of the time. Frank come near a typhoid fever he has not got over it yet he is pretty poorly he told father to hire a hand to help dig his potatoes and he would pay the help he could not get any one to do his work for him. Lizzie [Wiggin] says tell Uncle Lewis that she is agoing to let Johnny [Smith] have her crib this winter to sleep in, and she wants me to send you some tea in the letter she has heard me say that I wished you had some. we had a chicken the other day Frank said as we set down he wished Lew had some it was dinner enough for me. the papers talk as though there would [be] no fighting out there at present unless you follow the rebels to Richmond where they are retreating I do hope something may turn up to prevent any more big battles. Tell Asa when I go to S[andwich], I shall go and see his folks if possible. I must now tell you to keep good courage. you are there and no fears of being drafted almost all in this town have got certificates to exempt them from a draft Frank is about the only one left. I want you to write to me every chance you can get and I will answer all your letters. You ought to be thankful you are not in the 12 regiment for that is still in confusion Burleigh is agoing to travel this winter and his wife and Eddie are going to Weare to spend the winter. Goodnight from your sister Lucy J. P.S. I am going to write to George [Wiggin, of Meredith] tonight he is in the 6 regiment well and hearty

In B. B. Smith's next letter, he offered unconditional support not only to Lewis, but also to Asa Magoon:

East Weare Nov. 17, 1862 My Dear Brother—

Your kind letter of Nov. 6th has been received, and please accept many thanks for the same. You may be assured that I shall do all that I can to assist your family during your absence and we shall not fail to think of, and pray for you. You can never tell how anxious we feel for you, and how much we want you to become a good Christian.

I am now at East Weare N.H. where my family will probably spend the winter. Soon as we came home from the West, we came to Weare to see Dorcas folks, and found her sister Hannah very sick and D. has remained with her ever since. She has not yet been to Sandwich, and I fear she will not be able to go up there at present. I am happy to say that Hannah's health is improving, though it is very slowly.

I have decided to travel and lecture for our Mission Society this winter; but shall make it in my way to be around to Sandwich as often as I can.

I am now making arrangements to get a sleigh and harness, so as to be ready for the first snow, or for the first sleighing, at any rate. We had a little snow here about a fortnight ago; but not enough to amount to any thing.

Please give my very kind regards to Mr. Magoon, and tell him that I shall be most happy to do any thing for his family that I can.

Kindly give my warmest regards to all the Sandwich boys. Tell them to keep up brave hearts, and act well the part assigned, and above all, to look up to the "God of battles" for assistance and support. This is the best advise I can give them. I thank you for writing me so promptly. Do write just as often as you can. Don't fail to write often to your dear wife. You can never tell how much good your letters do her. If you want any thing don't fail to let us know it.

Dorcas sends much love to you and will write you soon as she can. Eddie also sends love to uncle Lewis.

Please excuse haste and Believe me. Your brother Burleigh.

Lewis sent Libby a letter bearing a Twelfth Regiment NHV letterhead, dated November 30, 1862. The second half of the letter is from Asa Magoon. In addition, the handwriting and some spellings are not Lewis's. It is apparent that Lewis was too sick to write and that Asa wrote the letter for him. Asa addresses "uncle John," Lewis's father, John Smith, who is an uncle of Asa's wife, Mary "Eliza" (Smith) Magoon.

12th Regiment New-Hampshire Volunteers *CAMP*

november the 30 1862

dear wife once more i sit down to let you no i hav not forgoten you my health is gainning i hav had a very bad cold but i am getting smart you need not wory any thing about me for I shall goet Asa Magoon takes care of me i thought i would not rite until i got beter so to day i am a goin to rite you a fiew lines to you to let you no that i want you to send me five dollars in money as soon as you can i dont no when we shall draw any so you send me five dollars tell the children to be good and mind you rite as soon as you gett this tell father and mother that i shall rite to them soon and all the rest tell them to rite to me as often as they can so good buy

uncle John i thought i would send you a fiew lines to let you no that I hav not forgoten you if you hav me i hope those fiew lines will find you all well you think of me when you go down seler to get som S and aples lewis and i takes all the comfort we can to gether we hav got us a stove in our tent so we ar come fortable you go over to my house and drink som cider for me so i must close by biding you good buy this from your friend Asa Magoon

Going to Asa's house for cider, which was undoubtedly "hard" by that time of year, was very likely a popular pastime. Apple cider was as ubiquitous as fall foliage, and simple anaerobic fermentation produced a ready content of ethanol. As such, "cider" and "cider drinkers" were common targets of the temperance movement. Below are only three of fifteen published arguments against cider consumption:

From the *Christian Herald*
Cider Drinking

This practice should be abandoned for the following reasons:

1. If but little is used it may easily be dispensed with, as it can do no good when used in small quantities.
2. If it is taken in large quantities, it ought to be abandoned immediately, lest it should lead to drunkenness.
3. Cider drinking is justly becoming very disreputable. In these days of inquiry and reform, the cider drinker is regarded much in the same light as the rum-drinker; and the fact that the love of alcohol causes the one to drink rum and the other cider, shows that they both belong to the same class.[8]

It must be noted that "temperance" had arrived in Sandwich by 1843, for nowhere in the town could ardent spirits be purchased at that time.

Adams Express Office—Boxes. Author's Collection.

However, in neighboring Moultonborough, "where the article" was sold, "too much of it is carried into Sandwich." It was openly stated that Sandwich people, more likely *some* of them, would "be after the Moultonborough *rum store* at the next term of the [General] Court."[9]

Boxes from home soon began to arrive for the men in the field. Eighteen-year-old Francis H. Buffum, from Winchester, a small town twenty miles south of Keene, in the southwestern corner of New Hampshire, enlisted in Company F and subsequently wrote most of the published history of the Fourteenth. He observed that a "man who did not get a box from home was a singular and much-pitied individual."[10] The supply wagons that rumbled into the army's camps carried more than just supplies; they brought morale in the form of mail and boxes. Buffum's "ornamental" description is worth noting:

> In these delicacies, so deftly packed away as to occupy every available inch of space, were incarnated a devotion as lofty as that of the Spartan mothers; an affection whose tenderness of deed was the truest expression of the finest age of genuine humanity; and we may suggest, without presumption or overstatement, that those impulses which centered in the more than three hundred thousand boxes sent from Northern homes during the war to individual loved ones in the army, were the same for love, heroism, and loyalty, which, expanded into the majesty of an irresistable tidal wave, gathered up the power of the homes of a great people, and buried the Rebellion hopelessly. In another figure it may be said that the black fortress of Secession was not only breached, but levelled, under the bombardment of—boxes.[11]

Lewis's wife, Mary Elizabeth, usually addressed as Libby or occasionally Lib and rarely Liz, wrote from Sandwich on December 4. Libby sent the five dollars Lewis requested, indicating that her letter followed Asa's. She mentions Pvt. Herbert H. Smith and William A. Heard, brigade quartermaster, both of Sandwich and Company K. The name Henry Gilman will also appear in later correspondence and is almost certainly 1st Sgt. James H. Gilman. Henry Gilman's career as a sergeant would be less than stellar and his subsequent reduction to ranks would not be of his own volition.[12]

> *Sandwich Dec 4 [1862] Dear husban*
>
> *I take this oppotunity to rite a few lines to you to let you no that we received your letter this after noon I was glad to hear from you but*

was very sory to hear that you was sick but it is gest what I expected and looked for to if you was hear where mother and I could take [care] of you how glad I should be Mother wants you to rite how long you have ben sick and what ale you you need not be afraid to let us no gest how it is if their is eny medsin we can send you we'l do it tel Asa that farther has not forgot him yet he says that he will go over to his house and get some sider you tel Asa that I thank him for riting to me and wish that he had rote to me before hear is five Dolars I will send you th[i]s time and if you want eny more you let us no soon we sent you some things for thanksgiving their was a box sent to Herbert Smith in the care of William A Heard in the box their was yours a chicken pie in a basin to loves of s[w]eet bread in a bundle your mitting and a scarfe a pieace of flanel to were [wear] round your body and pound of tobaco in another bundle 3 Qart pail of butter Mother and father and I sent you Susan sent a little box of pies and little caks to pip[e]s to fish hooks some peper and a diper to pensils Saly sent some things to bo[w]ls of butter to pies and a puding in a co[ve]red pail in Henry gilman box if you have not got thes things let Asa look them up for you rite as soon as you get this if you can not you get Asa to we are all wel and hope this will find you better the children is wel we are looking for B B evry Day home to get the colt I wil close by biding you good nite this is from your wife Mary E Smith

After the October 26 march from Washington, the regiment camped northwest of the capital in the vicinity of Lock #21, or Swains Lock, which lay upstream from the Potomac's Great Falls, about seventeen river miles above the canal's termination at Georgetown. That the regiment was "green" was incontrovertible. One soldier wrote: "i wish my gun and knapsack was in hell we had to lug them five miles the whole will way abought 50 pounds and the last mile it wayd 75." Almost two years later, the regiment would be marching twenty or more miles per day for nearly a week at a time. Lax discipline and short rations were also evident: "the boyes steal every thing they can get . . . it is as cold here as it is in Bradford [New Hampshire] and not half as much to eat . . . we dont have much to do now onley to steal."[13]

At this time, it was common for soldiers to request money from home, as they had yet to be "paid off." Many soldiers needed money not only to purchase sundries, but also to buy clothing, shoes, and medicinals. Delays in pay would, in fact, be chronic: the financially strapped federal government paid for supplies and munitions before it paid its soldiers—a problem that did not remain unnoticed by the government. In a "Special Message" to Congress dated January 17, 1863, President Lincoln noted the authorization of an additional one hundred million dollars for the army and the navy, adding that "every possible facility may be afforded for the prompt discharge of all arrears of pay due to our soldiers and our sailors."[14] Even allotments to families of volunteers were tardy. Sgt. J. Henry Jenks, of Keene, wrote: "I see by the papers that they are not very prompt in paying the alotments. I heard to day the reason was, they wanted to see who skedaddled so as not to pay the wives of such . . ."[15]

In mid-November, the regiment moved to Offutt's Cross-Roads, on the road from Great Falls to Washington. Just before Christmas, the regiment relocated twenty miles to Poolesville, Maryland, where they would remain for the duration of winter. This last relocation was not without grumbling—the men had already stockaded their tents for winter. The small, "pretty village" of Poolesville, situated inside a large bend of the Potomac, was better suited for protecting a number of river fords and ferries, one of which was Edward's Ferry.[16]

On December 7, Lucy Wiggin wrote to her (and Lewis's) mother, Eliza (Webster) Smith, of Sandwich. She mentions John, Lewis's oldest son, and Lizzie, Lucy and Frank Wiggin's three-year-old daughter. In a badly blotted, prewar letter to home, dated December 12, 1858, Lucy expressed loneliness. Part of her distress and somatic state was the result of Frank's long hours as a Meredith harnessmaker—"he is so drove in the shop . . . the boys go to their work at 6½ o clock in the morning and I am alone till eight in the evening . . ." Her distance from friends and family in Sandwich is evident. She remarked: "tell Lib I am most mad with her for I have looked every pleasant day since thanksgiving for her to come she can bundle up in a sleigh and be warm."[17] Her husband Frank's prediction regarding "winter camp" would prove accurate.

M. Ville Dec 7 1862 My Dear Mother

The children are a bed and asleep and I have just answered Mr Hogan's letter and will now answer yours. I was glad to hear from Lewis and his being sick was nothing more than I expected to hear I hope he

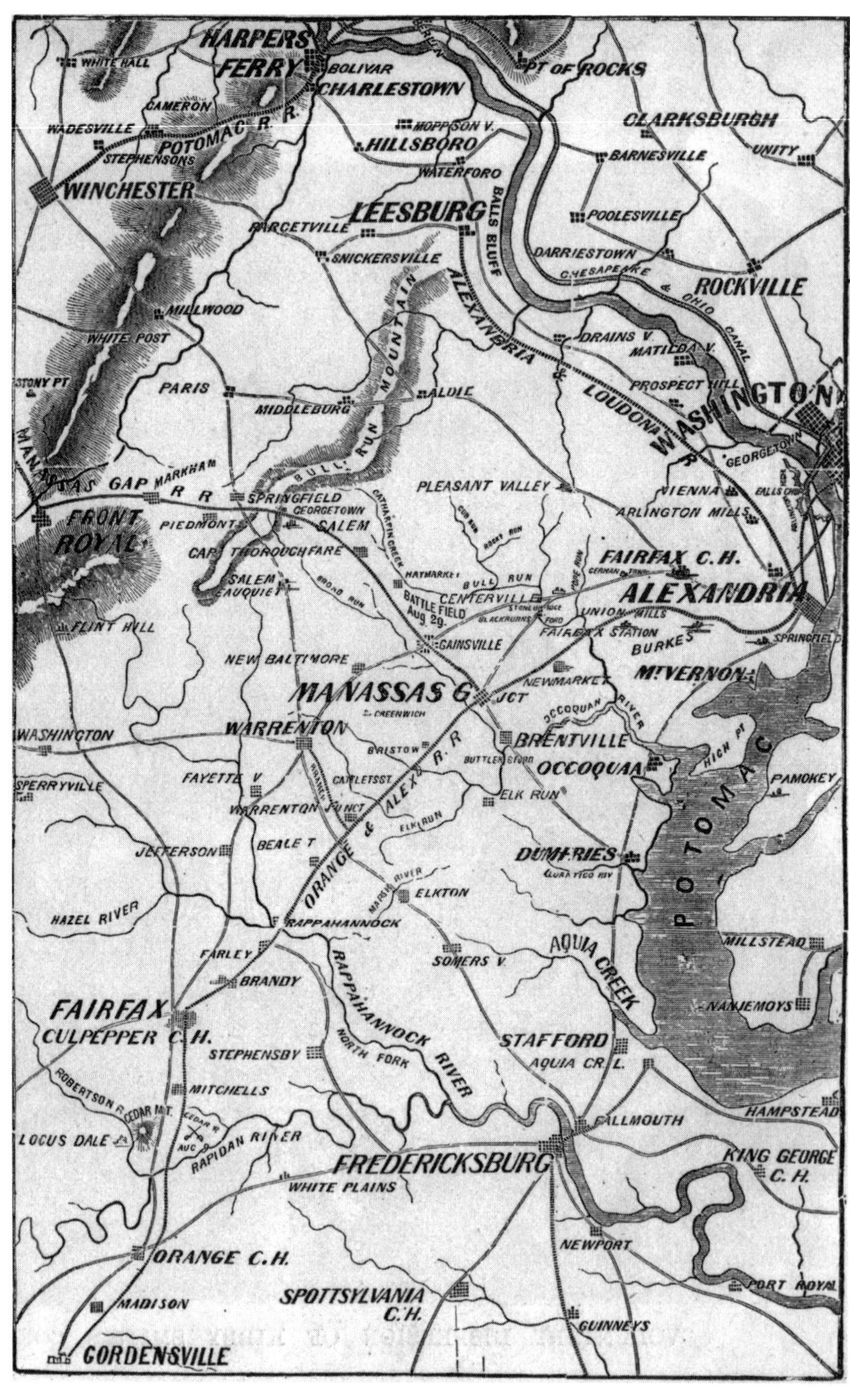

Seat of War in Virginia, Map. Author's Collection.

will not have a long time of it if he does he will probably be discharged if it is liver complaint so I would not worry more than I could help there was another sent home sick here the other day. Frank thinks if they have bought a stove they have gone in camp for the winter to keep guard there. let us hope for the best I shall write again this We got home well but the children both had bad cough for a few days Lizzie was quite croupy but I doctored them well with whisky and molasses and they are nearly over it now I think they took cold the day before we came home. John didnot get his boots till last night he couldnot find a pair in the village to fit so he had to have his foot measured and the Presscots made him a pair they charged 2,00 but J. thinks they are good boots. he is proud enough of them he is well contented he has not had a cry or a whipping since he has been here only he want to see Frank kill the cow and he sent him into grandsirs to warm his feet and he cried he thought he had lost Uncle Frank he says he wants to see grandpa & grandma his father and mother and the baby grandpa most for he is the oldest he dont care about the rest for they did not care about him he said Frank laughed when he come away but he will cry before he comes home he dont talk of going home before sapping he goes to the shop every pleasant day. he sees wonders down here he says he never had such a warm bed in his life. I told him grandma was coming down before long he said he should be terrible glad to see her. You tell Lizzie [Libby Smith] she need not worry one might about him for if he is sick I will take as good care of him as she would he and Lizzie [Wiggin] get along first rate. I had a poorly day yesterday but feel better today I had a turn of diarhea. Frank has a staffed cough all the time, keeps to work all the time Our cow was pretty fat I had about 23 pounds of rough tallow after it was tried out and I want you to come down and show me how to dip candles I wish you could come down before long if you cant come before come so as to be here Christmas time the 25 I want you to come and make a good visit. I am glad Irene [Chase] is getting better for I felt afraid it would go hard with her. I hope Sally [Irene's mother] didnot think hard because we didnot go over there. I meant too and I mean to go up there this winter. tell them to come down to Christmas if they can. I think a great deal about you this cold rough weather I wish I could run in often but I am alone and oftentimes sad God only knows

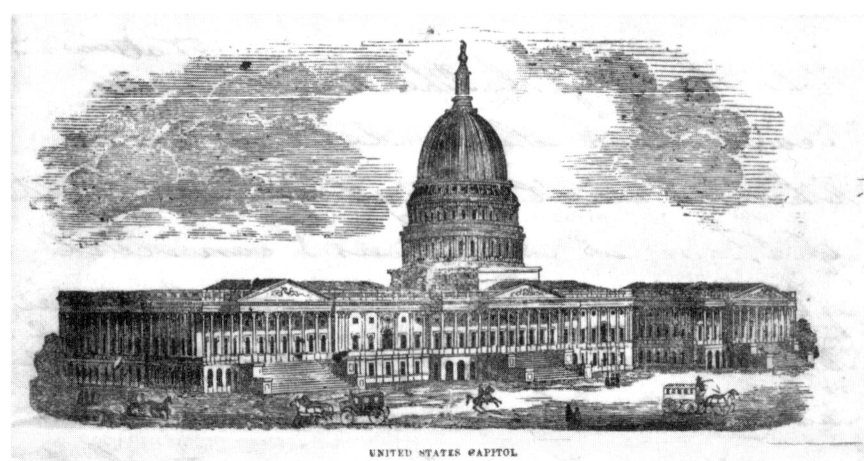

14th Regiment New Hampshire Volunteers, Col. Wilson.

COMPANY ------

Maraland Dece 8 ....1862.

My Dearest dear Libby I will wright a few lines to you to let you no how I am giting along I am ganing slowly it has bin sick three weeks yesterday I had the tyforefever I set up half day in a day we have nothing to strenking us up but I thinke it gott along now I have receved all of letters with much joy but was unable to answer them but I hope that you will fogive

Lewis Q. Smith letter of December 8, 1862, 14th Reg't NHV Letterhead, Sandwich Historical Society.

how I feel here evenings alone I get so as not to sleep at night and I think that being on those spells, a pain through my back and bowels, and palpitation tell father I wish I could help do his chores. tell him to come and stop as long as he can. I must stop writing for I am not feeling very well tonight and it is late the rest are all a bed and asleep. I want you to write when you hear from Lewis again Write often Your affectionate Daughter Lucy

An early December 1862 letter of Lewis's is from Maryland, and is written on regimental stationery, topped by an image of the Capitol.

14th Regiment New Hampshire Volunteers, Col. Wilson.
COMPANY . . . Camp *Maraland Dec 8 1862*

My absent dear libby I will wright a few lins to you to let you no how I am gitin along I am ganing sloly it has bin sick three weeks yesterday I had the tyfore fever I set up haf Day in e Day we have northing to strenhing us up but I should goit along now I have reseved of [blank] letters with much joy but was unable to answer them but hop that you will fogive the hole of the stuff that you sent reach hear safe tell them that I will wright to the rest of them as soon as I can tell farther that I thank him forty thousand tims for his p[r]esent an I thank you all but thar is northing that I can eat but the butter thar could bee north[ing] that you could send me that wood do me the good that your butter did tell the children to bee good children for I hop that wee shall come home some time an I want you to take care of your an not werry about me for I shall git a long some way Mr magoon rot home to you for some mony which I never should have don if I had knot bin sick but if wee have eny thing but powders an pill wee hafto by then [buy them] we can git along when we air well but when sick it is hard look if I had not lent eny mony I should had to sent to you for eny but we have not been paid once sent wee left Concord. I shall haft to close wright as of ten as you can so I will close by you good knight L Q Smith

I have just reseve your letter an evry thing come safe I was glad to hear from you an that you war all well so good knight

Writing from Maryland on December 14, Lewis described for Lucy and Frank the process of "stockading" their tents for winter. Split planks were laid edge to edge with the ends buried about one foot into the ground in the pattern of the tent, with an opening to match the tent's door flap. The planks extended about three feet above ground and the joints between were chinked. The tent was then placed outside and over the wooden walls, which were then banked up with earth, resulting in more headroom and a secure, tight dwelling. Such tents were occasionally placed end to end or doubled up to accommodate more men.

Lewis also commented on his slowly improving health and the rough nature of the country, "worse then Sandwich noch." The road through Sandwich Notch, a "gap," or pass, in the mountains allowing travel along the route from west of Sandwich toward the seacoast, passed near the Smith farm. It remains virtually unchanged from colonial days, and it is, indeed, rough. Pvt. William H. H. Bennett, of Sandwich, was just as critical as Lewis of western Maryland terrain: "the Country here is rough and hilly thinly enhabited. I would not give 3 cents per acre for it . . . the boys say it is the worst place they ever was in."[18] Lewis professed impatience with the conduct of the war. By this time, progress of the war, or lack thereof, had become an issue for both the Lincoln administration and the northern public.

Marland Dec 14 1862 Dear Brother an Sister

I take this optunity to answer your it has bin long enuf in answering your letter but hop that you will excues me for I have bin sick for the last fore weeks with the tyford fever an deyre but have [been] ganing I am so that have gut out doors I am ganing as fast as could expect I have not eny thing to make me gan but what I eat and that is not vary grat you wrot that you was up to farther to thankgiven I should like to bin thar with you but I am in the fetters fast and strong but thar is aday acoming that the i[r]on chane will bee brocken then we will return to our homes an hoping that day is not far distant then tell frank that the fish an partregs will haft to tak up perhaps you wood like to no what cind of houses wee live in wooding an cloth one[s] thay air bilt up three feet of pols then our cloth tents put on top of that we have a stove in ours so that it is vary comfetebel it cost us 60 cense apese five of us in the tent we have some cold hear enuf we had some snow hear a week ago last friday it blew Sattady an Sunday it seme like newhamsher wether but we air haveing fine wether her now but it is the worst lookin plase that you or I ever saw it is northing but neger hogs an woods an rock an if you doo not bleveit you may come out hear an see I wood not live out hear five year for the hole of mar[y]land thar is only now an then a house to bee seen it is worse then sandwich noch but we haft to put up with it thay sems as thou thay are trying to do some thine now thay air pushing the thing along now an it is hy time for them to do it wright as often as you can an I will do the same you must not wate for me for I canot writ so well as you can for I have not the time that you have L Q Smith

Lewis was a faithful correspondent and dutifully answered the letters he received. He became irritated with those who did not reciprocate. Libby also voiced impatience when a gap in correspondence occurred, most likely the result of vagaries in the delivery of mail to and from army camps rather than in the actual frequency of writing. An example of Lewis's prompt return of letters is seen in this one, to his mother.

Camp Maryland Dec 17 1862 Dear Mother

I reseved your leter nit before last an you cannot tell how glad I was to reseve it I have look for one from you for a long time an have just reseve it you wanted me to wright you how I was and what aile me I have wrot to Liby how it wes my helth is in proveny as fas as cowlob[?] expect I have got so that I can do a few chors the Caption [captain] has took me back to his Quartars to chor for him an molton webster thay are all that thar is in the tent they took me in when I was sick an spared no pains thay don every thing that thay could for me I was taken sick fore weeks ago last Sunday [Dec. 14] with the tyford fever an dyre it was ----- ----- vilent the knight befor ----- on picket down on the river thar is fore rigments of us ----- to guard the river an cenell [canal] an road leading from rocvill [Rockville] to woshinton have aboat five miles to take care of thar is knot much news to wright you for we have knot muche news hear with us we do not have half so much news as you do Asa is well an harty an send his love to all of you tell farther to keep up good curidg for I shall bee at home some time give my love to libby an children ass well of the rest tell libby to keep ---- up good curidg an never ssissdeit [cease it] an take car of her helth can you do the same I [want] you to wright as often as you can an I will answer so tell libby that I will wright to hir next Sunday if northen happens wright all of you I will close by biding you good knight from your Son Lewis Q Smith[19]

On the day after Christmas, Lucy wrote to Lewis, and Irene's health is again mentioned. Irene A. Chase was the eighteen-year-old daughter of blacksmith Jonathan P. and Sally M. Chase of Sandwich. Irene had an older sister, Sarah E., and two younger sisters, Marietta, or Mariett, and Lucy J. The bonds of the Smith and Chase families were strong, for in 1850, the three younger Chase girls, Lewis and Libby's nieces, Irene, Mariett, and Lucy J., were living in the Smith home. The Chase girls were in the Smiths' home of necessity: Jonathan's first wife, Mary W. Chase, certainly a Smith relation and probably Lewis's oldest sister, died on August 30, 1848, at age thirty-one. Jonathan married Sally M. Smith on Thanksgiving 1853. For those lacking relatives or extended family, the town's poorhouse was about the only option for orphans or children of a widowed working parent.

M. Village Dec 26 [1862] My Dear Brother

I will not delay to answer your letter longer for fear you may think I have forgotten my poor lone brother who may be while I am writing this letter be stretched upon a couch of cedar boughs suffering by disease. God knows it is not that I have forgotten you why I have not answered yours before it was other sorrows and anxieties that were claiming my attention. Irene Chase was very sick of typhoid fever and I went there the next day after getting your letter and did not get back till night before last. I then thought I would wait for a day or two to see how it turned out with her. today I hear she was almost throug[h] this life so far gone as not to know any one or to speak she is probably dead ere this poor girl so you will not wonder if my heart is filled with sadness tonight. when I think of a dear brother sick in a land of strangers with[out] the comforts of life and a dear niece one that seems to us more like a sister suffering the agonies of death and all I can do is to sit here alone and weep over them not being able to lend a helping hand in this time of greatest need. But the Lord wills it all for the best and we must try and feel resigned to His will. Yes Lewis Jonathon is wading through affliction, though our Countrys call did not take his friends and cause the bitter tears to fall. the hand of the Lord is doing it, and may he be brought to feel he must mingle his tears with all of the mourning hearts of our land Such gloomy times I never knew it seems to oerspread our land, and my prayer is that the time may speedily come when peace shall again reign in this deluded Country. where this thing will end God only knows. Johnny [Lewis's son] is here with us. he is well and well contented. he says he wants to see the folks but dont want to go home till sapping. he is a good boy I dont have any trouble at all with him. he minds the first bidding. he stays with Uncle Frank a good deal of the time at the shop they have a tame gray squrrel at the shop that will climb all over you he will climb into Jonnys pocket after nuts it pleases him very much. I dont send him to school for fear he will get hurt among so many bad boys I have a school at home for him and Lizzie they like it he speaks of you quite often since he heard you was sick yesterday morning he awoke up before we did and when I awoke up he asked me if I thought his father had got out where there were fighting he meant this last battle he felt much better when I told him no he is one that thinks more than he speaks. he sleeps in Lizzies crib in the room with us. I saw father when I was up to Sallys he come and brought Mariett over he said they were getting along well at home the children were all well. Frank is not contented up there since you left he dont know what to do with himself he has not been gunning or fishing since thanksgiving he is not well at all this winter he has a cold and cough the most of the time he is poor as a crow. I hear that your regiment expect to stay where you be this winter I hope you will try to keep up a good courage as you can hoping this thing will soon end. I saw George Dexters corps.[20] *it made our heart ache for the poor soldier, when I read of their freezing to death on picket duty O it did seem as though I should be crazy but if you dont have to move this winter I hope you will be more comfortable. I want you to write and tell me how you are getting along every chance you can get, and I will write often to you it does us some good to speak in the silent language of the pen Hoping the time will soon come when we shall see you face to face. I want you to write to Jacob I pity him. he could not speak of you for tears he said all had had a letter but him you know what he has to contend with. he is our brother still though he may err. Lucy*

Johny wants me to tell you Santaclaus brought him a stocking full of things for Christmas, and he went to the christmas festival and got a present from the tra—a rabbit in a basket Do write often L. J. Wiggin

The poor condition of New Hampshire's arsenals was the result of a long deteriorated militia system—"a dead letter for so many years."[21] In 1849, the *New Hampshire Democrat* editorialized: "At our last regimental musters, in many parts of the State there were hardly soldiers enough equipped and on duty to say 'we,' while in many instances fighting, gambling and drinking was the order of the day."[22] The newspaper called for abolishing militias, which the legislature accomplished in 1851. A decade later, in 1861, the legislature still debated reestablishing the militia.[23]

In late 1857, New Hampshire had two arsenals, one in Lancaster, "poorly stocked," and a second in Portsmouth, containing "a better array of 'war implements.' " Portsmouth had about thirteen hundred muskets, mostly percussion locks, but some flintlocks. New Hampshire had a total of ten thousand muskets, most of which were loaned out to towns, some of them "out for more than thirty years, and . . . wretchedly out of order."[24] In early November, the Fourteenth's muskets had been condemned but not replaced. It was said that the old smoothbores "were possibly more dangerous at the breech than at the muzzle."[25] One writer correctly argued: "Our future battles are to be fought at long range, and it is little better than murder to put an army with old muskets against an army with rifles and rifled cannon."

The writer, who signed himself "Cartridge," continued: "The South is better armed today than the North . . . But the North is rich, and neither false economy nor slow coach ideas should deter the purchase and supply of the best arms money can obtain."[26] Northern industry was attempting to meet the war's demands. The Amoskeag Company in Manchester, New Hampshire, employing more than two hundred machinists, had received a contract to produce Springfield rifles and was to have begun work on ten thousand of them by August 1, 1862.[27] By fall of 1863, the company would be starting its fourth contract and a production order of fifteen thousand Springfields.[28]

In the Fourteenth's winter camp, a new epidemic emerged—lice, a feature of the landscape until the end of the war. Almost a year later, a member of Company I wrote:

> I am getting uste to war fair I have laid on bords all summer but one ruber blanket under me sleep just as well as on a bed . . . with our clothes on all the time some times the lice pull us out of bed they are as big as sheep.[29]

Lice, however, were not all that itched. In the heat and humidity of summer, "flannels" and profuse sweating combined to cause "very troublesome" itching.[30] The remedy was simpler than for lice: cotton shirts—when available. Company H's Cpl. Henry Sanborn wrote of "ground itch," also known as swamp or water itch or coolie itch.[31] Predominant in tropical and semitropical areas, including the southern United States, this dermatitis (redness, swelling, blistering, and itching) of the feet is the result of larvae of *Necator americanus*, hookworm. Prevention was simple: adequate shoes, not going barefoot, and sanitary control of excreta.

On Sunday, December 21, the regiment marched upriver twenty miles to winter quarters at Poolesville, Maryland. Once there, they again stockaded their tents and settled in. The enemy lay across the river, but their immediate foe was disease, boredom, and cold.

~ *Three* ~

DEATH AND DARKNESS AT HOME

January 1, 1863, to January 31, 1863

. . . your place was empty it was atrying time . . .

—Lewis's mother, Eliza W. Smith, January 4, 1863

Nothing ever sounded more like yourself my dear brother than to hear you say I am willing to do my duty and take my chance with the rest.

—Lucy J. Wiggin, January 4, 1863

ON NEW YEAR'S DAY 1863, THE ROUTINE OF CAMP LIFE went on as usual, including the opportunity for correspondence. There were also endless drills and inspections—the latter every Sunday morning and on the last day of the month. The men were required to wear their cartridge boxes, each containing forty rounds, and carry their haversacks, knapsacks, and canteens. Even their old muskets had to be "kept bright." Only two companies, A and G, on the flanks of the camp, had been issued Springfield rifles; the other companies would have to wait.[1] On January 8, the first draw of pay began and some members of the regiment, now flush, deserted.[2] Further numbers were lost to the rigors of winter camp, suffering illnesses such as typhoid, diphtheria, brain fever, consumption, and even measles. The first six weeks of 1863 were monotonous as picket duty, camp guard, drilling, and "daily details for wood-chopping" filled their time.[3]

The Baltimore and Ohio Railroad, the Chesapeake and Ohio Canal, and roads paralleling the Potomac River were all essential to the Union's communication with the West and its productive agriculture and population. Between Baltimore and Washington alone, ten passenger trains, full to their "utmost capacity," ran daily. On the same route, an average of twelve "immense freight trains" carried "products of every conceivable kind."[4] Traffic by road through Maryland also required protection, as did crossings on the upper Potomac. Potomac River ferries and fords were obvious invasion routes from the south and offered opportunities for Confederate flanking movements on Washington. In the summer of 1863, Gen. Robert E. Lee's Confederates would cross the river to begin their invasion of the North. In the summer of 1864, Gen. Jubal Early would lead his rebel force across the Potomac and approach to within a few miles of the Capitol.

As 1863 began, the news from home was not good. Lucy Wiggin first commented on Irene Chase's health in December, and Lewis's mother later wrote that the onset of Irene's illness was November 23. On December 7, Lucy believed that her niece Irene was getting "better." However, over the next three weeks, Irene's situation worsened, until her death just after Christmas. Lewis could not attend the funeral and his absence darkened the already black cloud at home. Lewis himself remained sick.

Poolvil Jen 1 1863 Dear Libby

Seat my self agan to wright the third letter sinse I reseved eny from you an I wish you a happy new year an see if you will knot try an see if you canot writ a few lins how you air gitting along my helth is inproveing I have gut so that I do some duty an hop that thes few lins will find you all [in] good helth an prosparity time has seem vary long to me sinse I have bin sick but in hop[e]s that the time will soon come that I shall bee premetted to return home agane but we must keep up good curig that is half of the battle I want you to send me a little box if you can with a pa[i]r of footings [stockings] an a neck hanckchif an som butter if you have it to spar an aplsas som tobaco an tea an some of Dr Engils pills for the deyree for I am troble vary much with it if you cannot send eny thing els send the pills in the letter that you send an you ask farther if he want go over to Mr Magoon an see if thay have eny thing to send to asa if thay have put it in to gither, an send me your an Lucy M Smith Minuturs if you can posebly can an what else you air aminto thar is not much news to wright you the mail is call for good by L Q Smith

Discovering Bodies of the Slain in the Potomac River, Battle of Ball's Bluff, October 21, 1861, Alfred R. Waud, Library of Congress.

Lucy Wiggin was often outspoken on the war, abolition, and politics and expressed concern about Lewis's presence in the vicinity of Poolesville. Lucy was undoubtedly familiar with the Union's October 1861 disaster at Ball's Bluff, on the Virginia side of the Potomac. Following a rout by the Confederates there, many of the fleeing Federals died at Edward's Ferry—shot or drowned while attempting to recross the river. Former Oregon senator Col. Edward Baker, a good friend of President Lincoln, was shot dead and Brig. Gen. Frederick W. Lander, of Salem, Massachusetts, received a wound that took his life months later. Company C's Pvt. William Combs, of Winchester, New Hampshire, wrote from Poolesville: "their is a lot of rebels just acrost the river from us . . . they would like to get us over there to bolls bluff where Meny a brave boys bones lay bleaching in the son . . ."[5]

Lucy, writing from her home in Meredith Village, mentions the presence of "Riley" at Irene's funeral. Riley Magoon, Asa's older brother, like Asa, lived not far from Lewis and Libby Smith.

M. Village Jan 4 [1863] My Dear Brother

I received your letter night before last just as I had returned home from Sandwich whither I had been to bury Irene. Yes Lewis after a painful illness of a number of weeks they were obliged to close her eyes in death they have probably written you all about it before this. they take her death very hard indeed. I missed your presence very much on the funeral occasion. It was a solemn day to us all not only on account of her death but the thoughts of absent ones the brothers and sisters all together to follow the remains of Irene to the tomb but you. It seemed sad sad indeed when we consider what called you with thousands of others from our midst. Lib was not there she could not leave her baby [Lewis E.]. Dorcas was in Canterbury, and they told me Mary was sick. Jacob went up a day or two before funeral and helped father get up some wood but there is no snow here and it is bad drawing wood a wagon runs as well as in September. I called up to fathers and got supper they were getting along very well they were all well but father hes had a turn of Rhumati[sm] but was getting better the children were all well the baby [Lewis E.] grows like a little pig. Hipsy is a little cunning thing good as she can be. We carried John up home he had a fine time with the boys but he wanted to come back again I think you need not worry at all about home for upon the whole I think they get along finely they all worry a great deal more about you than they do about themselves. I felt very bad to hear you had made a move for I thought you were in no danger of going into battles but you are not so secure at Poolsville that is a bad place and dont you try to go on duty till you are able to you had better be in the hospital than on the battlefield I worry so about you I dont know what to do but keep up as good courage as you can hoping right will soon triumph it seems this thing cannot last much longer our papers talk strongly now of emancipating and arming the slaves to fight for themselves this is what should be done for by so doing we weaken the South they now go forth to fight their battles and keep the negros at home to do the work and by freeing them weakens the South and arming them strengthens the north and it seems that the thing must soon be settled in this way if it had not been for the treachery of our officers this thing might have been settled long ago. they will in time have their just deserts all I wish the unholy war would come to an end. Tell Asa I saw his wife to funeral and Riley to the grave they are all well Tell Moulton [Webster] I saw all of his folks at Sally's were all well George set up with the corps one night with another boy he is growing to be quite a man There is no news to write here every thing seems dull we miss our poor soldiers boys far away. You don't know how thankful I am for these pleasant days and nights it seems the hand of the Lord is in it for the poor soldier's good. Could I give my bed to you tonight and I take your couch I would gladly do it. I want you to write often as you can I wrote to you last week you have probably got it by this time try and take as good care of your health as you can. John is a good boy tries to be as big as anybody I am a going to write to his mother tonight he says tell you he wants to see you I must close write often as you can Lucy J Wiggin

Also conveying the news of Irene's death is Lewis's mother, who wrote to him on January 4, 1863:

My ever dear absent

I now sit down to write afew lines to let you know how we are getting along we are getting along well our health is good for us the childrens health is vary good they have not had one sick turn since you left home we have meet with a greate loss Irene Chase is gone to be no more she was taken sick Nov 23 with the lung fever she was down sick two weeks got better & she set up all day was taken with pain in her head and vomiting she vomited six days and knights they had docter Ingals and Mason they [did] all they could but she could not keep anything down we tried evrything we could think of but nothing seemed to have any effect when she stop vomiting she was so distressed from head to foot it seamed as tho she could not live one hour all that saw her said that she was the most suffering person that

Irene Chase Headstone, Jonathan Taylor Photograph.

ever they see she had the spinal complaint newralegy tuch of the liver complaint she died Dec. 29 buried Jan. 2 Burley come but your place was empty it was atrying time it did seem as tho they never could giv her up she had not her reason but little part of the time for the last week by what I heard her say at times that she has made a happy change O Lewis write and let me know jest how your health is and how you are getting along and if there is any thing that you need that we can help you to if there is jest let us know and we will send it if possible the weather is about as worm as september weather there is but vary little snow here there has not ben but few days slaying here this winter I would like to know what kind of weather your having out there and if you are comfortable there O try and keep up good courage hope I hope you will not have to stay a greate while longer have not heard much war news lately hope they are planing for peace so to let the poor soldiers come home Frank has taken the colt home Father could not sell him he was in hopes to get some steers for him but he coudnot so he let Frank have him for the land he is agoin to have the deed put on record it will not cost any thing [to] keep that it was the best he could [do] with him Burleigh has not taken his away yet he is wating for snow says he will pay for his keeping give my best respects and greates thanks [to Asa] for being so good to you when sick hope the Lord will reward him for his kindnesses to the sick give my best respects to asa M. tell him his kindness will never be forgotten for being so good to you when sick day before yesterday she [not identified] was well and rest of the family O how I wish you and Asa could jest step in and take a drink of cider and a good eate of apples and a good supper O I will forbear for my feelings are in disscrible I must bid you good by for this time do pardon all my mistakes I will do better next time write as soon as you can from your most effectionate Mother E W Smith

On January 13, Libby wrote to Lewis:

Dear Lewis I sit down to let you no that we are all wel and in good health I receivd your letter last nite I was glad to hear from you I hope your health is better I have rote to you evry week since you have ben gone I rote the last Day of Dec and sent you three Dolers in money you sent for a box of things we hav got them all redy to send you Eliza

> *had a letter from Asa last nite he thought we had not better send them gest now for he did not no wheir he should be you let us no as soon as you get this we hav got 2 lb of tobaco 1 of tea 4 of butter 1 of sugar 2 pair of footing [stockings] a handchief a number of other things to send to you I hope that you wil get your mony the children is all wel the little one has got to be a great boy rite as soon as you get this tel us wheir to direct your box and when to send it I must close biding you good after noon Mary E Smith*

The ability of correspondence to diminish distance to home is obvious, and reducing the separation improved morale for both Lewis and the family. After almost two years of war, attitudes both away and at home were changing, and the spring of 1863 would see the contest in the field renewed. The Lincoln plan to emancipate slaves in the rebelling states—they would not be freed in the border states and in Washington—had been presented to the Cabinet on July 22, 1862. Lincoln announced the Emancipation Proclamation on September 22, 1862, after the Union success at Antietam, signed it in its final form and issued it on January 1, 1863. The proclamation also allowed freed blacks to serve in Union forces.

The term *hunker*, which appears in Lucy's next letter, was slang dating from the 1840s and was synonymous with *curmudgeon* or *conservative*. The label evolved and came to identify those northern Democrats (the northern Democracy) who had southern leanings or antiabolition sentiments, although the reasons were varied. Several examples of the usage of *hunkerism* may better serve to define the term than a review of two decades of political agitation. For instance, a Plymouth, New Hampshire, soldier of the Fourteenth, angry at being "misrepresented . . . by the Copperheads" as "sick of the war," wrote: "But there are some good Democrats and loyal men who would be glad to see this rebellion put down, and with whom *country is first* . . . "[6] Such "strong" Democrats were antipodal to hunkers. A member of the Seventh Regiment NHV who "changed his mind as to the relation of the Negroe to the present contest" asked:

> Friends at home, are you going to town-meeting, this year? Go and vote against Hunkerism. The mean Hunkers stay at home and will not lift a hand to help put down the war, but find fault with the army and Government because they do not close the war.[7]

A last example, found in a letter from President Lincoln to Gen. Samuel R. Curtis, sought the truth regarding an allegation that Missouri Gov. H. R. Gamble's "unionism, at most, is not better than a secondary spring of action; that hunkerism and a wish for political influence stand before Unionism with him." Lincoln had every confidence that Gamble, a staunch Unionist, was "an honest and true man."[8]

In her continuing political commentary, Lucy recalled a discussion with Moulton H. Marston (1806–1894) while sharing a stagecoach ride. Marston was born in Moultonborough, New Hampshire, and lived in Sandwich from the age of five. He was Sandwich Town Clerk for ten years, postmaster for a period, and president of the Carroll County National Bank and then the Sandwich Savings Bank. He was a lifelong Democrat and a frequent representative to the county Democratic conventions.[9] He served as a representative to the General Court and for two years was Carroll County Treasurer. He also sat on the Governor's Council in 1875 and 1876.[10]

In Lucy's letter, which follows, she referred to several more individuals. One is "Ben Woodman['s] son," Pvt. John O. Woodman of Company E, Twelfth Regiment NHV. Born in New Hampton, young Woodman was sixteen years of age, and therefore needed parental consent (under age eighteen) to enlist. Apparently, he falsified his age and enlisted, but deserted on December 12, 1862, near Fredericksburg. He voluntarily returned in January 1864, entered active duty in April 1864, and mustered out in June 1865.[11] Illness was probably the reason he "deserted" and the cause for his late return to the Twelfth.

Pvt. John O. Woodman, Twelfth Regiment NHV. Author's Collection.

Lucy frequently mentions "George," but never reveals his surname. He is probably George W. Wiggin, Frank Wiggin's younger brother. George, wife Nellie, and their son Eddie lived next door to Lucy and Frank following the war. Born in New Hampton, George enlisted from Meredith in the Fourth Regiment NHV on September 14, 1861. He was discharged for "disability" at Hilton Head, South Carolina, on December 5, 1861. George was undoubtedly sick but must have recovered, for he enlisted again on August 25, 1862, and served with Company A, Sixth Regiment NHV, until discharged on June 4, 1865. George would see frequent fighting.

William E. S. Foss was born in Moultonborough and enlisted in the Twelfth Regiment, Company I, as a musician with the rush of men on August 14, 1862. On January 14, 1863, he too was discharged for "disability," and returned from Philadelphia to his home in Meredith.[12] Foss, a druggist, and his wife, Lizzie (for Elizabeth), would also be neighbors of Frank and George Wiggin and their families after the war.

Meredith Ville Jan'y 19 [1863] My Dear Brother

I received your letter Saturday night [January 17] and was very glad to get another letter from you. A frequent correspondence seems to shorten the distance that intervenes between us. You said you were well I am glad to hear your health is better but while rejoicing over one thing, we weep over another, for while thinking of your returning health I am sad to know of your hardships. Being on guard so much is enough to wear out a strong constitution. You spoke of its being an unjust war. Of this I have not expressed my opinion to you before knowing you were bound in it I did not wish to say a discouraging word about it, for one has enough to bear without one discouraging word. People here at the North are entertaining different views from what they did one year ago and think very many of them this can never be settled by fighting what is the use of it when there are more secesh here at the north than at the south. The only jubilant faces we see here at present is an old hunker when the federal army gets defeated after the battle of Fredericksburg the[y] crowed over it fairly gloried it, and even women that had husbands in the war said they hoped it would never end under the present administration. Such an one has no sympathy though it does come in our own family. It is not the republicans making and procrastinating this war it is the mean black souled sneaking democrat staying at home doing every thing they can to aid the rebels I was fairly disgusted with Moult Marston while riding in the stage to Sandwich a short time since by his talk he was more for prolonging than ending this terrible strife.

I often ask myself the question how long will God suffer this thing to be. Will He not soon visit this wicked and rebellious people in mercy this thing cannot last much longer there must be a change in affairs soon and I pray the day may soon come that the bondman may be free not merely slave do I mean by bondman but the poor white man galling in the chains of Government. My dear brother I have been a republican but not a rank abolitionist. if it is a going to aid in putting down the rebellion by emancipating the slaves so be it if not let them alone and cause the blood of every white man to be spilled for them the President in his Proclamation said as fas[t] as the slaves were emancipated they should be armed to fight for themselves this is what should be for by so doing the South is weakened while the forces at the North is strengthened. But enough of this you are aware of it all. Nothing ever sounded more like yourself my dear brother than to hear you say I am willing to do my duty and take my chance with the rest. God will bless you for that noble response. You spoke of so many deserting I fear they will have to suffer badly for it Government is about to use stringent measures with them could they desert and get out of the way and keep so I would not blame them they have been so humbuged. There is one here from the 12 [Twelfth Regiment] sick abed and the sheriff has the papers to send him back as soon as he is able. I pity his folks he is Ben Woodman son about 16. He forged his fathers name to the papers and his father cant hold him if he does he will be sent to prison for forgery[13] *We are all well as usual Frank has enough work to do but poor pay you must not look for him to write for I have to write all the letters to George [Wiggin]. George writes home that he is fat and saucy but tired and sick of war. Give my love to all I am acquainted with you for I have a deep regard for anybody in a soldiers uniform. I have heard from home since I last wrote I shall go up again soon Johny says tell you he wants to see you very much Lizzie says she will give you a chicken pie when you come home you write and tell me if you want some more envelopes in your next write as soon and often as you can and I will. Lucy J Wiggin. Bill Foss has got a discharge and got to Boston sick Lizzie meets him there today*

Lewis responded to Lucy's letter of January 19. Father Paine was Amos M. Paine, a Moultonborough farmer and Libby Smith's father. In March 1829, Amos married Hepsis Lee, who died of cancer on September 27, 1859.[14] By 1850, at age eighteen, Mary Elizabeth Paine, Lewis's future wife, was the oldest of the Paines' four daughters at home. The others were Julia M., seventeen; Hepsa, fifteen; and Lucy, thirteen. Demerit Paine, probably Libby's older brother and a laborer, was twenty-four. Nearby lived Parker Paine (d. 1876); his wife, Sarah; and their daughter, Sarah J. He is the "Parker" whom Libby occasionally mentions. Another name that appears is that of Ricker, probably Joseph L. Ricker (d. 1872) and his wife, Rachel H. (1830–1907), buried in Moultonborough's Bean Cemetery near Libby's parents, Amos and Hepsa Paine, and Parker Paine.[15]

Maryland Poolvile Jen 25 [1863] Dier Sister

I reseve your letter last knight an I was vary glad to hear from you an to hear that you was all well I am vary glad that I have one sister that will wright to me often for I have knot had but one letter from Salley two from Susan one Jacob sinse I left home I have reseved severel from B B but I have knot reseved eny from him for most fore weeks I never have had eny letter from farther Paine famley since I have bine out hear So you can see how much [they] think of me if you all new how good it seems to me to have a letter I do beleve that thay wood wright to me but if thay cannot [find] time to writ to me I shall haft to let them go an wright to them that wright to me thar is not much knews to writ to you Lucy for we have no knews hear only what we see hear that is anuff to sicken adog of the ware if the people thar to the north shod see an no as much about this cursed thing as wee do out hear thay wood feel difrent then what thay do know that is ashur thing it is all speclation from the begining to the end if thar is ever a end to it if it was knot for the big pay that the ofices have this war wood vary soon come to close but thay have big pay an keep drunk half of thar time and half of the other half that is the way this war is carrid on thay far[e] well while the por soldier is kick around by the cursed oficess when sick the dochters do knot car what bee coms of them in the first plase thay do knot no enuff to docter a dog that is the reson why that so meny dise thay air exspose to evry thing that can bee weet an coald knight an day you no but little what we haf to un der go hear you in newhampsher no you do knot the report is that Burnsid has cros the rasphannock [Rappahannock River] an taken forty thousand prisners and Ginrel Lee Ginerel Longstreet but it is to much to bleve. you wantid to no if I wantid some invelops sent no knot know for I have some know thank you vary kindly for your

> *offer tell Frank to kep stiff uper lip for I am coming home to go afishing with him next summer give my love to all ciss little Libby for me tell John to bee a good boy for I want to see him vary much except this ring as a token of rembrenc it is one of my own make writ soon as you can so good knight from your brother L Q Smith*

Smith was not the only one to voice the theme that the officers, if deprived of pay, would simply disappear, as would the war as a consequence. In his volume, *The Vacant Chair: the Northern Soldier Leaves Home,* author Reid Mitchell quotes an Illinois soldier: "They say cut down the pay of every officer to that of the private and the war will close in less than three months."[16] The same expression appears in *All Quiet on the Western Front:* "Give 'em all the same grub and all the same pay / And the war would be over and done in a day."[17] Pvt. James K. Newton, of the Fourteenth Regiment Wisconsin Volunteers, while under the white flag of truce, observed: "They [the Rebs] agreed with us perfectly on one thing. If the settlement of this war was left to the Enlisted men of both sides we would soon go home."[18]

This theme is different from another often voiced aphorism, "Rich man's war, poor man's fight," which related to the draft, whereby the payment of three hundred dollars, "commutation," released one from his obligation. As an alternative to the payment of the commutation fee, a conscript could provide a substitute, usually hired, to avoid serving. Opponents attacked the first option as "$300 or your life." The proponents of commutation asserted that the three hundred dollar fee set the ceiling for payment of a substitute, *facilitating* alternatives for the poor.[19] Commutation was finally eliminated in July 1864.

Three hundred dollars was somewhat less than the average annual wage at the time and is arguably not an unreasonable amount. Nonetheless, there is evidence that in Conway, New Hampshire, there were more volunteers, presumably the result of bounties, from the poorer districts than from the wealthier.[20] The impact of bounties, funded by debt in towns, was to increase the property-tax burden of those tied to the land, ultimately aggravating the problems of the poorer class of farmers.

Lewis was obviously very sick and incapacitated for months in late 1862 and early 1863, and was fortunate to have recovered. Treatments for almost any infectious disease were ineffective. Lewis's statement that "the dochtors do knot car" indicates that uncaring attitudes were probably worse for morale than were deaths by sickness itself. Furthermore, even after a year and a half of war, there were deficiencies in supplies: "We had rather a rough time when we first arrived owing to severe rains together with a scarcity of rations & tents . . . Our Hospital by the way seems to be a humbug as the Doctors have not a supply of medicines and from what little I have seen do not tend up very well."[21] Sergeant Jenks also commented on medical care:

> I take the best care of myself possible and hope to escape sickness, it is a hard place to be sick for you get no good care, and the Doct. will not admit they <u>are</u> sick, until their case has run so long, that recovery is impossible, one reason is, so many are continually playing sick to get rid of duty, and the Doct. has not skill enough to detect the counterfit.[22]

If the Fourteenth's men were sick and confined to their own tents, they were cared for, five regiments each, by Drs. Marshall Perkins of Marlow, New Hampshire, and Franklin C. Weeks of Chester, New Hampshire. Those sicker, in the care of Keene's Dr. William H. Thayer, went to the regimental hospital, a tent about fourteen by thirty feet, warmed by a stove and containing bedsteads built of boards. The tents were provided with "bedsacks filled with straw, and plenty of comfortable bed clothes & feather pillows, many of which the sanitary commission furnish." The "nurses," who at that time and situation (in camp), were not female, were "tolerably faithful." The exception was predictable: They were "rather too apt to take to whiskey bibbing, making rather free with the liquor intended for the sick."[23]

Although the regimental hospitals served fairly well in a static environment, camps or barracks, they failed miserably in battle. In that situation, it was expected that the wounded would be taken to their regiment for evaluation and treatment. As a result, some surgeons would be overwhelmed with casualties while others had no wounded, and some surgeons refused to treat men from other than their own regiment. This chaos was resolved by the time of the Shenandoah Valley campaign in autumn 1864, when an extensive transportation and hospital system, based on divisions rather than regiments, was in place—a model for the world's armies up to World War I. When Lewis and the Fourteenth experienced the thick of bullet and shell, Lewis would refer to the wounded as doing "first rait."

Last, in regard to circulating rumors and war news, "to much to bleve," Smith was correct. Gen. Ambrose Burnside's forces were stopped at Marye's

Heights on December 13, 1862. Having sustained twice the number of Confederate casualties, the Federals retreated from Fredericksburg back across the Rappahannock. Cpl. Benjamin Franklin Pierce, of Bradford, New Hampshire, and Company I of the Fourteenth, recorded in his diary: "A rumor that Burnside had taken Lee or Longstreet and their divisions is going the rounds."[24]

Poolvile Marland Jen 25, 1863 My dear wife

I reseved your letter last knight an was vary glad to hear from you an that you was all well glad to hear an think you air all well at home while I am so far from you. you sed that you hop that I should knot blam you for knot gitting youar letters why no surttingley knot if you writ them that is all that can bee recuired of you but if I could hear from you evry day I should bee plea[s]e but if you wright once a week I will be satfid with that. but I want you to besur to do that if you can

About that box if you have knot sent it. you may not send it untill you hear from me agane for we gut news to day that the boats is agointo stop runing this week on the connol [canal] an will knot run eny more for to month to com. for the reson I no knot it is the govement that has do it. you wantid me wright how meny and hoe [who] thay bee that tents with me thar is nine of us Asa an I James Walic [Wallace] Samul [S.] Smith E Duston [Ezekiel E. Dustin] James [E.] Chase Henry Mo[u]lton I have written to you about it onc befor an all about how our tents was bilt which you have gut without dout beefor this

you wantid me to writ to you how Molton Webster was he is tuff an ruggard as a b[e]ar he send his love to you all. if it was knot for him I do knot no what we should do for he is as good as a farther to me an so has Asa Asa is ruggid he send his love to you all. I reseve a letter from Lucy J last knight thay war all well thar is knot much news to writ you Burnside has crosed raphanac [Rappahannock] an taken forty thousan prisner an Ginerel Longstreat an Ginrel Lee but it is to good anews to bleve I am afraid thar is no more news to writ this time give my love to all ciss the little ones for me an tell them to bee good childrens I must close by bidding you good knight wright as often as you can please to except this ring as a toaken of remebrenc for it is my one [own] make this is from yours Lewis Q Smith

Lewis sent several handmade rings to relatives and friends. These rings were simply crafted by many of the soldiers from bone or horn and were often carved with elaborate designs in the manner of scrimshaw. In Lewis's next letter home, a brief one, he mentions his children's names: John, Frank, Hiram, Lucy, Hypsy, and the "boy." He does not know his youngest son's name! Lewis's sister, Susan A. Smith, was married to Albert F. Hackett, whom Lucy Wiggin would later describe as a "strong Democrat." The Hacketts are mentioned frequently in subsequent letters.

Poolvile Jen 27 [1863] Dear wife

> *Set down to wright you a few lins to let you no that I have sent you a few things in mr [Pvt. George] Haddoc[k] box that he starts for home to day you must knot think hard of me for knot sending you more for I had knot mony to by it. I have knot reseve that mony that you sent me thar was three letters rit of that I have knot reseve yet if you writ evry week as you sed you did whitch I do knot dou[b]t it at all thar is knot much news hear know one thing over an over I am tyard sick of what knews that we git hear thar is knorthing to bee relied upon thos things that I have sent to you is as follows the knife is farthers to eat his dinner with the Spenser [a double-breasted overcoat] is for farther tell him to w[e]ar it the white hanchiff one for you the other for Mother the little hanchief one for John one for frank an hyrame the beeds for Lucy the other hypsy the boy for your boy is so smart he ou[gh]t have something to pleay with. the thing I send to you I send them in your name in the care of Susan hackett Asa send his bundle thar to Susan tell hir to send it to his fooks as soon as it git thar thar is northing more to writ this time so good knight wright as often as you can I wrot you last Sunday [January 25] from yours Lewis Q Smith*

Closing out the first month of the New Year is a letter from Lucy. The events of December and January have taken their toll. Dejected, almost melancholic, she nonetheless remained strong and was a rock in the Smith family. There is ample evidence that a similar malaise in the winter of 1862–1863 pervaded the military as well as the home front. In Poolesville, Sergeant Jenks's mood was also flat, but on the rise: "My faith begins to strengthen a little that all things will come out right in the end."[25] Pvt. William Combs, serving under Jenks in Company C, wrote on February 27, 1863, that "it is pleasant here to day with the excepsion of the mood."[26]

Dr. William Child, of the Fifth Regiment NHV, mirrored the others' sentiments: "Gen. Burnside made a grand move a few days since but 'got stuck in the mud.' It was as bad as a defeat. How unfortunate this army is. Will fortune ever favor us. Gen. B. is now removed and at present Gen. Hooker has command. Everything goes wrong—and it is a fact, that cannot be disguised, that both officers and men are in a demoralized condition."[27] Francis Buffum wrote: "It was seen that the war was likely to continue beyond all of the expectations entertained when the regiment entered the service. There was a general dissatisfaction with the management of the armies . . . "[28]

Lucy mentioned that Frank had "run" harnessmaker John Dearborn "out of the village."[29] B. B. Smith noted Frank Wiggin's penchant for work as early as 1856: "I very much fear that L's husband is working too hard for his health. If he confines himself so closely to his shop I fear that his constitution will give way under it. Tell him to be careful."[30] Lucy's loneliness was in large measure attributable to her husband's long hours in his shop; she was anything but a loner. She was *the* consistent correspondent for the Wiggin, the Smith, and even the Paine families. A decade earlier, Lucy wrote of giving an "applebee," attended by eleven couples, and though the gathering may have processed apples, the event was similar to a quilting bee—that is, social.[31] Lucy also referred to "pairingbees," which were undoubtedly social functions, as well.[32]

M. Village Jany 28 [1863] My Dear Brother

I received your letter today and I thought if a letter from me did you so much good you should have one directly I feel it my duty to write to you often and I mean to do it as long as I am able to do it. it is all I can do to do you any good. I know how glad I am to get a letter from you, and why should you not be as glad to hear from us, you be I know and shall as far as I am concerned. Yes Lewis your letter reached here today in time for Lizzie Ann's wedding. she was married here this afternoon and has gone up to Sandwich she will stay with us for a week she will then go to Lake Village to live. I meant to have told you of her in my last letter but I forgot all about it till after I closed my letter. she says she will write to you very soon I sent your letter up home by her.

My mind this evening has been carried back some seven years when a like ceremony was performed here, and I can but shed tears of anguish to think what heartrending scenes we have been called to pass through since that time. Yes dear brother it is heartrending I am not merry as of old my heart is sad If I do laugh I am sure to have a good cry when I think of how many tears a falling while I am making merry and my prayer is that peace may soon be proclaimed and the poor worn weary soldiers be permitted to again return to home and friends where he may lay himself down in peace and safety the question often times arises to my mind, how long will the wicked triumph and the inocent be made to suffer but Gods ways are not our ways His ways are hidden from our sight they are past finding out. Your prolonged absence does not erace you from my memory Oh! no no it does seem some times those cold dark nights that I could not endure it when I am comfortable in a warm room perhaps my dear brother is on his lonely night watch suffering for the comforts of life. oh who can say they cannot realize the horrors of war surely not I. all I can say to you is keep up good courage hoping you will soon outride the storms I think something will be done soon to bring this war to a close today we learn that 800 officers are to be sent home as incompetent and I do hope their places may be filled with good substantial men fit to serve well the government. I feel glad you are not in the main army of the Potomac. I look in the papers every day to see if there are any change in your regiment. You say they dont write to you I cant see why they so neglect to write it is too bad I think why B. has not written he has been travling around from place to place I did not know where to direct a letter to him for four weeks. I have not heard one word from him since I wrote you last. I have been looking for them down every day but it has been horrid travling we have not had snow to make good sleighing this winter till this week. I mean to go up soon as I possibly can. Frank cant get out of the shop he has all he can do he works till 8 or 9 o clock every night. He says tell you he has run John Dearbon out of the village he has quit work and took down his sign Frank is as poor as a crow he has not been fishing or guning this winter he has not been out of the shop a day since fall only when to I. to funeral I fear he will be obliged to lay by if he is not careful I see my sheet is most full and I have not said half I want to I wish I

> *could see you tonight and tell you all about everything I want you to take as good care of yourself as you can so you may be permitten to come home. the children send their love to you Johny is terribly well pleased to have a letter he run to hear it read they are good children he says he wishes you could come home and see them poor boy little realizes the horror of war give my love to all of your boys that I know tell them they have a place in my heart. Frank bought the second colt kept him 4 weeks and sold him for fiftyfive dollars he didnot harness him but once. he weighed him he weighed 800 he grained him all the time he kept him I was glad to have him sell it for it cost so much to keep and we could not I must close by asking you to write every chance you get and I will be faithful in answering Uncle Steve Wadleigh is dead Good night from si[s]ter Lucy*

Lucy touched on another pervasive problem: "incompetent" officers and the need for "good substantial men." Because regimental officers were elected shortly after the enlistment process, there was no guarantee of battle efficiency beyond a popularity contest. On the regimental level, Buffum stated rather elegantly: "All of this sash-girted rubbish soon floated homeward on the happy currents of eagerly accepted resignations, and better men from the ranks stepped into positions they should have originally occupied."[33] Complicating the competency issue was the amalgam of vanity and jealousy in relation to rank and position among officers. In October 1863, the Fourteenth's adjutant, Maj. Alexander Gardner, commented:

> The state of affairs could hardly be more uncomfortable than they are. One needs health, strength and patience to endure it—constant plotting—one hardly knows what is coming next . . . Just run over our list of officers present with the Regt. and you cannot help having some pity for me if we are sent forward.[34]

Dr. Child, from Bath, New Hampshire, the Dartmouth-educated assistant surgeon of the Fifth Regiment, commented on the officer "problem" and elaborated on his previous remarks regarding the winter's malaise:

> Everything about our country seems gloomy—sad—But this is to be expected. It does appear astonishing to me that we have wasted so many men—so much wealth and have accomplished so little. The fact is we want the man—the great man who is able to combine and direct our strength and lead us on to victory—it maybe a slow but a sure success. We

> have not yet seen the man. Is there one? . . . It is so vexing to know how our men and means have been wasted in foolish blind attacks the consequence of incompetent commanders. This army seems doomed to defeat and misfortune while victory follows our western armies.[35]

Although 1863 would see numerous changes in leadership in the Union Army, successful generals remained few. However, as President Lincoln and Secretary of War Edwin M. Stanton began to weed out the "political" generals by early 1864, the war in the East would be prosecuted by officers successful in the West—Grant, Sheridan, and Sherman, among others. The fortunes of the Confederacy would slip in the summer of 1863, and a year later would be recognized increasingly as a lost cause.

~ *four* ~

Gloom Continues

Duty on the Potomac and Winter Camp at Poolesville, Maryland February 1 to February 28, 1863

> *. . . thair is northing incurigin for us hear every thing looks dark and darker evey day thar is but little hop of peas being declared as long as thay can git man to fite for thar cursed woorks . . .*
>
> —Lewis Q. Smith, February 8, 1863

LATE JANUARY SAW A STALLED FEDERAL MOVEMENT toward Fredericksburg, Virginia, in the second attempt to take that city. After more than a day of very heavy rain, the Army of the Potomac retreated with great difficulty in what became known as the "mud march." On January 26, 1863, Gen. Joseph Hooker (1814–1879) replaced Gen. Ambrose Burnside (1824–1881), who had reluctantly accepted command of the Army of the Potomac three months before. In the West, Union forces were moving toward Vicksburg, Mississippi. Vicksburg and Port Hudson were the last obstacles to federal control of the Mississippi. At sea, newly built and purchased ships rapidly augmented the blockade of the South, while the Confederate raiders CSS *Alabama* and CSS *Florida* continued to destroy Yankee shipping in the vast reaches of the oceans as well as in the approaches to Boston and New York. In mid-February, with President Lincoln's support, a conscription act moved through Congress and passed in early March.

After a meeting with General Hooker on April 6, 1863, President Lincoln, reflecting a shift in strategy, wrote: "Hence, our prime object is the enemies' army in front of us, and is not with, or about, Richmond—at all, unless it be incidental to the main object."[1] It has been said that Lincoln's "strategic thinking was sound and for a rank amateur astonishingly good." It has also been stated that the president "soon realized, if he did not know it at

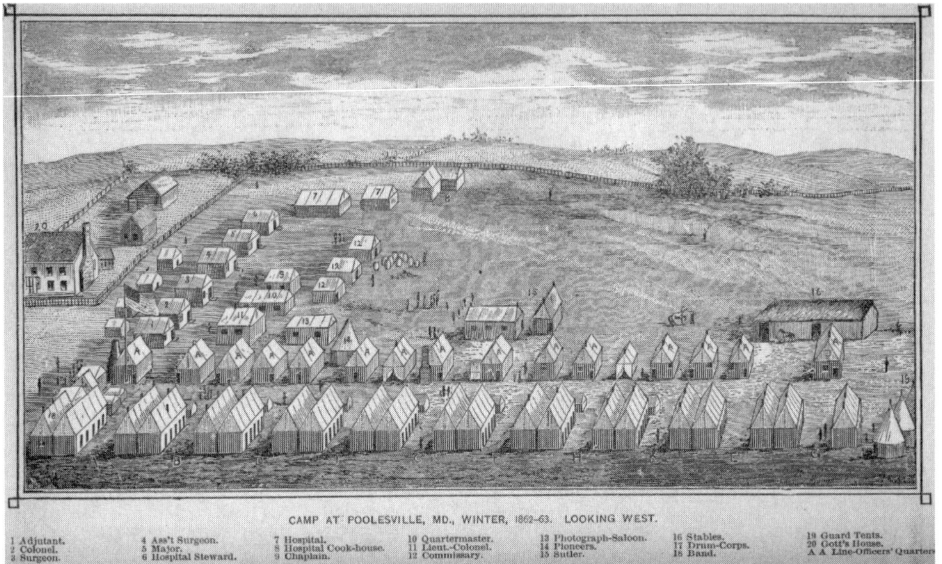

The Fourteenth's Camp at Poolesville, Maryland. Author's Collection.

the beginning, that the proper objective of his armies was the destruction of the Confederate armies and not the occupation of Southern territory."[2]

April 7 saw the first unsuccessful attempt to take Charleston, South Carolina, by federal ironclads. In late April, Hooker's army crossed the Rappahannock River, and in early May fought a major engagement with the Confederates at Chancellorville. Meanwhile, the Confederate dollar had fallen to a fraction of its value due to inflation, contributing to a bread riot in Richmond on April 2. Confederate currency would continue to drop in value: In October 1864, a Confederate soldier said "he had not seen any money for a year; but it didn't make much difference, as the money was so poor that he could not have a decent 'spree' on six months' pay."[3]

The troops in winter camp at Poolesville had their own problem with bread as the Union's supply system worked to catch up with its burgeoning population of soldiers: "we live prity well now but we had some living that has been prity hard . . . you can put hard bread into coffee and have the worms rise on top and when you brake the bread open the worms drop out." Undoubtedly as a consequence, "the boys stoled every kind of poltery and every swarm of bees . . . in this plase [Poolesville] killed sheep and hogs and cattle and stold all the goods thare was in one store and now we hafto gard evry house thare is in the place to pay for it."[4]

Lewis seldom mentions abolition in his letters and it appears that it was not a motivating factor for him as a soldier. Others were even less sympathetic to the plight of slaves. On November 23, 1862, Pvt. William Combs, of Company C, wrote home: They "do not want to bee free no more than we want to bee slaves i know a Negroe that is free and he sais he has to work harder to get a living then it [was] when he was a slave."[5] Sergeant Jenks, however, expressed a much warmer sentiment and was clearly moved by contact with slaves. While searching for a presumed Southern sympathizer who had shot a member of the Fourteenth (identified as Sandwich's Company K musician John L. Smith, who was purloining straw for bedding),[6] Jenks entered a shanty near the scene of the shooting:

> *I got cold I went into a Nigger shanty close to the house, which was occupied by a Negro woman about 50 years old, her son who had fits, and a man about 35. They had a nice fire in the huge fireplace all night. I wish I could tell you my feelings as I sat there alone at the dead of night, (the man went with Captain [Ripley] as guide) in that negro shanty, talking to that poor ignorant slave. It brought impressively to my mind the reading of Uncle Tom's Cabin. Little did I then think I should spend a night with them. Her husband lived four miles distant. She has had 14 children 7 of them have died, the rest are within a radius of 12 miles. Her daughter was in another shanty and had lots of little ones; her husband ran off 2 months ago; he did not live on the same plantation with her. The other Negro Henry was married to a girl 12 miles off, had 5 children. After he gets through with the toils of the day for his Master he makes brooms chairs and baskets to sell to procure tobacco, Sunday clothes for himself and wife, and some of the luxuries of life, such as sugar. Don't you think such men can take care of themselves?*[7]

In Lewis's first letter of February 1863, he queried Libby, ". . . if you git your mony of Weed." Both the town of Sandwich and the state of New Hampshire had authorized financial aid for families of volunteers, and William M. Weed (1814–1892) succeeded innkeeper Ezra Gould (1808–1888) as agent to disburse such aid in Sandwich.[8] Weed was alleged to have

William M. Weed, Gentleman, Sandwich Lower Corner. From the Twenty-Ninth Excursion of the Sandwich Historical Society (1948)

participated in a recruiting scam during the Maine Aroostock War scare of 1839, and at two Sandwich town meetings in September 1863 was accused of skimming aid disbursements. Nonetheless, Sandwich voters opted to retain Weed, regarded by some as "a most shrewd and wily person."[9] In 1850, Weed's occupation was "farmer" and he owned two thousand dollars in real estate. A decade later, he was a "Gentleman" with four thousand dollars in real property and $6,460 in personal assets.

In mid-October 1862, Weed was appointed lieutenant colonel of the Fifteenth Regiment NHV, a nine-month regiment.[10] However, he promptly declined the appointment.[11] Weed prospered in the decade that included the Civil War years. By 1870, the "Farmer & County Clerk" had considerable holdings: twenty-five thousand dollars in real estate and $10,400 in personal property—*significantly* more than any other individual in Sandwich save one, Isaac Adams (1802–1881). Adams made his fortune in Boston with his patented, steam-powered printing press (the Adams Press). Retired, he lived in Sandwich on "one of the finest farms and residences in the town . . ."[12] His fortune in 1870 consisted of a staggering $308,000 in real estate and $265,000 in personal property.[13]

Lewis's health remained marginal and there is little on his horizon that is positive—certainly not medicines and medical care. At the time, malaria still occurred in the northern United States, and prevention and treatment of malaria was beginning to be recognized. J. Henry Jenks, of Company C, wrote: "Doct. Thayer came back four days ago, and is now on duty, he is going to give the soldiers Whiskey and quinine three times a day to prevent sickness. I can tell them what will be better, a little less labour and better rations."[14] Pvt. Henry A. Clapp, serving in Company F of the Forty-fourth Massachusetts Volunteer Militia in North Carolina, described quinine's dosing:

Another very amusing scene occurs every night just after tattoo & roll call . . . when we all march up and take our quinine in a wine glass from the hand of the dispensing corporal who pours it from a great apothecary's glass jar. The quinine is liquified in whisky though no one would ever know it. It is the quintessence of all bitterness "and biteth and stingeth like an adder" in the throat.[15]

Poolvile Feb 1/63 Dear wife

I seat my self to writ a few lins to you acording to my promas all though I have not reseve eny from you this last week but I shall keep my promase as long as I am abele to wright my helth is knot vary good at the presant time I have bin lad up for to weeks with the dyree an that has troble me most of the time sinse I left home I have bin trubble with the gravele[16] but have gut about over with it our docters air knot woth a fly they dont care what becoms of us if thay only git thar pay it is powdars for evry one an evry thing oppium Quinnine is the med son that thay give for all cases it is monney is all that thay care for thay care nothing for the man nor mans lives no mor then you do a spiders it is fit for the neger when thar is knot half of them that wood leave thar marsters if thay was elibratid I have seen enuff to convinse me that this is the case and if thar is eny of the boy thar to the north thay had better stay thar untill thay no what thay are coming for not bleve thar cursed lys thar is knot much more news to wright you this time I could writ about this horible war a week in an week out but I forbear tell farther an mother to keep up good curig for I hop that this thing will soon bee dun away you must keep up good curidg for when I think of your roe to ho I do knot think of mine I wish that I was thar to help you but canot so keep up good curide an when I git home I will help you the more so never mind it I want you to wright if you git your mony of Weed now or knot an if you have gut your monney from Concord yet or knot an writ the hole about it Asa is well an doing well Molton Webster helth is good at the presant an thay boath send thar love to you all an say that you all must take car of your selfs thar is northing mor but ciss the children all for me an tell them to bee good childrin wright often as you can I no that it is bad for you to writ with so meny children I want you to wright in pertichler gust as you air gittin along all bout it so good knight from yours Lewis Q Smith

Libby responded with a brief letter dated February 4, 1863:

> *Dear Lewis I spend a few moments in riting to you we gett a long wel farther is smart he is goin to the corner with me to day Mary Ett is sick hear she had the Docter last night she is better to day she was taken vomiting the Docter did not say what aled her the children is smart all but Frank he has got cold and his throat trobles him he is so he can cut wood he wil do it I got all of them thing you sent they wer over to Atwards [Atwood's] I did not pay eny thing on them I received your letter Monday I was sory to hear you had orders to go away keep up good corage as you can give my love to Asa except a part yourself so good day this is from your wife Mary E Smith*
>
> *Unkle John sent that Cheese to you Parker [Paine] has lost one of his girls she died with [s]carlet feaver*

A week later, Lewis wrote again to Libby. The phrases "northing incurigin," "dark and darker," and "little hop of peas" need no elaboration. Lewis acknowledges Libby's "agoin to farming" by her purchase of a fifty-acre piece near Kiah Pond in the Notch.[17] Later in the year, Lewis would compliment Libby on her ability to maintain the farm. In a rare moment of subdued humor, Lewis teases his wife on her use of "my boys" as free labor.

> *Poolvile Feb 8 [1863] Dear wife*
>
> *I take my pen in hand to answer yours I reseved your letter that was daited Jen 30 I reseve it Feb 4 an was vary glad to hear from you and the rest of them and to hear that you air all well at home my helth has knot bin vary rich for three weeks past but am better now yesterday was the first duty that I have don for three weeks I have bin laid with the dyree an gravel complaint I have bin trubble with this complaint ever sinse I left home but am good deel better now I gess I shall go it now I was vary sorry that you co[u]ld knot send your box after you had bin to so much trubble in fixing it up but I thank you all vary much for your kindness in fixing it out you sed that you wood send me some postig stamps if you could I should bee vary glad for I have gut all out an northing to by them with It took all of my mony to by medson with I have taken Dr medson untill I gut sick of it an seem as though that it*

done no good I bou[gh]t a pint of brande an a lb of lofe sugger an pai one dollar an fifty cents

I takit that you air agoin to farming by your bying you a farm well I hop you will maket well an rase a grat crops for I shall bee ofel harty when I git home you must make your brave boy help you farm but if you woork my boys you will have to pay me when I git home So you look out how you work my boy thar is knot much news to wright you this time only the rebels air doin what is done thair is northing incurigin for us hear every thing looks dark and darker evry day thar is but little hop of peas being declard as long as thay can git man to fite for thar cursed woorks if thar was knot eny ofecers this thing wood bee settle but thay like thar whiskey an pay to well this is the reason and the hole reson why this thing has knot bin settle befor but then I will say no more this time a bout the helish works thare is not much more to wright you this time Molton an Asa is well sends thar best respect to you all tell farther and mother to keep up good curidg for I shall come home some time if I live war or no war wright as often as you can give my love to the children and ciss them for me except my love your self so good knight from yours Lewis Q Smith

Libby wrote on February 8, 1863:

Dear Lewis I sit down this eavning to let you no we are all wel and wish this mite find you the same I received your letter last nite and them things that you sent to me I was very glad to hear from you I am very sory that you are sick I hope that you wil get better soon I should think that [they] mite let you come home when you are sick most all the time farther thinks evry thing of his knife and spenser you sent him he thanks you very much for them the children is very much pleased with their things that you sent them they thank you for them the little one would thank you for his little baby if he could talk he is a great boy now he weigh 14 and a half and hipsy weigh 23 I told you once before but did not tel you rite I thank you very much for the trowesers and the others things I did not think you would ever let me weir the trowsers but I wil keep them til you come home and see how you look with them on dont wery eny about home for we get a long first rate farther has got up about 20 lods of wood to the door B is up hear now he has bin over

> *to the nor[t]h and got his colt shod he likes him very wel h[e] got his chek last thursday and I have got the mony if you want me to send you som I wil I could [send] a dolar to a time if it got lost it would not be much wednesday was the coldess day that we have had this winter was as that day you come from the north if you remember it tel me what kind of wether it was their that day Mr. Derbern was beried to day and Mr. Straw to the north*[18] *Mother was to the corner to day the[y] are all well I cant not think of eny thing else to rite now rite as often as you can I rote to you last week and to the week before I wil bid you good nite this is from your wife Mary E Smith*
>
> *Dear Asa I must rite a few lines to you to nite we are all [well] and I hope t[h]is wil find you the same I am glad that you are so good to Lewis I am glad that he has got one friend in that de[v]olish plase you be to him and I wil be your friend for ever I pitty you poor boys to stay their and the war wil have an end before a great while Mother was down to the coner to day she see Eliza [Magoon]*[19] *she is wel and all of your folks there is no newes that eny body can believe now days I must close good nite your friend Mary E Smith*

Lewis's sister-in-law, Hepsabeth (Hepsa) L. Paine, was another correspondent. Four of her letters (from 1863 to 1870) survive, and reflect her experience as a mill girl in Manchester, New Hampshire. In 1860, Manchester was hardly a large city, for its population stood at just under nine thousand. Hepsa's first letter was dated February 8, 1863, and two others were written in June and July—after she left Manchester and moved back to Moultonborough.

Her job in the mill rooms was less than enviable—long hours, incredible din, dust, and potential for injury. Serious accidents or even death lay a half-step away: In a Laconia cotton mill, a shaft turning at 140 revolutions per minute caught a young Ossipee girl's hair, resulting in "her body striking the Loom, wall and plastering at each revolution." The overseers were present and immediately stopped the wheel. Despite one leg badly fractured and, in Yankee understatement, "her body somewhat bruised," her doctors concluded that she would recover "without the loss of a limb."[20]

In early 1863, not tied to a farm or a farmer or Moultonborough, Hepsa is still a mill girl, though barely. Many mills had already shut down due to the self-imposed Confederate embargo on cotton, an embargo that was a Southern miscalculation.[21] With bumper cotton crops in the two years before the war, cotton remained in British warehouses, and pent-up demand for textiles, especially in the Far East, had been satisfied. Although the strain was certainly felt in Britain, where one in five was dependent directly or indirectly on textile manufacturing, that country officially proclaimed neutrality in May 1861 and, although recognizing the Confederacy as a belligerent, never recognized Southern independence.[22]

In New Hampshire, wool's resurgence kept some mills working and by the summer of 1862, the change was evident: "Wool is now higher than it has been for forty-four years. This is owing to the large demand for army goods, and to the advanced price of cotton. It will not soon fall so low again as it has been of late years and we shall be surprised if the flocks upon our New England hills are not greatly increased."[23]

> *Manchester February the 8 1863 Sunday afternoon Dear Brother*
>
> *I received your most welcome letter last night and I hasten to answer it I was surprised to think you had written to me I could hardly realize that it was from you was verry glad to hear from you but sorry to hear that you was out of health it must be very hard to be sick so far away from home no one to real sympathise with you I pitty you if wishing would do aney good I would wish you home verry quick my health is very good and injoy my self tiptop I am hear to work in the mill the mills ar about all stoped hear, in Manchester it is verry hard times indeed it makes some of them look blue I tell you it does I hope the war will end soon and give us peace once moore so the poor soldiers can all come home once moor it has bin a verry mild winter hear their hasent bin but about two weekes slaying hear this winter it is so sloppy hear to day that it is most imposible to get out of doers I am going home to morrow at ten O clock they have sent for me to come home and stay with Father a few weeks for John Clark is sick and Julia [Paine, one of Hepsa and Libby's sisters] has got to go up and stay with hime untill he gets well and Lenord is going up to move Rachel [Ricker, the domestic living with Father Paine and Julia] down to Portsmouth to live the 14th of this month So I am obliged to go home but no one knowes how bad I hate to go but my self I shall come back soon as John gets well and go to work in the mill again the over sear is going to keep my chance for me I shall go up to see Lizzie as soon as I can after I get home and*

let her read your letter for I suppose that she is ankcious to hear from you every day or two I well remember the day that you started for the war it was on a Sunday when you went through Manchester it was a cold day I was looking out of the window but did not no that you was with the rigment if I had I should bin down to the depot to see you I havent aney news to write to you that is interisting to you give my best respectes to Asa Magoone I remember him well the time you and he ["made sugar" lined out] burnt the cole pit up in the woodes how cold it was and he heat a rock to set on so you sed to plage him I supose well Lewis I must close for want of wordes to say pleas answer this and I will write moore the next time try and get a discharge and come home and stay and fight for the darned Negrows they would not fight for you from your Sis Hepsa L. Paine

Hepsa's opinion about "Negrows" not fighting is far off the mark. Formed as black regiments, they fought extremely well and in significant numbers—an estimated 168,000 served in the last two years of the war.[24] Their record was clearly established:

Whether Negroes Will Fight

> There is nothing new or surprising in the brilliant conduct of the blacks at Petersburg. They fought with desperate courage at Port Hudson . . . At Milliken's Bend they repulsed an attacking force of more than twice their numbers. At Fort Wagner the 54th Massachusetts won a renown such as no single white regiment has yet attained in this war.[25]

Libby next wrote to Lewis on February 15, 1863. Albert Magoon is Riley Magoon's second son, who, at age about eighteen, and barring other circumstances, would have been draft eligible. The Twelfth Regiment NHV fought at Fredericksburg in mid-December 1862 and again under General Burnside in late January's "mud march." The Twelfth served at Falmouth, Virginia, until April 1863. Of thirteen engagements, the Twelfth's highest casualty rates were sustained at Chancellorsville and at Cold Harbor.

Dear and afectnate Lewis I sit down to rite a few lines to you to pass a way the time I thought that you would be glad to hear from us we are all wel and I hope this mite find you ingoying the same blesing I rote to you last friday I have bin riting to Hipsy to nite you rite to her and she wil to you I have not ben over to farther [Paine] yet farther has ben over hear once this winter I have not [heard] fro ther since he was hear Julia has ben up to Clarks this winter and Rachel keeps house for Farther Ricker is to Portsmouth to work on ships Albert Magoon has got home he aint afraid of being drafted now you ma[y] be thankful that you did not go in the 12 Regiment they have ben a marching from place to place ever since they have ben gone th[e]y have ben in one battle to Fredricks berg their was not but a few kiled the[re] if it had not bin for their Conol they would ben all kiled but he would not take his men they wanted him to and so he saved them so Dorcus told me her brother Adams was their the Regment is Falmouth [Virginia] now the little children is all gone to bed the[y] all send their love to Asa and all rest that I no to Mr Perl there ex[accept] there greatist part your self Burleigh and his familey is hear now he had a lectur down to the coner [Corner][26] *to day he uses his Colt most evry day he goes wel I must close biding you god nite and wil rite some more to morrow*

feb 16 Dear Lewis I sit down to rite a few lines to let you no that we are agoin to send a little box of things to you to morow they will let them go I have got all of them thing that you sent for

Farther went to see Eliza to see if [she] was a goin to send Asa eny thing she did not send eny thing as long as I have got your money I should think its a pity if I could [not] send you a few little thing that you need to make you comfortable we have got enough to eat and drink and enough to weir if you keep having them s[p]els do try and see if you cant get a discharge we are all wel to day tel Asa that I sent him bar of tobaco to cher up his poor old sool I must close by biding you good day this from your wife Mary E Smith

On February 15, 1863, Lucy Wiggin penned another characteristically detailed and lengthy letter to Lewis. The impact of funeral processions is obvious, as is Lucy's criticism and contempt for Copperheads (Peace Democrats or southern sympathizers). In the North, resentment against Copperheads boiled over in early May. Clement Vallandigham (1820–1871), a former Ohio congressman and probably the North's most outspoken Copperhead, had repeatedly made antiwar statements. Gen. Ambrose Burnside, then in command of the Department of Ohio, had Vallandigham tried: the sentence, confinement for the duration of the war. However, instead of prison at

(3)
always keep them. I have made horrid
work with this letter for Mary Ann Irving
is here and she is jabber jabber pardon
me for delaying so long to write for they
have been up here till 10 oclock at night
and I could not get a chance to write
write often as you can I surely will
L. J. Wiggin M. Village Feby 15
My Dear Brother
I received your letter
3 days ago and should have answered
before but I have had company and still
have but they are abed, I was very glad
to hear from you again but pained to hear
your sick could I but administer to
your wants how glad I should be I think
of you by day and dream of you by night
I am particularly reminded of you
when I see friends bearing past the
bodies of their dear soldier friends
I feel to say Lord spare me this one
great trouble, it seems that your dis
ease is such that that you can render
but little service to your country
and I feel a little in hopes that you
may be permitted to return to us

Lucy J. Wiggin letter of February 15, 1863, Sandwich Historical Society.

Boston Harbor's Fort Warren, President Lincoln banished Vallandigham to the Confederacy.

Perhaps reflecting the changing mood of the country, Lucy expressed optimism about the defeat of the "rebellion" and again supported a role for black soldiers. In late March 1863, Lincoln wrote to Gov. Andrew Johnson of Tennessee: "The colored population is the great available and yet unavailed-of force for restoring the Union."[27] Near the war's end, the Confederates considered using blacks, but never could or would utilize them in significant numbers. Using them entailed liberating them, a blatant inconsistency with secession and the choice of war to maintain the institution of slavery.

M. Village Feby 15 My Dear Brother

I received your letter 3 days ago and should have answered before but I have had company and still have but they are abed. I was very glad to hear from you again but pained to hear your sick could I but administer to your wants how glad I should be I think of you by day and dream of you by night. I am particularly reminded of you when I see friends bearing past the bodies of their dear soldier friends I feel to say Lord spare me this one great trouble. It seems that your disease is such that you can render but little service to your country and I feel a little in hopes that you may be permitted to return to us ere long if your health is so poor I see no benefit for you to stay there if you were here I doubt not but you might have medicine that would do you good. let us all hope and pray for the best. I have not been to sandwich since I wrote but have heard from them brother B came down here to meet his wife and Eddie last week he told me they were all well and said he had written to you the night before, so I thought you would hear from us all. Jonathan came down yesterday to get Sarah for by the way she has been down here for a fortnight past they were all well at home. Henry Gilmans horse came near dying I dont know what did ail him. George Dexters wife has got a little boy poor woman. Our folks here at home think the prospect looks brighter for this rebellion to be put down than it has for some time past. Chase says Sandwich will go democratic but Frank thinks this town will go all right the most interest it take in political afairs is to have this most wicked war to come to a close which I think will soon be if the democrats tried one half as hard for the end of the war as they do to divide the north there would be brighter times.

> *It is as much as a man can do to live now any way flour from 10 to 12 dollars per bbl and sheetings 50 cents per yd and calico from 25 to 30, and every thing accordingly surely war brings misery Burleigh said they had got up a nice lot of wood and were getting along nicely Frank & Hiram [Smith] are as smart as a trap John dont like to have them praised for their smartness for fear they will get ahead of his times he is well and well contented says he shall go home in saping for grandma told him so he has been a very good boy has not spoken one bad word since he has been here he has not had to have a whipping since he has been here he has not been about with the boys much for they are not fit companions he goes with Uncle Frank he wanted me to send one of his cents to you he has got 25 I told him I would send a postage stamp for him. he thinks a great deal about you he and Lizzie write to you very often Lizzie prays for the poor soldiers and for Uncle Lewis & George that dont have tobacco. We are all as well as usual now. I see by the papers the negroes have conquered the rebels in one battle in Kentucky. if they all would pitch into them they would soon wipe them out every southerner but we have got to wait patiently. If I could see you tonight by walking many miles I would gladly do it and jump to camp on the ground and let you lie on my bed. I am here alone and dont know when our folks send to you I should be so glad to send to you I am a going to send you some tea in this letter instead of a sheet of paper and George sent for black peper to put in his soup if you would like some you just write and I will send some in a letter I was much pleased with my ring I shall always keep them. I have made horrid work with this letter for Mary and Irving is here and she is jabber jabber pardon me for delaying so long to write for they have been up here till 10 o clock at night and I could not get a chance to write Write often as you can an I surely will L. J. Wiggin*

Lewis wrote home a week after his letter of February 8. Again, he was irritated by lack of correspondence and his health was still problematic. Both Lewis and Libby expressed insecurity in sending money via the mails—fear that had some factual basis. The *Laconia Democrat* reported: "Last week one hundred and thirty thousand dollars was stolen between Aquia Creek [Virginia] and Washington. The money was in separate packages and belonged to soldiers who were forwarding it to their families."[28] The security of money transfers improved in 1864 with the introduction of U.S. postal money orders for amounts up to thirty dollars.[29]

Poolvile Feb 19 [1863] My Dear wife

I reseve your letter Tuesday knight maile the 14 it was knot daitid I was vary glad to hear from you an hear that you was all well. my helth is knot good at the presant but hop that theas few lines will find you in good helth an prosparity you wantid me to let you no if I had wrighttin to Hepsey yes I have an she has wrighten back to me She was in Manchester then but was agoin home the next day so she said an was goin up to see you as soon as she could and perhaps has bin thair befor this reach thair to you

I rot to Susan a few days ago but have knot had eny answer from it yet I have knot had but two letters from Chases folks Since I have [been] out hear one from Salley one from Sarah and I answer both of them long ago an do knot no why thay do not unles it is to much troble an cost without profit an that ma[y] bee so I rot to Jacob but he dos knot answer it perhaps it is the same with him I have reseve all of your letters that I no of except three at one time at time that you sent the mony that you sent last thar was three that I did knot git at that time an the one that had the money in was one of them

I vary glad that you air all gitting along so well I gest it is best for me to stay hear for it must bee that you git along better without me their [than] with me we air having it stormy hear for three days past it comence storming monday an rain all day tuesday it snow all day an knight an thar was six or seven inches of snow when it gut don snowin an it turn to raine it raine all day wensday an good shair of the knight an two day is Thirsday an that is not all it has knot cleard off yet. we git the maile three tims a week tuesday, thirsday saturday is the days that we git the maile I am vary much obelige to you for the postigue stamps there is northing els to writ this time give my love to the little ones except a share your self I will close by biding you good knight this from yours Lewis Q Smith pleas to wright as often as you can

Lizzie Ann Smith lived in Lake Village, Belknap County, New Hampshire. Lake Village, once part of Gilford, was renamed Lakeport in 1891 and became a section of Laconia in 1893. The Twelfth Regiment NHV was enlisted largely from Belknap County, and when the men left for Concord and camped there in late August 1862, it was at "Camp Belknap." The men of Sandwich had originally intended to join the Twelfth but were instead enlisted in the Fourteenth. At the time of Lizzie's writing, the Conscription (or Enrollment) Act was moving slowly through Congress. The legislation established a federal draft that was independent of state efforts. Sandwich's William F. Quimby, Company K, was later wounded at Cedar Creek by a shell. George N. French, also from Sandwich and Company K, was a headquarters clerk.

Lake Village Feb 19/63 My Dearest Brother

I received your ever welcome letter to day and you do not know how glad I was to hear from you- if you only knew how much good it does us to receive a letter from you, you would write often. I received a letter from Lucy yesterday. They are all well there at the [Meredith] Village and Mother is a going down there to make a visit next week. I have not had a letter from home since I last wrote to you. I shall write to Lizzie to day and let her know that I heard from you. Well My Dear Brother you do not know how I long for this war to close but if the Conscript Act passes I expect that everyone will be obliged to go to war. Oh how many thousands there are that loses their life upon the Battle Field. I hope and pray that this war will close soon. Oh how many glad hearts their will be when it does close- and they welcome their friend once more in Dear New Hampshire and I doubt not but what there will be a good many sad ones, but I hope and pray that you may be permitted to return to your Native Home once more. I wish that you could step in and eat supper with us to night. But I fear that I should be too happy to eat if I could see you. Ned says tell you that he will write to you Sunday and he wants to see you very much he says he wants you to come home so as to go a fishing with he and Frank this summer Now Lewis I want you to tell me just what you have to eat and do you have enough to eat. And do you sleep warm nights or do you suffer with the cold. There is one man here from the 12th New Hampshire Regiment and 2 too Holderness and one to Laconia. The report is that there is 2 from every Co. coming home until the whole regiment comes home they have 14 days furlough I wish that you could get a furlough home but it would be hard parting the second time. How is William Quimby. I heard that he was quite sick. Do you see George French very often. please give my best respects to him. You tell Asa Magoon that I want him to remember his promise I believe he said that if I ever got married that he would serenade me so I shall expect him to do so. Tell him I would like to see him first rate. Ned sends his love to him. I believe he saw him up to Father's. A thousand thanks my Dear Brother for the ring that you sent me. I shall keep it to remember you by. Ned wants to know if they cost you anything he says if they dont he wishes you would send him one make it bigger than you did mine he wants to carry it into the Foundry and show it to the hands that work in there. Have you got any paper and envelopes if not you write and let us know and you shall have some. Well My Dear Brother my sheet is nearly full and I shall be obliged to close. I want you to be sure [to] write just as soon as you get this and I will warrant you that you will get an answer. You must take good care of your health—and play sick and come home for you do not [know] how I want to see you You do not know how much I miss you when I go by home. Lucy wrote that Johnnie was well and contented. Little Lucy is just as cuning as she can be When I was up to Fathers she followed me around everywhere that I went. Ned thinks everything of her and Little Lizzie is as fat as she can be. Now dont fail to write just as soon as you get this Ned unites with me in sending much love he says keep up good courage From your Affectionate Sister Lizzie Ann Dont fail to write just as soon as you get this From Lizzie Ann

Almost all of Lewis's circle of writers supported conscription and were encouraged by the passage of legislation establishing a draft. The federal draft represented the nation's commitment to put more men in the field and to aggressively pursue the war. In theory, at least, it also took some of the burden off the volunteers and perhaps put a few Copperheads in arms. The Enrollment Act of 1863 was improved and amended multiple times before the war's end. Both it and the mistakes made and corrected would be the model for the Selective Service system of World Wars I and II.[30]

In Washington, the Thirty-seventh Congress was about to close, but at home the political contest was on. As residents of New Hampshire's towns well know, spring brings political heat to Town Meetings and warmth to sapyards.

~ *five* ~

Politics, Smallpox, Sapping, and Spring

March 1 to April 21, 1863

> *. . . the soldiers air all in good sperits for the union my curidg was never better then it is now if my helth was as good [as] the curidg I wood lick the South a lone . . .*
>
> —Lewis Smith, March 10, 1863

IN HER NEXT LETTER, LIBBY REFERS TO LEWIS'S ILLNESS and to "town meeting." She wryly taunts Asa Magoon by offering to "cary a Democrat ticket for him." Democratic sympathies would begin to decline after Lee's defeat at Gettysburg and the fall of Vicksburg in early July 1863. The Confederate loss at Mobile Bay, the capture of Atlanta in September 1864, and Sheridan's successful Shenandoah campaign would ensure Lincoln's reelection on November 8, 1864. By Town Meeting of 1865, Union victory would be nearly complete and politics would no longer fill New Hampshire newspaper columns.

Perhaps in advance of the public's political shift, it was becoming apparent that there were fewer Democrats in the army. One soldier wrote home in December 1863: "they are a very scarce article in the Army at present . . . The past six months have made a great change politically in the Army. Men who a year ago were bitterly against the Administration have failed to find even sympathy, much [less] encouragement in any other party."[1] William Combs also noted the change: "the soldiers think different of the war than they did when they inlisted."[2]

Back in the Granite State, however, in early 1863, Democrats still held sway. In Libby's words, "the Democrats wil goet strong . . . " In what was a straw vote for the New Hampshire governorship (absentee balloting would become law in 1864), the men of the Fourteenth cast 424 votes for the Democrat, Judge Ira A. Eastman, of Concord, and 305 for Republican Joseph Albree Gilmore (1811–1867), a railroad man and superintendent of the Concord Railroad.[3] In the New Hampshire (town meeting) elections of March 10, Carroll County endorsed Eastman, the Democrat, 2,403 to 1,785. Sandwich came in with 247 votes for Gilmore against Eastman's 220 and sent two Republican representatives, Ezra Gould and Nathan Mason, to the state legislature. Eastman won the popular vote by almost four thousand ballots but, due to scattered and Unionist votes, lacked a majority. Democrats gained some seats in the statehouse, but not enough to get Eastman the governor's chair (a one-year term until 1877). Without a majority, the election for governor was decided by the Republican-dominated legislature. The Democratic vote was in a measure antiwar and anti-Lincoln, but it also stood for states' rights and strict adherence to the Constitution. In regard to the latter, the *Laconia Democrat* editorialized:

> To assume that one man [Lincoln] can abrogate, by [Emancipation] Proclamation, the law-making power of fifteen States . . . of this Union, is to stultify the intelligence of every sound thinker on our peculiar polity; it is to say that he can violate the primary law [the Constitution] of our national existence.[4]

Sandwich Mar 1 [1863] My Dear Lewis

I sit this eavning to rite a few lines you no I received your to letters last week one I got tuesday the other thursday I was glad to hear from you I was very sory to hear that you was sick I hope that you wil get bett[er] soon I wish you could be to home so I could take [care] of you it would not be eny put out to me if I could have you but I am afraid that I cant have you hear e[n]y more see it seames as though I could fly when I think it when I no you are a sufiring I hope you wil live to get home once more so the reason why I did not rite before to you I could not get my letter to the [post] ofice farther has not ben very wel for a day or to he has ben troubled with his old complaint but he has got better now Mother is over to unkle John a visiting he is a goin over after her to morrow if it does not storm it has snow hear to day we have enough snow heare now if you want eny mony I wil [send some] in the next letter I dont want you to sufer for money as long as I have got eny the letters go puty rite now Julia lives up to clarks now Hipsy is along with farther now I cant think of eny news to rite this time the little children sendes their love to you give my love to Asa and except a good part your self tel Asa I shal g[o] over to town meeting and I shal cary a Democrat ticket for him the Democrats wil goet strong [this] year I canot think of eny thing els to rite now so I must close by biding you good nite this is from your ever Dear wife Mary E Smith

Ma[r]ch 3 Dear Lewis as I could not get my letter to the ofis yesterday I rite a line this morning we are all wel the children sendes there love to you ex[cept] my love your self if there is eny thing that you want and I can send it I wil if you wil let me no so good morning.

Also writing to Lewis on March 1, Lucy Wiggin added dimension to the political landscape and discussed the "conscript act." The Enrollment (Conscription) Act had passed Congress and awaited Lincoln's signature on March 3. Lucy referred to "Dan Beede," (variously spelled Bedee, Beedy, and Beade in New Hampshire), a Sandwich native, who was appointed adjutant of the Twelfth Regiment NHV when he mustered in on September 6, 1862. He resigned from the army on May 15, 1863.[5]

Maj. Edwin E. Beede was also Sandwich born—on January 8, 1838. Enlisting from Meredith on August 18, 1862, he was appointed first lieutenant of Company G, Twelfth Regiment NHV. He was described as "Brave, sometimes almost to rashness . . . always conspicuous where the harvest of death left its sheaves the thickest, and if he knew what fear was, it was to scorn it . . ."[6] Ornamental prose aside, he was wounded several times, captured, and paroled. On April 14, 1865, while serving on special duty in Washington, he was at Ford's Theatre. While a physician was removing Lincoln's coat and unbuttoning his vest, Edwin was said to have discovered the fatal wound: "Captain Bedee, who was at the same time supporting the President's head, felt something warm trickling into his hand . . .[7] Dr. William Child was also at Ford's Theatre on the evening of the assassination and left his own account of the tragic event.[8]

Capt. Edwin Beede, Twelfth Regiment NHV. Author's Collection.

Meredith Vill M 1 [1863]

My Dear Brother I again sit down to answer another letter from you. I am glad very glad to hear from you but pained to hear your health is still so poor I fear you will be of little service to your country if you remain in the army if there is no prospect of your getting better adapted to that climate I think that the government would [be] better off to send you home than to keep you there on expense. they need all of their men and more too but what is the use of keeping sick ones since the conscript act has passed I think they will be a looking into this matter for now government has a right to call out every able bodied man in the country they are not obliged to put [up] with anything for a volunteer you are there and have nothing to fear from conscription were you at home I hardly think they would accept you Frank says if he is called for he shall pay no fines. By the way the law is a substitute or 300 dollars fine, he would make a poor soldier I fear. Dan Beede the adgatant of the 12 is at home on a furlow he says Frank would not stand it to march at all with the load upon his back they have to carry. that is what is killing all the feeble soldiers. There was a union man a member of congress from New Orleans lectured here he says the South have almost every white man in the field from 16 to 45 and thousands over 45 are enlisted he thinks let the North fill up her ranks this spring and the point is carried at once he says take the negroes from them and make them fight in the union army instead of laboring for the South raising provision for them to carry on this unholy war. he says it is not Lincolns war he says had James Buchanan sent one hundred men down there at the first onset it might have put a stop to let the south know they would meet opposition at the North but what did he do instead in his message he said if a state has a mind to go out of the union there is no power under heaven to coerce him back into the federal government so he helped it on instead of trying to defeat it a black hearted traitor. The democrat party here at the north are bound that this war shall never come to an end as long as Lincoln sits in the Presidential chair if they tried as hard to put down the Rebellion as they do to defeat the administration this strife would soon come to an end. The sensible Democrats are coming out boldly denouncing a Democracy that is against the union the[y] call themselves & party the same thing as a republican <u>Albert Hackett of Sandwich</u>

is one of the number as strong democrat as he has always been I think you will see by this there is a tuening up Jack here at home N.H. will I have no doubt go as strong as ever Republican a Republican defeat here at the North would rejoice the rebels more than any victory they have ever achieved in any battle that is what they are trusting in is a divided North as for politics I dont care a straw for anything only to have means used to put down the rebellion. I heard Mr. Wheeler of Dover a strong Democrat till 1860 and that year voted a democratic ticket he said when leading Democrats would go onto the stand in convention and declare that they were rebbels as he had heard them do then it is time to renounce them he said he came before the people as a member of no political party in the world he was for the union and only for that, and could our poor soldiers have the heart felt sympathy he expressed for them they would make the wilds of Maryland resound with their cheers. I am a friend to any man that has sympathy with the soldiers. I have given you quite a political lecture. I have done it that you may know how things are going on here at home. Our folks have sent you a box which you have got by this time. I have not heard from father since I wrote you last I have been looking for mother down for a week. she has not been down since you left home you hear oftener from home than I do we are not very well I have a bad cold now the children are pretty well they want you to come home Johny is looking for sapping to come so he can go home he don't want to go till sapping. he has been a very good boy. Write just as often as you can for I am very anxious about you L J Wiggin

Lizzie Ann Smith's letter of March 1863 runs in a similar political vein as Lucy's letter, and she also refers to Albert Hackett—a political update. Albert F. Hackett, a Sandwich carpenter, and his wife Susan (Smith) had three children: Hannah E., Burleigh B., and Augustus M. If Lucy Wiggin was correct that Albert was a strong Democrat—that is, not a Peace Democrat—then it is possible that Hackett switched parties and carried a Republican ticket. Against this supposition is the fact that later, on January 7, 1864, Hackett was one of Sandwich's Democracy representatives at that party's senatorial convention at Watson's Hotel in Moultonborough.[9]

Among those mentioned by Lizzie was Pvt. William S. Leach, from Meredith, who had enlisted on August 14 and mustered in on September 9,

Pvt. Willie Leach, Twelfth Regiment NHV. Author's Collection.

1862. "Willie" was almost certainly with the Twelfth at the first battle of Fredericksburg, from December 12 to 15, 1862. Although he had the "best of care," he died of illness on February 17, 1863, in Falmouth, Virginia. Hiram Nelson, born in nearby Bristol, New Hampshire, lived in Meredith Village and enlisted from Bristol as a private in the Twelfth.[10] He mustered out in September 1865, and if he deserted, as Lizzie stated, he may well have changed his mind and returned to serve out his enlistment. On March 10, 1863, President Lincoln issued one of several proclamations regarding desertion. In what was basically an amnesty, anyone returning "now . . . absent without leave" would be restored to duty without punishment except "forfeiture of pay and allowances during their absence."[11]

Lake Village Mar 2nd/63 My Dear Brother

I received your ever welcome letter to day and I was very glad to hear from you but was sorry to hear that you were sick. It is indeed very hard for a soldier to be sick for he is far away from his home and he has no one to care for him. I do wish that you could get your discharge and come home. I received a letter from Lizzie last Saturday she wrote that they were all well with the exception of Father and he had a very bad cold. she said that the children were smart. I also received a letter from Sarah Chase Saturday she wrote that Burleigh was there to her house she said that he lectured there last Sunday. I was up to Lucy's last Thursday I found them all well. Little Johnnie is as smart as he can be. Every soldier that he sees come home he will ask them why his Father cant come home Lizzie [Wiggin] is getting to be a large girl. We are expecting Lucy and Frank down here soon. Willie Leach was buried at Meredith Ville one week ago to day. he went in the 12th Regiment, his Father said that he had the best of care but said that he actually thought that he suffered with the cold. Do you not sometimes wish that you could run home and get a good warm supper. I often think of you when I am eating anything that is good and wish that you could have some of it. We had quite a snow storm here yesterday it stormed all day long- but it is quite warm to day. Dan Beede is at home on a furlough he says that Hiram Nelson is at Washington to work for the Government without pay. And they say that he will be branded as a deserter before he leaves. how foolish he was to desert. I cannot see as he has gained anything by it. Do you hear anything about Politics out there it is all you can hear here. Some of the Democrats pretend to say that if ever the soldiers get back they will all carry a Democratic ticket how is it with you I think that I can tell you some news that will surprise you Albert Hackett and Mr. Copp have both turned they are a going to carry a Republican ticket this year. Ned says tell you that he wants to see you says that if it was not so far he would slip in and see you some of these evenings he says he will try and take good care of the Widows he wants to know if you received a paper from him last week if you receive them he will send you one every week- he says get your discharge and come home if you can. He says tell Mr. Magoon that he should be happy to receive a call from him What do you do for your stomach I wish that you was where that Mother could take care of you You tell Asa to take good care of you You must keep up good courage for I am in hopes that you will soon come home. If there is anything that you want you write home and if it is possible you shall have it but as my sheet is nearly full I shall be obliged to close by wishing you Good Luck. Ned sends much love to you. Write as soon as you get this for we are anxious to hear from you. Your Sister Lizzie

Lewis may have experienced some conflict with his family's concern for his well-being and their urging him to get a "discharge." Lewis's criticism of both officers and the war became muted, and he decided to remain a soldier and to see "this thing" to its end. Nor was it a simple matter to return home on furlough. Despite trains, a trip to New Hampshire, though not a long one, entailed significant cost. Sergeant Jenks wrote that a fare from Washington to Springfield, Massachusetts, was nine dollars, and to Worcester, Massachusetts, ten dollars. Estimating perhaps fifteen dollars to Meredith, it would have cost Lewis nearly two months' pay to visit Sandwich—money he had little of. In addition, Sergeant Jenks, Lucy Wiggin, and others intimated that the second parting might be worse than the first. It is not surprising that few soldiers returned home during their three-year enlistments.

Brother B. B.'s concern continued to be Lewis's health:

North Sandwich Mar. 6/63 My dear Brother

Sarah has just written to you and asks me to put in a line to you in her envelope, and I will not fail to do so, though I can only write a few lines.

We are sorry to learn that your health is so poor. Now we want you to let us know just how you are. Kindly tell us all about the sore that is coming on your stomach. Dr. Page told us about you and he thought you would have an abscess, and we feel anxious to know how it is getting on. I am at Jonathan's [Chase] now; but am expecting to go to Thornton tomorrow so as to be there to lecture on the Sabbath, if it does not storm to hard. We are just having our winter snows now. It seems more like winter now than it did in Dec. and Jan. but the days are getting so long now, that we cannot expect the cold weather will continue very severe much longer.

I have not heard from home for a few days; but they were all well at the last accounts. Shall hope to see your family again soon.

Don't fail to write as often as you can.

Remember my love to all the Sandwich boys.

Dorcas and Eddie send their love and kind regards to you.

In haste Believe me Your affec. brother Burleigh

The Fourteenth remained camped at Poolesville, Maryland. The state virtually surrounded Washington and was very much a border state. Home to many southern sympathizers, it remained marginally in the Union. Lewis's spirit was strong, although his physical state was still lagging—he had been sick for about four months.

Poolsvile March 10 year 1863 Dear Syster Lucy

I set down [to] wright a few lins to you in answer to your that I reseve last Saterday knight an was vary glad to hear from you agane an hear that you air injoying your helth as well as you air my helth is knot vary good but is some better then it was a while ago my Syd [side] an stommack is the same as it was when I rot to you befor it has knot come to soar to brak yet but I think that it will in time but what cind of a soar I canot tell but I hop northing vary bad but bad a nuf I gest thar is knot much news to wright to you this time it is [same] thing over an over thay air knot doing much out hear now our pickets pick up a few rebels spys evry day or to thay have taken some about twentyfive or thurty of them this past week I do knot no how meny we have taken sinse we have bin hear thay air spy[s] that come acrost the river to see what thay co[u]ld and find out what thay could an I gest that thay do find it a little harder for them to git back agan then it was for them to come over hear on to this syd of the river thay have take advantig of us for the citezens hear will cereat [secrete or hide] them if thay can we have gut the wors set of the rebels that thar is in the woorhd all around us thar is knot union person in this an I wish that thay was burnt at the stake the soldiers air all in good sperits for the union my curidg was never better then it is now if my helth was as good [as] the curidg I wood lick the South a lone but I shall haft to wait awhile thar is knot much more to rit you an I will close for my hed aks bad an I do knot no as you can read it So good by for this time do rit often from your brother L Q Smith

Today, there would be considerably less concern about a "sore," but Dr. Page's and B. B.'s concern was appropriate. In Lewis's time, a sore or abscess could seed the bloodstream or infect a heart valve with fatal results. Sores and skin lesions were also manifestations of some systemic diseases such as diphtheria and anthrax. If Lewis's "soar" was indeed an abcess, which appears to be the case, and if it was a complication from typhoid, then it can be said that he dodged his first bullet. After months of illness, Lewis's health was nearly restored and, although limited, he was back "on dutey."

John L. Smith was a Sandwich blacksmith who enlisted in Company K as a musician. James Marcellus Smith, a shoemaker, also from Sandwich, was the other Company K musician. Their instruments, a fife and a drum, reside in the Sandwich Historical Society's collection. Although both John and Marcellus were seventeen and enlisted on the same day, they were not twins or even brothers. John was slightly older, and by 1860 he had left home and was living with Oliver L. Ambrose, a Sandwich blacksmith, to whom he was apprenticed. Marcellus's brother by a year was Herbert H. Smith, a tinman, who also served in Company K.[12]

Poolesvile Mar 28 year 1863 My Dear wife

I will try and wright you a few lines to let you no how I am gitting along I am gitting along first rait my Syd an Stummick is some lame and the Soar is heling up first rait and my helth is veary good other ways I have gon on dutey agane to day for the first time for six weeks I am on supernumary that is a reserve gard to bee in redness if eny one of the gard is taken sick while on duty it is vary rainy to day it comense raining this morning an it has rained all day long vary hard and it is wet and muddy a nuf you may depend

I havenot reseved eny letter from you this week but I reseve one mary ett last tuesday knight staiting that you was all well thar and that you had gon over to your farther on a visit and was vary glad that you had a chanse and could go over and see your farther you must go as often as you can and see the old gentleman I no that it is bad for you to git away from home now but keep up good curidg thar is better days acoming some time thar is knot much news to wright you this time thar is every thing quiet hear now in this sexion but thar will bee a grat moove through the Southern State and I long for the day

March 29 Thar is knot eny thing new to day I have gest com off from gard this morning I was knot called upon but onse and so that I did knot haft to stand on gard but two ours out of twenty for so I gut off vary eassy I reseve a letter from Burleigh and Sarah Chase and Lucy and Lucy sed that mother was down thar with her when she rot to me and I was vary glad to hear that you both had gut out onse more Sarah Chase roat to me that Albert Hackett had the smallpox or the next thing to it I am vary sorry if it is so and I hop if [it] is so you havenot bin expose to it eny of you I want you to wright gest as it is as soon as you git this

I will say to you that John L. Smith is gitting along first rait know he has gut out doars agane he is down hear to our tent now he has bin down hear evry day for a week to see us the rest of the boys air gittin along first rait thar is northing more to wright to you this time give my love to the little children an pleas to except a shair your self wright as often as you can and I will close by biding you go[o]d day from your[s] in hart and hand Lewis Q Smith tell Mary Ett I will wright to her soon

Libby wrote to Lewis on March 24, very briefly:

Dear Lewis I take my pen in hand to let you no how the children is a getting a long they are all better they all gain up it they all set up some I think if they do not get cold I think they wil get a long wel Lucy is up hear now Saly went home yesterday Unkle Bean is dead he is beried to day I must close by byding you good day this is from your wife Mary E Smith

Smallpox, a highly contagious disease with a mortality rate of about thirty percent, is mentioned frequently in the correspondence. An epidemic of smallpox (variola) was dreaded, but it was only one of a number of lethal infections that could threaten a home or a community. Albert Hackett's illness with smallpox (or "the next thing to it") is discussed again in the letter below. Varioloid, sometimes known as "modified" smallpox, occurs in people with partial immunity—that is, those who have been vaccinated or who have previously had (and survived) smallpox. It had been known for about a half century that immunity to smallpox from vaccination or disease was not permanent and decreased with time. Thus, reinfection or varioloid was usually mild and very rarely life-threatening.

Sandwich Mar 30 [1863]

Dear Lewis I sit down to rite a few lines to let you no we are all wel I received your letter satturday [March 28] I was glad to hear tha[t] your stomark was better and I hop it wil keep so I would like to no what you think ales your side if you have time to rite a few lines to John and Frank they work puty busy they are out sho[v]ling snow this morning it snow here yesteday they send their love to you farther has tapt a few trees John says we might he wishes we would send you a sugar tod he ses that it would be nise to sweetning your coffee their is not eny news to rite to you now only Mr Ha[c]ket has got the very loid [varioloid] so Docter Paige ses I dont beleve it is so yet I dont no as you can read this John sendes you this postage the children so much nois I mus close by biding you good morning this is from your wife Mary E Smith

In Libby's next letter, we hear more about the health of the Hacketts and others, including "Evrit taner." Edward E. Tanner, the eighteen-year-old son of Joshua and Sarah Tanner, of Sandwich, enlisted in Company K on August 14, 1862, and died of typhoid fever at Poolesville, Maryland, on March 19, 1863. His remains were returned to Sandwich, but, as revealed below, not without some delay. The Adams Express Company forwarded mail, supplies, and boxes to soldiers and also shipped bodies home—initially in wooden coffins, later in sealed metal ones. The expense could be considerable (with increased distance) and soldiers were known to share the cost of sending home a comrade.[13]

Henry H. Tanner, age twenty-two, enlisted four days after Edward and was probably his brother. Henry was discharged with "disability" in October 1864 and is mentioned in later correspondence. The Tanners lived near Asa Magoon and Levi H. Smith, not far from Lewis and Libby. Dr. Thomas J. Sweat, of Sandwich, was a respected forty-year-old physician with a wife and six children as of 1860.[14]

Libby noted the progress of sapping, attitudes toward the Democrats, and the draft. However, comments about Albert Hackett's politics vanished when the Hacketts became sick. "Edy," B. B.'s son, and "our boys" are helping out with "saping." Sapping, in late winter and early spring, might be regarded as northern New England's fifth season of the year. Collecting sap from sugar maples, most productive on south-facing slopes when warm days follow freezing nights, was, and still is, very labor intensive. Forty or more gallons of sap evaporated by wood fire produced a gallon of syrup, which could be further reduced to maple sugar. For most farmers, syrup and sugar were significant cash crops.

Sandwich's Parker Beede was "probably the largest sugar manufacturer in the country." In 1860, he was said to have had "a yield of 2400 pounds of sugar of a superior quality."[15] In 1863, Sandwich's sugar production totaled 11,700 pounds; the adjacent town of Moultonborough could claim only 3,355 pounds.[16] In the 1864 season, twenty Sandwich maple farmers produced 15,300 pounds, with six of them contributing less than three hundred pounds each.[17]

Sandwich Apr 6 [1863]

Dear Lewis I take my pen in hand to let you no that we are all wel and hope this wil find you the same farther and Burleigh gets a long nisley with their saping the bois is in their glory now Edy and our boys gethered 2 barel of sap saturday B went over to the north dont you think they are smart I received your letter saturday nite I was glad to hear from you and very glad to hear you was better you wanted me to tel you how Hakets folks is haket has got wel Susan has got round the house again the children are all sick again Meave is very sick the other to aint very as yet we havent ben exposed to it yet as we no of farther was in their when he was first sick but did not take it it was lucky for us want it Hacket kicked it Christpher Felos [Fellows] he ketched of Doctor Swet on acct of his close [clothes] when he Docterd Thomson famly Mother has ben over to Evrit taner [Tanner] furnal to day he got hear friday the reason was the [body] did not get hear before george Burleigh neglected to send the money on to Was[h]ington Mother see Eliza [Magoon] over their to day Mr Gilman has maid 2 hundred weigh of sugar and got sap and surap en ought to make 2 more up hear in Mr. Beede sap yard our folks has not sugared of[f] yet but wil to morrow we dont hear much news now I belive that the first draft to be in June I hope they wil draft so to take the Democrats and let them fit for themselves they want you poor soldiers fite and they stay to home and have their liberty I think it every ones duty to do their one [own] part and if they would this war would soon come to an end I cant think of eny news to nite the little children has gone to bed they send their love to you the little boy has got so he sets alone he is a little dear boy he is to good to live with me same as you was but I hope that you wil live to come back once more I must close by biding you good nite from your wife Mary E Smith

Little Lewis E. Smith was now sitting up and would have been about six months old. From all references to him, it would appear that he was born after Lewis's departure for duty. Several weeks after receiving Libby's letter, Lewis sent a flurry of letters before the Fourteenth left Poolesville for Washington. In the capital, there was also an outbreak of smallpox. Since 1862, postage stamps were used for small change due to the "present scarcity of silver coin,"[18] prompting this comment: "Quite a number of persons in Washington have contracted the small pox by being obliged to handle a great amount of the small postal currency. It is a fine medium for conveying the disease all over the country."[19]

Poolesvile Ap 11/63 My Dear wife

I will try and and answer your letter that [I] reseved the 9 daitid the 1 of Ap I was vary glad to hear from you onse mor and to hear that you air all well thar at home but I am afraid that the next letter that I git I shall hear that you have gut the Small pox for I heard that farther was [told by] Susan that Albert give up work but I do hop that you all will stear clear of it but if you do try and bee as cafel as you can and take good car of your self as you can as for my helth it has knot gut to be vary good yet My sid and stummach is rather lame yet the soar on my stummach is about the same it run some yet but I am in hops it will git better in a few days thar is knot much knews to wright to you this time we air h[e]ar on the old spot whar we have bin but we air exspecting [to] go every day and whar we shall go we do knot no for never no mor then one knight befor hand and then often tims then not no whar we air gointo untill we git thar thar is knot much goin on hear know it is vary still hear with the exsceptions of moveing thar is the most of the ridgment air mooveing and shiftins a round and I hop that thar air fixing to bring this war to a close

Apr 12 well Libby I will try and wright you a few lins this morning to let you no that my helth is about the same this morning and we have gut orders to move to morrow morning at seven o clock under seald orddors so we do knot no whar we shall go but we shall no when we git thar then I will let you no whar it is thar is knot much news to wright this morning Asa and Molton is well give my love to the children and pleas to excep a shar your self I want you to wright as often as you can dyrect your letters the same as you have don I shall hafto close for want of time So good morning for this time from yours truley L Q Smith

Lewis posted a letter three days later, with another following it by a week. James Y. Webster, of Center Sandwich, was Moulton S. Webster's brother and served as a corporal in Company G, Second Regiment of New Hampshire Sharpshooters. James was forty-four years old when he enlisted on October 31, 1861. Wounded on September 17, 1862, at Antietam, he was discharged with "disability" in Baltimore on April 10, 1863.[20] Libby would meet him "to the coner" in early May. "Mr Purle" and "Mr Sawtel" are James W. Pearl and Benjamin F. Sawtelle, both in Company K and both from Sandwich.

Poolevile Apr 14/63 [Tuesday]

My Dear wife I have gest reseve a letter from you and brother Burleigh and I will hasen to answer it I vary thankful to hear that you was all well ther at home and sad to hear the deth of poor little Mav and the truble that that famley is in but I do them no good I am glad to think that our famley has steard clear of it while I am so far away from them as for my helth it is knot vary rich yet my side and stummuch is about the same the soar is about the same I roat to you last Sunday [April 12] that we was ordored to march the next day but we have knot gon yet but we air under marchin orders to bee redey at a minit worning we hafto keep evry thing pack in redeness if thay should call for us I reseved a letter from uncle and ant Wiggins to knight and was vary much pleas to hear from them agane James Webster is hear he come hear last knight and is goin home he has gut his discharge I have send you a little bundle in Mr Purle and Mr Sawtel box to bee left to the postofic I must close

Poolesvile Apr 20 [1863] My Dear wife

I will try and wright you a few lins this morning to let you no how I am agitting along about the same my helth is knot vary good yet my syd and stummach is rather lame yet but I hop it will bee better soon we have moved about two mils the hole bridgaid has come to gether all but one ridgmant and how long we shall stop hear I cannot tell we air hear to day and whair we shall bee to morrow I cannot tell. thar is no knews to w[r]ight you to day for we donot git eny know we have nise wether hear now evry thing is grean I have not reseve eny letter from you sinse you and B roat I cannot wright much to day wright often I donot no as you can read this for I haftto rit it on my nee for the want of somthing to wright on so I will close by biding you good day from ever yours L Q Smith

Lewis mentioned having to write on his "nee" for lack of a suitable surface, for there were no desks or tables in the camp. Even an overturned box was a rarity, as it would probably have been reused or consumed for firewood. One soldier wrote that his writing was not very good "for I have to use Alex['s] back for a writing desk, and of course he doesn't sit very still."[21]

Obviously, smallpox—the extremely contagious affliction that the Hacketts and others experienced—remained a threat in Sandwich. B. B. Smith understood smallpox and the process of vaccination and wrote of his experience during an epidemic in India in 1858: "This is a land of disease and death . . . "[22] Dorcas had been vaccinated in America with a good take, as had Eddie, in both arms, in India. B. B. had had no take with two or three vaccinations in America and no better result when vaccination was repeated during the 1858 outbreak. Thus, B. B. was vulnerable. Libby's description of vaccination is classic. If and when the four children "take," a vesicle (blister) or vesicles would be ruptured and the virus-containing fluid would be driven into and beneath the skin with a needle on the "other to."

Dr. N. G. Ladd, of Sanbornton Bridge, New Hampshire, described the potential risk from contaminated clothing:

> I shift my outer garments, vest and hat, before entering the house; I am careful not to touch any article of clothing, furniture, &c., connected with the patient—stop in the sick room but a few moments, and never to sit. But even this precaution is not particularly important in the first stages of the disease; but after the eruption begins to dry away and a peculiar smell escapes from the whole surface of the patient, these precautions become more important.[23]

Libby again mentioned the health of the Hackett family and other illness in the community. Another reference bears highlighting—that to the mills "all starting up." Mills provided fixed wages that attracted girls and young women, employment that was an alternative to rural farm living and "keeping house." Of the twenty-four Sandwich women in the 1860 census who reported an occupation, ten were "serving," seven were teachers, six were seamstresses, and one was a "homekeeper." Some of Sandwich's pre–Civil War population decline may be attributable to departing "mill girls." Before the opening of the mills, a woman's occupation was largely an oxymoron.

"J L S" is the previously mentioned John L. Smith, the Company K musician, and "Samuel" may be Samuel S. Smith, also from Sandwich. Eli N. Cotton, an eighteen-year-old from Moultonborough, enlisted on October

28, 1861, and served in the Eighth Regiment NHV until his discharge on February 10, 1863, in New Orleans, with "disability."[24]

Sandwich Apr 23 [1863] Dear Lewis

I sit down this eavning to let you no that we are all well and hope this wil find you the same I hope you are better then you [were] when I heard from [you] last Haketts children is geting a long wel they wil live if nothing new taks place they have had a very hard time of it Burleigh has vactnated 4 of our children to day if they take I shal have the other to from them they let him do it and never said a word they let him do eny thing for them Burleigh went up in to cut some bushes they all went after him Hipsy as wel as the rest all up to the sap yard when he worked their father went over to Unkle John day before yesterday Uncle was very mutch pleas with it that day he got your letter Eli Cotton has got home they do not think that he wil live long he has ben sick some time to New Orleans Langdon is sick some wheir I dont no wheir Farther Paine is smart Hipsy is their with him she do not want to stay their

She said [that] she got a letter from you the 26 of March she has answerd it last Sunday she wanted me to tel you for she did not no as you would get it She had a letter from Rachel she has ben sick with a very sore throat but has got better now Julia ben down and moved all of her thing[s] John had ben outdoers but once since he was sick with the lung feaver [pneumonia] Hip[sy] sais that it is hard for her to stay their when she could make three week the mills all starting up cloth has fel 20 cents on a yard I ges it has ben forty cents a yard if not more farther P[aine's] heifer has got a bool calf he thinks there aint no more like her in the world the Olde Cow has got one this year that wil beat her for buty I ges I have not heard eny war news latly but hope it wil come to an end prety soon so you can come home give my love to that Asa tel him it is time fore him to be getting out his manure and doing his plowing and geting ready for soing and planting except my love your self rite how J L S gets along and Samuel M E Smith your wife the children sends their love to you all of them

The following letter bears no date. However, from Libby's mention that the children's arms are healing from their vaccinations, which requires a week or more, the letter is from April 27, 1863, or slightly later.

> *Dear Lewis I sit down to rite a few lines to you to let you no we are getting wel the children armes is a taking wel wheire they wer vaxinated Haketts folks is getting a long wel a[s] could be expected I received your letter last nitte was glad to hear from you farther getting a long wel with his work he has had Harson Smith cattle 3 days to plough and Leslie drove them for him he has got the old ground all plowd and soad Oats out beyond the great brook on the hill I got that bundle that you sent in the box with Mr. Perl last nite I did not get your memoral perhaps it wil come I would like to [know] how you sent it if it was sent in a invelop or how Lewis I would try and get discharged if you can get home I think we could get something to heal up that sore dont stay thir if you can get a way dont stay their for the sake of mony is nothing do get discharged if you can this is from your wife Mary E Smith the children sendes thire love to you do rite to little L and H*

The winter of 1862–63 was a long one, especially in light of the realization that "the war was likely to continue beyond all expectations entertained when the regiment entered the service."[25] On the plus side, the rigors of winter camp and frequent drilling hardened and solidified the Fourteenth for its subsequent campaigns. On April 3, that solidarity was disrupted when part of the regiment was moved to picket duty between Seneca and Great Falls, farther down the Potomac. The separation was brief, as the remainder of the unit was ordered to Washington on April 13 and broke camp five days later. They bivouacked at Great Falls, which had been an active trading point on the river, but which was now almost deserted. The reason proffered was the "frequent interviews with both Union and Rebel shells, which had got into a habit of almost periodically screeching over and into the little hamlet with a sort of triple location on river, canal, and gorge."[26]

~ *Six* ~

WASHINGTON CITY

Duty in the Union Capital
April 22 to June 30, 1863

I donot no what to say to you for it look the darkest now that has sinse this war brok out it look dismel to us all the rebels air driveing hooker back they have gut into Pennslvany they no that our army is the weakest that it has bin for mor then a year . . . we nead more trops in the feald to do eny thing else . . .

—Lewis Q. Smith, June 17, 1863

THE REUNITED REGIMENT SETTLED AT CAMP Adirondack, situated "in an oak grove on undulating ground" in the northeasterly outskirts of Washington.[1] Although considered a model regiment, the departing One Hundred and Eighteenth New York Volunteers apparently were not "governed by the ideas of neatness and of sanitary regulation prevalent in the Fourteenth."[2] Whether or not the New Yorkers were actually responsible, another epidemic of typhoid promptly swept the Fourteenth's camp. Of all the New Hampshire men who served in the Civil War, 5.2 percent were killed or died of wounds; eight percent died of disease. For the Fourteenth, 4.4 percent died from battle and 10.6 percent died from illness. Forty officers, 928 enlisted men, and 418 recruits served in the Fourteenth over the three years of its existence. Desertions numbered 110, the lowest for any three-year regiment (of thirteen) from New Hampshire.

By mid-1863, one aspect of camp life that seems to have generated little complaint was food—a subject mentioned occasionally by Lewis. He would later complain about a corrupt officer as a cause of deteriorating meals, and in 1864, rations were occasionally slow to arrive in the press of battle. On the Confederate side, food supplies were a major problem toward the end of the war. At the surrender at Appomattox, most of General

Lee's Confederates had been without rations for days. Quite simply, whether at sea or ashore, Union forces had superior means of supply. Sgt. Francis Buffum summarized:

> Say what you will, Uncle Sam was a "good provider." The coffee and tea were excellent generally: so was the sugar and the meat. The range of supplies included all that could be reasonably expected. Never since battles were set on the earth was there such a *commissariat* for such an unparalleled host. Never were soldiers so well and so bountifully fed as were the Union troops in the war of the great Rebellion. There were cases of severe and perhaps unnecessary hardship, where hard service and inadequate rations were joined in one experience; but it was either an inevitable calamity of war, or the fault of a single officer. The government did all and more than could have been expected . . .[3]

Despite Uncle Sam's status as a good provider, soldiers of the Twenty-sixth New Jersey "had repeatedly stolen" fresh meat from the Second Vermont. Having discovered the recurring thefts, "the Vermont boys thereupon killed a dog, dressed it neatly, and hung up the quarters in the quartermaster's department." On the following day, the canine substitution was observed on the Jerseys' table and the deception became public knowledge. Whereupon, the New Jersey men were subsequently greeted by the Vermonters "with a bow-wow-wow, by way of friendly salutation"[4]

Washington at this time was a bit of a rough place, thus the necessity for military as well as civilian police. Intoxicated soldiers returning to their camps were often robbed of their possessions. Some were plied with poisoned liquor to obtain the same result. One of several jails guarded by Lewis and the Fourteenth, the Central Guard-House, was especially "well supplied with tenants." As Buffum described it:

> Scarcely a night passed that some serious assault, if not murder, did not occur . . . and many a bloody and broken head was brought in by the patrols. The city police and the patrols were not on the best of terms; and the patrols were obliged to preserve the peace, as well as see that soldiers were not abroad without passes . . . the general reception-room, presented an exceedingly cosmopolitan appearance at all times, with its hundred or so cut-throats, thieves, and other ruffians . . . At the door were two sentinels, with loaded pieces and bayonets fixed.[5]

Sergeant Jenks left his own description of Washington:

> The city is full of cut throats, there are any quantity of beings who will kill a man for $5. This is one of the fruits of the war. Should this war close, I fear the land will overflow with such characters, and the gibbet will do for them, what the bullet failed to do.[6]

Smith's Washington correspondence began with several letters in late April 1863.

> *Washeston Apr 22 [1863] Well Libby*
>
> *I have gut back hear to Washeston agane we gut hear last knight we was two days a coming we come down the Conell [canal] I road on the Boat all the way but about ten mils the most of them come a foote Asa and I road we was lucky this time but I do not no how we shall come out the next time we air hear to day and that is all that I can say we air hear to day and whar we shall bee to morrow I cannot tell I should like to stop hear but we do knot expect to but we do knot no whar we go nor whar we go untill we git thar but hotter the war sooner the peas so let them goit and have done with so that we that air neaded can return to our homes I will tell you of my helth which is inproveng a little my side and stummuch is a little better I think it will soon bee well agane if it dosnot gether up and brake agane and I hope it wont for I think that I have had my part of it since I left home thar is not much knew to wright the report is that thay air a fightin down to Fitsburg [Vicksburg] and Fredsburge and I hope that we shall succeed in takin them to plases and Charleston if we should succeed in taken them three plases this thing will soon come to a close Asa and Molton is well Asa send his best respects to you thar is northing mor to writ this time give my love to the Children wright as often as you can I will close by biding you good knight from yours Lewis Q Smith*

A brief letter of Lewis's is undated and unplaced. It is obviously written in late April, probably 1863. He feels "unworthy" and is apologetic, themes that ran through several letters written that spring. In late July, he would mention "licker" and not drinking the "cursed stuff." In February 1864, he is unquestionably abstemious: "I have not drink one glas of likker for one year." It is difficult to estimate the character and magnitude of the problem that Lewis may have had, but it is evident that both he and Libby put the matter behind them—not only for 1863 but also for the succeeding five decades.

My Dear wife [April 1863]

I will wright you a few lins to you a lone I have gest reseve your letter mald the 17 of Apr I was glad to hear from you agane if I cannot see you and toch with you I want to hear from you evry day and if I cannot every day as often as I can I do knot suspose that you want to spend your time in riting to me and I dont belam you for I no I am not worth riting to. you sed that your cow had gut a hefer calf you had better kept it and rase a cow from it but you may do as you air minto for you have the advantig of me for I cannot do as I am a minto if I could I wood see you befor I slep but I cannot you sed that you wood send me some money if I wantid you to if you have some that you do knot want to use if you will send me a little I will pay you back when I git paid off if we ever git paid off you may keep this sheat to your self do rit as often as you can from your[s] in hart and hand when this you see think me good knight LQS

14th Reg't, New Hampshire Vols, Col. R. Wilson

Company _K__ Camp Gale Washineton Ap 29 1863 My Dear Wife

I set down to wright you a few lins this morning to let you no how I am gitting a long first rait my helth is inproveing my soar is healing and doin first rait and hop that theas few brokens lines will find you all in good helth and prosparity I reseved your letter last knight daited Ap the 23 and was vary glad to hear from you all onse more and hear that you wer all well and gitting a long sowell thar at home. we air hear to washington yet but we do not no how long we shall stop hear for we have not had eny orders to go or stay but we shall git ordors soon without dout thar is a good deal of fighting goin on down South now and it is what aut to bin long ago our army is haveing good success now thay air first rait thay air whipping the rebels up finley thay air at it hot and hevey and it incurigeis us vary much and I hop that thay will foller it up untill thar is knot one rebel left on the fase of the erth I want you to tell farther and Burleigh to have the seed put into the ground if you can hyer help to do it for I am in hops that I shall bee thar with you to help you harvas if knot befor for it is better for you to hyar some help and have things agroin then it will bee to haf to by every thing I have roat to B about it so you can gest speke to him about it. I was paid off day befor yesterday two month pay I reseved six dollars and thar is twenty dollars do you whitch I lotted to you in the car of Burleigh you may gest spek to him about it day after tomorow thar will bee twenty six dollars mor do me two month thar is six dollars for me and twenty for you when you git it but we cannot git that until I git paid off a gane but tell B to look after the other thar is knot much mor to rit this time give my love to the children tell them to bee good children tell Farther and Mother to keep up good curige for I shall bee at home some time I want you to wright as often as you can and I will do the same tell farther and mother to wright and knot wait for me to for your air all rit thar to gether and I have so meny to right to it take about all of my time I will good by from yours Lewis Q Smith

Apr 29 [1863] My Dear and afectnat wife

I have gest reseved your afectnat letter daited April 26 and I was hyle pleas to hear from you agane an to hear how you air agittin along I am thankful to hear that thay do so well by you as thay do for I think that you aught to take some comfort now for you never did befor while I was thar with you and I no it now but the past I cannot recall you must forgive me for the past if you can for I feal bad enuf for it when I think of it it seems as though this is a gudgement sent upon me as I sed befor I was to mean to stay thar at home with you and if I donot do right I mist suffer the penelty you sed that you hope that our time wood bee out when the nine month men was so that I should come home but I should think that you wood rather I should stay for when I am hear thar is no one to trobel you plague you as I ues [use] to for I did not [let] you take eny peas knight nor day I must close for it is so dark I cannot see I want you to wright all of the pertichlers gest how it is pleas not let eny of them see this that dollar that I found in your letter I thank you a thousan times for it I told you that when I was paid of I wood pay you back but if you do knot want to ues it I will keep it for I did not git

The Old Capitol Prison, 1st and A Streets NE, Washington, D.C. Library of Congress Photograph.

> *but two month pay this time and I do not no when I shall git eny mor so I will close by bidding you good knight from your unworthy husban Lewis Q Smith when this you see think of me while faraway faraway from Lewis Q Smith to his wife Mary E Smith*

The first week of May was a milestone for the Fourteenth: the remainder of the regiment received Springfield rifles—"they are lighter and easier to cary."[7] Although major engagements with the enemy remained in the future, at least it would be through the sights of rifles, not muskets. For now, the men of the Fourteenth were assigned guard duty at the Old Capitol Prison, serving every other day "in addition to a march of three miles."[8] Following the burning of Washington by the British in the War of 1812, Congress established a temporary Capitol and occupied it for about a decade until completion of the present Capitol. At the commencement of the Civil War, the "old capitol" stood abandoned and derelict, but it was soon converted for use as a prison by the federal government. Though hardly "maximum" security, the prison nonetheless housed a variety of Confederate officers and spies, Union traitors, and deserters.

Interspersed with Lewis's letters are several from Libby dated May 8, May 10, May 14, and May 21, with only that of May 14 bearing the year 1863.

> *Sandwich May 8 [1863] Dear Lewis*
>
> *I sit down this eavening to rite a few lines to let you no that we are all wel and I hope these few lines wil find you the same I received*

your letter yesterday I was glad to hear from you I am glad that your health is better I hope that you wil not go in to battle & you can stay to washington I hope this war wil soon close for it is one awful thing Frank and Moulton was up hear last Sunday and went a fishing down to river they got a very good string of trouts Oliver has caught your great one that you see down to the cold spring he weight one pound and a half you spoke in your other letter as though that you did not use me wel enough you need not cast one aflection that you always used me better then I did you I am sory but I can not get it back I would give all of this wourld if I could git you home again do not wery about the children being noched round I wil give chaces crue some if they tuch your boys they do not dair lick them I ges they got their orders last fall Mary Ett has ben very good to the children she had better be Farther has been getting out his manure to day the boys has ben helping him he holed [hauled] it with folks ask a dolar a day for ox work we got levi [Smith] for 75 a day farther is a fixing the ground to plant corn out by the peace wheir it groed last year it snoed hear yesterday the Mountain [Mount Israel] white with snow to day give my love to Asa tel the old hero that I should like to see him give my love to Moulton tel him I see James [Webster] tuesday to the coner I hope that I shal see you to home be fore a while I must clos by [bidding] you good nite this is from your wife Mary E Smith

May 9 Lewis we are all wel to day farther is planting some early pot[at]oes to day Mother is a soing her flour seeds I have bin a washing my floers

Sandwich May 10 [1863] My Dear and afectnate Lewis

I take this opotunity to rite a few lines to let you no that we are all wel and I hope these few lines wil find you the same I received your letter last nite I was glad to hear from you I should like to hear from you evry day if I could I wil look for them things when they get hear Haketts folks is up hear to day it is the first time since they were sick Susan feals very bad and I should think she would She is to be pit[i]ed

Ed Moulton has ben up hear to day and Lib and Sarah is a goin down to stay with her a spel Jacob is up to the brook a fishing to day he has ben up hear once since you have bin gone the 12 Reg[iment] was most all stove up in that great Battle the newes came in here last nite that the rebles had taken Fredricks burge back again we dont get the right news & their is so much news I hope you wil not half to [go] there Hipsy sais she is par[s] girl now Lucy ses she wants you to rite to her again you rite as of[ten] as you can rite to me and let the rest go if you cant get time to write to them take this pace of paper and rite to the children I must close by biding you good day your wife Mary E Smith

By this time, General Hooker's Union force had crossed the Rappahannock and Rapidan Rivers to confront the Confederates at Chancellorsville, Virginia. Despite Hooker's nearly two-to-one superiority in numbers, Lee forced his retreat during the subsequent action of May 2–4. General Hooker arrived in Washington on May 13, on "official business," and conferred with the president.[9] There was, at the very least, the appearance of disharmony between Generals Hooker and Halleck regarding Chancellorsville: "It is quite certain that Gen. Hooker ordered a portion of the army across the river some days ago, but the plan was disaproved by Gen. Halleck, who countermanded the movement."[10]

Later, as Lee's army moved toward Gettysburg, Halleck and Hooker clashed over withdrawing federal troops from Harpers Ferry, prompting Hooker's request to be relieved. This request, in addition to continuing loss of confidence in Hooker since Chancellorsville, resulted in his replacement by Gen. George Meade (1815–1872) in late June, just days before the battle of Gettysburg.

14th Reg't, New Hampshire Vol's, Col. R. Wilson
Company ____ Camp Washington May 13 1863 My Dear wfife

I seat my self to wright you a few lins to inform you of my helth whitch is vary good for me I reseved your tow [two] letters to knight and was vary glad to hear from you all onse mor and to hear that you air all well and prospering so well thar we air hear in the Cyty doin gard duty but we do not no how long we shall stop hear so we cannot tell you we shall stop hear until we air needig mor some whair else mor then we shall hafto go let it bee as it will with regard to mr [Gen. "Fighting

Joe"] Hooker he is doing well and if the govement will let him a lone he will poot this rebelion down that is my opinion and that is the opinion of others the rebels did not drive him back acros the river he went back acros on his own hook and for a good purpos best none to his self but he has gon back acros the river agane and he is doing first rait and you will find it so in time this thing is on it last lages I hope

Thursday morning May 14 I gest say to you Ginrill Hooker arived hear to this City last knight at 11 o clock for what purpos I no not but I fear it is of no good but cannot tell. you tell Farther that if the old mar is agoin to have a coalt to knot work hir to hard on the farm if thar is eny oxon that he can hyar and not work himself to deth if thar is eny one that he can hyar and you can pay them if you have the mony to spar if not tell B to pay them and c[h]arge the same to me tell B to wright to me as often as he can and how you air all gitting with your work thar and every thing else that is of eny benifit to me I have not reseved eny letters Lucy nor Chases folks nor Hackett folks sinse I have bin in Washington but I have [been] wrighting to them all no answer from them you tell Eddy I will wright to him next time for I have not time this morning for I have gest come in of[f] from gard tell the children to bee good children and I will wright to them nex time you wantid me to wright often I think I do as often as you will want to hear from me I want you to wright as often as you can if it is evry day I shal hafto close by biding you go[o]d morning from ever yours Lewis Q Smith

Sandwich May 14 1863 My Dear Husban Lewis

I sit down to let you no how we are getting [along] very wel now we are all wel but Mother is not very good about the same as it was when you was to home her head achs a great deal Burleigh was to Gilmanton yesterday I expect he wil be up here in a few dais we shal get some cattle to do our work Farther expect to brakup to morow if nothing hapins for corn he has not used the old mair but a little yet the ground has ben to wet to do much on it yet he has not soed his wheat yet but has got the ground ready to so it when it comes fair weather the oats and the peas is up from 2 to 3 inches

Washington, D.C., Guards at Ferry Landing . . . Checking a Pass. Library of Congress Photograph.

> *it come snoe on the mountin thursday it staid til Saturday we shall get some seed in the ground when it comes weather so we can I can tel B what you rote as for the mony part I have got 9 dolars by me of your check money left yet I ges his other wil come by the time he gets home Jacob is up hear to day he ses that he has rote to you to or 3 times and got no answer he ses he is goin to rite to you again I wil take back that I told you about him being a Democrat B told me that he did not vote that way Jacob apears to think as much of you as eny of them the children sendes their love to you I must close by [bidding you] good day this is from your wife Mary E Smith Mother sendes her love to you do not use eny of your money to by eny thing to send home save it to get you some thing to eat*

At the time of Lewis's next letter, he was serving as a guard at the wharf between Sixth and Seventh Streets, Washington's shipping and ferry terminal. In addition to the many regiments passing though Washington, some to the front and others, as noted by Lewis, returning home for discharge, "the effects of war" were becoming obvious. Company I's Pvt. Christopher

Hoyt wrote: "young smart men with their legs or arms shot of[f] . . . and any quantity of wounded seen."[11] Hoyt, born in Hillsborough, New Hampshire, enlisted from the nearby town of Washington. He apparently survived the fall 1864 Shenandoah campaign, but died of diarrheal disease on December 17, 1864.

14th Reg't, New Hampshire Vol's, Col. R. Wilson
Company __ K __ Camp Seven Street wharf 1863

Washington May 16 My Dear wife

I will try and wright you a few lines to let you no that we air hear to the City a doing duty yet and my helth is pretty good at the presant time the soar whitch I have is doin pretty well thar is knot much knews to wright you this time every thing vary still and quiart I donot think that thar will be much fighting don agane at the presant acording to all acounts that we have now thar has been over twenty ridgments has come to this plase since we have bin hear that air on thar way home thar time has exspiard and air discharge and thar is ridgment after ridgment air haveing discharge dayle it is the nine month and two years man. I havenot bin to our ridgment since we come hear to the city I have not sene Molton Webester since I have bin hear but hear from them every day I reseved a letter from Hepsa and one from Lucy last knight Thay wore all [well] I answer them this morning and when you see Hepsa give her my thanks for wrighting to me

May the 17 Well it is a vary fine morning and I will try an find my letter thar is no news this morning to wright to you every thing vary still and quiart hear to day as yet I am on duty to day and I shall hafto cut my letter short and wright more next time give my love to the children and to all of my frends and pleas to except a good shar your self tell Eddy and the children that I will try and git time an rit to them next time Asa and Molton air well wright often I will close by biding you good morning from yours Lewis Q Smith I sent you a fry bason in Asa box so you can git it

Sandwich May 21 [1863]

Dear Lewis I sit down to rite a few to let you no how we are getting a long all wel but Mother she has got a bad cold and got a lame side you no how to pity her farther has gott to yoke of cattle to day he has soed his weet yesterday rite often as you can I wil rite more next time good morning this is from your wife Mary E Smith

Sandwich May [1863] My Dear and afectnate husban

I sit down to rite a few lines to let you no how we are giting a long very wel Mother is better then she was when I rote to you before I rote to you last sunday and sent you one dolar in it I am very sory that you lost your walet Farther got your letter last nite wer glad to hear from you I hope that the war wil have an end so if ever so you can come home Hipsy was up here friday she had got a letter from you she was very much pleased with her ring she told me that Jeremiah got knocked down by a shel but did not get wounded Lucy and Frank is up hear to day Frank has gone up to put his colt into Mr Gilman parster he and Ned Wiggin went a fishing down to the brook they [caught] a prety good lot of them and got to woodchucks he wishis you was hear to go with him ant so do I the children is all wel Farther has got his corn ground all plowd the Mr Smith and Fred plowd it and holed [hauled] out the dung we had Hed Smith cattle we shal get what we can in to the ground we haft to pay one dolar a day for help and for cattle Hed lets us have his for 75 sents a day I got a leter from lib last nite she was smart I canot think of eny thng els to rite you can rite a letter to Lucy on the rest of this this is from your wife Mary E Smith

May 1863 concludes with a letter from Lucy. Planting is under way, the impact of Irene's death in December is still apparent, and the fishing is good—unfortunately, not equaled today. "Ned," mentioned in both the preceding and the following letters, is Edward F. Wiggin, the fourteen-year-old son of Meredith farmer Benjamin F. Wiggin, and very likely Frank and Lucy Wiggin's nephew. Burleigh B. Hackett is said to be badly "pitted up," certainly the result of the recent outbreak of smallpox.

M. Ville May 31 [1863] My Dear Brother

I set down tonight to answer your last letter, the reason why I have not done so before you are probably aware before this as Lib wrote to you I have been up to Sandwich around a visiting but it dont seem up there as it use to Frank had to take Ned with him he is so lonesome up there they had quite a time fishing caught about 300. Father had

had quite a sick turn of diarhea and mother had a slow [long duration] fever Mariett [Chase] was at home when they were taken but came back when I came home father was better and mother was also gaining Mariett there is a great change in her since Irene died she does as well as she can for mother and Lizzie says she has been good to the children ever since you went away the little ones love her very much. The children are healthy and growing fast little Lucy would take a six quart pail half full of water and go from the gutter to the house like lightning she would get to the house while Liz was turning round. Lizzie had a good time with them she traveled the fields and pastures all over with them she wore out a pair of new shoes while she was gone Hipsy has got to be a fat little girl and little Lewis is the prettiest of the lot he so fat and good I love him very much he looks like my girl [Lizzie] father is getting along well with his work Frank would have helped him plant but ground was not ready I felt glad to find them all gitting along so nicely. Susan [Hackett] poor girl is looking miserably she is all worn out Hannah [Hackett] has a bad cough and mother says she should not think strange if she didnot live one year. Burleigh health is better but he is badly pitted up my heart aches for him Sallys [Chase's] health was very poor so much so was not to be able to go up to mothers she has had a numbr of bad spells lately.

I was obliged to lay my writing by last night Lizzie coughed so and to day Sarah has come from Lake Vile on her way home she had a letter from her father her mother was not so well. I hope to hear she is better in a few days. little Lizzie I fear has got the whooping cough coming on it is in her school we are having pretty warm weather here now it is very dry Frank works on the land and in the shop I think his health is better then it was in the spring. This is the third time I have tried to get this letter done and I am bound to finish This time I have got the blinds shut, last night we had a big thunder storm with high wind and threw me off the track. I think from the appearance of the thing there will be no more fighting on the Rapahanoc at present they had better beware of the third attempt I understand that Lee is coming over the river to attack Hooker if he does I think he will meet with a warm reception. Grant seems to be gaining ground slowly at Vicksburg the key to rebellion in my opinion I hope this thing will come to an end by and by. I am very glad to hear your health is improving slowly, write as often as you can get time I want you to write and tell me if you want some more envelopes if you do I will send some. keep up good courage and hope for better times. I guess you will laugh for I have had to stop writing again Mrs Randall comes if the blinds are shut and it is now too late to have it go today, but never mind it will tomorrow. Frank has gone to Sandwich Goodbye write as soon as you get this L J Wiggin

I liked to have forgotten about my ring I am very much pleased with it I want you to write and tell me what it is made of I[t] cant be rebels bones if it is their bones are as black as their hearts. the soldiers have sent home some here they say made of hosses hoofs I thought I would like to have you tell me all about it in your nex letter. I cant see with the tools you have how you could mak so pretty smooth one I shall look upon it many times and think of you sometimes I can hardly wait for the war to end L J W

The month of June opened with a letter from Libby and her first mention of Sally Chase's illness. "Ebin" is Pvt. Ebenezer Dale, of Company K, a Sandwich farmer who would sustain a gunshot wound to the arm at the battle of Third Winchester (Opequon Creek) on September 19, 1864. He died on November 23, 1864, and was buried at the National Cemetery in Winchester, Virginia.

Pvt. Ebenezer H. Dale, of Sandwich, N.H. Note erroneous date. Bruce Jackson Photograph.

Schools in Sandwich reflected the rural nature of the town, mostly single-room buildings and nearly two dozen in number—decentralized, scattered about the town. The Smith children would have attended School No. 12 (as had Lewis), on Sandwich Notch Road, less than a mile from the Smith home. Parents contributed firewood in proportion to the number of children they sent, and the teacher's board was put out to bid. School was held year-round (a winter and a summer session) with the exception of older boys, who were often needed for farmwork in summer.

With planting about finished, "farther" has begun work on the "road," which is undoubtedly the Notch Road. A road agent (or agents) contracted with or hired abutters of various sections of town roads to perform maintenance or improvements. It is not known if John Smith was the actual road agent for the Sandwich Notch Road—a service Lewis provided for several decades following the war.

Sandwich June 1 [1863] Dear Lewis

I take my pen in hand to rite a few lines to nite we are all wel hear to home Sally is sick and Mother has gone over their last friday we have not heard from her sence she had a pain in her side Dorcus is over their a keeping [s]chool and Edy goes to her they board to Morison I dont no where B. is he lecturing some wheir we look for him home this week our check has come last Monday he wil [look] to giting the mony when he gets home if you want eny mony let me no it and I wil send it to you I canot tel you much newes only old fany has got a colt it is a Mare colt it is a little thing it is a darke colar I cant tel you much a bout him til he gits strait out a little Mr [Riley] Magoon thinks he wil look difrent then he does now in a month from now he was hear yesterday to see him farther has got his corn planted finished it to day he has got a few more potatoes to plant and his beanes and then he wil be done a planting he has got to work on the road this week the bois dro[p]ped the corn and to day they have bin [to] school [and] help father after they got home it pleases them to help him John wanted me to tel you to rite to him I sent Edy letter over to him by James Webster he has bin up here his health is better he has got a lame toe Mary Sily com up with him she has got a very prity boy he has got curly hair it hang down on its [his] sholairs you no that is my fancy if you can git your Minature taken and send it to me I wil send you the mony eny time I shal send mine to you as soon as the colt gits old enough to go to the coner wodbry has got back so Sarah Dale told me she had Ebin minature up hear that he sent home it look very natral keep up good courage as you can for I hope that you can come home before a great while this is from your wife Mary E Smith give my love to Asa and tel him to be a good boy

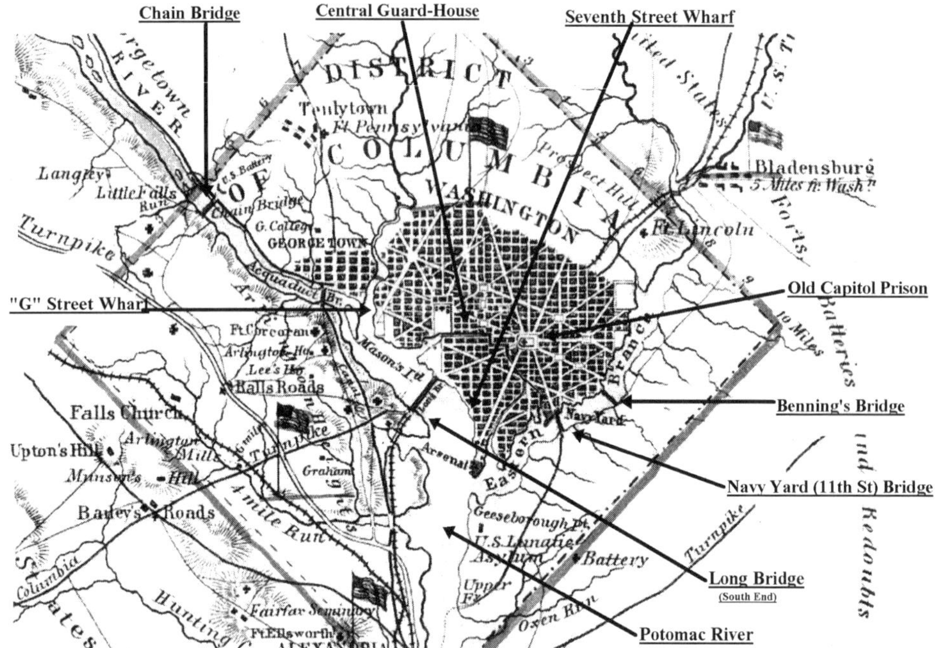

Sites Guarded by the Fourteenth Regiment, NHV

Duty Stations in Washington, Map. Adapted from Library of Congress Map.

In early June, there was considerable fighting in the vicinity of Fredericksburg, with almost daily clashes between Lee's and Hooker's forces. At this time, Lewis was still part of a detail that guarded the Seventh Street Wharf, which serviced ferries to Virginia and steamers to the lower Potomac River and Chesapeake Bay and to the principal northern ports. In addition to the wharf, the Old Capitol Prison, and the Central Guard-House, members of the Fourteenth guarded Long Bridge, the Navy Yard and Benning's Bridges, the G Street Wharf, and "all the departments of the government." For these "arduous duties," the Fourteenth received "flattering encomiums."[12]

14th Reg't, New Hampshire Vol's, Col. R. Wilson

Company _ K _ Camp Washington June 7 1863

My Dear wife I seat myself to try and writ you a few lins to inform you of my helth whitch is putty good and I hop that theas few lins will find you the same I reseved your last letter last knight and was glad to hear from you all and to hear that you were all wel thar at home an sory to hear that Salley was sick agane but hop that she will bee better befor this reaches you but am afraid that it will go hard with hir I was glad to hear that you was gittin along with your work thar at home and hop that you will continuer an prosper take good car[e] of your coalt as you sed you had one and pay Mr Magoon five dollars for the use of the horse for me an you may charge it to me if you air knot fraid to trust me that is if you think the coalt is worth it you roat that B was coming home tell him to wright to me rit how his coalt is gitting along and if it is fit to use or ever will be good for eny thing

thar is not much war knews to wright to you to day for I donot no what to writ we heard that thay air to work down on the raphanock it was last knight report that Fredecburg is taken thar was som woned soldiers came from thar com in to our whalf [wharf] that was woundid in the battle that all that we can tell you about it it has bin vary hot an dry hear this spring out hear Asa an Molton is well thar is northing else to rit about the minituer I will have it taken as soon as I can git a pas to go up on the streat I want yours an Lucy send them as soon as you can git them taken thar is northing mor wright as often as you can I will close by bidding you good knight from yours Lewis Q Smith

In the following letter, Lewis's comments of "darkest now" and "dismel to us" reflected the mood both in the field and at home; the Confederate invasion of the North was under way. Nor were Lewis's sentiments overstated—Sergeant Buffum concurred: "The cause of the Union and the faith of the people touched nearer down to utter hopelessness during the week preceding the 4th of July, 1863, than at any other period of the war."[13] Lewis's comment on Union troop strength, "we nead trops in the feald," was also correct. On June 15, 1863, there was a call for one hundred thousand six-month men that brought only about sixteen thousand. A call followed on October 17, 1863, for five hundred thousand three-year volunteers; it raised almost four hundred thousand.[14]

Lewis referred to Pvt. John Atwood, who at five feet five inches tall was the shortest man of Company K. Atwood's marital status was the subject of some disagreement between Lewis and Libby. At the time of the 1860

Federal Census, Atwood was single and living with his parents, Philip and Mary Atwood. From September 1862 to September 1863, John's state aid was paid to his mother, who appears to have been living alone at age sixty-eight. Lewis's assertion that John was not married in the summer of 1863 is likely correct. John Atwood survived the war and returned to farming in North Sandwich. In 1867, he married Pvt. Harrison Atwood's widow, and the first child of this marriage, "Harris," for Harrison, was born in May 1868.

> *Washington June 17/63 My Dear wife*
>
> *I will spend a few moments in trying to rit a few lins to you to let you no of my helth whitch putty good and I hop that theas few lins will find you all the same thar at home thar is knot much to wright you this time we air hear to the City doin duty at the wharf in regard to war knews I donot no what to say to you for it look the darkest now that has sinse this war brok out it look dismel to us all the rebels air driveing hooker back they have gut into Penslvany they no that our army is the weakest that it has bin for mor then a year for th[e] two year and nine month time is out and they have gon home the most of them and we nead more trops in the feald to do eny thing else*
>
> *thursday night [June 18] well lib as I have gest com of from gard and I will try and finsh my letter to you thar is northing knews to day onley we air haveing fine shower and it is a new thing to us for we havenot had eny rain hear to speak of for the last two month and has bin vary hot hear for a few days past and it is awfel dry hear it seem as though every thing wood burn up it has bin so hot and dry but it rains vary putty now and I hop it will all knight*
>
> *I have gest reseved your letter and was glad to hear from you a gane and hear that you ware all well thar at home I was glad to hear that Salley is ganing I hop that she will git over it that dollar I found inclose in your letter and you must forgive me for not thankin you for it for it slip my mind so that I will thank you twis this time to pay for it poor pay you sed that you did not want me to think hard of you a bout your pitchtur why no indead not I should lik it vary mich but if you cant git it you air not to blame I heard about Amos [Paine's] marridg befor Hepsa roat to me about it the other day In regard to John Atward he never was marrid but she sed that she was after John came*

out hear she went to Mr Willam Weeds to git hir stait aid and toald him that she was marrid to John Atwood but it was not so poor folish things you had better keep your calf to make a cow of and I want to hyar you to keep your coalt until I git home so that I can see it thar is northing mor this time wright often as you can give my love to all of my frends take a shar your self good knight from your ever true frend Lewis Q Smith

Libby was typical of women left at home: Some censuses simply recorded them as "keeping house." Work for women was difficult and without pause. Predictably, their problems worsened when their husbands departed for the war, even with financial aid, usually funded by debt, provided by the state and town. Libby Smith, as revealed in her letters, worked long hours and coped—albeit with assistance from relatives and occasional hired help. Libby refers to death and burial in one sentence and the weather in the next; early demises were too-frequent features of nineteenth-century life. In the following letter, a few of Libby's words are ink-blotted and unreadable.

Sandwich [Wednesday] June 17 1863 Dear Lewis

I [sit] down to rite you a few lines to let you no that we are all wel hear at home farther was over to chaces yesterday Saley was about the same when she gets up Chace has to take her up and set her in a chair to have her bed maid Mother is over their and farther see B (blot) he give him the check and he got the mony so if you want some mony let me no and I wil send you some I [he] has gone to Maine and cominge back friday he will come hear the Methodist minister wife is berid to day[15] *she was taken sick Sundy nite and died monday nite she had fits the weather is cool hear for the time of the year the wind bloed very hard hear yesterday farther is out a hoing corn three little ones is a plaing on the flore it is the fact (blot) has mearid John Atwood wife a (blot) shouldent you think I should feel proud to be aunt to John Atwood wife write often give my love to Asa and tel him to be a good boy your wife Mary E Smith Lucy and Hipsy send their love to you*

Libby wrote to Lewis less than a week later. The "cornel" is probably Col. Lewis Smith of Sandwich Notch, the son of Deacon Sam Smith, a brother of Eliphalet Smith, Lewis's grandfather.

June 23 [1863] Dear Lewis

I sit down this eavening to rite a few lines to let you no I have just received your to leters and was very glad to hear from you I thank you very much for it I wil git mine taken this week if I can and all of the children taken soon as I can and send them to you father has got his corn hoed once our thing[s] all looks very wel for chance they have to grow the weather seams like the fal of the year and it has ben dry hear yesterday we have had some showers to day Mother got home to day Salley [Chase] is beter she sets up some now Mother has got her a very prity little pig he looks like one that you had of the cornel farther is a goin to get one for me down to Ed martins he sais that they are nice ones we wil try and keep your colt for you if [you] do not stay away to long the darkest our just before day I hope day wil brake before a great while the call ma[y] turn upon the rebls and balance the other way bimb by keep up good corage as you can good nite this is from your wife Mary Liby Smith give my love to Asa

Another short letter home that is undated and unplaced may be from late spring 1863. The mare that was about to foal in Lewis's letter of May 13, 1863, has had her "coalt." Lewis repeated the apology elaborated in his last letter in April.

Mrs Mary E Smith

Wel Libby I though I wood wright a few lines to you a lone I was vary glad that you let farther have mony to git his boots and you better pay the rest of the taxes if you have mony to spair pay your bills as you go a long if you can and tak care of the rest of your mony and thake care of your self that is the best I can say untill I git home to tak car of you I will try and take better car of you then I did when I was with you ciss the little ones for me take a good harty one your self wright often as you can do rit how your little coalt groas if he gits eny oats and how every thing looks I will cloes by biding you good day from yours Lewis Q Smith Thare is one thing more have you gut your last check we was paid off last month thar is 20 dollars for you

Lewis continued to correspond with Hepsa Paine. She had left the mill and returned to Moultonborough. There is no mention of war, only her request that he come home soon—the fishing is good and berries are coming. The "Amos Marridg" that Lewis mentioned earlier is discussed in Hepsa's letter and the reference is to Amos Paine, but not "Father" Amos Paine. The younger Amos Paine would be drafted (and exempted) in November.

Moultonboro NH June 19th 1863 Dear Brother

I take my pen in hand this morning to answer your letter which I received some time ago was verry glad to hear from you glad to hear that your health is better I am hear all alone and have bin for two days Father has garn over on Osippy [Ossipee] Mounting a visiting his health is good and all of the rest of the folkes that I know of now and hope these few lines will finde you the same I have bin down to Manchester and staid three days went down to get my clothes that I left thare last winter when I come home thinking that I should go back again to work but have got disapointed that is my luck I was up to your house two weekes ago they wer all well and bright then the children grow like pigs you wont no them when you get home little Lewis is the prittest of them all I am going up this week some to see them you sed that you went a fishing and caught two one horn pout and one hog back I can beat that aney time went out the other night and caught eight perch great big ones the fish is plenty this summer Father goes most all of his time a fishing

Your uncle and aunt Wiggins is well and sendes their love to you they say they ar going to write to you soon

after noon now I have just got home from a baptism it was over to Abbott Shore there was four baptised Elder Tasker baptise them

I suppose you will want to no who is Married around hear well thare is Phinias Slitton is Married to a millery girl of Moultonboro and Amos Paine is Married to Harriet Varney of Sandwich

Julia and John was down last Sunday they wer well and sed they must write to you this week

You wrote that you was coming home to go Bluber[ry]ing with me and I hope that you will have the good fortune to come theire is a going to be a lot of them this year I shall haft to close for the want of wordes to say you must excuse my poor writing for my pen is so poor that I can hardeley make a mark come home soon as you can answer soon and not delay so long as I have I wish you all the luck that ever was from your sis H. L. Paine

It should be noted that mid-1863 marked the culmination of decades of effort on the part of Virginians west of the Allegheny Mountains to form a separate state. The non-homogeneous Scotch-Irish and German population of "western Virginia" were largely not slaveholders and had little communication with eastern Virginians. An early effort to form "Westsylvania" had failed in 1776. Virginia's subsequent apportionment to the U.S. House of Representatives, which counted the slave population as three fifths of their actual number, left the eastern counties in control of the state.

In short, western Virginia became West Virginia on June 20, 1863. Following this date, numerous towns, including Harpers Ferry, Martinsburg, Charlestown, and Charleston, lay in West Virginia, while Berryville, Winchester, and Middletown, among others, remained in Virginia. The new state line followed the ridges of the Allegheny and Shenandoah Mountains that parallel the western edge of the Shenandoah Valley.

In mid-June, as part of Lee's Gettysburg campaign, federal troops were pushed out of Winchester, Virginia, toward Harpers Ferry after fights at Newtown (now Stephens City), Cedarville, and Middletown, Virginia. The Southern invasion resulted in the Fourteenth's being hurriedly ordered to Fort Stevens, north of Washington. Originally called Fort Massachusetts, the site guarded the principal route into the city from that direction on what is now Georgia Avenue. The immediate threat was J. E. B. Stuart's crossing of the Potomac at Edward's Ferry between Lee's Army of Northern Virginia and Washington. Farther to the north, an invading force was assembling at another capital—Concord, New Hampshire.

~ *Seven* ~

Rebel Invasion of New Hampshire and Union Successes

July 1 to July 31, 1863

Thar is brilant knews from our army hoping it is true . . . this City has bin in grait danger

—Lewis Q. Smith, July 5, 1863

BACK HOME, THE GREAT NATIONAL HOLIDAY HAD A significance of a different sort: the "Rebel Invasion of New Hampshire." The *Boston Daily Evening Transcript* reported that former President Franklin Pierce (1804–1869) and a "force variously estimated at from ten to twenty thousand persons, occupied Concord, N.H., on the 4th of July."[1] Extra trains had run from Littleton, Plymouth, and Lake Village and carried ". . . in the aggregate of about 3700 persons."[2] The Democratic press estimated attendance at "about 30,000" with few "ladies" present due to inclement weather. In a speech before the Democratic convention, Pierce "sharply condemned the 'Lincoln despotism,' and gave due honor to 'that noble martyr to free speech, Vallandigham.' "The *Transcript* added:

> The exquisite timeliness of his assault on the government of the country, at the very moment it was engaged in desperate struggle for existence, against an invading enemy, and while the issue of the great battle was uncertain, must impress every patriotic mind. Jefferson Davis was once the Secretary of President Pierce; Franklin Pierce now seems to act as the Secretary of Jefferson Davis.[3]

Pierce blamed the war on "vicious intermeddling of too many of the citizens of the Northern States with the constitutional rights of the Southern States . . . in disregard of the Constitution." Pierce advocated the right of free speech and "urged moderation and a regard for all Constitutional rights, believing that all the States would one day be again united." His hope for a conclusion to the war was "to rely on moral power, and not on any of the coercive instrumentalities of military power."[4]

The *Transcript* was in no hurry to dismiss "The Copperhead Ex-President":

> He misrepresents the American heart; he is false to democratic principles and democratic ideas; he is recreant to the spirit of the Constitution; he turns his back to all that makes the glory of the republic, to cringe to the autocratic despotism of Southern slaveholders. Thus he has added to the history of his imbecility as a ruler an appendix to tell the story of his delinquency as a citizen.
>
> Posterity will be his impartial judge, and its retributory sentence will be ineffacable. When Andrew Johnson, Dix, Dickinson, Cass, Butler, Stanton, Holt, and a host of other Democrats, too true to democratic principles, to sell themselves to those alike the foes of those principles and the united nation, are gratefully remembered this politician will either be entirely forgotten or thoroughly despised.[5]

Several more items demonstrate how sharply northern political lines were drawn as Lee's defeated army recrossed the Potomac and news of the fall of Vicksburg reached the eastern press:

> The Lounger, in *Harper's Weekly,* has a scorching comment on the speeches of [Governor] Seymour and other politicians in New York on the Fourth of July. "These orators," he says, "forget the soldiers who are dying for the rights of all the people, in their eagerness *to howl over the wrongs of a man* [Vallandigham] *summarily arrested for helping the murderers of those soldiers*.[6]

New Hampshire's equally vituperative Democrats saw their position as "for their Rights and Liberties and against Abolition and secession."[7] Among some contemporary adjectives used by the Democrats for the Republican party are found the following: ". . . Emancipation High Taxation-Centralization-Confiscation-Negro-Equalization-Usurpation-Administration Party."[8] In response to accusations of disloyalty, a section of the New Hampshire Democracy's platform read: "we have only to point to the Democratic sons of New Hampshire who have fallen on every battlefield in this contest, and to the thousands who are now in the service."[9]

Yet another attack on Pierce was published in *New York Evening Post* and quoted in the *Transcript:*

> Isaac Hill, long the head and master-spirit of New Hampshire "Democracy," once declared that "he who does not support the Government in time of war is either a traitor or coward." Mr. Franklin Pierce, a leader of New Hampshire "Democracy" of today, declares that the war of the nation for its existence is "homicidal madness," and should be stopped at once. Is he, according to Hill's test, a traitor or a coward?[10]

Franklin Pierce had served in the Mexican War and was neither of the above, but he miscalculated the magnitude and vehemence of Northern abolitionists and opinion against the South. He also underestimated his fellow Yankees' tolerance to infringements upon their own liberties during the prosecution of the war. As the tide of war turned, Pierce faded from public view: "The day's [July 4] work had been done, the last shred of public reputation which Pierce had, save with his old political friends, was destroyed. From this speech he never recovered."[11]

Years later, the question arose of why had New Hampshire refused "to honor this distinguished citizen until sixty years had passed. The answer . . . is found in the bitterness of that troubled period . . . when a large group of people in its northern states, conscientiously and patriotically laboring for what they considered to be the best means of preserving the Union, so lost caste in the community that their names became bywords of reproach for more than a generation."[12]

A nonmilitary solution to the war was becoming ever more unlikely. While Pierce "was preaching his counsel of despair this word [of Gettysburg] threaded in and out through the crowd."[13] With that news and the surrender of Vicksburg on July 4, jubilation and glimmers of hope appeared in the North—the cloud of gloom was lifting. While the contest in Virginia would continue to be a virtual stalemate (Confederate attrition aside) for at least another year, Union forces continued to successfully press the Confederates in the West and the naval blockade further aggravated supply difficulties for Confederates in the field.

The Fourteenth continued to perform guard and provost duty and thus would not see actual battle until 1864. As evidenced by letters from home,

Lewis's family was both relieved and thankful. It is not clear that Lewis had the same sentiments, for at times he seemed anxious not just to see the "thing" through, but to get it over. Two days after Lee's Gettysburg defeat, Lewis wrote to Libby.

Washington July the 5/63 My Dear wife

I seat my self to rit you a few lins to you this morning to inform you of my helth whitch is vary [good] at the presant time hoping that few lins will find you injoying the same blesing all of you I reseved your letter last knight and found John and Frank picturs inclose in it I thank you vary much for them thay look vary nathuel and I wish I could see you and the children in the room of your picturs but as I can not I am vary glad to see them tell John an Frank that I thank them vary much for thar picturs and thay look vary smart and tell them to bee good boys untill I git home for I hop that the time is not far distant befor I shall bee permitid to return back to my little famley agane try and keep up good curidg as you can I am hear to the oald camp ground know Asa has gon back to the City a doin dutty agane I have not sean him since Tuesday [June 30] I heard from him yesterday he was well Molton is hear to the Camp he is well and the same old fellow he sends his best respects to you all I will tell you of our forth of July that we had yesterday it was a hard one it was vary hot hear and we had to start for the City at 8 o clock in the morning with our dress Cots on all buten up to our chin and with our guns and ecrypments on with forty rounds of catridges and march out to the citty and through it and returned at to o clock I will tell you mor when I see you Thar is brilant knews from our army hoping it is true I will send you three papers in one packig so you can see for your selves to days yesterday and day befor papers it dos not look so dark to us as it did two weeks ago one week ago to knight we was ordord of[f] a bout five mils to a foart to the rifle pits to surport them with the expectation of a natact [an attack] of the enemy but was not we was then nearly surrounded by them but thay air driven into dispar I hope thay air gon from hear so no danger arond hear now but this City has bin in grait danger I will tell more when I git home I shall hafto close for want of time rit all the knews rit often as you can and I will do the same I am agoin to rit to Hepsa to day give my love to all after you take a good shar your self I will close by biding you good morning from yours Lewis Q Smith to Mary E Smith

Libby's next correspondence with Lewis came in mid-July. The family and farm were doing fairly well, with the exception of sheep, lambs, and corn. Brief mention was made of the Twelfth Regiment NHV, which fought in thirteen engagements and experienced its highest casualties at Chancellorsville, Cold Harbor, and Gettysburg. The Twelfth had almost three times the killed and wounded as the Fourteenth, but only fifty "left" is not accurate.

Sandwich July 13 1863 Dear Lewis

I [received] your letter this morning I was glad to hear from you I am glad you are beter hope you can come home so[o]n we are all wel hear a ex[cept] the baby is not very wel but he is a great deal better then he was last week he has had a lung feaver he com very ni having the croop but he has got so he is to play on the floare with hipsy and Lucy Frank and Lucy was up yesterday he wanted me to tel you he had got all of your fish

we have got to checks since you have bin gone that is all twenty dollars in each if you want eny money let me no and I wil send you some I have got the rest of our pictures and I wil send them to you if you want me to you tel me in your next letter we get our money to weeds yet your colt groes folks thinks he is the best colt their is round we hav not sen the cafe since he went to paster he is up in Mr Taners [Tanner's] I was up their the other day did not [see] him Mary Ett went to find farthers old sheep he has lost her we expect she is dead she was most dead when she went from the barn she had to lambs and lost them both My sheep had a very nice lamb and lost it she is fat now Jacob come up hear and got her and shird her and put her in Asa parster and I pade him for it I did not begreteh [regret] it one mite for I think she was too good to go the old Mountain for some feed our things looks very wel our wheet looks wel and po[ta]toes the corn do not look so wel we have got a good garding the war news is abot as you rote Frank ses their is but fifty left of the twelfe reg[iment] give my love to Asa this is from your wife Mary E Smith

In the letter below, Libby refers to the draft riots of the previous week. In New York, where the victims were increasingly black, the number of killed and injured neared one thousand. One writer, Anna E. Dickinson (1842–1932), described the outbreaks of violence as "unparalleled in atrocities by anything in American history and equaled only by the horrors of the worst days of the French Revolution."[14] After rioters attacked an armory, newspaper offices, and an orphanage, the antiwar governor Horatio Seymour (1810–1886) declared martial law in the city. Marines and sailors from the Navy Yard and soldiers from nearby forts marched into the city and federal troops, some just returned from Gettysburg, were also called upon to restore order.

New Hampshire had its own rioting, though not as serious as that in New York or even Boston. On Tuesday, July 14, the first day of the draft in the Granite State, an excited mob, "consisting of the ignorant and the depraved, with not a few brawling women and boys," appeared at the draft office in Portsmouth. Initially deterred by volunteers from nearby Fort Constitution and Colonel Marston's Marines from the Portsmouth Navy Yard, the rioters returned on the following day and smashed the office window and hurled stones. One soldier, struck by a rock, fired several shots but injured no one. On Thursday, July 16, violence recurred and after nearly a dozen people were injured, some with "dangerous" wounds, "the mob was crushed."[15]

Although anxiety persisted in New Hampshire, it was neither general nor severe. In the resorts of the White Mountains, it was business as usual. The hotels were filled with guests and the past two weeks of rapidly melting snows had rendered the "numerous waterfalls . . . unusually attractive. North Conway is thronged with visitors, and that pleasant village seems at the present time to be livelier than ever."[16] New Hampshire's most prominent visitors were, of course, President Lincoln's family, who passed through Center Harbor en route to the White Mountains on August 2. A "very affable" Mrs. Lincoln was photographed atop Mount Washington and "while at the Tip-Top House . . . made a very pleasant impression."[17]

Sandwich July 19 1863

Dear husban Lewis I set down to rite a few lines to let you no how we are getting a long very wel the little boy is better Sarah Quimby is bered [buried] to day[18] *Mother and farther has gone to the funeral*

Aunt Jinny was bered friday I received your letter friday I was glad to hear from you but should like to see you better in this letter I am going to send you my little boy picture I ges you wil say he is a very pritty boy he is not so fat now as he was he has got so he can say par and marm and Ett he can stand by the side of a chair but canot creep yet I ges he will not he sits on the flore and ses par donnt you think he is a brit boy I am glad you hear so good newes from the army hope it wil keep gro better til the war is over with they have had quite a riot in Boston and New York a bout drafting kiled a bout fifty in New york but the ones that is left mite go and do their part as we [blot] I hope this war wil come to a close soon Jacob is agoin to help farther do his ha[y]ing the boys was very much pleased with their letters you send my boy one next time he look for his when he see the others have thers I must close for he is a cr[y]ing this is from your wife Mary E Smith Samuel Smith has got home and inlisted and Eliphlet to

In much the same vein, Libby's sister Hepsa Paine wrote to Lewis, and once more the subjects were health, fishing, and berrying. Cpl. Jeremiah S. Smith, a shoemaker from Sandwich and Company K, would be wounded at Opequon on September 19, 1864. He survived to be discharged in the summer of 1865.

Moultonboro July the 26th [1863] Dear Brother

I set down this after noon to answer your letter that I received soon after date I was verry glad to hear from you and hope that you will forgive me for not answering it before it want becaus I didnot think of you it was becaus I was neglectful and lazy Father and I am well and hope these few lines will finde you the same Father is out on the end of the point a fishing for pirch this afternoon he goes most all of his time he went up to John Clark's last week he went a fishing and caught one hundred and forty brook troutes while he was garn Lewis I begin to think that you wont come home to go bluberrying as you have talked about I have bin on the hill once and picked eight quartes they are verry thick this year

I havent seen aney of your folkes for along time so I cant tell you aney thing about them I presume you hear from them often Parker has sold our old mare so we havent got aney horse to go aney where with

> *now but I must try and go up to see Lib some how or rather Sarah Jame Dinsmore is down hear now on a visit She says Jeremiah [Smith] is sick and is coming home on a ferlow he is on his way now coming home I wish that you could have the good luck to come home to it is a verry warm day hear it is the warmest day that we have had this summer Father and Parker has just commenced haying it rains most all the time hear so it bothers them about their getting in hay you will get red of mowing down the grass this summer but prehapes you had rather do that then to be whare you ar you rote about your selebration I think you had a hard one of it I staid to home all day and braided hates I shall haft to close for the want of words to say you must keep up good courage and come home soon as you kill all of the rebbels excuse this poor writeing and all mistakes pleas answer soon So good luck from your sister Hepsa L. Paine*

Much of the Northern public viewed the draft as a very positive measure. It represented a commitment to vigorously prosecute the war and boosted morale at home and in the field. Men of the Fourteenth noted both the riots and the delayed draft: "be they ever going to draft in N. H. I wish they would and if they resist dam them shoot them they have got us out hear and dont care how long we haft to stay."[19] The source of the delay lay with New Hampshire's own citizens and with Governor Gilmore, who had asked Secretary of War Stanton to adjust the quotas for those numbers of volunteers previously supplied by the towns. The governor wrote: "If the delinquent towns can be first called upon the draft will proceed well; otherwise, the most patriotic towns will be punished for their early patriotism, and the other towns will have a premium paid them for their delinquencies."[20]

The result would have been an extremely complicated and cumbersome process. Quotas were to be adjusted (or reduced) not only by the number volunteering, but also on the total time volunteered—based on three-year enlistments. Converting nine-month, one-, and two-year enlistments to a three-year base would create huge delays. After initially agreeing to the idea, the War Department reeled under the practical application, "found to be a very extensive labor," for what was a fair solution to the draft. The War Department reversed its decision. Gilmore, who had championed New Hampshire's towns in the effort, was burned as political heat reached the boil.

On September 29, Governor Gilmore squared with the public: "The result has shown that I was too sanguine in my expectations; that I was mistaken in my conclusions, and that I have been unable to fulfil my promises to the people in this respect." He closed his address "To the People of New Hampshire" at the council chamber, and acknowledged that the scheme "would be wholly impracticable in its general and universal application, and that any attempt to make such exact apportionment of credit would necessarily result in such delay as would amount to a virtual abandonment of the draft, and in consequent disaster to the interests of the country."[21]

Also, coastal communities and states, more of whose sons volunteered for the Navy, were not credited for naval enlistments, nor were Union sailors eligible for bounties. In his Third Annual Message to Congress (December 8, 1863), President Lincoln wrote that: the "operation of the draft, with the high bounties paid for army recruits, is beginning to affect injuriously the naval service, and will, if not corrected, be likely to impair its efficiency by detaching seamen from their proper vocation and inducing them to enter the Army."[22] The disparity between navy and army enlistments was not corrected—and even then not completely—until February 1864.[23]

On July 26, Lucy Wiggin penned another of her detailed letters to Lewis. At the time, much of Washington was swampy and mosquitoes were plentiful, transmitting yellow fever and malaria. Malaria derives from the Italian *mal aria,* or bad air, considered to be the cause of these diseases, not mosquito-borne yellow fever virus or malarial parasites. Nor was the water supply suspect as the source of deadly diarrheal illnesses such as typhoid and cholera.

Morris Island and Battery Wagner to the south of Fort Sumter were not taken in July, but were eventually evacuated by the Confederates in early September. Fort Sumter did not fall until mid-February 1865, when Charleston was abandoned as a result of the surrender of Columbia, South Carolina, to Sherman's army. Although victorious at Gettysburg, General Meade was not between Richmond and Lee's army and did not (or could not) pursue the retreating Confederates.

M. Ville July 26 [1863] My Dear Brother

A letter is due you and I set down to write it. The reason why I didnot answer you as soon as I came from Sandwich is they were preparing to draft so I thought I would wait and tell you who was drafted but they have postponed it to allow towns their [volunteered] men they had sent so I thought I would write I learn by way of Henry Gilman that it is very sickly there in Washington also hearing by way of Henry [H.] Tanner that you had a diarhea am afraid this muggy weather will lay you up we have had a long rainy time here very much to the injury of some things our peas are all milldued and spoiled last year we sold about 20 dollars worth this year we shall have to buy for ourselves, but the loss is only money we wont moan for that. I dred the draft I expect Frank to be drafted the prospect looks very favorable for using the South up now the last evening paper said that our forces had taken all of Morris island if this is so fort Sumpter [Sumter] is surely ours and where then is Charleston the mother of the rebellion she too in my opinion has fallen General Mead is also between Lee and Richmond, and I do hope and pray that the hour is not far distant when peace shall resound from every hill top and through every valley, and the poor worn out soldier may return to the embrace of their home and friends if there is any one in this world my heart is in sympathy with it is the poor soldier that has sacrificed all to fight for our firesides as well as their own oh may it never touch a tenderer chord in my heart than it has already done When I was up home I found them getting along very well indeed they were all well but the baby he had been quite sick but was getting better I should have staid up for a few days if it had not been for the draft. it has worried me very much but all we can do is to trust in God he doeth all things well though at times things look dark and gloomy. I go blueberrying most every day I pick them to sell I sold enough one day to come to 72 cents so you see I am getting rich Frank has had as much as he can do in the shop till now he is not drove up so and I am glad of it for he is as poor as a snail. our crops are looking pretty well, when I pick green stuff I think of you and George by the way you w[a]nted me to write where George is he is down to Port Hudson we have not heard from him since the last battles when he wrote that he was fat and healthy never so well in his life he was on the Yazoo river the last time he wrote I saw your picture up home should not have known it away from there I think you must have changed since you left home very much almost one year has passed away since

> *you left may God grant that you may return before another shall have rolled around. I want you to write and tell me just how you are getting along and what your feelings are. write as often as you can and I will do the same, you will consider my feelings and forgive me. L. J. Wiggin*

Port Hudson, Louisiana, located on a bend in the Mississippi River about 150 miles upriver from New Orleans, was the last Confederate position on the Mississippi to surrender, on July 9th, five days after Vicksburg. Except for persistent guerrilla attacks, control of the river remained in Union hands for the duration of the war, thus dividing the Confederacy. The Yazoo River enters the Mississippi from the northeast some ten miles above Vicksburg and about 410 miles above New Orleans. Yazoo City, Mississippi, lies on the Yazoo River and was the site of a Confederate navy yard.

Libby's next letter is dated July 27, 1863:

> *Dear Lewis I received your letter this morning I was glad to hear from you their was ten dolars in it you of sending farther 2 but I wil give farther 2 of mine so if you have got eny more mony use it your self we are wel enought of[f] hear to home I shal go down to Mr Weeds again in a few days to get my money I thank you a thousand times for your money it is hard for you to work so hard for your money and not take the good of it we have got to checks and that is all perhaps the other wil come you tell me if you put the 2 dolars in the letter with the ten their was only ten in it I wil let farther have the money when he wants it that is rite aint it Jacob has bin helping him to day fix for haing he is a going to help him af[ter] this week he has got to help Uncle John the rest of this week Burleigh is hear to day he is goin to Virmont next week our hay is a coming in pretty wel the rains has maid it a great deal better do not wery about us hear at home if we ar sick I wil let you no it if the children is sick I wil do the best that I can for them they are all wel now the little one is prity wel now he has got so that he stood in the dore this morning a half of a our and see me churn I never had the board put in the door ---- Saturday he can I would like to no if you have got eny footings to wair if you have not I wil try and send you some you keep money enough by you so if you want to get you some shues you can get them or eny thing else you can in room [instead] of sending it home for we are wel enough of[f] here at home keep up good corage as you can I hope it wil not be long before you can*

come home it is hard for you to work so hard I must close by biding you good day from your wife Mary E Smith

Lewis's reference in the following letter to "nine shillins" is notable in that the United States Mint began issuing coinage seventy years before, in 1793. The colonies had used British exchange, mostly copper and silver, and the first shillings (silver) struck in America dated from 1652. Although the "proclamation rate" was six shillings to the dollar, the value of the shilling varied widely throughout the colonies. Lewis's reference to the shilling was not unusual: "Reckoning by the shilling is still not uncommon in some parts of the United States, especially in rural New England." [24]

Washington July 30/63 My Dear wife

I have gest return from the City agane from my duty I am doin duty to the City at the Centerel gard hoas yet and as for my helth is vary good for me it has not bin so good since I had the feaver last fall as it is now and I hope that theas few lins will find you all the same the mail has gest come in and I hapely found a letter in it for me from you and I am glad to hear so good a knews to hear that you all were all so well thar at home and if air all well thar it is all that I ask for yes yes yes I sent you ten dollars that is all and I have gut two dollars left I bot a pair of shues and paid 3 dollars for them no better then I ues to by for nine shillins this is the way that we sholdiers hafto tak it to pay dobble prise for every thing we hafto by I have not sat down to a table to eat but one meals of vittles since I left home and that was to day and paid fifty Cents for it but I have bought some vittles to eat a good meny tims and I will tell you the rest of the story when I git home I can tell you that I donot by licker with my mony nor I donot drink the cursid stuf no no no you wantid to no about feattings [footings] I git a long first rait I have two pair of them that you sent to me thay havenot come to mending yet thay will last me until winter. thar is one thing that I should like that is a pair of woling shirts for I cannot git eny hear that is good for eny thing and thay ask from four to six dolars a pare and if you could git some cloath and make me a pare and send out to me if you can git a chanse I would thank you a thousand times I want collard ones to wair out sid I can draw under shirts but thay air whit ones thay will do to wair for under ones this winter I cant wash white ones so thay will look well As for war knews it is good so far tell uncle Been that Calob was hear and staid with Asa and I last tuesday knight he is tuf as a bair his ridgment [Second] and the fif and twellf all three air hear in the City I donot no how long thay will stop hear I saw William P Ham he is well and he sed that he did not no whair Jed Dinsmore was[25] *he give out on a march and he had not hern from him sinse he is curled up under a leaf some whair thar is knot mich more to rit this time Asa and Molton air well thay sends thair best respect to you all tell farther and Mother keep up good curidge better days air coming you try and do the same kiss the little ones for me and take one to your self I will close by biding you good knight from yours L Q Smith*

With Bean's regiment, the Second NHV, and the Fifth, Twelfth, and Fourteenth all in the city, there must have been something of a New Hampshire homecoming.[26] The Second and the Fifth had fought at Gettysburg and paused for a few days in Washington in late July. The Fifth subsequently performed draft/rendezvous duty in Concord, New Hampshire, until November, when they were transferred to Point Lookout, Maryland. Point Lookout, on the southeasternmost point between the Potomac River and Chesapeake Bay, was the site of a major Union prison camp. The Twelfth participated in Burnside's "mud march" and was also at Gettysburg until ordered to Point Lookout—as was the Second—in late July 1863.

~ Eight ~

More Guard Duty in the Capital

August 1 to October 31, 1863

> *I must tel you what I heard that they had a house out their on a purpus for the 14 Rigment it was for the ofisers a lone and you other soldiers had to gard it when they wer in it.*
>
> —Mary E. Smith, August 15, 1863

SOME DUTIES FOR SOLDIERS OF THE FOURTEENTH were almost pleasant enough to be considered excursions. On one occasion, with the exception of Companies E, G, and K, men of the regiment escorted 1,260 prisoners captured at Chancellorsville to Fort Delaware, "Uncle Sam's seaside resort," at the head of Delaware Bay just below Philadelphia, Pennsylvania.[1] They also accompanied prisoners down the Potomac River and the Chesapeake Bay to Fortress Monroe (Virginia), the only fortress in the United States. At the time, the country's fortifications, or forts, "had reference principally to harbor defence." Fortress Monroe was constructed for that very purpose *and* for "its capacity for a garrison."[2] There, the men witnessed a Fourth of July salute by the great guns, swam in the bay, and enjoyed other uncommon diversions.

One journey turned out to be less than pleasure—the transfer of rebel prisoners by rail to Johnson's Island in the harbor of Sandusky, Ohio. After passing through Baltimore, the train derailed near York, Pennsylvania, after hitting a "turned switch." Fortunately, the train had not yet reached high speed, for the cars careened to the edge of (and not over) a steep bank above a rocky creek bed. "In the confusion of the moment half of the prisoners might have escaped into the darkness; but, by appearances, few had any inclinations in that direction: and Pennsylvania was a poor State for escaped Rebel officers. Had the affair been located back in Maryland, a goodly number of those leaders of Southern chivalry would never have seen Sandusky . . . "[3]

The valley of the Susquehanna River and the scenery about Harrisburg drew major admiration from prisoners and guards alike, while an "experience of twenty-seven miles in thirty-one minutes, whirling round bends with chasms hundreds of feet deep gaping in awful precipices at their feet, is something never to be *encored*." On August 1, 1863, "the expedition plunged into a hill-walled basin, and a dense bank of smoke and soot,—called Pittsburgh. A pleasant feature of our visit to that city was the immediate departure."[4] The prisoners were transferred at Sandusky and the return to Washington was uneventful.

In Washington, members of the Fourteenth served guard duty at the Old Capitol Prison until relieved by a regiment of the Veterans Reserve Corps, initially known as the Invalid Corps. The corps consisted of wounded but recovered or partially disabled men who could perform less-strenuous service, allowing troops at full strength to move to theaters of battle. The Fourteenth's men were also assigned duty at the Central Guard-House, the common city jail prior to the war, located at Tenth Street and Louisiana Avenue. The guardhouse was essentially a detention center where prisoners, both civilian and military, were held briefly, until charges or other dispositions could be determined. When the regiment left for "active service," they left the prisons "without regret."[5]

Meanwhile, back in New Hampshire, Lewis's family and the farm were doing well. Planting was months past and only the vicissitudes of weather remained before haying and harvesting began. Some of the summer's entertainments were berrying and fishing, and children had the outdoors for a playground. New Hampshire's first snow squall that summer occurred on August 30—"on that cheerful spot the top of Mt. Washington . . . The general weather there is cold as Greenland."[6] Correspondence from home began with Libby's letters of August 7 and August 12, 1863.

Jed Dinsmore, of the Twelfth Regiment NHV, was wounded in May 1863 at Chancellorsville. He was discharged with "disability" on April 18, 1864, at Portsmouth Grove, Rhode Island, the site of Portsmouth Grove Hospital, located on Narragansett Bay about six miles from Newport. The hospital housed and cared for well over one thousand patients in twenty-eight ward buildings, each 175 by 25 feet, with chapel, library, post office, dining hall for 850, and other amenities.

> *Dear Lewis I sit down to rite you a few lines to let you no how we are getting a long very [well] at present farther has begun haing he has gut in five lodes of hay the bois help him I received your letter last tuesday I was very glad to hear from you I have got your other check when you drar your money you keep more of it your self we do not need it so much as you do we have got 35 dolars on hand I ges that enough to do the haing if it not let it go on dun I wil send your shirts as soon as I can do you want me to send you some tobaco and tee if you do I wil let me no when I shal send them I shal go to the lore [Lower] corner to morow Sarah Jane has bin up hear to see me she told me Jeremiah [Dinsmore] was to Rhodiland in the hospital farther Paine has bin up hear he said that hipsa had rot to you we are all wel and hope this wil find you the same*
>
> *I thank you for your kiss I wil kiss you when you come home give my love to Asa tel him that I went a pluming with his wife last tues-day ask him if he dont wish he could go with us I got fifteen Qarts of plumbs Lewis I must close for it is tim to go to bed it is past ten and I have maid my soap to day had good luck be a good boy I trust you be so good night this from your wife Mary E Smith*
>
> *Sandwich Aug 12 1863 Dear and afectionate Lewis*
>
> *I take this opotunity to rite you a few lines to let you no how we are giting along very wel for our help farther has got in nine lo[a]ds of hay he think that is enought to keep one cow Jacob is a com up to help him last of the week he has got to cut oats this week I tried to git you some cloth to make you some shirts but I could not their is not eny in flanel to the co[r]ner I think likly their be some that I can get this fall I can send you the money to get some their fore dolars is cheep[er] then I could get them hear I was over to farther Sunday they wer all wel Julia was down their Julia Boy has got to be biger [than] Hipsy but he not so pretty as Hip[sy] poor Asa Broom is dead he died the 18 of July he was in the army som wheir if you want some Money rite and let me no soon and I wil send it to you I wil try and get you some shirts this fall*

> *that wil be good you must excuse me for not riting eny more this time I am sleepy I can not rite eny more to nite little Hipsy has got a sore coming on her toe and she kept me a wake last nite and little Lewis was sick nite before last but he is smart now the rest is all wel and I hop this find you the same I thank you for your kiss that you sent me I shal save all of mine til you get home hope it wil not be long befor you can come home their draft begun yesterday it is po[r]tsmouth rite as often as you can this is from your wife Mary E Smith 12 farther is a cuting his oats to day we are all wel to day*

Saving kisses until Lewis gets home is about the only mention of the conjugal separation that Lewis and Libby endured. William Combs, in good humor and quite a bit more bluntly, gave the subject a little more exposure: "you say you way 185 I should like to snug up to them fat legs of yours but there is nothing here that is at all attracting."[7] Sergeant Jenks wrote frequently of his loneliness and deeply missed his home and family: "I have many sad and lonely hours and long for home and those loving arms to clasp me at night . . ."[8] In the fall of 1864, after sleeping on the ground all summer, Dr. Child noted that he "never had better sleep . . ." He added: "I hardly know how a feather bed with clean white sheets would feel—and much less to be in bed with my wife."[9]

Private Combs commented on the temptations of a soldier's life: "i have not drank but one glass since I left the hospittle at Pheladelpha except what has been issued to us and have sold more then half of that I am temprate as to drinking smoking and going to bad houses well you will not believe that I supose but it is trew I have not been into a house in this city and have not smoked a pipe full of tobaco since the seder creak [October 19, 1864] fite."[10] During three years of separation in an environment where the next muzzle flash or shell burst or even a fever could bring death, there remained, as Dr. Child noted, "a thousand temptations in army life . . ."[11] Young James Newton, of Wisconsin's Fourteenth, wrote of his perceptions: "No person can ever realize it [camp vices] until they have been placed in some such a position as I am now . . . then they will see all kinds of inequity openly practiced without being reproved by any one . . ."[12]

In Lewis's next letter, below, he wrote: "thay air a doin somthing to Charleston." Rear Adm. Samuel Francis "Frank" Du Pont (1803–1865) led a force of ironclads that attacked Charleston, South Carolina, on April 7,

1863. Despite tremendous enthusiam for ironclads, the federal effort failed and Du Pont shouldered the inevitable blame. In spite of their armor, the Union ships' slow rate of fire was no match for the Confederate forts. The second attack, on July 10, led by Rear Adm. John Dahlgren (1809–1870), was no more successful and the Union force again withdrew. Gen. William Tecumseh Sherman correctly predicted that Charleston could not be taken by naval force alone, but when isolated by land, it would simply fall like a ripe pear into federal hands.

As a port, Charleston was secondary to Wilmington, North Carolina, which was closer to Lee's army in Virginia and had superior rail connections. However, Charleston, where the first shot of the war had been fired, was the symbol of the rebellion and a major political prize. After Sherman's army seized Columbia, South Carolina's capital, in mid-February 1865, Confederate forces simply withdrew from Charleston. Maj. Robert Anderson, who had originally surrendered Fort Sumter to the Confederates, would return to raise the Union flag there on April 14, 1865, four years to the day after lowering it in 1861.

Washington August 12 /63 My Dear wife

I have gest return from the City agane from duty and it is my day to rit to you an so I will or try to eny way I reseved your letter last Monday and glad enuf to for I began to think that thar was some trobel it was over a week that I did not hear from you it seame a long time I was glad to hear that you was all well and giting along so well thar. I was glad to [hear] that farther is gitin a long so well you did not say that Jacob was helping farther hay rit an let me no all about it you sed that the boys was helping farther hay tell them to bee good boys and mind thar gransir and give them good close let them have some shous to wear dont let them go without things to make them comtyful and lok out for your self as long as you have the means to do it with I send our money home for you and the childrin to take the good of it dont kep your mony when you need to ues it for it will knot be but a few days befor it will be pay day agane the first day of next month then there will be six dollars for me an twenty for you

So you use your mony when you need it and not save it for me nor eny one I reseved a letter from Hepsa two weeks ago and I answered it the same day that I gut it I havenot a brother nor a sister that takes the pa[i]ns to rit to me that she dos she will neve[r] be forgotten by me while I live in this world John and Julia hasnot answerd my letter yet never mind that it save my ritin to them you ask Jacob what the reson why he doesnot rit to me I have ritten two letters to him since I have bin out here and I have not had eny answer from them if he cannot spend time hyar him a day and let him rit

As for war knews thar is northing new thar is not much goin on now it is so hot that thay hafto lay off thay air a doin somthing to Charleston [South Carolina] but what we donot no you didnot rit whither you gut eny [news]papers from me or knot in regard to the tea and tobaco you nead not be to the trobble to send it for I can by it hear send the shirts when you can git a chanse The Captin [of Company K, Oliver H. Marston of Sandwich] has gone home you will be likly to see him give my love to all of the famley tell farther an mother to not think hard by my not riting to them for I donot git time to do it rit often so good knight from yours Lewis Q Smith

Several of Libby's letters follow:

Sandwich [mid] Aug [1863] Dear Lewis

I sit down to rite a few lines to let you no we are all wel and I hope this wil find you the same I received your letter last wednesday I have not seen Miss Perl I did not no wheir but Jeremiah Smith wife is a goin to washington I am a going to send you a few thing by her she oferid to cary them Mother sends you the Haris pouders I send you some pils a pair of footing the Bois the shugar cak[e]s farther ses he gets a long first rate with his ha[y]ing he has got in to the barn 13 loades of hay he has got his oats he had t[w]o good load of them we have very good weather hear now not hotter then com[m]on we have had it very weat one or to [days] ago but his bin dry for a week past Hipsy to[e] come to a sore but it has got better now she did not rest much of eny for to or th[r]ee nites I wished you ben hear to helped me but I got along very wel John Ma[r]ston wife is dead she [B. Ellen Marston] had the consumsion [tuberculosis][13] *the Bois spreads all of the hay they work very wel you must rite to them when you can my eys is all aslleep and I must close by bidding you good nite this from your wife Mary E Smith*

Haying continues and "pluming" is good "over to the pond and up by the school house." Libby is probably referring to Dinsmore Pond and School No. 12, both a mile or less from the farm. Libby takes a poke at Lewis for guarding a conjectured house of prostitution frequented by officers. Apparently, rumor has it that the men of the regiment guarded it while officers used it—if true, certainly not morale enhancing. During the war, Washington had nearly five hundred brothels, and prostitutes numbered about five thousand, about equal to five full strength regiments.[14] Descriptions of vice reached the home press, though perhaps not without some hyperbole:

> Fourteenth street, Washington, is said to contain throughout its whole length south from Willard's [Hotel], not one house that is not a house of ill fame. A contract has just been made to build a house of the same character that is to cost $80,000.[15]

Sandwich Aug 15 Dear Lewis My Husband

i sit down this eavning to rite a few lines to let you no we are all wel and hope this wil find you the same farther is gitting a long very wel with his haing he thinks that he shal about finish this week Jacob is a helping him this week I ges I shal help him some dont you think it wil be great help I have washed to day and went pluming over in south pasture and over to the pond and up by school house and got about to Qarts of blakbrys they wil be very thick when they get ripe I wish you was hear to and get some of them you wanted to no if I was a goin to cut eny up to My farm I shal cut one tun this year father pasters Franks coalt up their he gives him money to buy a tun of hay for the use of it it would cost more then the hay would come to if he had tri[e]d to cut it this year for help is nine shilings [a] day but I do not no how much farther is to give Jacob I wil tel you when they get dun haing farther was up to John yester day they wer all wel he see Parker to the coner to day they are all wel over to farther Paine Hep[sa] has got company from Manchester one of my cosin and boy I would like to no if you new G[e]orge Cochrin he was her husband he is dead now he lived on chesnut street in Manchester Lewis I did think you was a bad boy why I told you to be a good boy I dun it for fun I think you love your wife and children to wel for that they to you I must tel you what I heard that they had a house out their on a purpus for the 14

> *Rigment it was for the ofisers a lone and you other soldiers had to gard it when they wer in it I should [think] you all would feal bad to think you could not go in it now Lewis you tel me if it is so rite it by it self this is from your wife so good nite Mary E Smith we are all well*

Lewis served daily duty at the Central Guard-House from mid-June through most of August. The Old Capitol Prison, in contrast to the guardhouse, had its entertainments: the Confederate spies Rose O'Neal Greenhow and Belle Boyd. Imprisoned from January to May 1862 at the Old Capitol, Rose was said to have contributed to the Confederate victory at First Manassas (Bull Run) by passing intelligence of the federal advance to Confederate Gen. P. G. T. Beauregard. More than simply affable, she was attractive, and charmed officers and gentlemen of the North and South alike. Rose was deported to Richmond in May 1862. Sent to Europe to court favor for the Confederacy, she drowned while attempting to enter Wilmington, North Carolina, aboard a blockade runner in the fall of 1864.

Belle Boyd, Confederate Spy, Library of Congress Photograph

Belle Boyd (1843–1900), born in Martinsburg, Virginia, was another well-known Confederate spy. Belle was arrested for spying in July 1862, held at the Old Capitol Prison for a month, and released for lack of evidence. Apparently continuing her clandestine activities, she was again apprehended in August 1863 and initially held at Carroll Prison.[16] It is rather unlikely that Rose or Belle would have blinked an eye at guards such as Lewis, who continually paced the perimeter and the interior of Old

Capitol Prison. However, in the presence of men of rank, Belle was treated more like a guest than an incarcerated spy. Sergeant Jenks, although not mentioning Belle by name, left a notable description of a "female spy" in a letter to his wife.

> *Camp Adirondack November 8, 1863 Dear Wife*
>
> *. . . Since I last wrote you I have been to the Old Capitol Prison on duty. The Prison is situated about twenty rods [110 yards] from the Capitol building, and is ocupied principally for Rebel prisoners. There are nearly 500 there now; some of them quite smart looking men, with the exception of their dress, which is very shabby; some of them have nothing but shirt and pants on; among them there are several officers, but they cannot be distinguished by their uniform. I had the pleasure of talking with the noted Female Rebel Spy, who is confined in the Carroll prison close bye. She comes up to the C. [Old Capitol] prison most every day under guard of two men to see the R. Officers. She is a Lady of very fine appearance, smart, and can talk as though her tounge was hung on a pivit. She will probably have to stay in confinement untill the war is over. I should judge her age about 30. She was arrested once before and released, but now, the evidence against her is conclusive. A Mr. Wood suspected her, and pretended he was a Secesh, and she communicated her plans to him, after she got through he told her she was his prisoner and might go with him. She seems very cheerful and to all appearance enjoys life up to the hub, as the boys say. She has such a winning way with her, that she readily gets into the good graces of the overseer and warden of the prison, and they love to talk with her, and allow her many privileges, which others are deprived of under less offence. Woman has a magic charm, when she puts in practise all those facinating powers to which our Creator has endowed her with. Yours Truly J. Henry Jenks*[17]

In his next letter, Lewis expressed no regrets about leaving "the gard house" for duty at the Navy Yard Bridge. The Washington Navy Yard and the Navy Yard Bridge, today's Eleventh Street Bridge, lay just south of the Capitol on the shore of the Anacostia River, about two miles above its confluence with the Potomac. Farther up the Anacostia, which is the "eastern branch" of the Potomac, lay Benning's Bridge. Both bridges bore traffic to and from Maryland. On the Potomac, the southernmost crossing

Bridge Over the Eastern Branch, Potomac, Washington, D.C., (Navy Yard Bridge), Library of Congress Photograph.

to Virginia was by Long Bridge; to the north, it was by Chain Bridge. All of these crossings were guarded and passage was controlled.

> *Washington August 29 /63 My Dear Wife*
>
> *I seat my self to answer your letter that I reseved last knight was glad to hear that you air all well and giting a long so wel thar at home. my helth is pooty good but I have gut pooty wel drag down a doin duty I have bin doin duty to the Centerl [Central] gard house for 10 weks about every day but I have gut out of that for the presant I am to the Navee yard Bridge I come hear Thursday and my duty willnot bee half so hard hear I am with Lieu M. S. Webester Benjaman Sciner [Sgt. Benjamin C. Skinner, a Sandwich tailor] Jary Smith thar is nine of us hear an Mrs Smith an Mrs. Schiner air hear and it seams like home and I gest that we shall live beter then we did up to the camp thay take holt and cook us pys and Brown Bread and you may ga[u]ge our thankfulnes of thar company thar is knot knews to rit you this time that*

is new to you Fort Sumpter has folen and the oald flag of liberty is onse mor a floiting over it onse more and fort Wagner has surenderd and they air bombaring Charleston and that to will hafto surender and I think that this thing must soon come to a close I hop it will at eny rait we air whiping them in every plase that we come to and thay cannot holdout much longer it is imposebel for them

in regard to my shirts I will by the cloth and git them maid hear as soon as I can git the mony to do it with and I cant tell when we shall git paid off agane thay say not for one month I am most destitut of shirts but whar thar is a will thar is a way so thar will be some way previded for me it is vary comfetebel wether it is coldenuff days and knight is quit cool it is cold enuf knight for under shirts and drawers how is the wether thare you sed that you had bin a pluming wel I am glad you air smart a nuf to go you tell John an Frank to bee good boys an pick me som plums and save them untill I git home and tell Hyram to be a good boy an help you Molton is well Asa is thay send thar respects to you all I shall hafto close give my love to all take a good shar your self rit often rit all of the knews this is from yours L Q Smith it is roat in a hurrry

In the letter above, Lewis noted that Jeremiah Smith's and Benjamin Skinner's wives had arrived. Wives were allowed in the camps but were subject to orders to leave on a moment's notice—sometimes creating hardships that outweighed the morale benefit of their presence. Jenks wrote in a letter dated November 21, 1863, that the Fourteenth's colonel, who had "been very indulgent to let them stay," ordered all women from the camp by the twenty-fourth. With several women as sick as some of the soldiers and unable to leave, another problem surfaced: "then who will take care of them, Soldiers must attend to their duty for the Government . . ."[18]

In the following letter, Libby remarked on an outbreak of diphtheria in Moultonborough. Weeks later, the *Laconia Democrat* reported that "diphtheria is prevailing at a fearful extent in Moultonborough and Ossipee" and "also making its appearance in this place [Laconia] . . ."[19] In January 1864, the same newspaper commented: "The doctors are recommending whiskey both as a preventative and cure for diphtheria. The remedy is immensely popular."[20] In February 1864, Lemuel Chase, of Sandwich, would lose "four children by this disease in one week, three of them being buried in one grave." Reflecting on the state of medicine, the *Democrat* added: "It is singular that our physicians cannot find a remedy to stay the ravages of this disease."[21] In 1921, more than two hundred thousand cases occurred in the United States, with fatality rates of about thirty to forty percent, whereas with immunization in general use, only about two dozen cases occurred in the entire 1980s.

Death from diphtheria was often rapid, as in the case of "the fellow that used to work in the cook house" of Company H. He entered the hospital on Friday and died the next Tuesday: "he had a sour [sore] throat for a number of days before he went into the hospital the Doctor said that his throat was half closed up before he came up there. He let it go to long we boys sent him home. His Father got out just in time to see him die."[22]

Diphtheria commonly commences with a sore throat, as in this soldier's case. It may proceed to "bull neck," massive swelling of tissues of and about the throat, rapidly progressing to death. More commonly, death results not from respiratory obstruction but from diphtheria toxin and its attendant cardiac complications and systemic failure.

Sandwich Sep 20, 1863

Dear Lewis I sit Down this eavning to rit a few lines to let you no that we are all wel and hope this wil find you the same I received your letter last tuesday I was glad to hear from you again and hear you was wel I think it a long time to not get but one letter if you can get time to rite to letters a week I wil send you some stamps if you want me to I should rote to you again last week but I let your little boy fall of the bed and he hurt his shoulder and it maid him very wersome but it has got better now and he got a sliver under his townal and it paned him to I expect that has got better now the res of the children is all wel John and frank cut the corn stoks last week all but 3 or 4 roes dont you think they are smart boys their is not much news to tel you Lucinda Briant is sick and 3 children with the dyptherea she has lost one hur bois it is very sickly over wheir she lives that is lee mils [Lee's Mills, Moultonborough] I can tel you a litle news Gorge Bean is drafted and Joseph Clark[23] *I dont think that Jo wil go farther come up hear friday and went home this morning he ses that if you could have one of his hook to fish with he should be glad I hope that you can come home before a great while so you can go a fishing hear I must close by byding you good nite this is from your wife Mary E Smith*

Col. Robert Wilson, of Keene, N.H. Author's Collection.

Still in Washington at the end of September, Lewis again mentions "Mrs Purle." Her husband, Pvt. James W. Pearl, a Sandwich farmer, at age thirty-nine, was eight years Lewis's senior. Not listed as wounded or killed and perhaps ill, he would receive a discharge on the day after Christmas 1864. Lewis mentions officers who left the regiment—essentially, good riddance. Jenks also commented on officer disaffection: "to appearances it seems no settlement then it did a month ago, but thre[e] have resigned the last month, because they were obliged to, there are now some 8 vacancies among the commissioned officers . . ." Jenks indicated that the regiment's colonel, Robert Wilson of Keene, New Hampshire, was the source of those so obliged: "a hard one to fight against, he hangs on like a bull-dog."[24]

One officer who saw more bite than bark in Colonel Wilson was Company G's Capt. Solon A. Carter, also from Keene. Carter wrote: "I was not satisfied with the treatment I had received at his hands . . ." Carter resigned in July 1864 to accept another appointment: "knowing the condition of affairs in the [Fourteenth] regiment and that there was no immediate prospect for a change." He referred to "the quarrels and bickerings to which every officer . . . was obliged to encounter under Col. W[ilson]'s administration."[25] Officers as well as soldiers may have had a little too much spare time on their hands—a situation that battle would quickly alter.

Washington Sept 29/63 [Tuesday] My Dear Wife

I seat my self to rit you a few lins by your request I thoth that I wood commenc it to day so to finish it to morrow so that you wood git it Saturday I rot to you a Sunday and I will wright every day if you want me to as for my helth it is good as it has bin for some time and the boys is all well hear on this post and thay air gainin in camp as the wether gros colder I hop that thay will come up agane thar is 13 of us hear on this post all from our compny Moulton Webster is hear he is well only gut a bite on his foot or rather aheel

I roat to you to send my over coat and boots I wish you wood send me some mor haras pouders [Harris powders] I deveided them that was sent with Asa [and] Molton and I am afraid that I shant have a chanc to git eny mor this winter I should like some black charis [probably lozenges] if you have them to spair I donot nead them now I donot no how soon I may so I wood like to have them on hand in time of need thar is no knews to rit to day so I will wait untill to morrow or thar is one thing thay air turning about all of our oficers out of ofic thar is in the redgment thar is 11 sent home this last week and I wish that thay wood send the rest of them

Wensday the 30 well Libby thar is knot eny thing knew to day thar is no knews for me to wright to you Mrs Purle is goin home to morrow and [Pvt.]Henry Plummer is goin home to morrow on a furlow and he mit as well stay after he git thar we air all well hear on this post I have waited all day with patienc for a letter and gut dispontid at last I have not reseved eny letter this week and as you sed the time semes long to me you may gudg I shall hafto close to git supper wright often as you can give my love to all pleas to take a good shar your self good knight from yours L Q Smith

Oct 1 we air all well this morning hop theas will find you all the same thar is northing knew this morning for me to wright so good morning from your husband Lewis Q Smith

Any person crossing at the Navy Yard Bridge had to show a pass, although it would be assassin John Wilkes Booth's escape route from the city two years later, when security was lax. The bridge would remain guarded, but passes were not required after April 1, 1865, just days before the assassination. The bridge also served as a route for contraband, especially liquor, which the men became very adept at discovering. At times, it was found hidden in hollowed-out loaves of bread and even buried under manure. In Washington, a "vigilant officer . . . extracted seven canteens of whiskey from a lady's hoop-skirt the other day—21 pints in all—She bore it like a martyr."[26] Lewis wrote twice in early October:

Washington Oct the 2/63 My Dear Wife

I seat my self to rit you a few lins to let you no how I am and whar I am I am well an am hear to the Navee yard bridg yet a cookin for the boys perhaps you wood like to no what our duty is hear it is a garding the bridg hear by the Nave yard to pevent thar beaing eny licker or eny other goods smuggle acros the river it is the easton branch of the Pertomack river thar is northin new to day I though I wood wright you a few lins every day so you may no how I am a gittin a long every day I shall send my letters so you can git them Tuesday an Saterday

Oct the 3 My Dear wife I seat my self a few moments to wright a few lins to day to let you [know] what is goin on thar is northing knew our army is on a moove agane thar is a grat meny ridement air goin down front thar was one thousan Cavelry gest past hear agoin front thar has bin a number of thousan past hear to go front I gest thay will have a wakeup down thar soon Old Jo Hooker has gon down that way to take the Command agane he sese that he is agoin to speek to the rebs through a tone of canonnadan [cannonading] an mesitry [musketry] I hop he will and so that thay will under stand what he mene well libby I ges you donot think that the time seams long to me to not git one letter a week it has bin over a week since I have reseve eny from you and I dont no what to think of it if you air sick you sed that you wood rit to me and I want you should do it if you can if you cant git some one to do it for you if you air sick I want to no it if you air well I want to no it for I worry a nuf for fear you wood bee do rit as often as you can if you donot rit but a few lins rit how you air all agitin a long and how things lok I reseved a letter from Jacob some time ago and answer it have hern northing from him sinse well libby I have gest gut a letter from you while I have bin ariting I was glad enuf to reseve it and hear that you air all wel I think you air quite smart on farming you never roat how much corn you plantid this year I gest you forgut it you tell the boys to be good boys an help thar granfarther all thay can tell farther and mother to keep up good curridg as thay can you try and do the same for better days air coming some time I hop I shall have to close for it is time to git super rit often as you can give my love to all take a shar your self good day from yours Lewis Q Smith

Once again, Lewis voiced his irritation at and resentment of those who did not return his correspondence. There are faithful correspondents and there are those who simply cannot be bothered. Considering distance, orders to move on short notice, and disruptions of weather, it appears that the mails were fairly rcliable.

Washington Oct the 9 year 63 My Dear wife

I seat my self to wright a few lines to let you no that we air all well hear on this post hear to the bridg thay air a bout the same in Camp as thay have bin. thar is no knews this morning and I have northing to rit I and Jarymiarh Smith gut a pas and went out into Contry a bout three miles to a horse raise we startid at one o clock and gut back at five yesterday it did seame good to git out of this stinkin City after bein obelige to stay in the City so long and knot alowed to go out of it I shall hafto say as you did time seams long to knot git a letter when the maile comes wendsday from thar and the rest of them gittin letters and I non I suspose that you git tyard of wrighting so I will poot up with it for I cant help it

Oct 10 well Libby thar is no knews to day in the pappers we air all well this morning I reseved a letter and things you sent I gut them last knight thay all come safe and I thank you all for your kindness the kindness of you all the garlesis [galoshes] air gest what I nead I thank you for them as for the foottins I have one pair that I have never woar the last ones you sent to me my old ons will last me a while longer I rot to you to send me some more haris powders and som black charis thay did not come I donot no as you gut my letter in season to send them if you have eny to spare if you can git a chanse to send me some with out it bein to much troubele tell farther that I thank him for carring our box to the Vilague and if you have the mony to spair if you will pay him for it if I live to git home I will try to pay you tell Mother I thank hir for the things she sent to me it is all that I can do as long as I am whair I am tell the boys I thank them for what thay sent tell them that thay must be good boys I was vary sorry to hear that little Hepsa and your boy was sick I hop thay will be better befor this reach you rit gest how thay air when you rit and rit how your corn and potato air this year how my pertatoballs do this year and so on. I ges that the rest of them have forgutten whair I am except Lucy. J. and Hepsa. L. [Paine] thay two air all that wright to me know except you

I never have reseved that letter that John and Julia war a goin to wright to me I gest thay have forguten to writ it dont you

Oct 11 we air all well hear this mornin thar is no knew this morning all quiart hear but how long it will be I cannot tell good by for this time from L Q S

In his next letter, Lewis refers to censorship of the press—there were ongoing efforts to control the news by the federal government. As early as March 1862 and after planned troop movements appeared in print, the War Department began to censor reports telegraphed from the field. Also, it was well known that the captains of the Confederate raiders CSS *Tacony* and CSS *Alabama* were aware of the sailings of Union cruisers sent in their pusuit. They simply read the newspapers taken from captured Yankee ships. However, even a suggestion of censorship was enough to create credibility problems for both the press and the government.

The reference to "Ginerell Mead is to bol run" is neither the Battle of First Bull Run (Manassas), of July 1861, nor Second Bull Run, in August 1862. It is probably the inconclusive Bristoe campaign of October 1863, in which Lee drove Meade back from the Rappahannock. In this ten-day struggle, Confederate losses considerably exceeded Meade's.

Washington Oct 16 1863 Wel Libby

I will comenc one more letter but I hant gut much to wright onley I am well and I hop that this will find you all the same thar at home I cant rit you eny knews for we do not git eny t[h]ar is not eny in the papers thay say that thay air not alowed to print the knews gest at the present time for thay have comense thar fall fighting and how thay come on I cant tell you thar is a grat meny folts reports comes out in the papers for mischif so thay have poot a stop to it I reseved your letter yesterday I was glad to hear from you all agane an to hear that you wore all well agane I wish I could hear from you every day an hear how you air gitting along thar you sed that you wore agoin to send me some pouders and Chares Plummes I trid to git some hear but could not you said that you wore agointo knit me some featings and send me I shall bee vary glad of them when it comes cold wether the reason why I roat to you to send my Coat an boots so soon it was reportid that we wore ordored off down front an we wantid to git them if w[e] could befor we went but we did not go the reson why I donot no but we air hear yet

Oct 17 wel Lib I a goin to wright a few more lines if it is knot so bright as for my helth it is good we air all well hear on this post hop you air all the same I have not much to wright a bout the fighting for I donot no much a bout it thay air a fighting every day our army a haveing good success as yet Ginerell Mead is to Bol run thay air bound to have one more fight thar and our men gut in thar first this time and gut persesion of it first this time and Mr Lee will hafto back out I gest we have men a nuff thar to hold it a ganst eny army thay can bring on and thay air wel perpaired for them in other plases our army is in good a condision as it ever was as far as I can lern by all sorsis but we have sonthing to do yet befor this rebelion is poot down but I hop it wont take agrat while to do it I wood give you the pertichlers about thar fighting if I could but I have knot lernd them yet when I do I will rit them to you. It is a vary plesant day as plesant as summer it has bin wet and rainy for two or three days past but it is gittin to bee more helthy then it was and I hope it will continuer so well I must close agane give my love to all of my frends after taken a shar your self wright often from yours good knight Lewis Q Smith

Lewis mentioned in the following letter (and in several previous ones—the spellings vary) "Harris Powders." Dr. Mark Harris was a "Thompsonian" healer in Sandwich Notch, very close to where Lewis Smith lived.[27] His "old remedy of burdock seed, poplar bark and gum aloes" was still in use by some elderly residents of the Notch in the 1920s.[28] Black Cherries are probably lozenges or another proprietary preparation. Thompsonianism flourished in the first four decades of the nineteenth century and was *the* prominent system of herbal medicine.

Lewis pointed to corruption by Cpl. Henry Gilman, a sure source of poor morale. Gilman would soon pay the price for shorting his comrades' meals—"busted," or reduced in rank, to private. On the opening of the war, many career army surgeons had been immune to change and progress for years, and attempts to improve general health and army cooking in particular had begun with prodding by the civilian U.S. Sanitary Commission in 1861. In March 1863, Congress passed legislation revising "sanitary" practices—from personal hygiene, latrines, garbage disposal, and tents to cooking. The Army of the

Potomac's medical director, Dr. Jonathan Letterman (1824–1872), transmitted Maj. Gen. Hooker's General Orders No. 52, dated May 15, 1863: "The cooking, especially when in camp, should be done by companies and not by individuals or by squads, and for this purpose two men should be detailed from each company as cooks . . . "[29]

In theory, the change brought specialization and economies of scale (Negroes could be added as "assistant" cooks at ten dollars per month) and, it is hoped, improved quality to meals. The recollection that Lewis, having recovered from typhoid only months before, *became* a cook might give one pause—if not outright weakness at the knees. However, who does or does not become a typhoid carrier is most unpredictable: the example of New York's "Typhoid Mary" (Mary Mallon, 1869–1939), who was never even sick, and the recognition of the bacterial cause of typhoid, was decades away from the Civil War experience. In addition to typhoid, Lewis mentioned trouble with the "dyree" several times during his enlistment. His experience was representative: one estimate of the frequency of this "universal ailment" was an "annual average being 73.8 per cent."[30]

Washington Oct 24 1863 Dear Sister [Lucy J. Wiggin]

I seat my self to try and answer yours that I reseved some days ago I was glad to hear from you agane and to hear that the helth of you all is as good as it [is] as for my helth it is good it bin the best for the last four weeks the best it has bin sc[ince] I have bin in the survis I am at the Nave yard Bridg adoin duty I am a cooking for the boys yet Mother sent me some haris pouders by Mrs Purl and I have taken a dose onse a week and it has don me the most good of eny thing I have taken sinse I have bin out hear I have bin troble with the dyree or it has bin the other way with me Asa Magoon was vary slim for a long time and I dvided my pouders with him and he comence taken it and he has gut to bee as tuff as a bair agane he [is] in Camp a doin duty he was down to see me yestrday he sends his best respects to you all and wood like to call and tak[e] tea with you and so wood I but we live wel hear on this post we have a nuf to eat the govement firnish a nuff to make us comfible but we have not and it is holey oin to our oficers the boys in camp do not have a nuff to make them comfitble and our o[r]dly Mr. Gilman I mean Henry Gilman is taken it out of our mouth and poot in to his pocket and our Captan hant forse a nuff to say why you do so

> *As for war knews thar is but little thar seams as though we air giting the best of it whar thar a ingagement air but Mr. Lee has bin folin back and has burnt and disstroyd all of the bridgs as he crosed them so our army could not foller him and a cordin to the reports it will poott our army back one month and I am vary sorry for it I shall hafto close for it is ten o clock and the boys air carin on so I [can't] hear my self think so you must excues all mistaks I will try and do better next time give my love to little Lizzy an ciss hir for me give my love to Frank and his farther folks wright often and I will do better next time good knight from your Brother Lewis Q Smith this is rebel paper*

As autumn advanced to winter, the Fourteenth remained camped, necessitating marching to duty stations and a "good deal of travel through the mud."[31] Their tents were old and "leaked badly, hardly any are tight."[32] With cold weather imminent, the comfort of barracks lay months ahead—in fact, in the next year. Thankfully, Lewis's health had improved, but illness continued to strike others. Capt. Oliver Marston commented: "We have a good many sick in the Regt. now, it is very sickly." Marston echoed some degree of impatience with the war: "I am not feeling homesick or tired particularly—but would like to see the whole thing closed up honorably. I do not want to come home until it is done so, but the sooner the better."[33]

~ *Nine* ~

The Holidays and Year's End

November 1 to December 31, 1863

I like my frends famely and Country and am willing to bee one with others to stand hir defense . . .

—Lewis Q. Smith, November 14, 1863

On occasion, men were sent back to Concord to the "military rendezvous"—today a recruiting station—allowing brief furloughs home. While there is no record of Smith's returning to the Granite State for recruiting, some members of the Fourteenth did travel north. However, as a result of the draft, conscripts rather than enlistees began to enter the army, although their total number was never very great—one estimate is 3.67 percent of all Union troops raised from 1863 to 1865. When substitutes (9.35 percent) are added, since they were a direct result of the draft, the total becomes 13.02 percent.[1]

Conscripts were not highly regarded by the volunteers—perhaps *despised* is the better term. Francis Buffum wrote: a "reckless, almost worthless, element was being enlisted into the Union army . . ."[2] James Newton had a similar opinion: "Yesterday the drafted men were mustered into the U.S. Service, there are some pretty goodlooking men among them, but as a general thing they aint much to brag of. They have been fighting and raising cain generally, ever since they have been here."[3] Jenks offered his views of the draft's impact on the Fourteenth:

> We had an acquisition to our Rgt. last week of an hundred *conscripts* or rather Substitutes, but one third of them have run away, they are a drunken set of fellows, knock down and rob one another in the night, and are

Drunken Soldiers Tied Up for Fighting and Other Unruly Conduct, Alfred R. Waud, Library of Congress

> nothing but a nuisance in camp. It makes the guard duty much harder then formerly, as I have to tie them up to trees &c. &c. They keep the guard house full all the time.[4]

When escorted to the front by "picked" guards, few of these men skedaddled, but later, when accompanied by members of the Invalid Corps, wholesale desertions occurred. On October 17, 1863, President Lincoln was compelled to call for three hundred thousand more men, and there would be additional calls for men until Christmas 1864. The situation never really improved. Of 625 substitutes sent from Concord, New Hampshire, to join the Fifth Regiment NHV in early January 1865, 137 deserted enroute, eighty-two deserted to the enemy from picket lines, and thirty-six deserted to the rear. Four, "utterly worthless," were discharged with "glaring" physical incapacities, and a few more, including "impracticable imbeciles," were returned to Concord. Thus, from August 1864 to year's end, only 359 of the original 625 remained.[5] Worse yet, since bounties had risen significantly, the potential financial loss per deserter approached one thousand dollars, or $26,600 for the 266 deserters from the Fifth alone. Multiplied by a dozen or so regiments, the result was not loose change to governments already strapped with debt.

Lewis began his next letter on November 6, 1863, and finished it the following day. His embarassment over not knowing "your boy name" and his reference to "your boy" is thinly veiled—the child is better than one year old! A sense of duty emerges from this letter: Lewis must stay to see the war through.

Washington Nov 6 1863 My Dear wife

I agane seat myself to try and wright you a few lines to let you no how we air we air all well hear on this post I did reseve a letter from you last knight with 3 Dollars inclosed in it I have not reseved eny befor for two weeks and I was vary uneasy about you so you may wel suppose that I was rejorsed to git one and hear that you wore all well thar at home and gitting a long so well I roat to you yesterday I roat that we wore a goin to move we air ordord of but when we shall go I cant tell our oficers dont no we may go to morrow and we may not go this two weeks we cant tell I thank you for the mony that you sent me it is all the reckumpenc I can give you now for it you sed that your boy name was Lewis E Smith and you gest that I did not no what his name was why should I you never told me what it was I belive what is the E in his name for I wish you wod wright and tell me so I shall no what to call him. you wantid to no if I went on gard knights I havenot sinse I have bin a cookin I do no other duty now but cook I have compny a plenty day and knight I donot care eny thing a bout compny hear I wood as soon be a lone as to have compny co[u]ld I bee with you and the little Children I wood knot ask for eny other compny

You sed when I git home you wood let me do the cookin for you I wish I was thar to git your dinner for you to day I wood gladly do it for you but I am hear an hear I must stay untill this war is settle and when that will be I cant tell but you must keep up good curidg I will do all I can to help you when I do git home I will wait untill to morrow and see what that bring forth then I will finish my letter Nove Fryday eve 7 well Libby I will try and finish my letter thar is not eny thing knew we air hear yet and air all well hear to this post you wantid to no whar

> *Molton was he is hear with [us] is hear to the bridg and has bin ever sinse I have bin hear and the same old boy we had a visiter to day it Mr James Hart he come from Lowell[6] he gut hear to day and I need not say that we was glad to see him for you no we wore he sed that he saw my babes when he was up to Sandwich and I wish I could see them but I am glad to hear from them and you to I gladly reseved your other letter to day and found two dollars inclosed in it I hartly thank you for it for the letter and money I hop it will bee so that I can repay it agane you did not say as you gut your check or not I should think it was time long ago pleas to wright next time about it and wright often as you can give my love to them all after taken a good shar your self ciss the little on[e]s for me take one your self I must close by bidine you good knight from yours Lewis Q Smith*

Lewis noted that he is still "to the bridg" and anticipated that the Invalid Corps would relieve the regiment. Lewis also expected to remain in Washington through the winter. In his letter of November 9, Lewis discussed sending his pistol home if ordered to the field. A pistol was useful to a guard in a city, on a bridge, or on a wharf, but not in an infantry action: "from the best authority (the Chief of the Bureau of Ordnance at Washington) . . . side weapons of all kinds for troops are useless and pernicious."[7] Earlier in the war, some Massachusetts politicians insisted that their infantry volunteers be equipped with pistols as well as muskets or rifles. Military experience dictated that volunteers with two types of weapons would be at a disadvantage with dissimilar rounds, powder charges, and ramrods in the heat of battle. Most infantry carried only long arms in the war.

> *Washington Nov the 9 1863 Dear wife*
>
> *I agane seat my self to try an comence one more letter to you to let you no that we air hear and air all well hear to the bridge and hop that theas few lines will find you all the same thar at home we havenot found out when we shall leave this plase perhaps not at all but we air expecting to but we shant no untill it is time to start we air gittin vary good knews now thay brot in 18 hundred prisners to day that our army took day befor yesterday down to raperhanock thay had quit a battle thar and our men give them a hansom whipin and took 18 hundred prisners one battry our lost not over 300 thay will git anuf in time*

Nov 10 Wendesday eve I seat my self to try an finish my letter we air hear yet and I ges we shall stay a spell I think we shall stay hear this winter but dont no we air haveing gest as much as we can do to take cair of the rebels prisners that our army air taken from Mr. Lee thar is 1100 a coming in to knight to ad to the other 1800 whittch makes 2900 that Ginerill Meed has taken this week and sent hear to this City and how meny more thar is that he has I donot no but meed is wel and I hop that thay will continer so an this thing will soon bee closed up and be at a end I long to have it come it seems as though I could not wait for it to come

Nov 11 thar is not much news to day all good that we git we air all well hear to the bridg and we air still hear in washington and I think that we shall stay hear this winter but I dont no thar is a good meny storrys of our mooveing but we wore all abel body man a round washington was ordord off and the envelid coar was to take our plases but we air hear and I think we shall stay hear the Citsons say that thay cant let us go thay dont no how to git a long without us and thay hang on for the [war] department to keep us hear to do the duty in the City and I shall not think that we air goin to leave hear untill we start and when we git and git out of the City then I shall beleve it and not befor so you need not worry eny more our goin I shant. I reseved a letter from Lucy to day Frank was vary slime I was sorry for that she was as well as uesel and little Lizzy [Frank and Lucy's daughter] she sent me a letter and 50 Cents in mony I shall answere it to morrow I have bout me a pistil and if we should go [to the] front I shall send it home and a box an shant at presant if we dont go so you need not look for it until it come I shall have to close for want of room wright often as you can give my love to all kiss the little ones for me and cindly take one your self tell the children to be good an mind thar mother good knight from yours Lewis Q Smith

In Lewis's next letter, he noted Hepsa's mention that "uncle John Wiggin" was unwell. John M. and Polly F. Wiggin and their two sons lived next door to Lucy and Frank Wiggin. John, a carpenter by trade, and Polly were older than Frank and Lucy by a little more than two decades.

Washington Nove 14 1863 My Dear wife

I agane seat myself to try and answer your letter that I reseve to day roat the 7 and 9 I was glad to hear from you agane hear that all well and harty and gitting a long so well as for my helth it is good and hop theas will find you all wel thar. we air hear in the City yet and I gest we shall stay hear a while longer but dont no how it will bee I have sent you two letters this week and dout lis you have gut them befor this I reseved two letters from you last week but thar was two weeks befor that I didnot git eny and I felt vary unese about you as you may well suspose and if you have ritten and I hant gut them you air not to blame thar is not much knews to wright to you this time I wright so often it is one thing rit over and over I reseved a letter from Lucy this week and have answer it I reseved one from Hepsa to day she sed thay wore all well thar but uncle John Wiggin he was pooty sick but she an farther wore both well and harty She sed that Amas Paine was draftid exzemtid and Joe Clark[8] was draftid and exceptid an he cryed baby so thay let him go a spunkey boy he had better stay at home untill he gits weend for it is no plase for babis out hear for we have no craidels to rock them in we dont want such

I shall answer Hepsa letter to morrow I shall not delay in answering hir letter for Hepsa and Lucy an you air all that thar is that wright to me now and I will not let eny of your[s] nor thars go unanswered Hepsa shose more respects and frend ship to me then some of my own brothers and sisters I clame hir as a sister and a frend if thar is eny one that wants to hear from thar frends and famely it is a sholdiear when he is in the gap of defenc of his Country thar is no one nose what a sholdier is untill thay try it on and then thay see how it fits perhaps some like it but I dont I like my frends famely and Country and am willin to bee one with others to stand hir defense

It is a vary dark an rainy knight an lonsom thar is a nuff hear with me but that dosnot hender me from bein lonsom thar is so meny that is a suffering this dark and rainy knight I am comfitbel but thar is thousands that air not that have no shelter from the storm I pity them I no how to I will say no mor at this time. it is gitin puty lait it is 11 o clock and I will draw to a close tell farther an Mother to keep up good curidg and hop for the best an knot work to hard give my respect to all ciss the little ons for me tell them to be good children wright as often as you can good knight from yours Lewis Q Smith

A very brief letter followed a day later:

Nove 15 [1863] Mrs Lewis Q Smith wel Lizzy

it still raines this morning thar is no news to day we air all well to day hear to the bridge Asa was down hear yesterday and brot a letter from you and one from hepsa he was well and sends his rspects to you all he wantid me to wright to you to see if you had eny mony on hand that you did not want to use if so if you wood let his wife have it to pay Jonothan Been up[9] *if so how much if you have it that you dont want to use you can do as you pleas with it rit what about it in your next good by for this time from yours Lewis Q Smith rit often if I acuses you rongferly about riting I am sorry pleas to forgive me this time*

Lewis wrote again on Tuesday, November 22. His tone is optimistic and he refers to Henry Plummer, another Sandwich farmer in Company K.

Washington Nov 22/63 Dear wife

I agane seat myself to try and answer your letter that I reseved the 21 first and to let you no whair and how I am I am hear in the City on the same post that I have bin on and my helth is vary good at the presant time hoping that theas few lines will find you all enjoying the same blesing I was vary glad to hear from you all agane [and] hear you air all well I reseved some black charis and haric powerders by the way of Henry Plummer he gut hear to the City Thursday and I went up to the Camp yesterday and see him he sed he was up to see you and had a vary good visit thar you sed that you gest that your check was to the Corner I should think it was time for it to be it has bine over two month sinse we was paid off that time and we was paid off agane the 19 of this month whitch [was] last Thursday and thar will bee 20 dollars more for you if you ever git the check for it so you can look for it untill it comes you sed that Burleigh had mooved I wish he could staid thar this winter but he noes best what to do so you must try and git along the best you can this winter I should like to spend the winter with you but as I cannot you must try and make the best of it and I will try and do the same and we both will come out bright and shiney at last onley

> *keep up good curridg I think you have. We air hear in [the] City and I ges thar is no danger of our gitting out of it we shall stay hear this winter I think thar is the rest of the ridgments are releved from duty hear in the City by the invelid coar and air redy to take the feaild and I dont no the reason why we donot go thar is one thing the Citisons will not give us up to have us leave the Citty if thay can posable help it Thar is not much knews this morning our army air haveing good success every whair at the presant time thar is a report that thay are a fighting down on the raperdam [Rapidan River] but we have not lernd the perticklers about it yet the rebels prisners air coming in every day and deserters to Thay tell some hard tailes about the rebel army I gest that thay air about on thair last legs as they (blot) will hafto to give it up soon and I dont cair how quick. I shall hafto to draw to a close I see Asa yesterday he is well he give me a peas of his wife cheas it seem good So you can tell hir I gut some of hir cheas wright often give my love to them all after taken a shair your self good day from yours Lewis Q Smith*

The Fourteenth's historian, Francis Buffum, remarked on the regiment's apparent popularity in the city: "According to the highest testimony, the military guard and special duty in the city of Washington had never been performed so satisfactorily as it was by the Fourteenth."[10] J. Henry Jenks, of Keene, also wrote proudly of the regiment: "We are called the best Regt. that ever was in the City. Although some of the N.H. folks call us a bandbox Regt, baby Regt, &c and seem to feel real bad that we have not been in battle and killed off most of us, but I am satisfied to stay here, and let folks talk, for our reputation is made."[11]

Lewis also referred to the burning of the Sandwich Quaker (Friends) Meetinghouse, which occurred on the night of November 14, 1863, months after the summer draft riots in the cities. The fire was more likely the result of antipathy to Quaker pacificism.[12] The Sandwich Quakers had refused to sign the Association Test in 1776 due to their "Quaker proclivities in most instances."[13] On the national level, in keeping with their tradition, Quakers refused the Civil War draft as well as the payment of commutation or the provision of substitutes—in other words, exemption without qualifications. Quakers were offered commutation or alternative service until the Amendatory Act of February 1864.[14]

Washington Nov 24/63 My dear wife

I agane seat my self to try and answer yours that I reseved yesterday the 22 I was glad to hear from you all agane to hear that you wore all well as for my helth it is vary good with the exceptions of a bad coald whitch we air about all trobble with hear to the bridge. we air hear in the city and I ges that we shall haft to stay hear thar is no danger of our leaveing hear at present our rigment is all split up thar is five out of each compny to be taken out for detective hear in this city and the rest of us has gut to do gard and pertroll duty in the City so I see no chance for us to git out of the City this winter. thar is not much knew to wright you to day our hole army is on a moove and the rebels air on the retreat as fast as they can I ges thay air gittin some what discuridg if thay hant thay will thay have to come to it eny old how. I wood like to no how your Copperheads feal about it if thay feale fore the South as much as thay did when I was thar poor Creaturs how I pity such I wish thay wore out hear rit in front of the balls and bernits [bayonets] it wood be gest the plase thay ort to be plaised into I should like to see it you sed the quaker meetin house was burnt how did it take fiar was it sut on fiar or how we herd that it was sut a fire by the Coper heads

Nove 25 Wel Lib Thar [is] no knews of eny a mount to day we air all well hear to day hop that this may find you all the sam thar. it is a fine day for the season hear to day it was weat and rainy yesterday how is the wether thar it is genely coald thar thankgivin to morow is thanksgivinday an I wood like to bee thar with you but can not I hop that you will have a good time I am a goin send you a rebel bill of fifty cense to pay your expensis with to morrow I though[t] you wood like a little spending mony it is good for northing only to look at it is thar ginewine mony I will send you a biggar one when I can git it you must excues all blundrs for the boys make so much noyes I cant hear myself think so I will draw to a close give my love to all tell farther and mother to keep up good curidg better days a coming keep up good curig your self thay cant keep me but two years longer So good day wright often from yours L Q Smith

In the letter below, Lewis wished he could have provided Libby with "a good fat Turkey" even if he "had to hook it." Lewis's honesty proved to be a virtue. Sometime later, New Hampshire Gov. Frederick Smyth (1819–

1899) pardoned Russell T. Varney of Sandwich, who was serving a two-year sentence in the New Hampshire State Prison "for stealing a turkey from an open shed." The published report noted: "He learned such tricks in the Army." [15] The irony of Varney's situation was that Thanksgiving was "well celebrated" at the prison—with "roast turkey."[16]

Washington Nove 28 1863 My Dear wife

I seat my self this evening to try and answer yours that I reseved this evening I was vary glad to hear from you all agane and to hear that you are all well if I could hear from you every day and no that you all air well it is all that I wood ask for I wood be contentid but I hafto content my self the best that I can. as for my helth it is vary good at the presant time hoping theas few lines will find you all the same thar the boys air all well hear on this post thar is 21 men hear to the bridge 14 from our Compeny one from Co A one from Co B one from Co D one Co I one Co C one Co F to from Co I[17] *you sed that you wish I was thar to your Thanksgivin I wish I could be with you I woodnot cair what I had [to] eat or drink I [am] hear and hear I am willing to stay if you all air well untill this thing is settle and settle for ever and have it for ever settle I think you was coming out large to kill your poor old hin that you cant winter for me if I com home now I wood don better by you if you had come out hear to see me I wood gut you a good fat turkey if I had to hook it whitch I have never dun sinse I have bin in the army to take eny thing that didnot belong to me what I gut I baugh and paid for it and I have gut a long gest as well and a little better. perhaps you wood like to no what I had for Thankgiveing some bake meat and beans that the govement found us and I cook them myself and it was good anuff for me the rest of them went in for bake chickins and chickins py and I felt gest as well as thay and save my mony for some other use I had rather have my mony than to spend it in that way. I have roat two letters to you this week and I sent you a fifty cent bill in my last one it was rebel mony and it is good for northing to you and I found a fifty cent bill in yours of good mony and I felt rather a shame to think I had sent you mony that was good for northing dont take it as a front and I will do better for the time to come. well Libby as for war knews it is good it is glouris I will send you a paper in sted of wrighting it our army is doin first rait every whair and the Coper heds air down for ever down. I shall hafto draw to a close it is a dark rainy knight give my best respects to all tell the children to bee good children wright often and I will good knight from yours Lewis Q Smith*

In the above letter, there is a notable message: since "you are all well," Lewis will stay "untill this thing is settle." The connection to friends and family, especially their well-being, is strong—a bond that was certainly weaker among the jumble of conscripts and substitutes. William Combs, of Company C, wrote home from Georgia on March 2, 1865, and stated this relationship just as succintly: "i am very glad to here every time that you are all well that gratifies me the most of any thing that I can here."[18] On the next morning, Lewis wrote again, and it is obvious that Lewis and others of the Fourteenth were becoming optimistic. Although Charleston was not "aburning," morale was nonetheless on the upswing.

Sunday morning Nove 29 [1863] Dear Libby

we air all well this morning hop you air all the same thar we have good knew[s] from all pornts this morning Charleston is a fiar it has bin aburning 62 ours at the last acounts we had of it and the rebs air gitting hail Clumby [Hail, Columbia] every whair in regard to your pig do as you think best and in regard to your bying corn if you have gut cloth anuff for you and the children you look out for enuff to eat and you look out for your self that is the best advise I can give you look out for your self I shall hafto close by biding you good morning frome yours Lewis Q Smith ciss the little ones for me and take a harty one your self keep up good curig I shall be with you befor long so you must take all of the cumfort you can befor I git thar

Still in Washington, Lewis wrote in early December:

Washington Dec 6/63 Dear wife

I againe seat my self to wright a few lines to let you no how we air a gittin [along] hear as well as we can and hop you are doin the same thar at home we air all well hear on this post hoping that this will find you all the same thar at home the boys air pooty helthy in camp Asa has bin layd up a few days with a bad coald but he is beter he will bee on duty agane in a few days he will come down hear to stay with us I expect I hope he will thar is not much knews to wright this time our army is doin well as we can expect I have not reseved eny thing of eny letter for a week past from you or eny one else so I have not much to rit it is vary plesant har for the time of year we have not had eny snow hear this year yet but a little rain this fall I have gut to wait untill I git dinner for I am doin the cookin alone know but I expect that Asa will come down hear to help me

well I will try and finish my letter perhaps you wood like to no what we had for diner some fresh meat stue fry we have a nuf to eat hear but it is one thing over an over we by some things for a change I took that 50 cents that you sent me and baught some butter with it to eat with bread it went first rait but the butter that we git out hear dont much like the butter we git at home butter is worth 37 ct lb or that is what thay ask for it and 10 ct a quort for milk and other things acordingly a soldier cannot bye eny thing hear without paying a good deal moar then a citsan doas a soldiear stands rather a lousa chance hear in bying eny thing out hear I hafto pay 1.00 a Lb for tobaco an the citsans 80 cents I ges I shall hafto leave off usan it as I did Licker Thar is one thing I will tell you if you will keep it to your self that is Hen Gilman is reduse to the ranks he is a privet as wel as I he can not have eny control over eny one he has gut to sholder his gun as wel as the rest and he aught to long ago he will think how he has treatid others he is knot to be pitid eny and he is not. I will tel you more when I see you I shall have to draw to a close give my respects to all except a shair your self and wright often as you can good knight from yours wright Lewis Q Smith

Washington Dec 16 1863 My Dear wife

I agane seat myself to wright a few liens in answer to yours that I reseved last knight I was glad to hear from you all agane and hear that you was all well Sorry to hear that mother was having the headake So much I was in hops that she wood not be trobel with that so much as she uesto she must be vary carful of hir helth as for my helth is good with the except a bad coald the boys air all well hear on this post thay are quit[e] helthy in Camp to what thay have bin hear before

thar is not much knews to wright this time for we donot git much but what we do git is vary good our army is doin well as can be expectid

Grant is driveing long Streat and his army to eturnity what Grant take as prisners it is rportid that he took 4000 prisners and all of longstreat artilry and I gest he will not have much army in a few days if thay keep on much longer I hop this will sink him and his hole army to the oald boy and keep them thar after thay git them thar but we cant tell how thay will come out but thay have gut to give up some time if thay dont thar will be no one of the rebes to tell eny tails

Suppose you wood like to no what we had that was good to eat for dinner to eat to day we had a boile dish turnips and cabig we went out and baight it and if you had bine hear you should had some with us but I suspose you had somthing better at home I was glad to hear frome Hepsa to hear that she was up to see you and I wish I had bin thare to but could not so you must injoy your self the best you can it is all you can do I hop the time is not far distant befor we shall meat agan I have answer Hepsa letter to day I will not let a letter go unanswer that I git from eny one you or Hepsa a specely You sed you was agointo send me some things in Ebin Dails [Ebenezer Dale's] box I have not reseved eny thing by eny one but by Plummer and if you have sent by eny one els wright and wright what you sent and hoe [who] you sent it by and if you send eny more send it by it self or with Asa and no one else Asa is hear with me he is well and send his respects to you all I shall hafto draw to a close by biding you good knight from yours Lewis Q Smith

Dec 17 we air well this morning hoping this will find you all the same thar at home

Lewis's last letter of 1863 was written on Christmas Day. In the course of the year, his health had been restored and he and his Sandwich friends were doing well, almost "first rait." Lewis was even capable of a little humor, as in the case of Confederate money and his suggestion to use his picture for scaring crows. Complaints are noticeably fewer.

Pvt. Harrison Atwood II, a Sandwich farmer, was born in Gray, Maine, on July 11, 1836, and married Augusta A. Batchelder in Sandwich on April 8, 1858.[19] Harrison was fortunate to obtain a furlough on this occasion, but his luck would not last.

Washington Dec 25 1863 My Dear wife

I seat my[self] this evening as it is the first day of Christmas to wright you a few lines to let you no how we air agittin along out hear as wel as you can expect we air all well hear on this post Liu M S Webester has gon into Camp to do duty a few days I hop he will come back soon for we air lonsom without him. thar is concidebele agoin on hear in this City to day it is agrait day with the Citsons hear thay think more of it then eny other day in the year

I had the first dinner to day that you wood call a dinner sins I left home I will tell you what I had a baike turkey a sparib pertatos gravay some cabig pies an sweet caks and warm biskit and I will tell you how I come by it thar is a man that lives hear that has the charge of the bridg that we air a garding of by the naim of Hudson he gut up a dinner and ask me and two more up to tak dinner with him and wodnot take no for a answer he is a nise man he is not like the most of the citsons for he lets licker alone

Thar is knot much knews to writ this time every thing is vary quiart and still it is quit cold out hear thar is no snow nor has not bin but it has bin vary cold hear for eight or ten days past but I expect you have gut snow a plenty thar wright and let me know I have not reseved eny letter from you this week yet but I hop to git one tomorow I shall finish my letter to morrow knight

Dec 26 well Libby thar is northing knew this evening we air all well but I did not git a letter to day I hope you air all well thar at home I heard that Harison Atwood was goin home to morrow I am a goin up to see him and git him to carry a little bundle he will leave it to Mr Folsom Asa and I send together I shall send you my pitcher and a pistil for you to keep for me I mene for you to keep the pistile and you may do as you like with the pitchtur hang it up to scair crows with I send it for a knews year presant it is not much of a presan I no the prise of that pistil was 35 Dollars when it was knew I paid 6 dollars for it if eny one will pay you 20 Dollars you may sel it I will poot a line into the bundel from yours with much love Lewis Q Smith

In late 1863, the Fourteenth witnessed the "finishing touches to the exterior of the grand dome of the Capitol. The work of years was complete, and the familiar but unsightly stagings and hoisting-rigging soon came

U.S. Capitol Building under Construction, 1860. Library of Congress Photograph

down."[20] Visible from the Navy Yard Bridge, Thomas Crawford's statue, Goddess of Liberty (or Armed Liberty), "was raised upon the Dome of the Capital [sic] . . . then a flag was run up at just twelve; for a signal to the different Forts around the city that they might fire a salute . . . and they did fire I reckon right smart sure."[21]

Company G's 2nd Lt. John W. Sturtevant, of Keene, had commanded the detachment serving at the Seventh Street Wharf from May to November, but was now working at the Washington provost marshal's office. The only officer there on Christmas Day, he galloped away to "a splendid dinner of chickens, oysters & and galloped back again only being gone an hour." He noted that the day "seemed very much like Sunday, all the stores were closed, and every body was out on the street, firing crackers and getting drunk."[22] He also sent word that Keene's Col. Robert Wilson "has been dangerously sick with diphtheria but is now out of danger." Wilson

Lt. John W. Sturtevant, of Keene, N. H. Author's Collection

recovered, but would resign his commission with a "surgeon's certificate of disability" later in the new year.[23]

In Boston, after deliberating for twenty-four hours, a Superior Criminal Court jury found Patrick Malone guilty of assaulting a police officer during the July draft riots. Malone got three years in the house of correction.[24] A week of subfreezing weather had been "remarkably pleasant," and ice skating was reported to be "excellent" on almost all ponds.[25] Back in Washington, a member of the Fourteenth wrote home on the last day of the year. He had previously noted that "thare is any quantity of girles round camp," but now he pined: "we have dances hear most every knight but the girls come up missing."[26]

On Boston Common, at noon on New Year's Day, it was rainy, foggy, and dull, at least until the firing of a one-hundred-gun salute. January first was the anniversary of the Emancipation Proclamation: "the cannon's voice appropriately celebrated the enfranchisement of large masses of persons heretofore held in bondage."[27] Also of note was an endorsement for Messrs. A. Williams & Co. that appeared in the *Boston Daily Evening Transcript* on January 1, 1864:

> A large stock of Diaries for the year in such various forms and sizes as to suit all classes . . . all of which have a calendar . . . with all the conveniences of a business pocket book, will be found very perfect and convenient. The smaller and cheaper kinds will answer all purposes of a business man."[28]

Of course, such pocket diaries could serve the purposes of soldiers as well.

~ Ten ~

WASHINGTON AND HARPERS FERRY

January 1 to February 28, 1864

I wish you was hear or I was thare but you are thair and I am hear and we will make the best of it . . .

—Lewis Q. Smith, January 27, 1864

. . . it is pooty cold and wind heare we air heare to Harpersfary to knight but whair we shall be to morrow I cant tell you we may be heare and we may knot we shall be some whair . . .

—Lewis Q. Smith, February 14, 1864

CONFEDERATE RAIDS INTO WEST VIRGINIA, IN LATE January and early February 1864, were "potent in shaping the destiny of the Fourteenth."[1] The Confederates' intent both in West Virginia and in the Shenandoah Valley had been as much to draw Union troops away from the vicinity of Richmond as it was to preserve the valley's resources for their own use. This objective was better expressed by Confederate Lt. Gen. Jubal A. Early:

> The object of my presence in the lower valley . . . was to keep a threatening attitude toward Maryland and Pennsylvania, and prevent the use of the Baltimore and Ohio Railroad and the Chesapeake and Ohio Canal, as well as to keep as large a force as possible from Grant's army to defend the Federal Capital.[2]

Almost from the beginning of the war, the Confederate strategy in the valley had been a success and a huge Union embarrassment, first at the hand of Gen. Thomas "Stonewall" Jackson and later by Gen. Jubal Early. Both men were aggressive and not risk aversive, even entering battle with inferior numbers and resources. On the federal side, picket duty along the Potomac and simply guarding Washington were no longer a viable strategy, and 1864 would be the year that the balance of victory would weigh heavily on their side, finally. For Lewis and the Fourteenth, it would also be a year of surprises.

On January 6, Pvt. William Combs, Company C, of Winchester, New Hampshire, wrote to his wife: "bilding barox . . . now our men are out helping bild them they will bee done soon."[3] The regiment shortly occupied the newly constructed barracks at Sixth and O Streets, and Camp Adirondack was a thing of the past. The new location was only temporary, however, for the Fourteenth was destined for other service. On February 1, the Fourteenth left Washington by train for the upper Potomac. Due to a burned bridge at the confluence of the north and south branches of the river, the regiment could proceed no farther and returned to Harpers Ferry on February 7 and ultimately to Washington on February 25. Washington remained vulnerable, and the Fourteenth was subject to move on short notice. Reflecting a state of uncertainty, Private Combs noted the countermanded order referred to below: "we had an order to move last week but it was Countrymanded . . . "[4]

Lewis's correspondence began the year on January 2—misdated 1863. The events described indicate 1864: the rebs were not "rather discouraged" in early 1863, but were arguably becoming so by early 1864. Reacting to news from home, Lewis expressed frustration and anger with the unidentified "Bil," who appears to be responsible for some missing sheep. As a method of branding, holes, slits, and notches were placed in various combinations on the ears of sheep to identify their owners should any sheep stray.

Washington Jen 2 1863 [1864] Dear wife

I seat myself in answer to yours that I reseved Thursday I [am] glad to hear that you wore all well as for my helth it is vary good hoping this may find you all the same you wantid to no how your sheap was mark it was farther oald mark a noch [notch] under the righ[t] ear a slit in the other farther noes what it is I think Bil is a mean dog for doin as he did he had better go an find yours if ever he expect to see me in Sandwich agane he will be sorry for it befor he dys a mean scamp to try and take advantig of you an farther while I am out hear it showes what he is I reseved the featins you sent by Quimby and some cheas I have not seen him yet you sed that mr Tanner was a coming out send a dish of your applesas and a sasige if you have gut eny on hand and I will send you somthin in return when he goes home thar is not much knews to wright to you this time every thing is vary still and quiart out hear we was ordor away from hear last thursday [December 31] we was orderd to go to harpers fary and the ordor was recolde and countermandid so we did not go we hant gut out of this city yet why we wore to go thar was becaus thay expected a rebel raid acros the river into Mayland but thay havenot cros the river I gest they wont at presant if thay do thay will get met with worm reseption I ges the rebs air gittin rather discuridg acording to all reports and I donot belame them eny for it for thay have not eny thing to incuridg them thay have gut all the man thay can git

I shall hafto draw to a close for want of time I have roait in a hurry for I dont git time to eat hardly Since Asa has bin unwell I have had all of the work to do for him an me too I dont no as you can read this I am in a hurry wright as often as you can I will close by biding you good knight from yours with much love to you all Lewis Q Smith

Concern for "farther's" cough motivates Lewis to recommend his favorite cough remedy, although the "receat," the recipe or formulation, is not revealed:

Washington Jan 13/64 Dear Wife

I agane seat my self to wright a few lines to you allthough I have not much to wright as for my helth [it] is vary good hoping that theas few lines will find you the same I have bin looking for a letter from you to day in hops to hear from farther I wish you wood wright as often as you can for I want to hear how air gittin a long if eny of you air sick eny time and I want you to rite gest as it is and gest how you all air I have gut a receat for calf [cough] medson I will send it to farther for he is allway trobeld with a calf in the winter it is the best thing for a calf I ever found we air trobeld a good deal with a calf out hear he can take two tea sponful at a time take it when he calf you can git it to a potacary [apothecary] try it if he has gut a calf I reseved a letter from Ricker and Raich to day thay was well I shall answer it to morrow. if you have gut it by you that you dont want to use you may send me five dollars for a pertickler use we shall not git paid off untill next month Asa is smart agane he sends his respects to you all I will rit more next time. so good knight from yours Lewis Q Smith

Ten days later, Smith was still concerned for his family's health. His anxiety is manifest, as is his desire to help—to telegraph him should anyone become acutely ill. Becoming "slim" is often the result of cancer, but in the nineteenth century, slim (thin and not robust) foretold an early demise from consumption, as tuberculosis was then known.

Washington Jen 23 1864 My Dear wife

I seat myself to wright a few lines answer to yours that I reseved one Thursday one to knight one had three dollars inclosed in it the other two I thank you vary much for it but I am sorry I sent for it I fear you will need it more then I did I was very sorry to hear that farther was so slim and dos not gane eny have you tryd eny of that calf medson that I sent the reseat to make if you hant I wood for it is the best for a calf of eny thing I ever tryd take two tea sponfuls every time he has a calfing spell I was very sorry that the children had gut coald for thay must be vary trobelsom I wish I could bee thair with you to help you take caire of them but canot when duty cals we hafto go I hop we shall have the privelige of meating and spending meny long and happy day in safty to gether the time seams long to me I think it dos to you thare is a day a comine when I shall be free from this an the war hoop an bludy steal will be no more shant we be glad yes we shall I am glad you have gut so good a boy thar with you I wood keep him gest as long as he will stay if you can git eny thing to pay him with I will try an save every sent I can

I was sorry to hear that Susan was so slim how do thay git a long the same old thing thay air to be pittid thare no one no my felings at times I baire it as pasint [patient] as I can has farther found his sheap yet rit and let me no thair is no knews to rit you a bout the war nor eny thing else we air having fine wether out hear it is fair an plesant the snow is all gon it seems like may wether thair in old New Hampshier thair is not much mud hear to City it is a bout all dryed up it is nise walkin hear in the peapel say that it has bin the coald is [coldest] that it has bin for a number year the ise is a bout out of the river

Jen 24 wel Libby thar is northing new this morning it is fair and plesant an we air all well hear hoping this may find you all the same thaire I want you to wright often when eny of you air sick rit gest as it is if eny of you air vary sick I want to no it if farther is worse and dangeres I want to no it if eny of you should be take dangers sick I want you to telegraft on to me and I will try and come home I should rathe not come gest now if thar is no spesal need of it if thar is let me no it. give my love to all of my frends take a good shair yourself tell farther and mother to keep up good curidg this thing wont always last I will close by biding you good morning From yours in love Lewis Q Smith

An undated, unplaced letter of Smith's can be identified from its context as written from Washington, probably in January 1864. Lewis described the gifts that he intended to send home—gifts that he later identified as sent on January 27. This letter is the one enclosed with the "bundel."

Wel Libby I though I wood rit this and poot the letter in the bundel I have a number of things to send you I cant send by him and I will send a box by and by I send you Asa and my pitcher my pistil and holster and belt to you two pipes that I maid myself all a lone one of them is for farther Paine the other is for Levi H Smith the one that I have gut my name on is for farther donot think hard of me for not sending more for he cant take them so keep good curidg look out for your self and babys I hop to bee with you some time Libby I wish you wood make Hepsa give you hir pitchtur and send it to me for I want to see it I would rather see hir then them that do knot think a nuff of me to rit to me I think mor and say the les so good knight give my love to all of my frends take a good shair your self wright often as you can from yours with my best wishis Lewis Q Smith

On January 27, Lewis discussed health and weather, the contents of a box sent home, the conduct of the war, and impending marching orders. General-in-Chief Henry W. Halleck (1815–1872) ordered the Fourteenth, a battery of artillery, and the New York Veteran Cavalry to Harpers Ferry "by railroad," on February 1: "These troops will go ready for immediate service in the field."[5] At the time of the order to move, Gen. Jubal Early's Confederates threatened the Baltimore and Ohio Railroad and a major depot at Piedmont, West Virginia, on the upper Potomac. As a result, the Fourteenth spent less than a week in the vicinity of South Branch station about two hundred miles from Washington: "we remained here in this lonely place expecting a raid on the R. Road."[6]

Interspersed with Lewis's correspondence (and that of other soldiers) is the issue of uncertainty, not knowing when or where the regiment might be ordered. Soldiers and sailors adjust quickly to orders yes or no, but "maybe" is difficult to endure. Until a decision is determined and announced, the future is subject to speculation, rumor, and anxiety, the latter manifested by the frequency that the men write about it. However, one thing is now voiced: optimism, "we can do it." And soon enough, they will.

Washington Jen the 27 1864 My dear wife

I agane seat my[self] in answer to yours that I have gest reseved I was glad to hear that you ware all as well as your air I am vary glad that farther is better he must be vary careful and not git down agane he must not think that he can do as he onse could for he cannot tell him for me to be as carfel as he can My helth vary good at the presant time hoping this may find you all the same thar at home I have bin vary much worrid a bout home since father has bin sick but has dun no good but could not help it you sed you had gut them things I sent whair did you find them you wantid to no if i sent a knife no I did not I sent a pistill a belt a holester a lether thing to poot the pistill in I poot the pistill into it. in the box thar was two pitchters one for you the other for Mrs Maggoon one had your name on it the other had hirs two pips tyd together with your name on them two pipes stemes and three bowess was Asa the three pips and one pitchter is for Asa wife the rest is yours did you git them all and whar did you find them wright and lett me no all about it and what gut and if you had to pay eny thing for them

Wel Libby thar is not [much] of eny knews to wright you about the war thar is not much agoin I expect thair will bee some ripup befor a grait while we agane air under marching ordors whair I no not the most of them think we shall go this time but I do not but for all of that we may leave the City befor to morrow morning we cannot tell one day whair we shall bee the next but if we do go I will send you a few lines before we start so you need not worry about us till we go I hop that thay will poot every man into the feald this Spring and give the rebes gest what thay want and have it dun with we can do it It is vary plesant out hear it seems like Spring I wish it was as warm thair as it is hear I suspose that it is vary cold thar and a good deal of snow how much snow have you do you have them big drif this winter I have not sean eny drift this winter thar is no snow hear and it is warm enuf so to not freas eny knight I wish you was hear or I was thare but you are thair and I am hear and we will make the best of it the boys air as well as uesal Asa is well so is Molton Asa sends you his best respects give my love to all of my frends take a shair your self Ciss the little ones for me take one your self I will close by biding you good knight from yours Lewis Q Smith

In her next letter, Lucy again mentions "George" (Wiggin), her brother-in-law, "with the N. H. 6 Reg't," who had been in Jeff Davis's "mansion." Among its nearly twenty engagements, the Sixth Regiment NHV had fought at Second Bull Run, Antietam, Fredericksburg, the siege of Vicksburg, and, in July 1863, Jackson, Mississippi. On July 12, 1863, cavalry of the Thirteenth Army Corps seized Jefferson Davis's home, called Brierfield, and library, near Jackson. In addition to finding thousands of books and "bushels" of private papers "from both Northern and Southern traitors," they found several gold-handled canes—one of them presented in the antebellum era to Davis by his friend Franklin Pierce.[7]

Many of the Sixth were granted thirty-day furloughs on January 16, 1864, which were subsequently extended to March 18. Lucy also commented on the Copperheads and on father Smith's health, apparently precarious but now improving. Also mentioned is Asa Magoon's mother-in-law, Betsey Moulton Smith, who died on January 4, 1864, at age seventy-four, and was buried at the Levi Smith Cemetery in West Sandwich. Her husband, Levi Smith, had predeceased her, on January 18, 1856.[8]

M Village Feby 1 1864 My dear Brother:

I again sit down to write to you, yesterday being Sunday was my day to write but I had such a cold I put it off till today, but finding myself but very little better this morning I fear my letter will not be very interesting, nevertheless I will do the best I can. Yesterday I was forcibly reminded of you by the return of George home on a furlough with the N. H. 6 Reg't we were very glad to see him but the idea that it is to be but a few days seems worse than not to have had him come at all going away the 2d time is worse I think another summer will end this cruel war so you can all come home to remain at home your own masters. Sometimes I think we hav[e] a great many bond men at the present day in our free states. were it not for the miserable northern copperheads this war would have been at an end before this, or I might [have] said would never have been at all. George went to the war one but comes home bitter against them, laying it wholy to them now prolonging the war. It does seem passing strange to me why men here that have sons and Brothers in war can do anything against the administration. every blow that is here against it is doing a great wrong and injustice to you out there, and only an ignorant mind will see it so, but enough of this you know it all yourself.

You spoke of your health it was just as I feared all of the time it does seem hard that a man in sickness cannot be his own master, but keep up good courage right will yet rule George has been in Jeff Davis mansion he was there when they set fire to it he said it a splendid house and Library but they had to go. George has seen some pretty tough times but he has come out of all looking well he has been in 5 battles he has good courage he says they have got to come to it and that before long too.

Give my respects to Asa. I pity his wife very much it seems very hard to have her mother taken from her when he is away, but that her children are older and can be a help and comfort to her. When father was taken sick I was afraid he would never get over it I thought what could they do with out him when you was away they would have been provided for but it could not seem so much like home, but he is getting better I was going up Saturday but it snowed I cant get away only of Saturday on account of boarders Jacob is still here Burleigh is going

Meeting of the Potomac [center looking downstream] and Shenandoah [enters from right beyond bridge] at Harpers Ferry. Note the wall tents in the right foreground and the arsenal buildings at the near left. Library of Congress Photograph

> *to teach school here this Spring he is drawing him up some wood now across measly Pond [Lake Waukewan][9] he has a very good chance to get it there Frank would have gone out and helped him draw it but his father would not stay in the shop I shall be obliged to close for my headaches so I can hardly see and I must lie down write just as often as you can Your sister Lucy*

On February 7, the men returned to Harpers Ferry, "a scene of desolation [and] ruins in every direction."[10] The Confederate threat had diminished, however, and the Fourteenth was at Harpers Ferry briefly. On February 13, Halleck ordered them to return to Washington "as soon as cars can be furnished."[11] One soldier wrote: "We was glad to get out of that durty hole." He also reported: "We have [had] some fine rid[e]s over the country to uncle sams expence."[12] Harpers Ferry had been known as "Peters Hole," "Shenandoah Falls," and "The Hole" as well as "Harper's Ferry." Initially settled in the mid-eighteenth century, Robert Harper had operated a Potomac ferry there.[13]

The rugged terrain of that beautiful region is impressive: steep hills punctuated by small hollows and fast-flowing creeks. There is little flat

Harpers Ferry, West Virginia. View of the Town, Railroad Bridge in Ruins. Library of Congress Photograph.

On the Potomac, at "Uncle Sam's Expense." Author's Collection.

ground anywhere—even burial plots often lie *along* the contours of the hillsides. With the Baltimore and Ohio Railroad and the Chesapeake and Ohio Canal passing through Harpers Ferry, the area was a critical transportation junction. Although an important location, Harpers Ferry was difficult to defend: any force occupying one of several surrounding heights could shell the town at will. As a result, Confederate and Union forces alternately occupied the town and surroundings until final possession by the Federals after Lee's defeat at Gettysburg in July 1863.

In his letter below, written from Harpers Ferry, Lewis remarked that he had not had one "glas of likker for one year," and, with the demands of duty and the family's continuing need for money, it is clear that he was no longer tempted by drink.

Harpar fary Ver Feb 8 [1864] Dear wife

I seat my self to rit you a few lines to let you no whair I am I am hear to harparfary we gut hear last knight at dark and laid in the cars all knight this morning we slung knapsach and come up on olevers hith [Bolivar's Height, the controlling elevation overlooking Harpers Ferry] an pitch our tents and we air hear to day and whar we shall bee to morrow I cant tell we dont expect to stop hear but a day or to we may go befor morning we cant tell but I will wright when we stop and let you no whar we air that is the best I can do My helth is vary good hopping this may find you all the same I have not hern from eny of you sense we left washington I hop you will rit as often as you can perhaps you wood like to no how it look hear it is a ruff hole as I ever saw the norch [Sandwich Notch] road is a smoove plase to this it is not eny thing but ruggid mountans hear we have been up the river about 80 miles abuve hear and it was mountains all of the way I cant tell you what we went thare fore or what we air hear for we was ordord to go so we go that is all I can tell you it has bin wet and cold ever sinse we left the City it is and has bin a vary cold day and it a little coald to knight for us to sleep in our pupy tents but we air good for it we h[a]nt had two knights sleap sinse we left the City but you can tell them all that the 14 rigment is good for it thay have felt so bad to think we had so easy time we have dun the duty of two ridgments in the City and we can do it in the feald thar is no knews to rit and I will close for it is so cold my hands air so cold I [c]ant rit so you can read it my tabel to rit on is my knees so you must not think I am drunk by the looks of my riting for I am sober or out to be for I have not drink one glas of likker for one year thank god I am don with that. do rit as often as you can dyrect your letters as uesal give my love to all Ciss the little ones for me take a harty one for your self good knight from yours with much love to you all Lewis Q Smith Co K 14 Rid N H V

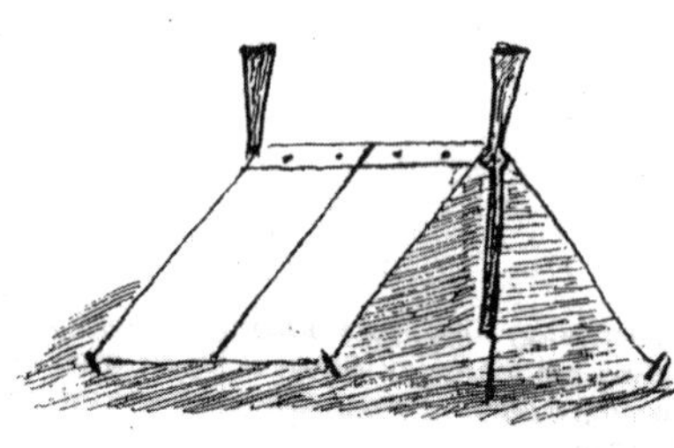

Shelter Tent

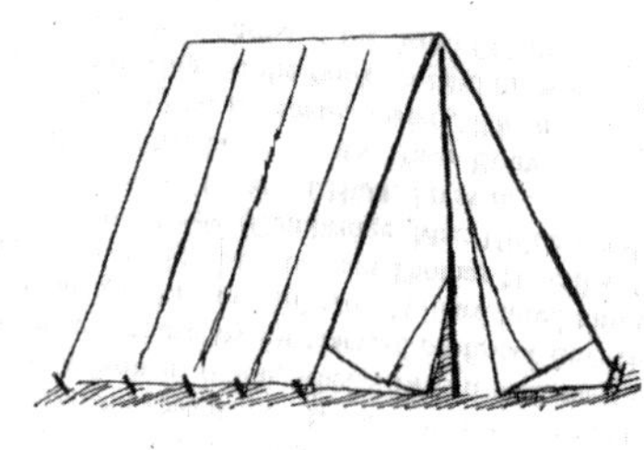

"A" Tent

Wall Tent

Civil War Tents. Courtesy Wentworth Library, Sandwich, N.H.

Pup tents or shelter tents were carried for use in the field and lacked the space and comfort of the "A" tents or wall tents used for winter camp. Smith's relative James Marcellus Smith was also at Harpers Ferry and, like Lewis, remarked on the intense cold. Marcellus, one of Company K's musicians, noted that the band ceased playing after a few minutes—their instruments froze. At night, despite two fireplaces in their room, water pails froze solid, and outside, a man's whiskers were frosted in a matter of ten minutes.[14] Considering that these were New Hampshire men, it must have been *cold*. Captain Nye, from Roxbury, New Hampshire, noted briefly: "We had three days of extremely cold weather."[15]

Lewis's pride in both his service and that of his regiment is obvious despite criticism that the Fourteenth had "had so easy time," which was substantially correct. The regiment had not experienced battle in its first fifteen months of service. So far, the men had been fortunate.

Harparfary Ver Feb 14 1864 My Dear wife

I seat my self to wright you a few lines in answer to yours that I reseved fryday [February 12] while I was out on picket I went out last Thurday and didnot git in untill to day at 3 o clock I went out on the outer lines of infertry pickets it was within 3 miles of the rebels lines it is about 6 miles from our incampment whar we went thar was 160 of us that went and stad 3 days and I am pooty well tyard but never mind it I shall feale better after I git restid it is pooty cold and wind heare we air heare to Harpersfary to knight but whair we shall be to morrow I cant tell you we may be heare and we may knot we shall be some whair I was glad to hear that farther was better and you all was gitting a long so well thair you mist be as carful of your helth as you can and git along as well as you can I gut a letter from Lucy and one from Libby Ann I will try to answer them to morror thar is northing new and I am so sleapy I cant hold my ieys open Asa is well sends his respects to you all I must close by biding you good day from yours rit often Lewis Q Smith I will try and do better next time if I can git time

Libby wrote on February 22, 1864:

Sandwich Dear Lewis I seat my self to right you a few lines to let you no that we are all wel and hope this wil find you the same I am afraid your health is not so good as it has bin I received your letter last friday I was glad to hear from you again keep up good courage as you can perhaps you wil come home some time I heard from Susan to day She was smart Chace was up hear yester day and Mariett went home with him I hope that Mother wil have some rest now for she kneedes it farther talks of goin over to father paine tomorrow if it is a good day I havent bin over their since last summer I dont get eny news now days the boys is all well and smart your Frank cant be beat on cuting wood by eny of the boys they are boath good to do the chores I wil close by [bidding] you good night give my love to Asa and Moulton this is from your wife Mary E Smith

February 22 was, of course, Washington's birthday, and was duly celebrated as such—"a day of sport," catching a greased pig and bag races. Soldiers of Company C won both events, and the unfortunate pig "was served for our Co. men."[16] On February 24, the Fourteenth returned to

Washington and to Wilson barracks on Sixth Street—barracks they had helped construct the previous summer—"nice and clean." It was reported to be a handsome facility: "We have a nice cook room, and a dining room tabels and seats all nice it looks like a hotel."[17]

The next orders for Lewis and his comrades were probably a surprise and undoubtedly well received: first, home to New Hampshire; second, on to a more salubrious climate in New Orleans, the Crescent City. (The nickname derives from the location of New Orleans on a large bend of the Mississippi, about which it forms a crescent.) Having been surrendered to federal forces on April 29, 1862, the war had essentially been over for two years by the time of the Fourteenth's arrival in 1864.

Maryland and the nation's capital were only a few hundred miles from home, but now the Fourteenth would venture several thousand miles—by sea. This voyage would not be an excursion: "not half a dozen in the regiment had ever stepped on the deck of an ocean steamer . . ." One third were "helplessly sick, while not more than one-fourth entirely escaped . . . and the rails were constantly fringed with sufferers heaving—not the lead. The condition of things below was indescribable."[18]

~ Eleven ~

Battle with Ballots and Duty at the Crescent City

March 1 to June 6, 1864

Mr. Lincoln was more afraid of Northern Copperheads than of Southern battalions.

—Sgt. Francis H. Buffum

We was inspected by the Inspector General last week, and he told our Adj. It was the best Reg't. he ever inspected. Our men are prompt in duty, faithful and trustworthy, and just such a Reg't. as is needed to do duty, in, and around a city. Not a man of ours, has been drunk since our arrival.

—Sgt. J. Henry Jenks, May 1, 1864

FRANCIS BUFFUM WROTE THAT "WHEN THE FOURTEENTH Regiment entered its first battle, it had probably reached the highest state of discipline and *esprit du* [sic] *corps* of which it was capable."[1] However, the Fourteenth would first wage war "not with bullets, but with ballots."[2] Arriving by train at Concord, New Hampshire, on March 1, the men received twelve-day furloughs—to attend town meetings and to vote. In March 1863, the Republicans had not done well in the Granite State. The Republican candidate for governor, John A. Gilmore, received 29,035 votes against his Democratic opponent's 32,924. Counting thirty-seven scattered votes and 4,446 for the Union Democrat, Gilmore lost by 8,372. However, as previously noted, Gilmore was elected by the legislature, *not* by the popular vote. New Hampshire's performance in 1863 had not gone unnoticed by the press:

> With this showing, adverse to the Republicans, the Democrats profess to be confident of carrying the State. And it is evident there must be a considerable change of opinion, since the election a year ago, to prevent such a result. This, the Republicans aver, has been the case in all parts of the Granite State. The friends of the Administration will be grievously disappointed if their candidate for Governor does not handsomely distance his opponent, and if the Legislature is not overwhelming in their favor. They are exceedingly encouraged by the large number of Democratic soldiers that have returned home to support the Republican ticket.[3]

The stakes were actually a bit higher, as New Hampshire Sen. John P. Hale's seat was also up for grabs—senators were elected by state legislatures and direct election would come with the Seventeenth Amendment in 1913. Hale, a noted, early abolitionist, had originally been a Democrat, but broke with that party over the proposed extension of slavery into Texas in the mid-1840s. He subsequently entered the Republican party and became one of its most prominent members by the late 1850s. Hale's career came to an end on June 9, 1864, when the New Hampshire Republican caucus failed to nominate him for reelection. Hale, a known enemy of Navy Secretary Gideon Welles, had been the chairman of the Naval Committee of the Senate and was tainted by an allegation of influence peddling. More importantly, during his decade in the Senate, his political base at home had eroded.[4]

In addition, reflecting New Hampshire's modern primary, the state was "the first to open the political contest for the Presidential year,—and the election of great national importance as involving a seat in the upper branch of the Congress,—the canvas has been one of great activity even for New Hampshire, which is noted for the thoroughness of its partisan trials of strength."[5] The weather on Election Day cooperated; it was one of the most delightful mornings of the season. In addition to the Fourteenth, men of the Tenth and Thirteenth Regiments returned to New Hampshire from North Carolina, as did the Third and the Fourth from elsewhere—almost all reenlisted veterans.

There was no prolonged wait for the March 8 election results. The vote count, transmitted by telegraph, was available by the next morning: "The Union cause, safe in the principle which enlightens and enforces its doctrines within and upon the people, has triumphantly succeeded. The majority for Governor Gilmore counts up . . . something like six thousand votes."[6] Secretary of War Edwin M. Stanton sent Gilmore a congratulatory telegram thanking him and the "patriotic people" of New Hampshire for "their great loyal victory."[7]

Not surprisingly, Lincoln and the Republicans were critized for allowing soldiers to go home to vote. The Third and Fourth Regiments numbered 690 men, and it appears unlikely that the numbers, even with the Tenth, Thirteenth, and Fourteenth, would have been sufficient to account for the governor's margin of 6,315. Later, in November 1864, Lincoln released soldiers from those states that did not allow absentee balloting, but again, the returning troops are not thought to have decided the election.[8] In the popular vote, Lincoln would defeat his Democratic opponent, Gen. George B. McClellan, with 2,216,127 votes versus 1,808,725. In the Electoral College, the vote would be 212 for Lincoln, 21 for McClellan.

His leave over, Lewis Smith left his family and home in Sandwich on March 16 and rejoined the regiment in Concord. Only a few desertions occurred and the claim could be made that "it was a stronger organization with seven hundred men than originally with nine hundred and eighty." Most of the "useless and unworthy material" had been weeded out in the first year and a half of service.[9] At this time, Lewis commenced his diary, a pocket size measuring four inches by five inches wide open and bearing six days' entries in that space. The entries, though brief, nonetheless described sights and sounds, exposure to cold and heat, and death by disease and battle.

Lewis experienced months of guard and picket duty and frequent drills. Later in 1864, he would be called to arms in the early-morning hours—only to stand down many, many times. When the bullets and shells did fly, his comments remained simple, without emotion and without heroism. He used the first few of the diary's January 1864 pages to record his purchases of clothing, boots, a haversack, and a shelter tent. In the remaining January pages, he just as methodically listed Company K's killed and wounded in the battles of August through October 1864.

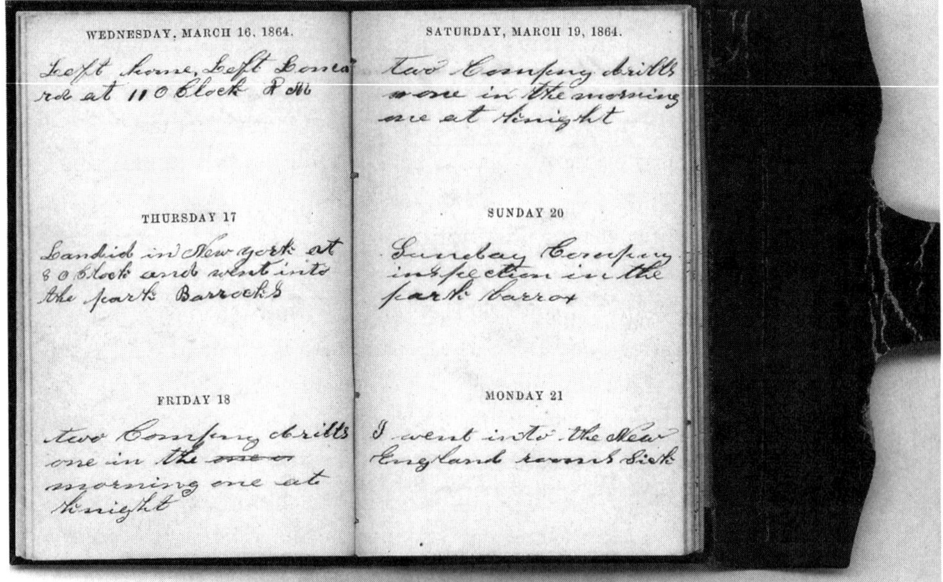

WEDNESDAY, MARCH 16, 1864.

Left home, Left Concord at 11 O Clock P M

THURSDAY 17

Landid in New york at 8 o Clock and went into the park Barrocks

FRIDAY 18

two Company drills one in the ~~mo~~ morning one at knight

SATURDAY, MARCH 19, 1864.

two Company drills one in the morning one at knight

SUNDAY 20

Sunday Company inspection in the park barrox

MONDAY 21

I went into the New England rooms Sick

Diary, March 16, 1864 to March 21, 1864, Sandwich Historical Society

Lewis continued to write home, but with much less frequency whenever the Fourteenth was in proximity with the enemy or in actual battle. And despite the apparent dependability of the mails, disruptions occurred by the hands of the adversary. One example from the Shenandoah Valley might suffice: "A mail escort was ambushed by bushwhackers. Three men were killed, three officers and four men were badly wounded and robbed, and the mail carried off."[10]

"Wednesday March 16, 1864: Left home. Left Concord at 11 PM
"March 17: Landid in New York at 8 o clock and went into the park Barrocks"

From the barracks, Lewis wrote a quick letter to Libby:

New York City Mar 17 [1864] My Dear wife

As I could not go back home I will try and comfort you in wrighting to you I am well and may the Lord Smile on you all with the same blesing we arived at willams pornt at 9 O Clock last nit and took the boat and arived hear to the citty this morning we expect to leave hear

> *to morrow for New Orlens Do try and kep up good curridg you shant lack for mony I didnot git paid off but Burleigh will furnish you with all you want untill we air paid agane*
>
> *Libby I cant rit much to day you will pardon me do rit often rit gest how you air rit if but a line dyrect your letters gest as you have don untill you hear from me agane ciss the little ons for me from ever yours Lewis Q Smith I will rit to all when I git to a stopin plase*

"March 18: two Compny drills one in the morning one at knight
"March 19: two Compny drills one in the morning one at knight
"March 20: Sunday Compny inspection in the park barrox
"March 21: I went into the New England rooms sick
"March 22: Coald an Snowey Line Storm
"March 23 and 24: [blank]
"March 25: I went over to brooklin Citty with Liutenant M S Webster and took dinner with his frends
"March 26: We left the Barrox at 12 o clock it rained vary hard we went on to the boat and laid on the boat all knight
"March 27: We left New york at 1 o clock PM for new Orleans"

It appears that few would miss New York. Company G's Lt. John Sturtevant wrote: "I have got tired of the city & shall be glad when we are onboard."[11] Sandwich's Capt. Oliver H. Marston was also impatient: "Cannot tell when we shall go but probably some time this week, the sooner the better it will suit me, for I have seen enough of N.Y."[12] Companies K, E, and G boarded the transport *Liberty*, "just built and is as nice as any parlor I ever was in."[13] The three companies sailed on what quickly became a tumultuous voyage—Lewis made no diary entries from March 28 through April 5.

After arriving at New Orleans on April 7, the men moved about six miles upriver on April 9 and camped in a clover field four hundred yards from the levee—Camp Parapet, on the upriver edge of Carrollton, Lousiana. The camp was "situated in a most beautiful grove of Orange, Fig, Live Oak & a great variety of other trees & flowers . . . also the magnolia . . ."[14]

"April 6, 1864: We arived heare at mouth of the Mississippi at 3 o clock PM
"April 7: We arved heare to New Orleans at 2 o clock PM

"April 8: Landid at 12 o clock and went into the Cotton press for a barrox and staid all knight"

Lewis wasted little time before writing about the trip south, and began to number his letters. It is apparent from the gaps (those letters presumably numbered and missing) that the surviving letters are about one third, possibly fewer, of the total written.

I will number my letters 1

Carelton Luceaner Ap 8/64 My Dear wife

I agane seat to try an wright you a few lines to let you [know] whair I am an how I am am hear five miles from New Olens City and am well hoping this may find you all the same thair at home we landid hear to the whalf wensday [April 6] knight and came on shore yesterday and come up hear to day we gut hear about 5 o clock and some had to go on duty as soon as thay gut hear I have gut to go on duty to morrow I ges we shall do duty hear rit a long hear an in the City

I suppose you wood like to no what time [we] had a comeing a vary bad one it was vary ruf it storme three days and the wind blue three days whitch maid six days as ruff a sea as our Captin of the boat ever had we had a good new boat it was all that save us thar was 600 of us on board and the most of them was vary sea sick I was not eny the voig [voyage] dun me good we was 10 days a coming we was 12 days on the boat Burleigh noes what it is to rid[e] on the watter but he dosnot no what it is to go as uncle Sam's frait thar is no one nose what it is untill thay try it

the first part of the rigment that startid before we did have not gut hear yet thare was 7 company started one week befor we did and have not gut hear thay startid in a old boat and the boat gut smash up and thay had to run into fortris monro thay all gut ashoar safe by other boats goin out to meat them lucky thay was when we gut to the mouth of the miss river and found thay had not gon up we felt bad we expectid thay was in the bottom of the sea but when we gut hear we heard that thay safe then we was thankful an glad to think we was landid safe

I reseved your letter about fiftene minits befor we left New york I was vary glad to hear that the children was better I hop you air all well you did not say how you stand it I am a fraid you will git down sick

> *your self try an take cair of yourself as you can and rit often as you can and I will do the same dyrect your letters to the department of the Gulf New Olens LA. Co K 14-Reg N H V you scead [should] not worry about me I think I shall like hear vary much and I think we shall stop hear some time tell farther an mother an all the rest I will rit to them soon I mist close good knight from yours Lewis Q Smith my love to you all*

> "April 9: We left the Cotton pres for Carollton a doin duty thair we arived hear to Carrollton at 4 o clock releved the 12 Maine
> "April 10: Sunday Compny inspection
> 'April 11: A washing our cloth[es] and fixing up our quortors in the City of Carrollton"

Departing New York on March 20 aboard the side-wheel steamer *Daniel Webster,* the remainder of the regiment was considerably less fortunate—billows not bullets. Two days after sailing, a severe storm struck the transport. Company I's Private Hoyt provided the details:

> [W]hen the storm was the worst the steam pipe burst and filled the hole whare we had to stay with steam smoke almost killing us we could not stay on deck the wind blew so and the sea would wash over the deck I have seen it hot but I never sufferd as I did that knight.[15]

After drifting helplessly for three days, the storm abated and the ship limped into Port Royal, South Carolina, (not Fortress Monroe as Lewis wrote) for repairs.[16] Cpl. Albert H. Tyrrell, a miller from Charlestown, New Hampshire, Company B, wrote on April 7, 1864: "I do not wish to return by water if there is any other way open to us . . . I dont think I will ever be a sailor. I would rather risk the bullets than the waves."[17] Sailing again on April 2 and encountering a second storm, the steamer stopped at Key West for coal and water. Here, the men had a day ashore amid orange groves and coconut trees.

Departing on April 8, they arrived at New Orleans on April 12. Indeed, Smith and the men of companies K, E, and G had left later and arrived earlier than those aboard the *Daniel Webster.* Arriving too late to join Gen. Nathaniel P. Banks's expedition up the Red River and in the absence of troops that had left New Orleans for that campaign, the Fourteenth (and other units) provided protection for the city. Lewis and his fellow soldiers would settle at Camp Parapet, adjacent to the city of Carrollton, Louisiana, about six miles above New Orleans. Lewis would serve as a guard at the hotel and depot and on the cars to and from New Orleans.

Since its capture in 1862 by the forces of Adm. David Glasgow Farragut and Adm. David D. Porter, New Orleans had become the principal federal base of operations and home to an average of thirty-five hundred Union soldiers. Upriver from New Orleans and lying on the east or left bank, Camp Parapet, initially a Confederate fortification, was strengthened and enlarged by federal forces. Anchored by a redoubt near the river, an earthen parapet zigzagged away from the water over a mile toward Lake Pontchartrain to a swamp and another redoubt: Fort Star, or Star Redoubt. Across the Mississippi lay Fort Banks, with a covering line of fire for Camp Parapet.

The parapet, thirty feet wide at the bottom, fifteen feet wide on top, and about eight feet high, had a thirty-foot-wide, six-foot-deep moat in front. Behind the parapet lay a muddy campground initially occupied by mildewed tents and later by wooden shelters. Mosquito netting was in use and allowed some protection from mosquitoes, which were "so very thick."[18] Farther away, a refugee camp of former slaves began to fill up, as did a nearby cemetery. Conditions at the camp had improved by the time of the Fourteenth's arrival, but malaria, yellow fever (the "vomito negro," or black, bloody vomit), and typhoid still took their toll, earning the location the moniker Camp Fever. Deaths numbered several per day. Funeral processions would soon be silent: playing of the "dead march" was bad for morale and would be banned. Drills were conducted in the morning and early evening—the forthcoming summer heat stifled almost any midday activity.

> "April 12: I went on duty today for the first time at the depot
> "April 13: drilling and doin figtig [fatigue] duty
> "April 14: two drills today one in the morning one at knight"

On April 14, Smith penned a letter home. Other writers mentioned the burial at sea—familiar to sailors, the experience left lasting impressions on New Hampshire's landsmen.[19]

> *No 2 Newolenes Ap 14 1864 My Dear wife*
>
> *As thar is a boat agoin out to morrow I will rit a line or to to let you no how I am my helth is vary good hoping you all air the same thair at home I roat to you last Saturday but you havenot gut it yet I roat*

to you about the rest of our rigment thay have gut hear thay gut hear yesterday all but one he died an thay through him over board the ridgment is adoin duty hear thar is three compnys deataile hear whair I am by the Provo[st] marchel the rest of the rigment is about one and a half of a mile to a foart and I ges we shall stay hear this summer it is vary plesan hear flowers an peas in the blow thar gardins is vary nise thay have splendid doar yards of flowers every thing look vary nise this onse was a splendid plas and properus but it has pas by it is ded and down it will never git over this I like hear very well as wel as eny whair in the army but I have not gut but 18 month longer to stay in this Show so you must keep up good Curidg

I reseved a letter from brother B I gut it yesterday it was roat the 25 of Mar it is all that I have gut since I gut yours in New york about fiftine minits befor we left but you mist rit rit as often as you can an I will git them some time I shall rit gest as often as I can git a Chanse to send them if it is every day So you may no that I rit whither you git them or no I do hop that the Childran air abel to be out doars before this I think of you all the most of my time I think of your hardships but I cant help you eny how do you git along for mony do you git anuf to git a long with if not gest speak to burleigh and he will let you have som untill I get paid off then I will send you all I can and try and take care of your self and be carful as you can and not git down sick if you do I dont know how you will git a long and what will becom of you all be cafful as you can give my love to all an take a shair yourself ciss the little ons for me take one yourself tell farther an mother kep up good curridg So good by from ever yours Lewis Q Smith

Cpl. Albert Tyrrell, of Company B, also described the fine spring weather and noted "there are plenty of mosquitoes here already." In contrast to New Hampshire's rocky soil, he wrote: "The land here on the river is the richest land I think that can be found things seem almost to jump from the soil instead of coming along up in the slow and steady New England style. There are quite a number of fields close by our camp where the white clover is up a foot high."[20]

"April 15: I am on duty to day at the depot

"April 16: Schirmish drill at morning an knight at the City of Carrollton

"April 17: Sunday inspection to day rope [high-rope] performance at the hotel

"April 18: Genrill inspecton to day I am on duty to day

"April 19: Schirmish drill at Carrollton

"April 20: I am on duty to day for Gineril Robbarts acting as his odly mounted

"April 21: Asa Magoon an George Haddock came to the Co to day Come from home

"April 22: I was porntid Corporal this day by our Cormanders[21] two drill Co drills

"April 23: I am duty today at the depot Schirmish drills in the morning and at knight

"April 24: Sunday Company inspection it is rainy to day

"April 25: two schirmish drills one in the morning one in the evening.

"April 26: Liu Jason D Snell [of Pembroke, New Hampshire] died to day at 1 o clock AM two Co drills one at 7 AM one at 6 PM

"April 27: Liu Jason D Snell was sent home to day I am on duty at the depot to day"

In all likelihood, the "rope performance" that Lewis referred to in the above entries was at the New Orleans and Carrollton Railroad Hotel and Depot, constructed by the railroad and located near the intersection of St. Charles and Carrollton Avenues in Carrollton. The railroad ran six miles from the New Orleans central business district to Carrollton and was the line he took while riding as a guard on the cars. Another line, the New Orleans, Jackson (Mississippi), and Great Northern Railroad, passed through Camp Parapet.

No 5 Carrollton Newolens Apr the 27 1864 My ever dear wife

I agane seat to wright you a few lines to let [you] no how I am my helth is vary good hoping this may find you all the same thare at home I rsceved your letter last knight daitid April the 11 I was very thankful to hear that you all wore gitting along so well thar at home I am glad that the children air giting a long so wel I hop thay will bee smart an rugid [a]gane I no you have had a vary hard time to take care of them I wood bin glad to help you but could knot I hop the day is not far distant befor I can be with you and help you So kep up good curidg and not worry about me look out for yoursef

April 28 To day is thursday we air all well hop you air all the same I will try and finish my letter so to send it out in the first steamer that go out I will say to you that we paid our last respect to Liutenent Snell our first Liutenent he dyed Tuesday knight last at 9 O Clock he is a goin to be sent home he was sent off to be inbalm yesterday we folard him one mile and we had the band to play for us. he is gon whair thare can no one abuse him eny more on erth he has bin shamful abused for the last year an thay will have it to answer for some time I hope I havenot eny thing to reflect upon he an I was allways on good turms

We air haveing fine wether it is gitting to be vary worm days but it is cold knight we need our over Coats hear now as much as we did in the winter when we air on duty knights we air on duty some times every other day some times onse in three so our duty is not so hard as it was in washington when we air on duty we air on twenty fore ours I do like the duty and plase better then eny whair we have bin but I would like to hear from home oftener but I shall hafto poot up with it our compny is quatard in a house by our selfs we air laying on the floars but we air agointo bild some bunks so we can keep a little cleanner we shall stop hear for the presant

I was vary sorry to hear that Lucy Jane had gut that offal diseas of dipthere I hop she has gut well of it befor this sickness and disesis will go whair ever thay air sent we mist be carful as we can of our helth be as carful as you can I shall rit to Hepsa agane in a few days I hop we shall be paid off in a few days so I can send you some mony Asa an Liutenent M. S. Webester air well send their respects to you all I must close my love to you all a hary cis to you rit often dyrect to New orlens from yours L Q Smith

The likable duty described by Lewis was not without incident. As in Washington, smuggling alcohol was one such frequent activity:

> A remarkable fullness in Eliza Scott's person attracted the notice of the sentry whose beat she was obliged to cross, in order to reach her soldier friends. A somewhat ungallant investigation revealed a half dozen bottles of whisky stowed away in Eliza's bosom. Before Judge Atocha she claimed that she had purchased the whisky for her own use, and had no intention of giving or selling it to the soldiers. With the exception of a pointed reprimand, and the confiscation of the burning fluid, she got off Scot free.[22]

A letter from Sandwich dated May 1, 1864, follows:

> *Dear Lewis i set down to right a few lines to you to let you no how we are we are all wel and i hope this wil find you the same i received your letter last tuesday i was glad to hear from you father and Mother has got home from the Village to day Lucy Jane is better so she sets up three or 4 hours in a day the rest are all wel the snow is all gone and the grass is up green folks is a turning their young cattle of to paster I had to by a half of a tun of hay and paid a seven dolars for it the old cow has got a dark red calf you can tel me what i had better do with it perhaps i could git five dolars for it when it is fore weeks old father Paine ses I had better keep it and sel the other one it is so much better culer he thinks it wil make the best cow you can tell me what to do the children is all wel and harty you spoke about sending home your money keep all you want and kneed for we can get a long with les now i am goin down Weeds to day we do not get eny good knewes now so good day this is from your wife Mary E Smith*

"April 28: Ginerill inspection one drill Schirmish drill

"April 29: two drills one in the morning an one at knight we drawed clothin to day

"April 30: Monthly inspection to day I am on duty to day at the depot to day

"May 1: Sunday Compny inspection of knapsacks havesack cantens guns and equipments

"May 2: on duty on the Cars goin from Carrollton to New Orleans to day

"May 3: I have bin up to the paripits to the rigment to day two Co drill

"May 4: I have bin to New orlens City to day to see the city two schirmis drill

"May 5: I am on duty to day at the depot

"May 6: two schirmish drills one in the morning one at knight

"May 7: I am on duty at the depot today

"May 8: I have bin on duty to day to the roap performance Sunday Co inspection

"May 9: two schirmish drills one in the morning one at knight

"May 10: one Co drill an one Schirmish drill a prtroll pout out to day"

Lewis's next letter home was on the tenth:

No 7

Neworleans La

Karrollton May 10 1864

My ever dear wife

I will hasto
n to answer your dear letter
that came to hand to knight
baitlid the 25 of Aprill how
thankful I am to agane to
heare that you air all ingoin
g good helth agane my helt
h is very good hoping this m
ay find you all the same at
home I reseved one letter from
Burleigh to knight staiting
the condition of poor Lucy
s sickness when I heare of
eny of my frends air at
home under paines of sicknes
it maks my hart aks within
my felins I can hardly control
but we will try and make
the best of it I hop this cruil
war will not allways last

Lewis Q. Smith letter of May 10, 1864. Sandwich Historical Society

No 7 Newoleans La Carrollton May 10 1864 My ever dear wife

I will hason to answer your dear letter that came to hand to knight daitted the 25 of Aprill how thankful I am to agane to heare that you air all injoing good helth agane my helth is vary good hoping this may find you all the same at home I reseved one letter from Burleigh to knight staiting the condision of poor Lucy J sickness when I heare of eny of my frends air at home under paines of sicknes it maks my hart aks within my felins I can hardly control but we will try and make the best of it I hop this cruil war will not allways last I have not time to rit much to go in this mail for it gos at 9 o clock to knight it now 8 o clock

May the 11 well Libby I will try and finish my letter I was caled out so I could not finish it to go last knight So I will finish it and have it redy to go in the next mail I am on duty to day at the deppot whair I hafto come every third day it taks 10 men an 2 Coprils to go on the cars to New orleans City one Copril an two men at a time thair is a train that goes every our it taks 12 men and 3 Coprils to gard hear to the depot and I have gut to be a Copril I was a porntid when we first gut heare and actid as such ever sinse my work is not so hard as before dont you feale big to think I have gut so hy a ofice but a Copril is no better then a privit I wood never taken it if it had not bin easer for me and it is sed that our pay is a goin to be raised privit 16 Copril 18 Sarggnt 20 dollars pr month I hop it is so we have not gut paid off yet and we dont no when we shall some of the oficers say not untill July so you must git some mony of Burleigh if you want eny an not suffer and go hungry for want of it for I shall git paid off some time then you can have some and no thanks to eny one well Lizzy thare is no knews to wright to you about the war we donot heare eny thing how or what thay are a doin we air out of the reach of the knews every thing is vary quiart in this department at the presant time

As for the boys in our rigment thay air vary helthy at the presant time the Sandwich boys air all well but Frank Sawtell[e] he is vary sick Asa an Molton air smart thay send thar love to you all I must draw to a close give my love to all of my frends Ciss the little ons for me tak a harty one your self tell the Children to be good from yours rit often Lewis Q Smith

"May 11: I am on duty to day depot two Schirmish drill

"May 12: I come oft from duty this morning sick with the dyree tw Co drills

"May 13: Danel [R.] Gilman Alfred Wallas [Wallace] Ezekiel [E.] Dustin Frank P. Robson [Robinson, of Pembroke] come to the Compny to day"

On May 14, another death occurred: "Frank Sawtell [of Sandwich] died to day at the horspittle at Camp paripit." Lewis's entry for May 15 is equally terse: "Frank Sawtell is sent home to day or is carrid to the City to be in balm on duty to day Sunday inspection." During the latter part of April 1864, in the city of New Orleans, diarrheal illness topped the causes of lives claimed, followed by smallpox, consumption, and pneumonia.[23] Sawtelle was about thirty-one years old. His wife, Judith H., had predeceased him on December 9, 1859, at age twenty-two.[24] While the cause of her death is not known, it would commonly have been infectious disease or childbirth. Lewis's diary resumes without emotion.

"May 16: We was paid off to day I reseved 12.00 Twelve dollars 40.00 inlottid [allotted] to Reve B.B. Smith No drill

"May 17: two schirmish drills one in the morning one in evening

"May 18: gineril inspecton to day I was on duty to day at the depot Compny drill

"May 19: I came off from duty to day two schirmish drills one at 10 AM at 6 PM

"May 20: one Co drill one Schirmish drill

"May 21: I am on duty at the depot to day two Co drills

"May 22: Sunday inspection to day of guns an equipments"

However, not all was routine on the lower Mississippi, as soldiers, faced with monotonous drilling and inspections, too much time, often too little sense, and the usual temptations, got into trouble. On May 22, the Sunday *Daily Picayune* reported on "The Soldiers and the Police again":

A guinea pig had been stolen from a house of ill fame by three soldiers who had been visiting the woman. The assistance of Officers Mason and Bohm was procured to arrest them, and when they were found, it was with a contraband woman of the same profession, named Charlotte. The police attacked the greatly superior force opposed to them, consisting of the aforesaid Charlotte, Wm. Shemenberg, Co. C. 83d Ohio, R. Malone and W. E. Martin 23d Wis., but were at first repulsed. Shemenberg had a knife, and the rest, particularly Charlotte, stoned the officers with great paving stones. Bohm's brother, who came to his assistance, was knocked down and nearly killed, but finally all the soldiers and the woman were arrested, but not until Shemenberg had also been knocked down while attacking Bohm with his knife. There was a report that the soldier was dead; but we learn that this should be used with the addition of the word, drunk—dead drunk.[25]

On May 24, Maj. Gen. Edward R. S. Canby (1817–1873), who was wounded by Confederate guerrillas the following November, ordered all details back to the regiment and to prepare for "field service, and, so soon as it is ready for the field, will proceed, without delay, to Morganza [Louisiana] . . ."[26] The Fourteenth was headed several hundred miles north. It would report to Brig. Gen. William H. Emory, commander of the Nineteeth Army Corps, and would serve with the Second Brigade of the Second Division of that corps. In addition to the command changes, the Ninety-seventh U.S. Infantry, aboard the transport *Clinton,* joined the First Battalion of the Eighth U.S. Heavy Artillery at Camp Parapet. Both units were black. As noted earlier, the combat record of black troops in Louisiana (and elsewhere) was commendable.[27]

By mid-May, the weather had become hot, but not close to what it would be in a matter of weeks. Lewis commented on the flat, low ground so characteristic of the vicinity. In fact, much of New Orleans is below sea level, and the levees along the river were, and are, the highest terrain features in sight.

No 9 Carrollton La May the 22/64

I agane seat my self in answer to yours that I reseved the 20 daittid the first day of the month I was vary glad to heare from you agane and to heare that you wore all well thair at home how I do regoic [rejoice] to git a letter from you an hear that you air all well at home as for my helth it is vary good at the presant time hoping this may find you all injoying the same blesing thare at our dear old home how glad I am to hear that thous [those] little loved ons was onse more restoard to thare helth agane an may the hand of provedanc rest and smile on you all and give you all helth an streneh for your hardships that you haft to undergo I feal them but can do you no good but my simphy is with an for you I hop the day is not far distant befor I shall be permitid to return home with peas declard then I will help you bair your trobels and hardship Libby thare is not much news to rit for we git but a little and what we do git is rather old when git it every thing is vary quiart around hear in this department thay are gitting a good meny troops in hear to this plase some a coming most every day and for what I cannot tell for sume purpus

The condision of the boys in ours rigment is very good thay are quit helthy for the climat it is vary hot out hear it is so flat and low ground we do not git much air thare is no hils or mountians to be seen hear or to have the cool breas to come from it is all most sweltring in the middle of the day but we have gut to git season to it then we can go it. To day is a day that we should call Sunday or the Sabbarth I cant tell you what thay call it out heare for I never hear them call it eny thing but I can tell you how thay spend this day in hunting and sporting thay air haveing a rop[e] performanc[e] hear this after noon thare is a thing that they call a lady hear and you may call hir what you air a minto that walks the roap thay say the rop is one 100 feat long and 30 feat hy that she walks I have had to go and stand gard three times for hir to walk it but I am dun with it. We air doin the same duty that we have bin doin the Liutenant M. S. Webester is on duty to day he is well Asa is well thay both sends thar respects to you all rit how Asa folks air when you rit we have been paid off as I roat you in my other thar is 40 dollars acoming to you I must draw to a close give my love to all tell farther and mother to keep up good curidg the darkest our is gest befor day you must keep up good curidg as you can tell the Children to be good and mind thar mother ciss them all for me and take one yourself rit often as you can and I will good day from yours ever yours Lewis Q Smith

"May 23: two schirmish drills one at 6AM one at 5 PM
"May 24: I am on duty to day at the deport two Co drills
"May 25: I came off from duty to day one Co drill
"May 26: two Compny drills one in the forenoon one in the after noon
"May 27: I am on duty to day at the depot we air releved by a negro regment ordored to our regment
"May 28: I came of from duty this morning one Co drill
"May 29: Sunday inspection of guns an inspection
"May 30: I came off duty to day at the depot two Co drills"

In her next letter, Libby commented on Frank Wiggin's bout with diphtheria, after Lucy's encounter with the same disease a few weeks earlier. She also mentions Freeman Lewis, who was about eighteen years old when he made his trip to Concord, presumably to the Asylum for the Insane, "a farm of one hundred and twenty-one acres," that had opened in 1842.[28] For the year ending May 1, 1864, there were one hundred five admissions, sixty-nine discharges, and two hundred seventeen patients remaining. Freeman was the son of farmer Enoch Lewis and lived near the Smiths and the Hacketts. There is no knowing how long he was in Concord, but it is certain that he was at home when the census taker came by in 1870. Freeman died on April 28, 1882, at age thirty-five—outliving two sisters, who died at ages nineteen and twenty-three.[29]

Also noted was Sgt. Oliver Watson, who enlisted on August 27, 1861, one day after Cpl. James Elat White—both from Sandwich and both in the Third Regiment NHV. The two Sandwich shoemakers were more than close: they, their wives, and a total of seven children shared the household of Oliver's mother, sixty-one-year-old Elmira Watson. Elat was "wounded severely" on May 13, 1864, at Drewry's Bluff, Virginia, and lingered three months before dying at Fortress Monroe, Virginia.[30] Oliver Watson was the luckier, and although he would be wounded at Deep Bottom, Virginia, on August 16, 1864, the day Elat died, he finished out his enlistment and returned to Sandwich and his family. One can scarcely speculate on the range of emotions in the Watson-White residence with the homecoming of one soldier but not the other.

Sandwich May 30 [1864] Dear Lewis

i seat my self to right a few lines to let you no how we are getting a long very wel we are all now i hope this wil find you the same Burleigh went home yesterday he has bin up hear helping father plough and plant they have planted a good peace of corn and got their early potatoes planted and peas soed and got the ground plough for potatoes B is goin to come up to help finish planting i received your letter yesterday No. seven do not wery about us having money we get along wel for it i have enough to get a long wel i shal draw again wednesday Frank Wiggin is sick with dypthrea Old Mrs Aabbot is dead she died happy as a clam i got a letter from Rachel yesterday they well Leonard is to work in the Navy yard Freeman Lewis is crazy down to Concord in the Hospital Mariett was over to the North they wer all wel over their Jacob was up hear yesterday they are all wel to the coner Jacob ses all the men in this County is drafted 13 got to [go] or hire a subs[tit]ute they are a fiting in virgina Elat White is wounded and Oliver Watson is mising Grant is a puting for Richmond i hope he wil get their before a great while i hope they wil wind this war up soon as they can give my love to Asa and Molton ex[cept] a share your self i do not [know] of enything els to right so i wil close by biding you good day this is from your wife Mary E Smith

June 1 Dear Lewis we are all wel this morning and i hope this wil find you the same i was over to father yesterday he was out hoing corn Uncle John is smart Aunt Sally sendes hur love to you Aunt wants you to right to her

"May 31: I came off from duty to day monthly inspection to day
"June 1: two schirmish drills to day one at 6 AM one at 6 PM
"June 2: Battalion drill an drespraid rainy
"June 3: I am on duty the Corporal of the gard battalion drill drespraid
"June 4: Battalion drill an drespraid rainy
"June 5: Sunday inspection rainy
"June 6: Henry Sammser left for the horspittle to the City of New Orleans rainy
"June 7: Left Camp Paripit for Morganza at 11 o clock AM on the Sinsnaty [Cincinnati?] boat under Major Gardner"

The June 7 departure was up the Mississippi. On the following day, the men disembarked two hundred miles upriver at Morganza, Louisiana, south of the confluence of the Red and Mississippi Rivers. There, in a major reorganization, the twenty-five officers and 573 men of the Fourteenth joined the Nineteenth Army Corps. The Fourteenth, with Col. Robert Wilson still in command, had Brig. Gen. Henry W. Birge (1825–1888) as brigade commander and Brig. Gen. Cuvier Grover (1828–1885) as division commander. The Fourteenth would remain a part of (and fight with) the Nineteenth Army Corps until mustered out at war's end.

~ *Twelve* ~

SEARCHING FOR THE ENEMY, AFFAIR AT BAYOU GROSSETÊTE, AND RETURN TO WASHINGTON

June 7 to July 31, 1864

> *I donot think thair is much of a rebel forse heare it is mostly gyrillars thay air vary trobelsome thay fiar into our pickets every day or to I donot think we shall stop heare much longer I think we shall go up into Virgina soon . . .*
>
> —Lewis Q. Smith, June 30, 1864

MORGANZA, IN POINTE COUPEE PARISH, LOUISIANA, lies on the west bank of the Mississippi, above Port Hudson and Baton Rouge, about three hundred miles from the Gulf of Mexico. The town is protected from the river by a massive levee and today remains primarily an agricultural community. In 1860, Morganza had a population of 4,094 whites, 721 free blacks, and 12,903 slaves.[1] During the Civil War, it was a large Union base, and it stood as testimony to the power of the federal government and the U.S. Navy. The Union's ability to transport men from New Hampshire's granite hills and other northern states to the great artery of the South was, and is, impressive. At the time of the Fourteenth's arrival, this stretch of the river "had the look of business, being 11 steamers anchored on the banks . . . and the camps of the soldiers lined the west bank . . . for 3 or 4 miles.[2]

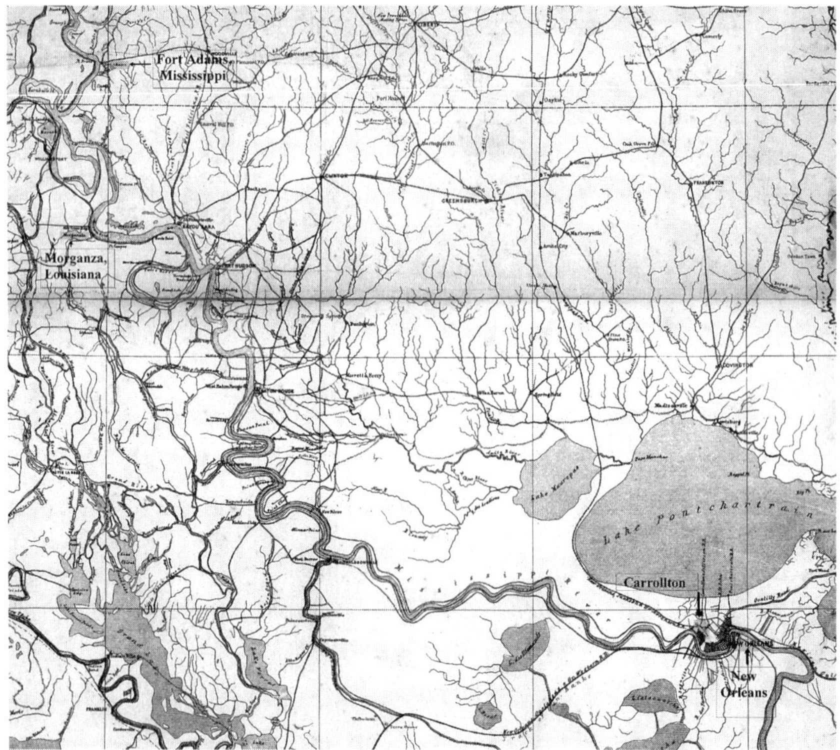

Map of the Mississippi River. Morganza is in the left upper center and Fort Adams, in southwest Mississippi, is left of top center. New Orleans and Carrollton are lower right. Adapted from Library of Congress Map.

In late May 1864, Gen. Nathaniel Banks's army would return to Morganza after the failed Red River campaign, intended to drive the Confederates from western Lousiana, but stalled in mid-April before reaching Shreveport. In a fighting retreat, the Federals moved downriver only to pause above Alexandria, where the falling river level trapped Union gunboats above the rapids there. Hastily constructed dams successfully raised the water level, allowing most of the vessels and men to escape by mid-May, and denied the Confederates a major triumph. Banks's forces were reassigned to other areas while the Nineteenth Army Corps remained to hold Morganza, fighting a number of skirmishes with small Confederate forces in May and June 1864. Lewis's diary resumes with his arrival upriver.

> "June 8: We aried heare to Morganza at 7 o clock PM we come off and pitch our tent S. A. tents rainy

Camp at Morganza. Author's Collection.

"June 9: I roat home to day we had drespraid rainy
"June 10: 3 men on pickits Asa has gon rainy
"June 11: Choar [Corps] drill four miles from hear rainy Post revue by Gin Grover
"June 12: Sunday inspection the mail come in no letter for me I roat B an Hepsa rainy
"June 13: drespraid rainy"

After a week of rain and routine camp duties, Lewis became sick—fortunately, for only about a week. The season was advancing and the "men here seemed rather sickly."[3] Buffum remarked that the "service . . . in Louisiana was more deadly than any active campaign in more northerly latitudes . . . even with frequent battles."[4] At this time, Sergeant Jenks considered life insurance: "to get my life insured if you can, then should I be taken away you may have something to do with, still I shall not fling myself away on purpose to put a snug little sum in your pocket."[5] Death by illness still dwelt everywhere.

Henry P. Page, a student from Center Harbor, New Hampshire, was a private in Company K. Page was successively promoted to sergeant and first sergeant, and became a second lieutenant in Company I on May 27, 1864.[6] He then served as commandant of guards at Camp McClellan in Davenport, Iowa. Page did not return to New Hampshire, but settled as a clergyman

Lt. H. P. Page. Author's Collection.

with his family in Nebraska City, Nebraska.[7] Also noted is Sgt. Jesse A. Fisk, Company A, a farmer from Dublin, New Hampshire, who became a second lieutenant, Company E, on January 12, 1864, and Company K's first lieutenant on May 27, 1864.[8]

The "revue" of the Nineteenth Corps was "a splendid pageant" with "thirty thousand men" marching "in columns by division." The colorful Maj. Gen. Daniel E. Sickles (1825–1914), his right leg amputated almost a year earlier at Gettysburg, reviewed the troops and was "the recipient of a hearty ovation . . ." The heat was described as "intense . . . nearly intolerable," and the "men wilted like cabbage-leaves . . ."[9] Troops standing at attention, whether for inspection or for a ceremony, quickly begin to faint away. The hotter it is, the faster it happens. Already sick, Lewis missed it.

> "Tuesday, June 14, 1864: Post revue by Gin Sicels fair wether I am sick with the dyree excus by the Surgent
> "June 15: I am sick and excus from duty by the Sargent Shoaray
> "June 16: Ginerel inspection to day I am sick excues by the Sargent I reseved a letter from my wife
> "June 17: H P Page comison to a Liutenant in Co G I am sick excus by the Sargent
> "June 18: Battalon drill and drespraid I am excues from duty by the Surgen
> "June 19: Sunday inspection Liu Fisk come into our Compny to day we reseve marching ordors to a minit worning to day"

On June 19, the regiment boarded a steamer and headed north in search of an elusive enemy. Smith's diary for June 20 indicates they found a few: "We left hear last knight up the river 15 ms went ashoar schoutid took 4 rebs som horsis an muls took the boat went up 20 ms on the boat all night." On the next day, they "went ashoar at sunrise a chouting 3 rebs—six muls and left for morganza at 7 o clock gut into Camp at 11 o clock at knight." Lewis's "a chouting" (scouting) was officially reported as the June 19 "Affair at Bayou Grossetête" (Bayou "big head"). Lewis's record and the official report of the "affair" display a congruence that is reassuring; it confirms the veracity of the accounts.[10] Gen. William H. Emory's report was equally brief:

> HDQRS. Nineteenth Army Corps and U.S. Forces,
> *Morganza, La., June 19, 1864.*
> Captain: Colonel Crebs has just returned; captured 5 prisoners, and also captured Richard McCall, one of the parties he was sent after. Drove in about 100 head of cattle and a few horses and mules. I send General Grover with the force to operate on the other side of the river.
> W. H. Emory
> *Brigadier-General, Commanding*[11]

Following the return of the expedition downriver, Smith wrote: "In camp to day at Morganza I comense a letter to my wife." It is "No 16," and, of the sixteen, numbers 1, 2, 5, 7, 9, and 16 survive—slightly more than one third. Lewis's understated "very nise time" was to others a voyage "beautiful beyond description." A soldier of the Fifteenth Regiment NHV wrote from Carrollton: "On either side you see the massive live oaks with festoons of grey moss hanging from their branches, which together with the orchards of orange trees loaded with their rich, golden fruit and bright green leaves, made the scenery calculated to remind one of the description of Paradise."[12]

The Fourteenth's next foray, "on the other side of the river," took them to the extreme southwest corner of Wilkinson County, Mississippi. Their destination was Fort Adams, built in 1799 to keep an eye on Spanish-held territory on the western side of the Mississippi River. After transfer to the French and the subsequent Louisiana Purchase in 1803, the fort lay abandoned until reoccupied by the Confederates almost six decades later. Lewis's description was apt: the upland hills, thick with oaks that conceal any remains of the fort, rise to about four hundred feet in elevation. The foray north was successful despite finding little or no enemy and was a valuable exercise in rapid, coordinated movement. It was also a respite from the routine of camp duty, which all too quickly resumed.

No 16 Morganza June 22/64 My dear wife

On our return to Camp acording to my promas in my other letter I seat myself to wright a few lines to let you no whair we air we aire heare to morganza our mooveing was only on a Chout up the river a hunt-ting gyrillars we went up the river 40 ms thair was 3 bridgads of us went the first second and third but we couldnot find eny foarse a few scharterin on[e]s we gut 8 an some horses and mewels we startid a Sunday 4 P M and went up about 15 ms and landid an went a hunt-ing the Johenneys there was 7 boats loaded of us and 4 gun boats an after Schouting all day a monday we startid on the boats up the river about 25 ms to a plase coled foart Adams we landid about sun rise and went out schoutting again untill 7 o clock at knight an startid for Camp and reached Camp at 11 P M we had a very nise time while we was gon up thar we went into Mississipi it was 15 ms above the mouth of read [Red] river to a plase coled fort Adams we found some small hils up thair it is the first hiles I have seen since I left New york and I never saw enything that look so good to me as that did

June 24 wel Libby I will try and finish my letter I have bin wait-ting to git one from you but have not gut it yet but hop I shall soon as for my health it is vary good hopping this may find you all the same thair we air hear at Camp a doing figtig duty most of the time we have a drespraid and inspection we have had a Gin [General] inspection an drespraid we have a good deal of red tappe hear more of that then fighttin as for news the laittest news we have had from the north is the 19 of the month so you git the news sooner then we do it is vary quiart hear on this river our boats git fiard into every day or to with but little damige Henrey P Page is prmotid and left our Co to day as for the helth of the regment it is a good deal better then a few days a go thay wore sick with the dyree air good deal better Asa an Moulton air both well Capt O H Mastin [Marston] is sick in the hospittle he is gitting better he will live through it tell farther and mother to keep good curidg we air a goin to have peas soon an I will rit to them next keep up good curridg Lib it is hard for you ask Jacob Susan Sally why thay donot rit me I have roat to them ciss the little ons for me take one yourself tell them to be good Children rit often as you can for I must close good knight from yours your husband Lewis Q Smith

As Lewis noted above and again on June 28, Capt. Oliver Marston was indeed sick. Unable to write home, Pvt. Benjamin F. Fellows wrote for him. On July 8, Marston remained on the fourth story of St. James Hospital in New Orleans. Undoubtedly, his unspecified illness was gastrointestinal. Having just received several "very unexpected" letters from friends and family, his spirits were buoyed: "nothing will cheer a soldier up as it will to get good cheerful letters from home." At the time, Marston was slowly improving and the doctor had just ordered a "Brandy & milk diet."[13]

> "June 23: drespraid and moveing our tents O. C. Mason porntid first Sargent an W. J. Brown Corpril to day[14]
> "June 24: Ginrel inspection to day by gineril inspecter drespraid
> "June 25: Gineril revue by the hol divison I am picket
> "June 26: I came of from duty this morning Co inspection an drespraid Cowin [Wentworth Cowan] poot in gard hous H O Backer [Baker] comes to the regment[15]
> "June 27: Co drill from 7 1/2 to 8 1/2 AM battalion drill at 6 PM Samuel S Smith Copril an Woring J brown[16]
> "June 28: Battalon drill at 6 1/2 AM the Captin [Oliver Marston] left the Co and went on the hospittle boat sick drespraid Co drill at 6 PM
> "June 29: Batalion drill Lieu Fisk took account of stock in the Co dresspraid we are poot into the first bridgad
> "June 30: Ginrill inspection and mustering in for pay drespraid Druker sworn into the nave[17]
> "July 1: two drills one at 6 AM one at 6 PM drespraid I was on firtig after wood this fornoon"

By now, the southern heat and humidity were oppressive, and Lewis was not alone in describing it. Jenks wrote: "It is awful hot hear–we drink M. [Mississippi] water, looks just like water out of a mud puddle."[18] Cpl. Albert Tyrrell commented: "the River water . . . is all we get . . . a man gets his peck of dirt before he is aware of it."[19] Another man added: "we settle the most of it with alum."[20] A mud puddle may reflect the river's color, but it bears no testimony to the immense volume of sediment carried. An 1864 scientific estimate, presented to the Association of American Geologists and Naturalists, is probably as good today as it was then: the average daily "discharge of mud is eight hundred and sixty-four thousand tons . . ."[21] For Lewis and the Fourteenth, New Hampshire's clear-flowing mountain streams still lay a year or more away.

Guerillas Firing on the Louisiana Belle. *Courtesy Wentworth Library, Sandwich, N.H.*

Morganza La June the 30 1864 Abcent Farther

I will spend a few in seating myself and try and writ a fewe lines in my broken maner it is my first atempt to writ you it is not becaus I have forgotten or dont think of you for I think of you and the rest of my frends every day it is oin to slackness. As for my helth it is quite good for this climat hoping this may find you in good helth and sperits. we air heare to Morganza one hundred and seventy miles up the Missis-sipi river from New Orleans we come up hear the seventh day of this month we was staison at the City Carrollton five miles from the City of New Orlens. When we gut up hear we went into the 2nd bridgad and 2nd divisen and 19th army Choar and since that we have bin poot into the first bridgad 2 divisen 19 Army Choar thare is about 30 to 40,000 men heare in this Choar we have bin heare in Camp the most of the time since we have bin heare we went up the river about forty miles on a schout a huntin rebels but we did not [find] much foarse we found a few gyrillars we took eight prisners and some horses and muls we was gon three day and returned to our camp and have bin doin picket duty sinse I donot think thair is much of a rebel forse heare it is mostly gyrillars thay air vary trobelsome thay fiar into our pickets every day or to I donot think we shall stop heare much longer I think we shall go up into Virgina soon we have it vary hot out heare and bad watter and bad air it is lo swampy ground and all of contry is swampy the watter that we git to drink is river watter and it is all we do git and it is vary muddy watter it looks like the watter in a mudpudele in the roads after a shour.

Thair is no news to rit for we donot git eny of them hear thair is no moove[ing] and no fighting heare in this department I will give you a better histry of this contry when I git home then I can wright to you I want you to have your fishooks all redy aganse I git home give my love to Parker [Paine] and wife also to uncle an ant Wiggin to tell them all to rit to me and if you air able to rit I want you to dyrect your letters to L. Q. Smith Co K the 14 Reg N H Vol New Orlens in the department of the Gulf La I will close from your son Lewis Q Smith my love to all pleas to answer this

No one disputed the torpor-rendering temperatures and humidity, not even the local press:

> The heat of yesterday [July 4] was less oppressive than has been the case for the past few days. Though no rain cooled the furnace-breath of the air, its heat was somewhat moderated by the welcome presence of a few black clouds, which tempered its brain-oppressive warmth with the cooling influence of airy breezes.[22]

Lewis and the regiment embarked at Morganza and ran downriver to New Orleans, where they crossed the Mississippi to the town of Algiers, Louisiana. Algiers, now a suburb of New Orleans, was annexed to that city in 1870 and is still served by ferries. At the time of the Fourteenth's visit, it had wharves and dry docks, commerce and shipbuilding, and was the river terminus of the New Orleans, Opelousas, and Great Western Railroad. It was at Algiers that Adm. Raphael Semmes took command of the CSS *Sumter* to begin his career as a raider of Union commerce—culminating with his command of the CSS *Alabama,* sunk by the Portsmouth, New Hampshire-built USS *Kearsarge* on June 19, 1864.

"Saturday, July 2, 1864: We reseved Marchin [orders] to day to report to New Orlens we air waitin for a boat

"July 3: We left Morganza at 6 PM we struck at 1 AM march one ms and thare wait untill the boat was redy for us

"July 4: We landed in New Orleans at 10 AM an then after reporting crosed the river an went a shoar an pitch tents

"July 5: Algiers we air waiting for transport to Fortrus monro or some other plase

"July 6: we air still awaiting for transport I am detealed at six o clock PM to go on duty at the wharf

"July 7: I am on duty at the wharf agarding hay and grain I was releved at 4 O. C. PM

"July 8: Algiers we air heare awaiting transport some whair drespraid at 6 O. C. PM

"July 9: Algiers. La. we air heare awaiting for transport expecting to go every our drespraid"

Destined to miss the crisis by several weeks, the Fourteenth waited at Algiers, unaware of the critical situation of the federal capital. Gen. Jubal Early's Confederates had driven Gen. George Crook's men from the Shenandoah Valley and crossed the Potomac into Maryland. Despite facing an overwhelming force, Gen. Lew Wallace's Union troops, in a determined delaying action, stopped Early at the Battle of Monocacy on July 9, buying time for Washington. Wallace's action allowed desperately needed reinforcements, some of them elements of the Sixth and Nineteenth Corps, to reach the capital's perimeter defenses just in time to counter the Confederate threat. On July 11, Early approached to within sight of the Capitol, and on July 12 scrutinized the defenses and skirmished before Fort Stevens on the city's Seventh Street approach. However, Early saw enough newly arrived bluecoats to reverse course and retreat that night.

"July 10: Algiers La Sunday inspection dresparaid

"July 11: Algiers La. we air still redy to march drespraid

"July 12: Algiers La Strick tents at 1 P.M. redy to march to the boat. pitch our Shelter tents to nit

"July 13: Brok Camp at 9 O. C. AM and went to the wharf 6 Co went aboard at 8 P.M. and left we stop on the wharf all nit

"July 14: we left the wharf at 7 AM and march one mile and pitch our Shelter tents to wait for transport to take us off

> "July 15: Algiers La We air hare waiting for transport expecting to go every minit"

As news of the June 19 sinking of the CSS *Alabama* by the USS *Kearsarge* off Cherbourg, France, reached New Orleans, Southern heat continued. On July 14, the *New Orleans Times* commented on the historic naval engagement and the weather: "A pleasant shower yesterday relieved the city, to some extent, of its previously parched appearance, but the windows of Heaven were not opened sufficiently to do all the good that was required. A great many of the cisterns, on which our good people depend for their daily drink, are utterly empty, and the change from cistern to river water is by no means pleasant."[23] Not surprisingly, there were those who sought the muddy waters for relief from the heat, waters that are deceptively enticing but move at five to six miles per hour.

> The currents of father Mississippi set as no currents of any other river. The unwary who lave in the turbid waters of this, the Father of Waters, undergo no little danger from the numberless eddies and whirlpools often springing up suddenly and as suddenly disappear, and which often engulphs the hapless adventurer who trusts himself to their embrace. The most practiced swimmer is often overcome by these sudden freaks of our great river. There is little pleasure in bathing in the Mississippi, and considerable danger. The Coroner yesterday held an inquest upon the body of Henry Buerling, an unfortunate soldier of the 176th N.Y. volunteers, who was drowned while bathing . . . [24]

The Fourteenth was unexpectedly broken up, though for only about one month. The "right wing" and the Seventy-fifth New York boarded the steamer *Continental* bound for Fortress Monroe, while the "left wing," companies E, F, G, and K, boarded the steamer *General Lyon* for their two-week voyage to Washington. Named for Gen. Nathaniel Lyon, the first Union general to die in the war (on August 10, 1861, at Wilson's Creek in Missouri), the steamer initially served the Confederacy as a gunboat. After capture at Island No. 10 on the Mississippi, she became a Union transport and was briefly the flagship, in April 1863, of Rear Adm. David D. Porter.

The regiment's "right wing" would move from Fortress Monroe to City Point, Virginia, and participate in a reconnaissance across the James River to within a dozen miles of Richmond. The men of Lewis's Company K and the left wing would march through Washington and Georgetown before bivouacking near Chain Bridge.

> "July 16: Algiers La on duty to day we struck tents 4 1/2 PM gut on to Steamer Gineril Lion at 4 PM and started down the river
> "July 17: we past Port Hutson [erroneous] at 1 AM crosed the bar at the mouth of the river at 6 AM thare was two vesels stuck on the bar faire all day
> "July 18: we air in the gulf of Mexico it is fair and plesant calm sea
> "July 19: ruf and rainy all day we run into the gulf Stream at dark we air runin South east all day
> "July 20: faire wether hedwin all day we air in the gulf stream runnin east all day
> "July 21: faire an plesant we past keywest at 7 AM we hit the cost of florida at 12 O C we air all of the afternoon on the cost
> "July 22: plesant untill 4 PM it comense rainin at 4 and the win blos it is gittin ruff
> "July 23: it is still a rainin it rained all knight the win bloses hard it vary ruff sea
> "July 24: it still rain it is vary ruff it rain all knight and all day to day
> "July 25: it is faire onse more it is gittin quit calm agane we air within 150 ms of Cap hatras
> "July 26: it is still calm and faire we reach Cape hateras at dark to knight
> "July 27: I am on duty to day it is calm we past Cap Henry 12 we arived at fortris monro at 6 left thair at 10 PM
> "July 28: we reach pornt lookout at 10 AM at Ecguirguirquick [Aquia Creek] at 8 PM and cast anker to bury a man
> "July 29: We left Equiarquick at 4 AM past Mount washington an fort washington at 10 AM arive at washington 12 N left wharf 10 PM for Chan bridg
> "July 30: Chan bridg we arive heare at 3 AM we left hear at 7 PM for washington we arive thair at 11 PM and laid on the Saywalk untill morning
> "July 31: Wasington we left heare on the Cars for Manoxsa [Monocacy] bridg at 4 AM we arive heare at 6 PM and pitch tents whair the battle was fought the 21"

Lewis's enigmatic spelling "Equiarquick" is Aquia Creek, a small western tributary of the Potomac River. A small Confederate battery protected the railroad there that ran to Fredericksburg, Virginia. Union forces occupied Aquia Creek in 1862, using the location as a supply depot and later establishing a field hospital at the site. Chain Bridge is a landmark crossing of the Potomac River at the head of navigation on the river at Little Falls. The actual chain suspension bridge was the third built at the site, in 1808, and destroyed in a flood several years later. By the time of the Civil War, the bridge was of wooden-truss construction and was a heavily guarded crossing to Virginia.

The Fourteenth's destiny lay farther west, in Virginia's Shenandoah Valley. The topography of the valley was important to the travel of armies and to battles fought therein. Flanked by mountains, the valley and its river run from southwest to northeast and to Harpers Ferry at the confluence of the Potomac and Shenandoah Rivers. The valley was a natural corridor aimed at Hagerstown, Frederick, and nearby Monocacy, Maryland. To the east of the Shenandoah, rivers spill away almost perpendicularly to the Blue Ridge Mountains across northern Virginia to the sea. These rivers—among them the Potomac; the Rappahannock and its tributary the Rapidan; the Pamunkey; and the James—constitute significant obstacles and hazards to north–south troop movement. Armies either faced a river or had one at their backs.

Thus, the Shenandoah Valley was "the safest, easiest gateway to the North for the Rebel armies . . . the granary of the Rebellion, previous to the fall of 1864." The Fourteenth would soon have "some reason to understand why the Johnnies' wheat-wagons did not roll toward Richmond after that time."[25]

~ *Thirteen* ~

Battles of Third Winchester (or Opequon Creek) and Fisher's Hill

August 1 to October 17, 1864

I do not wonder that you feel great anxiety in regard to the future, still it is not wise to borrow trouble, it cometh fast enough without, and you may not see what you fear; then all your anxiety will be for naught, only to wear you out, and make you less fit for duty.

—Sgt. J. Henry Jenks, May 1, 1864

[T]he rebels air hevely reingforsed they atacked us last Thursday [Ocober 13] and thay gut hansomly whiped and I am athinking thay had better let us alone if thay no what is good for them . . .

—Lewis Q. Smith, October 16, 1864

AWAITING A TRAIN AND OF NECESSITY SLEEPING ON the sidewalk outside the Washington Baltimore and Ohio station, the Fourteenth departed on the morning of July 31 for Monocacy Junction—in Lewis's diary, "Manoxsa bridg." Monocacy Junction, also known as Frederick Junction, lies three miles southeast of Frederick, Maryland. At the junction, where a spur line runs north to Frederick, the B & O Old Main Line Railroad crossed the Monocacy River. The Monocacy flows south from Gettysburg, Pennsylvania, past Frederick to the Potomac. The Georgetown (or Washington) Pike to Washington and the National Road to Baltimore also crossed the Monocacy near the junction.

Monocacy R. R. Bridge, Alfred R. Waud. Library of Congress

The Fourteenth detrained at Monocacy and pitched their shelter tents near the river "in one of the loveliest bits of riparian scenery . . . in the South."[1] Again boarding a train on August 4, Company K and the left wing returned to Harpers Ferry. Some of the men steadied themselves in the speeding, "rickety" cars by holding on to bayonets thrust through the roofs. From Harpers Ferry, the regiment marched southwest four miles to Halltown, West Virginia, on August 6. On the following day, Gen. Philip H. Sheridan assumed command of the "Army of the Shenandoah"—officially, the Middle Military Division.

"August 1: Manoxsa bridg we air hear no atak has bin maid yet our waygans train has gut along got heare at 1 O C PM
"August 2: Manoxa bridg ordered to march at 10 O C AM ordor is countermandid report came in of capturin 3000 prisners fals report
"August 3: Manoxa bridg Gineril enspection Ordered to moove with 2 days raishon the ordor is countermandid I went on gard at 6 PM
"August 4: Fredrick guntion [Junction] on gard Ordered to move with 4 days raishon left for Harparfary at 6 PM gut heare at 8 come in the Cars Stop on Bolevar hyth western [West] Virginia
"August 5: Harparfary we air to the paripit laying on our arms remaned heare all day and knight the rebel Army is at Hallstown [Halltown, West Virginia] 4 ms from heare
"August 6: Hallestown we had ordors to march at daylite so we did up heare and formed 3 lines of battels I am on gard
"August 7: Halltown I came off from gard this morning Copril of first releafe our waggon train gut along to day at ten O Clock"

In the following letter, Lewis mentions "Charlestown," a locality six miles southwest of Halltown in West Virginia. Regardless of Smith's inconsistent spelling, Charlestown, now Charles Town, is *not* to be confused with Charleston, the capital of West Virginia, at considerable distance from "Charlestown" and the campaigns in the Shenandoah Valley.

Halltown Western Virginia Aug 7/64 My dear wife and famely

I again seat my self [to let you know] whair I am and how I am my helth is vary good hoping this will find you all the same thaire at home we air heare to Halltown—miles above Harperfary we left Fredireck Juncton thirday knight [August 4] at 6 o clock got to Harperfary at 8 come on the cars when we got thair Fryday knight till 3 o Clock in the morning when we was routid up to make our Coffee and be redy to march at day light so we was redy to go and Startid came up hear and formed a line and pith our tents ans we air heare now but whair we shall be to knight I cannot tell when we got heare to Harparfary the rebels held this place but have retreatid back to Charlestown 4 ms from heare whair we expect they air now they have a large forse 3000 or more but we air enuff for that number thair is the 6 an 8 [Corps] and apart of the 19 army Chooars our Choar has not all got heare yet the rest of our regment has not got heare thair is but 4 [the left wing of the

> *Fourteenth] Companies of us heare E F K and G air the Companies that is heare we have got a large forse heare and is agroin larger every day we air bound to Clean the rebels out of this part of the country or git cleaned out our Selfs they have ---- ---- -- heare and I think thay have got to suffer for it I shall not be able to rit [much] this morning for I expect them to call for the maile every minit I have just come off from duty this morning so I have but little time but I must say the time seems long to me since I have hern from home the last letter was the fourth of July daitid the 16 of June it is gitten most two month but you air not to blame for it but you must rit every chance you git and dyrect to Washington and I will git them sometime and I will rit as often as I can git a chance or git paper to rit on I am out of paper money and tobaco and the rest of the boys air in the same way so I cant borow we ought to bin paid off a month ago but was not so it bring us up estanding I roat to you twice since we came into this department and roat for you to send me some money if you had it to spaire dont send it to come short yourself but send some paper to rit on if you want me to rit Asa and Moulton air well both tent with me give my love to all tell farther that I want to no how every thine looks tell them all to rit if thay will if the rest wont I trust you will rit often kiss the little ones for me and take one your self tell them to be good Children and they must mind thair mother and do as she tells them I will close by biding you good morning from ever yours L. Q. Smith*[2]

On August 13, Lewis commented about the loss of wagons to "mosby band," or Mosby's irregulars. Striking quickly and without warning, Confederate Ranger John S. Mosby (1833–1916) conducted highly successful, mounted raids behind federal lines in Virginia and Maryland. As the war closed, Mosby never surrendered, but disbanded his men instead. After the war, he practiced law, became a Republican, and even campaigned for Grant for president.

> "August 8: Halltown Va we air heare awaiting for the rest of the army to come up thair has 5000 cavely came in to day a cavely fit to Charlesto[w]n
>
> "August 9: Hallestown Va we air heare get redy to fit I leve to go on picket at 2 PM I went one half mile was on a reserve

A Civil War Hanging. Library of Congress Photograph

> "August 10: Halltown we left the picket posts 5 AM for a march past through Charestown on the road to winskchester march 16 ms an went intto camp
>
> "August 11: On the road to Charlesto[w]n we march 7 ms when we formed a line of battle the Cavelry had a schirmish no gineril engagement march on 8 ms forthere [farther] went into camp
>
> "August 12: we startid on at 5 AM and went on to mideletown gut in at dark our regment was deataild for picket Started out at 8 PM
>
> "August 13: we was releved at 6 PM went into camp the 8 Choar tok a spy we lost part of our waggon traine 30 of took by old mosby band
>
> "August 14: Middletown we was routid out on a line of battle at 3 O c and stood untill daylit then brock ranks and pitch our tents we hung a rebel spy"

Sheridan's army continued to move up the valley (southward) with cavalry and infantry skirmishes occurring as General Early's Confederate force retreated. At Cedar Creek, which flows from the northwest to join the Shenandoah's North Fork just south of Middletown, the Federals halted.

The Second Division of the Nineteenth Corps and the Fourteenth's right wing had not yet arrived. Early's men were established across the creek, and further pursuit—the valley splits in two here and Massanutten Mountain is the divider—would expose Sheridan's force to an attack from either flank, a potential trap.

On August 14, as the armies faced each other and skirmished near Cedar Creek, General Grant notified Sheridan that reinforcements commanded by Gen. Joseph B. Kershaw (1822–1894) had left Richmond to join Early. Sheridan, lacking a good defensive position, decided on a midnight retreat back down the valley to Halltown—pursued by Early and his reinforcements. Sheridan's move was perceived in the North as another Union defeat rather than a calculated tactical maneuver in the face of a stronger force. As the withdrawal proceeded, the right wing of the Fourteenth, which had spent the first two weeks of August in Washington, rejoined the regiment on August 19 near Charlestown. Sheridan was fresh to the valley and faced a new enemy. Prudently, he studied the terrain and probed his opponent with cavalry. When Sheridan was prepared, his troops would move again, weeks later, and there would be battle.

> "August 15: Middletown we was coled out on a line of battle at 3 1/2 AM and stood untill day lit fix up our camp ground had a inspection we startid at 11 PM for winchester
>
> "August 16: Winchester we left camp last knight at 11 O Clock for this plase past through Middletown village an to Newtown village at daylit gut hear at 7 gut our breckfast and went into camp for the day
>
> "August 17: Winchester we startid at 4 AM we was caled out at mid knight redy for a start past through winchester village at day lite to Baryvill [Berryville] 12 N went into camp for the knight
>
> "August 18: Berriville [about twelve miles east of Winchester] we formed a line of battle 4 AM Struck tents at 6 marct 2 ms Stop for Gin Grover to come up with his foarse [which included the right wing of the Fourteenth] march until dark went int camp for the nit
>
> "August 19: near Charlesto[w]n I out on gard at 2 AM we mooved one mile and joined our regment and went into camp with our old Bridgade Asa went on picket"

For readers in the Granite State, a news item appeared on August 19:

Washington, Aug 14—Positive news has been received that Lee has sent two divisions of reenforcements to the Shenandoah Valley. Sheridan at latest advices was at Winchester and the rebels at Strasburg. The distance between the opposing forces being only fifteen miles a battle is expected at any moment.[3]

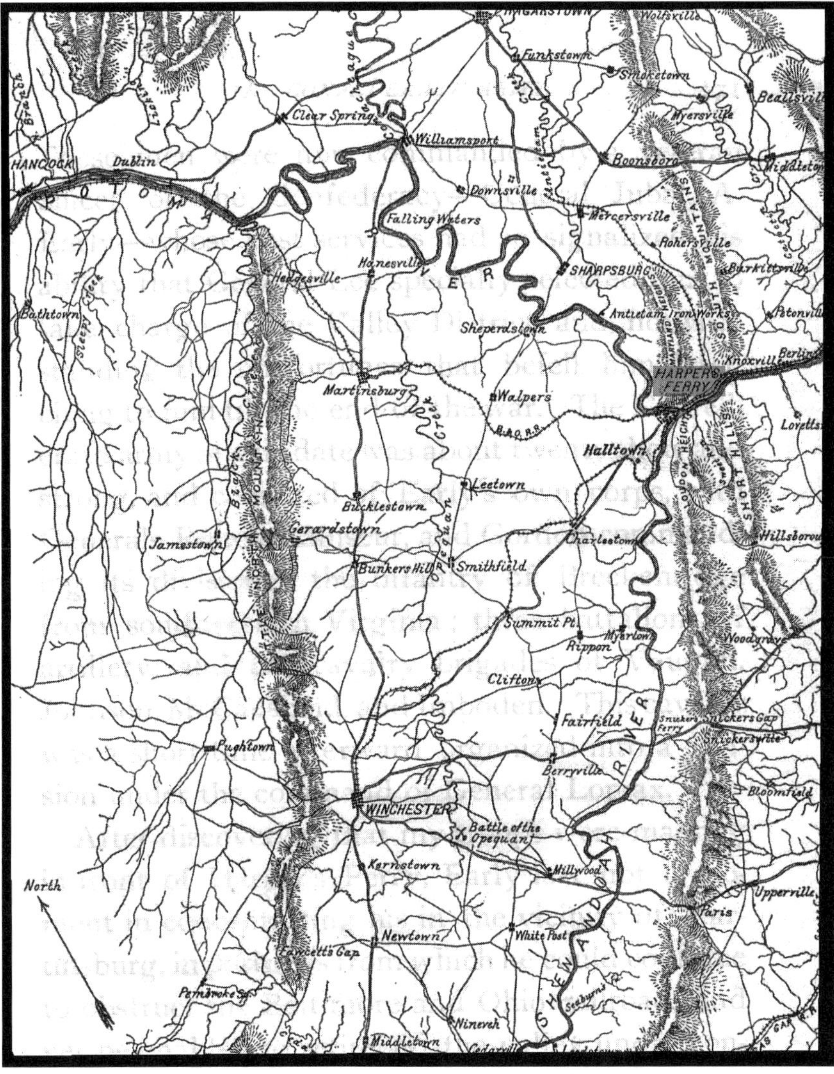

Map of the Lower Shenandoah Valley. Author's Collection.

For the next several weeks, amid frequent skirmishing and cavalry engagements, Sheridan bided his time, waiting for Kershaw's division of infantry and a battalion of artillery, which had been ordered to return to Richmond, to depart. Smith's diary records the essentially static positions that characterized late August. Buffum wrote: "On August 20 the Fourteenth lay quiet, receiving a big mail from home."[4]

> "Saturday, August 20, 1864: Charlesto[w]n we air on a rest the mail came in to day for the first time for one and a half months gut int camp from gittin a leave
> "Aug. 21: Charesto[w]n thare has bin fighting on our left one half of a cavely regment captured by the rebels we come[n]sed bilding work[s] at noon.
> "Aug. 22: Hallestown we left last knight at 11 o c we gut heare at 2 AM we lid down till 6 O C then we went to bilding brestwork heavy schirmishing all day
> "Aug. 23: hallstown we was caled up at 3 and stood till day lit schirmishing an fighting thrugh the day"

Lewis's estimate of the rebel force (below), "sed to be 70 or 80,000 in number," was high. In fact, the Yankees had superior numbers. In mid-August, Early had an estimated twenty thousand men, which would later be reduced by about four thousand with the departure of Kershaw's reinforcements and further diminished by battle losses. Sheridan's force was estimated at about forty-three thousand as of September 10, 1864.[5] Buffum wrote that "there was very little difference in the strength of the opposing forces" and he may have been correct.[6] Sheridan also dealt with the question:

> The difference of strength between the two armies at this date [early September] was considerably in my favor, but the conditions attending my situation in a hostile region necessitated so much detached service to protect trains, and to secure Maryland and Pennsylvania from raids, that my excess in numbers was almost canceled by these incidental demands that could not be avoided, and although I knew that I was strong, yet, in consequence of the injunctions of General Grant, I deemed it necessary to be very cautious; and the fact that the Presidential election was impending made me doubly so, the authorities at Washington having impressed upon me that the defeat of my army might be followed by the overthrow of the party in power . . .[7]

Hallestown Aug 23 1864 My Dear wife

I agan seat my self to rit you a few lines to let you no whair I am we have gut back heare to halltown agane we gut back heare yesterday morning at 2 O Clock and came onto the same hill we left 12 days ago and we was follard by the rebels thar was hevey schirmishing all along the lines and cavely was fighting all day yesterday and air still afightin this morning but no generil ingagement as yet the rebels have gut a hevey forse it is sed to be 70 or 80,000 in number but we air in hops to have anuff for them we air on good fighting ground as can be we air within five miles of harpars fary and if we git licked we can fall back thair and they cant git us out of thair but we donot intend to git licked our brigad is on the center of the lines we have not had to fiar a gun at them yet but expect it every moment the guns air a cracking all around us all in sit[e] of us we shall find out what the result will be in a day or to thay have gut git a whiping or we have we have all of the advantige of them if we can git them to fight on our ground we have had a vary hard time of it for the last 12 days we have not had a knight rest for the time we left up two ms above Charlesto[w]n at 10 O Clock nite before last and gut heare at 2 yesterday morning and lied down untill day light then we went to work an poot up a brestwork it took us till noon that was all we dun for the day we had a hevey shour it lastid all of two ours and we had a rather coald bed for the knight for we hat to thro away every thing we had but our shelter tents and rubber blankets for the wether was so hot and our march so severe we could not stand it to carry more I will give you more perticklers when I git time perhaps you wood like to no what oficers has the comand of our Choar Gen. Emery [Emory] the Choar Gen Grover the devison Gen Birdges [Birge] the Brigad our army consis of the 6, 8, 19 Choars. Shirdron [Sheridan] is in Comand of the hol forse heare I shall hafto close for want of time I want you to rit why you do not get your inlotment as well as the rest of them for thay have gut thare rit often as you can my love to you all from yours Lewis Q Smith

It should be noted that many writers of the Civil War era, whether soldiers or news reporters, reflected a decade or more of anti-foreigner sentiment, of which the Young America movement of the 1850s was the culmination. Lewis and his peers' grandfathers fought in the Revolution and in the second "War of Independence" in 1812. Immigrants of the 1840s and '50s had no such bonds with their new country and were the major force in the draft rioting of midsummer 1863. While conscription in the South was truly at the bottom of the barrel, that in the North was, perhaps, nearing the nadir in terms of quality. Upon this background, New Hampshire's *Concord Monitor* reported "gross misconduct" of a detachment of troops, "composed of every nationality but our own."

In Concord, "some 80 who had been mustered . . . effected their escape while in camp in this city and several were shot in the attempt."[8] The remaining recruits, described as "New York roughs, foreigners, bounty-jumpers, and substitute-brokers," left Concord on August 21 under heavy guard. After reaching Haymarket Square in Boston, "some fifty" dropped their muskets and equipment and bolted. The guard and a large contingent of police immediately opened fire, hitting ten. Ten more were fairly quickly rounded up: among them, one from an outhouse in Warren Square, one from a stable at Chardon Street, and "five in Campbell's saloon on Hanover street, where they were busily engaged in shifting [changing] their clothing."[9] The remaining soldiers, 146 of whom were unable to sign their names at muster, were placed aboard the transport *Constitution* destined for Fortress Monroe.

> "Aug. 24: Halltown Caled up at 3 and stood untill day lit gut breckfast and went on firtig all day bilding brestworks digin rifel pitts
> "Aug. 25: Hallstown fightin yesterday evry thing quiart to day hard fight three ms from heare we air on firtige bildin brestwork befor our rgment
> "Aug. 26: Hallstown. part of our regment is on picket the rest of us air to work on the brestworks a fit ocurd to the left of our bridgad
> "Aug. 27: Halltown we air expecting to move every moment we left at 8 O C went 6 ms two ms beyond Charlestown went into camp
> "Aug. 28: Charlestown we air lying in behind the brestwork thair is some fighting in front of us Asa went to the horspittle to day
> "Aug. 29: Charlestown tharr is hard fighting captuard some prisners 800 and 60 waggans I was on hedquartard gard
> "Aug. 30: Charleston I came off from duty this morning very quiart as yet to day
> "Aug. 31: Charlestown every thing quiart to day we air lying behind the brestworks we had a gineril inspechsion mustard in for pay"

On August 25, Company I's Pvt. Christopher Hoyt wrote of his experience at this early point in the campaign: "up knight and day we have marched not far from 100 miles since the 14 and dug rifle pits now we are four miles [Halltown] from Harpars Ferry with the rebs close to our ass they have ben skirmishing for four days."[10] Hoyt's fatigue translated to pessimism:

> You may fight them for ten years and then you cannot kick them out and it is no use to fight what have they done I can tell you they have killed of[f] about 100,000 men and that is about all why dont they settle it some way I hope they will get a new president this fall eather have it better or worse and it cannot be any worse the dam Generals will stradle their Horces and then you have got to march[11]

Late August brought a several-day lull in skirmishing and fighting. While marching from Charlestown to Berryville late on September 3, the Fourteenth paused for an hour's rest. A pitched battle with Kershaw's division ensued, and the Confederates were pushed back to Opequon (pronounced oh-PECK-un and sometimes spelled Opequan) Creek.[12] Buffum recorded: "In that blood the camp near Berryville was christened."[13]

> "Sept. 1: Charleston we air hear to the brestwork all quiart this morning every thing quiart through the day
> "Sept. 2: Charleston every thing quiart through the lines the rebels have felback no fighting to day
> "Sept. 3: Charleston we was called up at 2 O C for a march we left at 6 AM went in two ms of Barivill village when a fite took plase rebels defeat
> "Sept. 4: Barivill we liad last knight on our arms we air bilding brestwork and fortifieing we worked all day we air wel fortifid
> "Sept. 5: Berivill I am on picket thare hevey schirmishing a fit our bridgade was order out the rebs retreated"

The first two weeks of September saw continued skirmishing and cannonading. Lewis continued to work on fortifications and "brestworks," and to serve on picket lines. On duty from September 5 to the morning of September 6, his diary reads: "I was releved from picket at 4 AM it rain all knight it rains to day I suffered the most last knight since I bin in the sirvis." On Sunday, the seventh, Smith wrote: "Bariville thare is every thing quiart to day I have bin in Camp all day an roat a letter":

Barivill Vr Sept 7/64 My dear wife

I will hason to answer yours that I reseved last knight I was glad to heare that you wore all well as for my helth it is vary good hoping this may find you all the same we left Charlestown last Saturday morning [September 3] arived heare at dark formed a line of battle and throad up some rails for some pertechtion then lyd down on our arms an in a line of battle in the morning we went to work an bilt fortifications an we have gut this strongly fortifid and monday morning [September 5] I was sent out on picket came in yesterday thare was a smart fight as we come in it was on our left you will git more of the pertichlers then I can rit we had a smart schirmish last monday while I was on picket our bridgad was all ordort out for surport our lines fel back to the line of pickets that I was on then our men was reinforce an maid a ralley and the rebels felback and left all I see brot acros the lins kiled or woundid was three one kiled two woundid yestrday every thing was quiart it rained all knight befor and all day yesterday the Second bridgad has gon out to try them to day and we air lying to be redy at a moment worning I will finish my letter the regment that went out have gut back thay found northing I reseved your letter that you sent with dollar in it datid 28, 29 it will not pass out hear northing but greenbacks you need not send eny more for you will need it yourself I will try and leave off using tobaco and git along some way you mist rit often as you can I will do the same Asa went to the horspittle when we left halltown with the piles I hant hern from him sinse Molton is well I shall hafto close by biding you good knight my love to you all from yours pleas except this L Q Smith

After the 1832 Jacksonian Democrats' defeat of the renewal of the Bank of the United States and the government's consequent reversion to "hard" money, only state or local banks issued scrip or paper money, backed (redeemable) by silver or gold. At the onset of the war, the federal government faced a shortage not only of men and supplies but also of money. Silver and gold were hoarded and the U.S. Treasury's holdings were depleted, for, by law, the government paid its debts in metal.

The result was the Legal Tender Act of February 25, 1862, and an initial $150 million in paper money. Printed in green ink on the reverse and not redeemable, "greenbacks" quickly became the accepted currency—"northing but greenbacks." There were, of course, subsequent constitutional challenges to the government's authority to issue paper as legal tender. By mid-1863, courts in both New York and Ohio had decided in favor of the government and the greenback.[14]

Col. Robert Wilson, a lawyer from Keene, New Hampshire, served as commander of the Fourteenth from its formation. He assumed command of the district of Carrollton, Louisiana, from April 9 to June 12, 1864. Subsequently, he was commander of the First Brigade, Second Division of the Nineteenth Corps, in June and July 1864, and was discharged, with disability, on September 6, 1864. Highly respected, he returned to Keene and served in the New Hampshire Legislature the year prior to his death, in 1870. Maj. Alexander Gardner, of Claremont, New Hampshire, succeeded Wilson and was promoted to colonel on September 12, 1864. Sustaining multiple wounds at Opequon on September 19, Gardner died on October 8.

> "Thursday Sept. 8: Barivill every thing is quiart to day we have foar hard tack for two days rashons come to knight
>
> "Sept. 9: Barivill all quiart Cornel Robart Wilson has resind and gut a onarible discharg he left the regment at 4 PM
>
> "Sept. 10: Barivill all is quiart in front hevey cananadan to our rit this forenoon but every thing is quiart now 4 PM
>
> "Sept. 11: Barivill all is quiart on our lines we air pitching our tents over to day and fixing up our Camp ground
>
> "Sept. 12: Barivill every thing is vary quiart on our lins we have bin fixing up our streats. drill and drespraid
>
> "Sept. 13: Barryville all is quiart on our lins to schirmish drills a fight near Bunker hill 8 miles from our Cavely [Second Ohio] took one regment one Stand of collar [colors] th[e] eight South Carlina [Infantry] regment
>
> "Sept. 14: Barryville all quiart this morning I wenon picket at 4 PM every thing is quiart through the day
>
> "Sept. 15: Barryville I came in from picket at 4 PM all was quiart they expectid that we should be atacked last knight"

Capt. Theodore A. Ripley, of Winchester, New Hampshire, and Company F, would be captured during the battle of Cedar Creek on October 19, 1864. Ripley, mentioned below, was exchanged in March 1865, at which time he was promoted to colonel. Following his discharge and drawn by the agricultural

Capt. Theodore A. Ripley. Author's Collection

promise of southern soil and climate, he managed a plantation in Georgia. Many Yankee soldiers found farming in the South seductive. Keene, New Hampshire's John Sturtevant, of Company G, had felt the lure: "I think I should be perfectly happy on one of these vegetable farms and I know I could make any quantity of money. This country will be filled up with Northern men after the war is over."[15]

Captain Ripley was shot to death on the night of July 23, 1866, and in the history of the Fourteenth, he is listed as "Killed by [the] 'Ku Klux.'"[16] Company B's Cpl. Albert H. Tyrrell had received a letter from his brother warning of the risk of working in the South:

> [A]s for going down to take charge of a plantation you will have to risk your life for there are lots of sesesh who would delight to shoot any northern man who would go onto a rebel plantation. There would be a great many here who would go to raising cotton if it were not for the risk they would have to run of being shot some dark night.[17]

A case has been made, however, that former members of Company F were instead the murderers. The motive for the purported revenge killing was the result of Ripley's allegedly ordering men to unnecessary deaths: "If that officer had forgotten his canteen of whisky that morning (at Cedar Creek) it is possible the order would never have been issued."[18] General Sheridan, who clearly understood the impact of wasted lives, wrote: "Soldiers are averse to seeing their comrades killed without compensating results, and none realize more quickly than they the blundering that often takes place on the field of battle."[19]

September 16 was important for Sheridan, for on this day he was able to confirm that Kershaw's force had left for Richmond. He also gleaned the intelligence that Early's "force is much smaller than represented."[20] Sheridan's source was a female spy within Winchester, Miss Rebecca Wright, "of the Society of Friends and the teacher of a small private school." The message to Sheridan, compressed into a pellet and covered with tin foil, was carried across the lines by an "old colored man" in his mouth.[21] Weeks of waiting for just such an opportunity were over. Three days later, Sheridan attacked.

> "Sept. 16: Barryville all is quiart on our lins to day two Co of us had a schirmish drill at 9 AM a bridgad drill from 2 till 5 PM
> "Sept. 17: Barryville all is quiart Gineril inspection by Cap Ripley and stocked our tent
> "Sept. 18: Barryvill thair is fighting to our left and we air ordored to moove we still air heare at dark
> "Sept. 19: Barryville we left 2 AM mooved on to winchester [Virginia] whair the afful fight cuired [occurred] it lastid all day we drove them 3 ms 5 kiled 13 woundid out of our Co K"

Miss Rebecca Wright. Author's Collection

The third battle of Winchester (or Opequon Creek) began, as Lewis wrote, at two o'clock on the morning of September 19, 1864. Sheridan's Sixth Corps led the Nineteenth and Eighth Corps up a narrow canyon on the Berryville Pike (the Winchester–Berryville road, today's eastbound Route 7) to the crossings of the Opequon, cleared by cavalry units in advance. In the canyon, there was a traffic jam and a delay that cost the Federals several hours in getting into position: the Sixth Corps on the left, the Nineteenth in the center, and the Eighth to the rear right. The intent was to move on the left, but the force of the attack was to be in the center—by the Nineteenth. The Nineteenth would strike furiously, but would eventually be repulsed, until it was reorganized and then supported by the Eighth. The Eighth, with cavalry, would also succeed in flanking and rolling up Early's left as the Nineteenth again prevailed in the center.

After crossing the Opequon and then Abraham's Creek, the men of the Fourteenth passed a field hospital where "the surgeon's knife was in full play," treating the wounded from the cavalry battle of earlier in the morning.[22] At approximately noon and facing an open field, the Fourteenth was two miles east of Winchester and deployed about six hundred yards north of the Pike. Following the order to charge, the regiment entered a "galling fire" as they began to cross the field, while subject to enemy artillery fire from their right. In the half-mile advance across the field, soldiers began to drop: "exposed to a cross fire in the first charge it seemed wonderful that more were not killed."[23]

The untested Fourteenth "did not even halt." Francis Buffum, accompanied by three men who quickly fell, wrote:

> And now the boys began to feel the thrill, the enthusiasm, the exultation, of battle. Those who had escaped, and kept in their place, had passed the period of fear; and the wild intoxication of a great contest was nerving them on.[24]

As they entered the next band of woods, the fighting became more intense—even hand to hand. Punishing artillery fire continued from a range of not more than six hundred yards. Entering a second open field, the charge faltered and the order was given to fall back and regroup. The Nineteenth Corps and the Fourteenth had struck the strongest of Early's army. One witness described the action as "the bloodiest, the darkest, the most picturesque, the most dramatic, the only desperate moment of the day."[25]

While the Fourteenth regrouped, Gen. George Crook's Army of West Virginia (the diminished former Eighth Corps) moved up to reinforce the Nineteenth and the Union right. "At three o'clock the hour of defeat for Early struck," as Crook's men attacked with "a mighty battle-yell, which never ceased for ten minutes . . ." Simultaneously, "our whole army assumed the offensive."[26] Also to the right and to the enemy's rear, the soldiers saw the flash of sabers as the cavalry of Generals Averell, Merritt, and Custer

Sheridan's Campaign—Battle of Winchester—Position of the Nineteenth Corps General Emory. September 19, 1864—THE CENTRE. Author's Collection.

"drove the enemy from their guns like a flock of sheep."[27] Had the Union center, held by the Nineteenth at great cost (nearly two thousand casualties), folded, the battle would have been lost. The Eighth "carried the heights and the fort which crowned them" and "Early's battle was rapidly reduced to a simple struggle to save himself from utter rout."[28] By six in the evening, federal forces occupied Winchester.

At 7:30 P.M., Sheridan telegraphed:

> To Lieut. General U. S. Grant:
>
> I have the honor to report that I attacked the forces of Gen. Early on the Berryville pike at the crossing of Opequan Creek, and after a most stubborn and sanguinary engagement, which lasted from early in the morning until 5 o'clock in the evening, completely defeated him, driving him through Winchester and capturing about 2500 prisoners, five pieces of artillery, nine army flags and most of their wounded . . . Our losses are severe . . . I cannot yet tell our losses. The conduct of the officers and men was most superb; they charged and carried every position taken up by the rebels, from Opequan Creek to Winchester.[29]

Jubilation over the victory passed quickly, as the reality of the missing became apparent. At ten that night, the men of the Fourteenth were ordered to fall in for roll call—an assembly that was "mournful beyond expression." When no response to a name occurred, "the silence of suspense was depressing . . . at least one-quarter of the uninjured in some companies had not come in."[30] Of fifty-three officers and men of the Fourteenth who died, nine were from Company K, more than from any other company. In wounded men, Company K had ten; highest was Company H, with sixteen. In total, the Fourteenth had ninety wounded, "largely in excess of any other regiment."[31]

News of the casualties reached home: "Winchester is one vast hospital. There cannot be less than 5000 wounded in the town. Every hotel and vacant store and house are overflowing."[32] There was good reason for Winchester to be "one vast hospital," and the estimate of five thousand wounded is about right. Previously, hospitals had been established "without system after a battle, and much confusion consequently resulted." By the time of the Shenandoah campaign, a "division system" was in place, affording "the means of caring with the utmost celerity for large numbers of wounded thrown suddenly upon the medical department . . ." As the battle

Flag Raising in Winchester in presence of General Sheridan, on Thanksgiving Day, at the Field Hospital by Shawnee Spring. James E. Taylor Sketch. Courtesy of the Western Reserve Historical Society.

opened on September 19, "field hospitals were established . . . on or near Opequan Creek," protected by woods and accessible to ambulances "in the vicinity of good roads." From there, moderately severe cases were triaged to Baltimore and the very severe and very slight to Sandy Hook, just across the Potomac from Harpers Ferry, and to Frederick, Maryland.[33]

Two factors complicated care of the wounded at the Battle of Opequon. The fighting continued into darkness and many wounded lay "concealed in the thick woods where they had fallen." The second consideration related to the speed of the victory: the enemy was pushed so fast that the bluecoats' ambulance runs quickly lengthened. "At nine p.m. the same night the general commanding ordered . . . all the wounded taken to Winchester, and the field hospitals broken up as rapidly as possible." As a result, "churches, public buildings, and such private dwellings as were suitable" were used to house the casualties—organized by corps. Four hundred hospital tents and "ten additional surgeons arrived on the 23d," and the resulting camp hospital, "pitched on a well-selected site," at Shawnee Springs, became the "Sheridan Field Hospital."[34] It was "the largest hospital under a single unified control in any Union force during the entire war."[35]

Many of the dead were buried in a trench and later relocated to the Winchester National Cemetery. Some remains were later removed and reinterred in "their native hills."[36] Among the men of Company K to die would be Lewis's cousin, Moulton S. Webster. Badly wounded by rifle fire, Moulton returned home to North Sandwich, dying there on October 31, 1864, and "is there buried."[37] Cpl. Oceanus Straw, also from Sandwich, died two days after the battle "in hospital," and was buried at the National Cemetery in Winchester. He left a widow and two children at home. Harrison Atwood 2nd, had a leg shot off and expired the day of the battle. He also lies in the National Cemetery. Harrison's survivors were a wife and three children.

Lt. Moulton S. Webster, North Sandwich Cemetery. Jonathan Taylor photograph.

Cpl. Oceanus Straw. Bruce Jackson photograph.

The victory at Opequon (Third Winchester) was an important one, and control of the Baltimore and Ohio Railroad and the Chesapeake and Ohio Canal returned to the Union side. With little pause in Winchester, Sheridan's army began the pursuit of Early up the valley on the following morning, September 20. Early had retreated and occupied a defensible position between Fisher's Hill and the town of Strasburg—protected on

Cpl. Harrison Atwood 2nd. Bruce Jackson photograph.

his left by Little North Mountain and on his right by the Shenandoah River and Massanutten Mountain.

The gaps that Lewis referred to are breaks in the Allegheny Mountains to the west (the Union right) and in the Blue Ridge Mountains to the east (the Union left). The Blue Ridge gaps offered escape routes from the valley, and at Manassas Gap lay the Manassas Gap Railroad to Manassas Junction, one of Early's principal means of reinforcement and supply. "Near the gaps" undoubtedly meant Manassas Gap and Chester Gap, which are just east of Front Royal, about fifteen miles southeast of Strasburg and Fisher's Hill.

Obelisk Honoring the Fourteenth Regiment New Hampshire Volunteers, Winchester National Cemetery. Bruce Jackson photograph.

Monument Detail. Bruce Jackson photograph.

"Tuesday, Sept. 20: Winshister Village we left at day light dryveing the rebels befor us 18 ms to the gaps fough[t] them all of the way
"Sept. 21: Near the gaps we startid at 9 AM went 2 ms fought all day without driveing them one ms and lyd down for the knight
"Sept. 22: Near the gaps we advanse 2 ms comens fighting at daylight fought all day compleatidly routid and drove them all knight"

In late afternoon of September 22, Sheridan's army opened the battle of Fisher's Hill. Soldiers of General Crook's Army of West Virginia (Eighth Corps), concealed from view in the trees on Early's left, flanked the Confederates and quickly took a battery on little North Mountain. As the Fourteenth emerged from woods in line of battle at "elbow touch" on the Union left, they were exposed to sweeping cannon fire from one thousand yards away. To take the battery, they had to descend a rough exposed incline before ascending the other side to attack the enemy's guns at Early's center atop Fisher's Hill. Dread filled the ranks as the rebel gunners "were getting the range with fearful accuracy."[38] The Federals had more than six hundred yards to go.

Suddenly, the men "heard a strange cheer" and a Union flag appeared over the Confederate artillery position. Crook's flanking movement "struck Early's left and rear so suddenly as to cause his army to break in confusion and flee."[39] Union casualties were light: fifty-two killed, 457 wounded. The Fourteenth sustained two wounded and none killed. Sheridan's men pursued the main body of Confederates fifteen miles to Woodstock and on the next day to Mount Jackson. A federal cavalry force had been sent via Front Royal and the Luray Valley to close off Early's escape up the valley at Newmarket, but the attempt was unsuccessful.

News of the victories at Opequon and Fisher's Hill traveled quickly. On September 23, Secretary of War Stanton received a number of dispatches regarding the battle at Fisher's Hill. One read: "[Confederate] Military line down. The whole affair is complete and overwhelming."[40] The news had also reached Richmond, and Kershaw's force, which had been detached and was still en route eastward to join Lee's army, was ordered back to the valley.

"Friday, Sept. 23: Woodstock we left at 12 N march to Edensburg [Edinburg] went int[o] camp for the knight

Sheridan's Wagon Trains in the Valley, Early Morning Mist and Smoke, Alfred Waud, Library of Congress.

> "Sept 24: Edensburg we left at day light march till noon had a fight at Strawsburg [Strasburg] and *stove thar army all to peasis northin to it* (italics added)
> "Sept 25: Harson Burge [Harrisonburg] we arived hear at 3 PM our regment went into the Corthouse yard and stayed alone an went to doin provo[st] duty"

Unlike Meade after Gettysburg or the ever recalcitrant McClellan, Sheridan had ordered a night march in pursuit of the rebels at Fisher's Hill. The advance was quite rapid, so much so that the soldiers, who had drawn no rations since before Opequon, were forced to wait for their supply train. Arriving at Woodstock at four in the morning on the twenty-fourth, they "slept until ten o'clock, like logs."[41] Early arrived at Mount Jackson on the same morning and prepared to make a stand. The Fourteenth crossed the North Fork of the Shenandoah in waist-deep water and, encouraged by prompt Union shelling of every Confederate position visible, pursued Early's force all day. When they reached the enemy's front, the Confederates had disappeared. The "stand" was a rearguard action only; the main army was still in flight.

Also, on September 24, Union cavalry flanked Early's left, cutting off his retreat south to Harrisonburg and forcing him east toward Port Republic and the Blue Ridge. On the twenty-fifth, the Fourteenth arrived at the town of Harrisonburg, where, except for a night at Mount Crawford, they remained until October 6. For Lewis, duty would be almost continuous; added would be rain, cold, and hunger. Doubtless, many soldiers would uncomfortably recall their discarded impedimenta in the late-August heat four weeks prior: "we hat to thro away every thing we had but our shelter tents and rubber blankets."[42]

> "Monday, Sept. 26: Harson Burg we air hear adoing duty I am on picket to day the army is all lying heare
> "Sept. 27: Harson Burg I am still on picket to day we have bin on duty 36 ours and march 18 ms an went rit on duty
> "Sept. 28: Harson Burge we had ordors to moove the hole army but was countermanded an we air still in the Vilag
> "Sept. 29: Harson burge we left at daylight an advanse 8 ms and went int[o] camp the Cavely is afighting ahed
> "Sept. 30: Mountcroffard [Mount Crawford] we left 12 N and felback to Harisburg and went into camp I was detaled on picket it is cold an rany
> "Oct. 1: Harisburg I am still on picket it is cold I was releave from picket at 5 PM it has rained all day it is vary cold
> "Oct. 2: Harisburg it still rainy we air waiting for surplys this is the secon day without raishon Captin has come we air paid off to day I had 51.25 paid
> "Oct. 3: Harisburge we was caled at 3 AM ordor to march at day lit the ordor was counter manded at 12 N an pitch tents agane rany 300 prisners brot in
> "Oct. 4: Harisburge we air heare everything is quiart and plesant to day thar was eight hundred prisners brot in yesterday
> "Oct. 5: Harisburge We air still heare all quiart to day the Cavelry is a makin a clean sweep of this valley"

A "clean sweep" was Yankee understatement. Acting on Grant's orders, Sheridan's cavalry fanned out and began a series of movements back down the Shenandoah Valley, destroying anything of value in their path—homes generally excepted. Sheridan's report to Grant, often quoted, reads, in part:

> In moving back to this point [Woodstock, Virginia] the whole country from the Blue Ridge to North Mountain has been made untenable for a rebel army. I have destroyed over 2000 barns filled with wheat and hay and farming implements, over 70 mills filled with flour and wheat, have driven in front of the army over four herd[s] of stock, and have killed and issued to the troops not less than 3000 sheep. This destruction embraces the Luray and Little Fort Valley as well as the main Valley.[43]

Sheridan noted another aspect of the valley campaign: "Since I came into the Valley from Harpers Ferry, every train, every small party, and every straggler has been bushwhacked by the people, many of whom have protection papers from commanders who have been, hitherto, in that valley. The people here are all getting sick of the war."[44] From the soldier's side, Pvt. Marcellus Smith wrote:

> *All that the rebs come into the valley for is to harvest. I heard one Md soldier say that they detail men from the ranks and send them up to plant & hoe. They dress in citizens clothes & then the Rebs come up and harvest it & these men are detailed to do guerillering while the stuff is growing and when we go by they stand scowling at us and how . . . They get their old shanties torn down once in a while besides all this stuff stolen that is good for anything. But woe to the straggler that falls into his hands. They will kill him as sure as fate for they are raving mad. We burned one nice barn the other day. Coming up the man went and riled a spring so that we couldn't get water. He has got two sons in the C. S. service. It was about a mile from Charlestown. I wish that they would burn everything as we go along. I don't think that many innocent ones would have to suffer of any up in this part of the country.*[45]

The Fourteenth had settled down to provost duty in Harrisonburg and the Confederates had retreated to a secure position on the high ground of Brown's Gap in the Blue Ridge. Sheridan's supply line, meanwhile, could not be stretched much farther than Harrisonburg, much less east over the Blue Ridge. Although the gaps provided exit routes from the valley, not all of them were avenues for artillery and heavy supply wagons. By October 8, only Confederate cavalry were close to the rapidly down-valley moving, barn-burning Federals. The result was heavy skirmishing and a major fight on October 9 at Tom's Brook, near Fisher's Hill. Union cavalry, once a limp left hand but now a clenched right fist, defeated the Southerners and chased them twenty miles, "the Woodstock Races." One Confederate officer noted in his memoirs: "our troops had more dread of Sheridan's cavalry than of his infantry and our cavalry was unequal to them."[46]

> "Thursday Oct. 6: Mount Jackson we left Harisburg at day light gut hear at dark 25 ms we past through New market at 2 PM went into camp at 9 PM
> "Oct. 7: Mount Jackson left at daylit past through Edensburg at 3 PM on to woodstock an went into camp at 8 PM for the knight
> "Oct. 8: Woodstock we left at day light an come to fisher hill at 7 AM an fornd a lin an stopt

"Oct. 9: Strawsburge we gut in heare at dark last knight it is vary cold hear to day we have capturd 700 prisners sinse last Saturday morning
"Oct. 10: Middletown we air heare this morning it is vary cold a hevey frost last knight we capturd 300 prisners 17 armberla[nces] 40 wagans 15 peases of artillary
"Oct. 11: we air in camp I am on camp gard to day all is quiart an faire and plesant Dr faire [Thayer] come[47]
"Oct. 12: Middletown all is still and quiart and I was releaved from gard at 10 AM"

The next day, October 13, brought an engagement at Hupp's Hill, located northeast of Strasburg and just across Cedar Creek from the Union camps. The once quiet afternoon was interrupted by exploding Confederate shells among General Crook's tents to the east of the Nineteenth Corps. Because daily skirmishes were a feature of the landscape, the response (but not the outcome) was somewhat routine. Considering the rebel force to be small, for woods obscured the area, two brigades were ordered off to challenge the Confederates. However, the brigades, totaling about two thousand men, became separated and a single brigade faced many times its number in Confederates. Mauled and forced to retreat, the men in blue suffered 209 casualties.[48]

"Oct. 13: Middletown the rebels atacked us at 2 PM. an thar was a hevey fight untill dark we brock camp at 10 PM moved one ms
"Oct. 14: Middletown we air lying on our arms at 10 AM we march back to whair we was in camp an pitch tents at 1 one O Clock
"Oct. 15: we was cald at 5 AM an stood in alin of battle until sunrise but all was quiart along the lines through the day
"Oct. 16: we was caled up at 1[1] AM and sut to work a bilding brestworks gut them dun at 4 expectid a fit"

Smith managed to write home in the midst of privation from cold, shortage of rations and clothing, and "hevey" fights. His optimism and confidence are apparent and his transformation from farmer to soldier is, quite obviously, complete. Lewis's next letter is dated September 16, in conflict with his diary. Events fit October 16 rather than September 16.

Middletown Va Sept [October] 16 1864 My dear wife

I agane seat my self to let you no how I am my helth is good hoping this may find you all the same at home I have not had eny maile for some

> *time from eny of you it is bad agitting it heare we air heare a makeing astand we was cald up at 2 o clock and went to fortafieing we expectid to be atacktid to day the rebels air hevely reingforsed they atacked us last Thursday [October 13] and thay gut hansomly whiped and I am athinking thay had better let us alone if thay no what is good for them*
>
> *We air about 65 ms from Harpars fary I think thay will make astand heare this winter I hardly no what to rit for I [h]ave not but five minits to rit in thare is one thing I want you to send me some postid stamps for I cant wright agane untill I git some I gut some paper and invelops paid 3 cents a sheat for it. I have gut som mony to send to you gest as soon as I can send it with safty I am in hops to soon for I expect you need it vary much for it must bee hard times with you it is with us we have had a vary hard time sinse we have bin in this valley and I am in hops that we shall have it easeare when we git into winter quartars whitch will doutless come soon then we can git time to wright and wash our cloth[ing] we air a suffering some for want of cloathing whitch we cant git ges yet it is most inpsible to git raishtions to keep us from suffering but it will be differant soon then I can rit you more I shall hafto close give my love to all take agood shair your self ciss the little ons and take one for yourself from me so good day from yours L Q Smith I have not hern from the woundid sins roat to you befor*

Despite the Federals' obvious success in the valley, Early's force, though having suffered losses, remained a threat. Sheridan's lines of supply and communication were already stretched uncomfortably in a valley that "was the paradise of bushwhackers and guerrillas."[49] Sheridan was also under pressure to use the valley as a base to operate into central Virginia toward Charlottesville and Gordonsville. As a result of these realities, he left his army, on October 15, for consultations in Washington. The Army of the Shenandoah remained at Middletown, camped just east of Cedar Creek between Strasburg and Middletown. At this place, the valley is much wider to the west, the Union right, than to the east. From this recognized weakness on the right, any enemy attack was expected to come. However, for a few days, at least, quiet would prevail.

~ *Fourteen* ~

Battle of Cedar Creek: Eve of Near Defeat and Final Victory

October 18 to December 31, 1864

Probably no army turned into its blankets with a more perfect feeling of security than that which possessed Sheridan's troops on the night of October 18.

—Sgt. Francis Buffum

Soldiers opportunities during action, to study a battle as a whole being impossible, ow[e] to his narrow environments in the hurly burly of the conflict, shrouded in battle smoke.[1]

—James E. Taylor

GENERAL EARLY'S CONFEDERATES, THOUGH REDUCED in force, had a weapon that gave them an edge—especially at Cedar Creek, where the opposing camps faced each other. That resource, on top of the northernmost promontory of Massanutten Mountain, was Signal Knob. From Signal Knob, reached by a foot trail from the valley, the rebels had a clear view of Sheridan's camps, his troop and cavalry dispositions, and artillery positions. Better than an observation balloon, it was the Civil War equivalent of a spy satellite. On October 17, the rebels were unusually observant. Confederate Gen. John B. Gordon and Stonewall Jackson's noted cartographer, Jedediah Hotchkiss, climbed to the overlook, about seventeen hundred feet above the valley floor. From there, they spotted a Union weakness and immediately planned to exploit it.

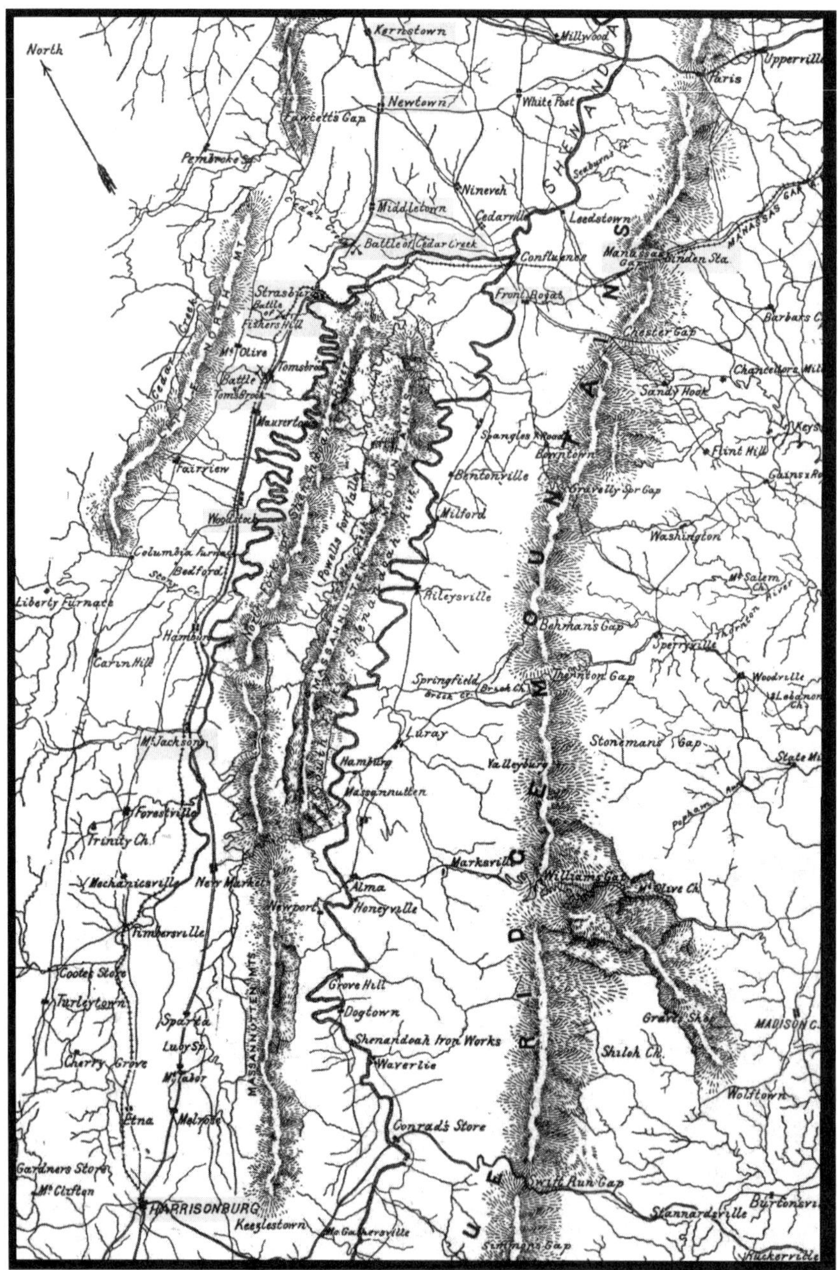

Map of the Upper Shenandoah Valley. Author's Collection.

On the evening of October 18, Sheridan, who had stopped for the night at Winchester on his return trip from Washington, warned his commanders to be on the alert for an attack. That same night, Crook's Eighth Corps lay camped on the Union left, facing Cedar Creek, nearly a mile above its confluence with the North Fork of the Shenandoah. To Crook's right successively lay the camps of the Nineteenth Corps, the Sixth Corps, Merritt's cavalry, and Custer's cavalry, although the cavalry's camps were several miles back from the creek and the infantry. The only cavalry on the left were deployed toward Front Royal about ten miles distant—the Union commanders' concern was for an attack directed to their right. "On the 18th reconnaissances on both [Union] flanks discovered no sign of a movement by the enemy."[2] Gordon and Hotchkiss scouted the Federals' positions a second time on the same day. The route to the enemy's defensive flaw, on their left, would go—for infantry but not artillery—especially in darkness.

Company K had moved with Sheridan's army down the valley (north) from Woodstock to Fisher's Hill, to Strasburg, and then to Cedar Creek, several miles southwest of Middletown. Smith's account of the Cedar Creek battle opens with his entry for October 17 and a letter from Middletown on the eve of the battle. Asa Magoon had just returned to the company, an event noted in both Lewis's diary and his letter. Lewis expressed concern for friends and family, and he sent money home, saying that "it is hard work to send money from heare with safty."

Lewis also mentioned the hardship of the campaign, "most three month sinse" it "comense," and the cold. There had been a fight about once a week, frequent skirmishes and troop movements, and little sleep or rest.[3] Tired and uncomfortable, he acknowledged that he had no time "to rit," and from the months ahead, little correspondence survives—from Lewis or from any other soldiers. In several hundred letters and a handful of diaries, there is hardly enough comment about battle to fill a single page. Some of Lewis's fatigue was the result of having been called up almost every morning at four o'clock (or even earlier) to stand at arms. Unwittingly, however, the order for an early rise was canceled for the morning of October 19.[4]

> "Monday, Oct. 17: Middletown It has bin all quiart to day Asa Magoon come to the regment yesterday I send 25 dollars home to day by Captn
> "Oct. 18: Middletown all is quiart along the lines we air si[g]ning for cloathing to send in to draw cloathing."

Union soldiers had a forty-two-dollar annual clothing allowance, "which, ordinarily, is a sum sufficient for it . . ." Adequate clothing was a touchy subject "as in recent battles, the soldiers, by orders of their officers threw away some of their equipments, &c., in order the better to prepare them for the conflict . . ." Of necessity, they subsequently drew additional "supplies, thus exceeding the legal stipulated amount of money."[5] When men drew more than their allotted forty-two dollars, the overage was deducted from their pay.

Prices for clothing were fixed: "Forage cap $0.56, uniform coat 7.21, trousers 3.55, flannel shirt 1.46, flannel drawers .95 . . . knapsacks 2.14, blankets woolen 3.60 . . ." The War Department "directed that clothing lost by the casualties of war be replaced without expense to the soldier." This decision opened "an opportunity to lose all one's old clothes in a retreat or other pleasant circumstances, and our dear Uncle Sam would give us new."[6] The quartermaster would usually accumulate requests for articles of clothing or equipment and then place an order with the supply base in the rear, such as the one at Harpers Ferry.

Sheridan's Army. Quarter Master Stores, Harpers Ferry, Alfred R. Waud, Library of Congress.

Various supplies as well as commissary items were generally shipped from Baltimore and stored in the arsenal buildings at Harpers Ferry. To reach Sheridan's men, materials then went by rail to Stephenson's Depot, six miles north of Winchester, and were then transshipped by wagon teams up the valley. As late-autumn nights brought frost and discomfort, the process could take weeks. Supplementing the official supply system were sutlers, civilian peddlers, usually licensed or permitted, who operated from wagons or tents (or a cabin in a fixed post) and sold items and essentials not usually available through army supply.

Middletown Vr Sept [October] 18 year 1864 My Dear wife

I agane seat to wright a few lines to let you no of my helth whitch is vary good hoping this may find you all the same it has bin avary long time to me sinse I have hern from eny of you but I suspose you have wrightten but I have not reseve it yet it will come some time it has bin som what dificult agitting the maile to us sinse we have bin afighting but I hop we shall git it more reglar now it will be som time fore us to go into winter quarters then we shall git some rest I hop

We have had avary long hard campain one of the harddist of the war it has bin most three month sinse this campain comense I cannot give you a histry of it in wrighting when I see you I will tell you in words Every thing quiart this morning along the lines we aire wel fortifid hear and air still amaiking it stronger every day we aire caled up every morning at 4 or half past and form a line of battle and stand in a line untill sunrise it is gitting to be vary cold hear and we are git rather destertut of cloathing we have not had eny chanse to draw eny for some time we had to thro away all we had but what was on our backs

We was paid off two weeks ago last Sunday four month pay thair is fourty dollars inlotid to you the same as uesul I have sent you twenty five dollars 25c to Mr Mastin [Capt. O. H. Marston] the Capting sent it with his to his farther for it is hard work to send mony from heare with safty he sent it to the express ofice by the settler [sutler] you will hafto go after it yourself for he will give it to no one els I want you to take this money and ues it to make you all as comfatible as can for I donot want you to suffer if I hafto take good care of yourself as you can and keep (blotted) and not worry eny about me for I ges (blotted).

Asa has got back to the regment Sunday his helth good thos that gut woundid are gitting along first rait the last I heard from them I want you to writ as often as you can wright gest how you all air and how you air all agittin along rit as it is you sed that mother was sick to Lucy J in your last letter I was vary sorry to heare it I hop she is better befor this you may think it hard my not riting oftener but you wood knot if you new how it was it has bin most imposibele for me to git a chanse to rit or send it after it is roat but I will do the best (blot) give my love to all take a good shair your self from yours Lewis Q Smith

As Lewis signed and sealed his letter and turned in, there was no hint of what the new day would bring—that "perfect feeling of security" that Buffum described on the night of October 18 would be shattered. Despite Sheridan's concern and his warning, there was "the perfect confidence that Early had been so gloriously whipped that he would never dare attack . . ."[7] Although some in the Union camps were restless, almost no one dreamed of the surprise that occurred the following morning. Many would be awakened as Confederate soldiers fired into their tents. Lewis described that day, about which volumes have been written, with a two-line entry:

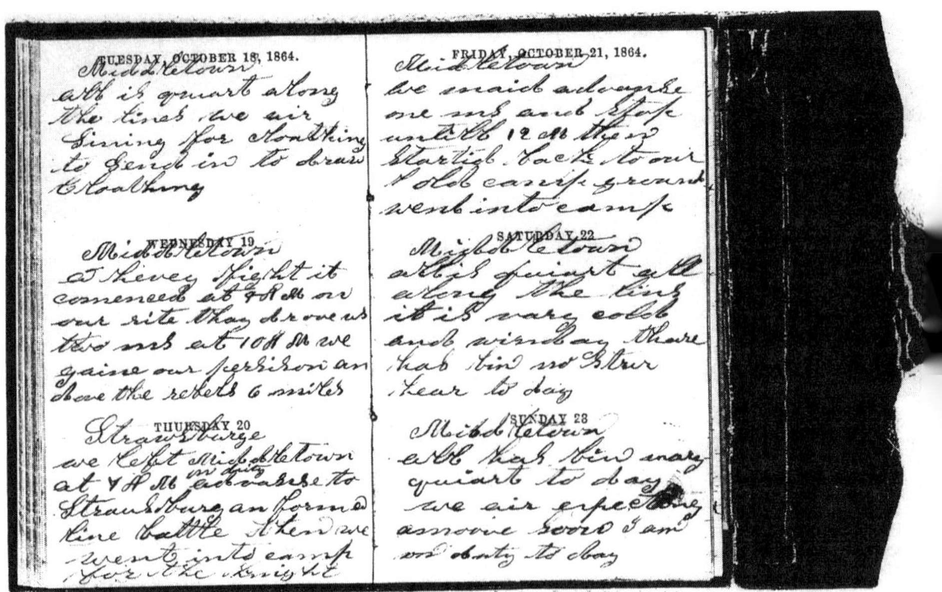

TUESDAY, OCTOBER 18, 1864.
Middletown
all is quiart along
the lines we air
[illegible] for somthing
to send in to draw
Cloathing

WEDNESDAY 19
Middletown
a hevey fight it
comenced at 4 A M on
our rite thay drove us
two mils at 10 A M we
gaine our persision an
drove the rebels 6 miles

THURSDAY 20
Strawsburge
we left Middletown
at 7 A M in duty advanced to
Strausburg an formd
line battle then we
went into camp
for the knight

FRIDAY, OCTOBER 21, 1864.
Middletown
we maid advance
one mil and stop
until 12 M then
startid back to our
old camp ground
went into camp

SATURDAY 22
Middletown
all is quiart all
along the line
it is vary cold
and windy thare
has bin no stur
here to day

SUNDAY 23
Middletown
all has bin vary
quiart to day
we air expecting
a move soon I am
on duty to day

Lewis Q. Smith's diary entry for October 19, 1864. Sandwich Historical Society.

> "Oct. 19: Middletown a hevey fight it comenced at 9 AM on our rite thay drove us two ms at 10 AM we gaine our persison an d[r]ove the rebels 6 miles"

Early's men threaded a needle, walking at night on a rough, narrow path on the west slope of Massanutten, with the North Fork of the Shenandoah at times almost below their left elbows. Silently crossing the frigid river where it began to curve eastward around Massanutten, they approached the Union left from both the flank and the *rear*. The moon had set, there was a dim glow of approaching dawn, and a veil of fog concealed their progress. Three other Confederate columns approached the Union lines, two in the center and one on the Union right, where an attack was expected to occur. The coordinated Confederate assault began at about five o'clock, and many Union soldiers, roused and routed, fled, leaving behind camps, artillery, and supplies. Not all of Sheridan's army had been asleep. The Second Division of the Nineteenth Corps, which included the Fourteenth, had been awakened shortly after three and by 4:30 stood at arms behind the breastworks.[8] Its intention had been a reconnaissance of the Confederates' position in force, but instead the rebels quickly found the Federals.

The Confederates first struck Crook's Army of West Virginia (Eighth Corps) on the Union left, followed by the Nineteenth Corps at the Union center. Men of the Fourteenth soon heard musket fire, and, off to their left, witnessed Confederates leaping over the works and firing into the tents of sleeping men. After the first volley, they heard the Rebel yell and "knew that Early's host was upon us."[9] There was silence in their front until shells started coming in. Soon thereafter, to their rear, they heard a musket volley, another Rebel yell, and saw a "well-formed Rebel line advancing."[10] The First Division of the Nineteenth Corps, now awake, formed to face the rear. As the rebels approached, the Union men suffered heavy losses and fell back. In turn, bullets struck the Second Division and the Fourteenth, which retreated. The battle, becoming a rout, was now about ninety minutes old.

As the Fourteenth successively fell back, it managed to stay alive. When its commander, Capt. Theodore Ripley, was captured, Capt. Oliver H. Marston of Sandwich took command.[11] When it appeared that the only colors left on the immediate field of battle were those of the Fourteenth, General Birge ordered soldiers of the first brigade (Second Division, Nineteenth Corps) to rally to the regiment's flag. At this point, the first brigade

The Confederate Army under Early, Surprising the Federal Forces at Cedar Creek, on the 19th of October, 1864. Belle Grove Mansion on the left. Author's Collection.

Belle Grove House, General Sheridan's Hd. Qts. At Cedar Creek . . . Gordon's troops sweeping the 19th Corps before it by the house at dawn. James E. Taylor Sketch, Courtesy of the Western Reserve Historical Society.

Sheridan's Ride. Battle of Cedar Creek, Alfred R. Waud, Library of Congress.

and the Fourteenth had been thrown back fifteen hundred yards, and much of the Nineteenth had been pushed almost three miles. Occupying higher ground and in a better defensive position, the Sixth Corps, on the Union right, fared better and initially repulsed the enemy. The Sixth was soon forced to retreat, but without suffering the disorganization of the other two corps.

About eleven o'clock, after his famous ride from Winchester, at a gallop, for he had heard the far-off din of artillery, Sheridan arrived on the field of battle. As Confederate energy began to ebb, the Union retreat slowed. As Sheridan rode along the *front* of his re-forming lines, his soldiers became revitalized and inspired. At four in the afternoon, when Sheridan gave the order to advance, the Union position was about one thousand yards from the Confederates, and again the Nineteenth Corps and the Fourteenth would be in the thick of it. As the Confederate left was turned, its entire line began to collapse and fall back. Union soldiers recovered much of their supplies and equipment and all the artillery lost earlier in the day. By nightfall, the Fourteenth had sustained as many casualties as any of the other five regiments of its brigade.

Washington, D.C., Civil War Ambulance Wagons and Drivers. Library of Congress photograph.

Among the dead was Company C's Sgt. J. Henry Jenks, who had often written of his insecurity in battle and more than once feared that he might never return to his family. "In the last charge, in the last moments of Rebel resistance," Jenks was "the last man who fell in battle in the Fourteenth."[12] Struck in the head by a "round shot" (cannonball), he was not borne home—buried instead at Winchester National Cemetery. Jenks, in an earlier letter home to his wife, Almina, had virtually written an epitaph:

> *Camp Adirondack Washington D.C. July 12th 1863 Dear Wife*
>
> *. . . I should not fear death, this kind of life has a tendency to wean one from the love of life, the soldier rushes into battle caring little for bullets, and what becomes of him; we have become so use to war that a thousand killed in battle is of little account, hardly worth noticing. Still a thousand hearts may be struck at the same time by a poisoned arrow whose wound will never heal. The bullet seeks out among the crowd the high in rank, and lays him low; he falls and dies, all covered with glory, and his body is bourne off the field and embalmed and sent home to his loved friends, who bury it under military escourt, and great pomp,*

surrounded by hosts of sympathizing friends, and the bosom companion hardly knows she is a widow in the great whirl of excitement. The poor lonely private falls, it may be, in fighting to save the life of his General; his body left on the battle field to be trampled on by the fierce charger, and a[d]vancing foe, and when the days slaughter is over, his body with scores of others, fill one common grave, and the news is bourne home through the publick press of his being lost on the field of battle. His anxious wife hears of the battle, and seeks the list of the lost, and there sees the name of her only loved one on earth save her children, and hope dies within her bosom, and greater pain does she suffer in her lonely cot, during the sleepless hours of that night than will ever be known to the world.[13]

Jenks's words were closer to the mark than he could ever have anticipated. In the center of the Winchester National Cemetery is a common grave located by four simple corner posts. Within this area lie the remains of 2,238 unidentified and unknown Civil War soldiers. A nearby plaque bears testimony to the burials with the words: "Even Though Their Names Are Unknown, The Sacrifice Of These Soldiers Will Never Be Forgotten." J. Henry Jenks, who longed for his family and his home and at times despaired of returning, is not among the 2,238. He lies instead in a small plot designated #1202.

Sgt. J. Henry Jenks, of Keene, N.H. Bruce Jackson photograph.

Lewis's cousin James Marcellus Smith, not quite twenty years old, later ordered to the U.S. General Hospital in Claysville, Maryland, wrote home on October 22, 1864. Musician soldiers (Marcellus was one) were frequently detailed to hospital duty and by October 1864 were also drilled as stretchermen. Three years earlier, battlefield medical care and evacuation of the wounded were disorganized and not even marginally competent. Ambulances were owned and controlled by the Quartermaster Corps and driven by civilian teamsters hired for that purpose. As a result, in 1861 and 1862, ambulance drivers had led the flight from both first and second battles at Bull Run—"villainous conduct."[14] Those wounded who could walked. Efforts to establish an ambulance system, controlled by division or brigade medical directors and utilizing trained litter bearers, finally resulted in the Ambulance Corps Act of March 1864.[15]

Sheridan hospital, Ward 20, Winchester Va   Dear Parents

> *I have just written a letter for Asa Magoon. He was wounded through the left arm, a flesh wound between elbow and shoulder . . . Our Regiment was cut up awfully It is getting to be cold here. The wounded are suffering awfully tonight. Some haven't got a thing to put over them. There are thousands suffering from the cold and wounds. It is awful to think of. This is a cruel war. I can see, you can imagine . . . Hospital life is a hard life for me but it is my duty & I shall do it as well as I can. I had rather carry a gun any day I have missed one fight by being kept here & perhaps saved my life.*[16]

Union sutlers, who had arrived at the camp with full wagons the night before the battle, may have contributed to the victory. It has been noted that some of the Confederates paused to loot the Union camps of the newly arrived goods—the pause's impact is still controversial. In the Fourteenth's history, this statement appears: "the Rebels devoted more energy to pillaging the camps than to following up their victory; giving Sheridan time to re-form the lines," rest his men, "and repel their [Confederate] charge in the afternoon."[17] General Early, perhaps self-servingly, attributed the time spent looting as a factor in his defeat.[18] Finally, it should be conceded that Early's men had marched all night and fought all morning, and by afternoon were hungry and tired. Their momentum and their victory were irretrievably lost.

The battle of Cedar Creek essentially marked the end of Confederate strength in the valley and was a major contribution to the ultimate Union victory. One Confederate participant, Maj. Henry Kyd Douglas, wrote: "One thing is certain: it was to us an irreparable disaster, the beginning of the end."[19] For service at Cedar Creek on October 19, 1864, Sheridan and his army received the congratulations of Lincoln, Grant, and Sherman and the thanks of Congress. The battle was also the inspiration for the poet/artist T. Buchanan Read's poem "Sheridan's Ride."

"Oct. 20: Strawsburge we left Middletown at 7 AM on duty advanse to Strawsburg an formed line battle then we went into camp for the knight
"Oct. 21: Midletown we maid advanse one ms and stop untill 12 N then startid back to our old camp ground went into camp
"Oct. 22: Middletown all is quiart all along the lins it is vary cold and winday thare has bin no strir hear to day
"Oct. 23: Middletown all has bin vary quiart to day we air expecting amoove soon I am on duty to day
"Oct. 24: Middletown it is quiart along the lines I came off from duty to day it is vary cold an windy"

Home in New Hampshire, both "the Franconia and White Mountain ranges" were now capped with "spotless snow," magnificent in daytime but, when illuminated by a bright moon, showed "a bleak and weird appearance." As guesthouses closed for the winter atop Mount Washington, on one of the clearest days of the season, October 17, "the ocean view" was "so extensive that upwards of thirty vessels were counted off Portland [Maine] harbor."[20] In the Shenandoah, Union tents were folded as regiments began to be parsed out to other fields of battle.

"Oct. 25: Middletown all quiart and it is plesant thare has bin no stur with the army to day all is quiart
"Oct. 26: Middletown Every thing is quiart along our lines a part of the six a part of the eight coar has gon over the mountain to day
"Oct. 27: Middletown every thing is vary quiart along the lines the third Bridgad of the Second divison 19 Choar left this morning for Harpar fary
"Oct. 28: Middletown all is quiart this morning coald and windy I went on picket at 4 PM gut on post at dark three ms from camp
"Oct. 29: Middletown I am on picket Stood at arms all knight form aline of schirmish at 4 stood untill 6 AM
"Oct. 30: Middletown all is quiart to day I gut in from picket last knight after dark we had avary cold time of it
"Oct. 31: Middletown all is quiart along the lines to day we had a ginerill inspection and was mustard in for pay to day"

Third Winchester (or Opequon), Fisher's Hill, Cedar Creek, and other engagements had not been without significant cost to Union forces. Approximately thirteen hundred men were killed and another ten thousand wounded: "The total number of amputations after these battles was 388 (3.9%). All these were primary and generally skillfully performed."[21]

The numbers are straightforward: about one in twenty-five casualties lost a limb. In early October 1862, in the aftermath of Antietam, Dr. William Child wrote: "dressing bullet wounds and stumps. The worst part is the bad smell."[22]

However, Dr. Child's estimate of the frequency of amputation was disconcordantly higher than that noted above for the Shenandoah campaign: "The wounds in all parts you can think, but seven tenths of all have suffered amputation."[23] Some of the discrepancy may be attributable to the term "primary" used above—that is, immediate amputations as opposed to later or secondary cases when extremities, for example, became infected. Of all the New Hampshire regimental histories, only that of the Third Regiment provides a detailed list of wounds and wounded. Of 609 wounds, amputation is noted in twenty-one cases (3.5 percent), an incidence about equal to that of the Shenandoah campaign. Of the twenty-one, three were thumbs, eight were fingers, five arms, four legs, and one foot.[24]

From the official medical reports for the Shenandoah campaign (two years following Dr. Child's comments), it is clear that improvements in ambulance transport, field hospitals, and hospitals behind the lines had been made. There is also a suggestion that the incidence of amputations decreased and some evidence that amputations were better performed, though certainly not by modern standards of technique and hygiene. A contemporary description was published in Frank Moore's *The Civil War in Song and Story:*

> How an Amputation is Performed.— Imagine yourself in the hospital of the Sixth Corps after a battle. There lies a soldier, whose thigh has been mangled by a shell; and, although he may not know it, the limb will have to be amputated to save his life. Two surgeons have already pronounced this decision; but, according to the present formation of a hospital in this camp, no one Surgeon, not two, can order an amputation, even of a finger. The opinion of five, at least, and sometimes more, including the Division surgeon, always a man of superior skill and experience, must first be consulted, and then, if there is an agreement, depend upon it, the operation is necessary. This did not used to be, in the earlier months of the war; but it is so now . . . the man . . . is approached by one of the Surgeons, and told that he will be attended to, and whatever is best will be done for him. They cannot examine his wound thoroughly where he lies, so he is tenderly lifted on to a rough table. So, then, the decision is communicated

> to him that he must lose his leg. While the operating Surgeon is examining, and they are talking to the poor fellow, chloroform is being administered to him through a sponge . . . The inhalation goes on, and the beating of the pulse is watched; and when it is ascertained that he is totally oblivious to all feeling, the instruments are produced, and the operation commences. Down goes the knife into the flesh, but there is no tremor or indication of pain . . . the Surgeons are cutting, and carving, and sawing away. The leg is off, and carried away; the arteries are tied up, and the skin is neatly sewed over the stump. The effect of chloroform is relaxed; and when the patient opens his eyes, a short time afterwards, he sees a clean white bandage where his ghastly wound had been, and his lost limb is removed. He feels much easier, and drinks an ounce and a half of good whisky with gusto. This is a real instance of amputation, and the chief characteristics of the description will answer every one.[25]

> "Nov. 1: Middletown all is quiart this morning it is vary cold to day no pickets sent out of our regments to day
> "Nov. 2: Middletown all is still quiart to day it is cold it is squala this after noon and cold
> "Nov. 3: Middletown every thing quiart along the lines I am on camp gard to day an it is cold and rainy I went on gard at 1 PM
> "Nov. 4: Middletown every thing quiart I was releved from gard at 2 PM to day and went to gitting out stockaiding for my tent
> "Nov. 5: Middletown all is quiart on our lines to day John Goss [Pvt. John W. Goss of Sandwich] and I have bin astockaiding our tent an fixing it up to day
> "Nov. 6: Middletown all is quiart this morning thar has bin slit schirmish in front this after noon
> "Nov. 7: Middletown all is quiart to day we have past a choar revue to day it is wet and rainy"

Company K remained at Middletown for approximately three weeks—November 8 would be its last day there before moving on to Newtown (since 1880, Stephens City). On that day, the men voted for president: "We was caled up at 4 AM ordored to moove at daylight and was red[y] all day we votid for presedent 194 Lincon 16 Mclelin in our regment our Co 22 [to] 1."[26] The regiment had numbered only about 350 men when it returned from Louisiana, and although it had been supplemented with recruits, the number voting reflects the condition of the Fourteenth after several months of almost continous fighting. In addition to being under strength, some soldiers were not of voting age (twenty-one).

New Hampshire's election results were noticed: In a "Special Dispatch to the *Transcript*" on November 8, the Granite State was "looking well." As of two in the afternoon in Concord, quiet prevailed. There was optimism for the Republicans:

> A full vote will be thrown. Lincoln party jubilant. The State is regarded sure for Lincoln, and returns thus far received indicate quite as large a majority as last spring when the soldiers were all furloughed.[27]

In Sandwich, the voting was closer. In 1860, the Republicans had received 260 votes to 152 for the Democrats. In 1864, the numbers were 251 to 213—it was still a divided town in a divided country. Had Early succeeded on October 19, for he came very close, the consequences might have been enormous. Sheridan was not the only one apprehensive about a major reverse prior to the election of November 8, 1864. Gen. Ulysses S. Grant later wrote:

> I had reason to believe that the administration was a little afraid to have a decisive battle fought at that time, for fear it might go against us and have a bad effect on the November elections. The [Chicago] convention which had met and made its nomination of the Democratic candidate for the Presidency had declared the war a failure.[28]

The political risk of an adverse outcome in the valley was quite likely appreciated by almost everyone. At the battle of Fisher's Hill, it was reported that "one of our [Union] generals, when he saw the rebel line break and run . . . exclaimed, 'There goes another plank out of the Chicago Platform!' "[29] Unquestionably, the November elections were a sound defeat for Copperheads and Peace Democrats. Lincoln was reelected and the war would continue until victory was attained. With Union control of the Mississippi, the ever-tightening blockade and seizure of southern ports, the fall of Atlanta in early September, and the defeat of Early in the Shenandoah Valley, the Confederacy was crumbling and doomed.

> "Wednesday, Nov. 9: Newtown we brock camp at 10 AM and march we fell back two miles belo Newtown Village and went into camp
> "Nov. 10: Newtown we air redy to march at day light I went out with a forrige train to day we mooved a short distant an went into camp

"Nov. 11: Newtown we mooved a short distant fightting in our front we air in a line of battle hevey schirmishing on our wright at dark
"Nov. 12: Newtown we air afortifing expect an atack every minit our men pitch into the rebs and drove them and took some prisners[30]
"Nov. 13: Newtown our Cavely went out last knight and d[r]ove the rebs took 5 peases of artillary not much fighting to day
"Nov. 14: Newtown all is quiart today no rebels in sight we have bin afixing up our tents I reseved a letter from my wife to day"

President Lincoln and the North were jubilant over the victories in the valley, which Lincoln acknowledged in General Orders No. 282:

War Department, Adjutant-General's Office
Washington, November 14, 1864

Ordered by the President, I. That the resignation of George B. McClellan as major-general in the United States Army, dated November 8 and received by the Adjutant-General on the 10th instant, be accepted as of the 8th of November.

II. That for the personal gallantry, military skill, and just confidence in the courage and patriotism of his troops displayed by Philip H. Sheridan on the 19th day of October at Cedar Run, whereby, under the blessing of Providence, his routed army was reorganized, a great national disaster averted, and a brilliant victory achieved over the rebels for the third time in pitched battle within thirty days, Philip H. Sheridan is appointed major-general in the United States Army, to rank as such from the 8th day of November, 1864.

By order of the President of the United States:
E. D. TOWNSEND, Assistant Adjutant-General. [31]

One member of the 143rd Regiment New York Volunteers did not get the above news, nor had his fellow soldiers on their march of destruction from Atlanta to Savannah. Reading a rebel paper on December 19, 1864, they learned of the reelection of Lincoln, McClellan's resignation, and Sheridan's promotion. The soldier summarized the prevailing mood: "Bully for that."[32]

Back in the Shenandoah, newly promoted Maj. Gen. Sheridan promulgated two orders of note, both dated November 17. The first, General Order No. 25, officially established "the army now serving in the Valley" as the

"Army of the Shenandoah" and their "present camp" would thereafter be known as "Camp Russell."[33] The camp, southwest of Winchester near Kernstown, was named for Maj. Gen. David Allen Russell (1820–1864), who sustained a chest wound at Opequon on September 19. Despite his injury, he remained on the field in command of a Sixth Corps division during "a critical moment of the battle," until a shell fragment passed through his heart.[34] Camp Russell would be home to Lewis, the Fourteenth, and thousands of other soldiers through the end of the year.

The second order, No. 11, was an award of flags and badges, Lewis's "Corps bage" mentioned below, to the officers and men of the Nineteenth Army Corps. The badges would be issued by the chief quartermaster and for enlisted men would be "cloth, two inches square, and worn on the side of the hat or top of the cap." Color variations designated units by division and brigade, and enlisted men who chose to could "supply themselves with metallic badges."[35]

> "Nov. 15: Newtown it is vary cold hear and squalla but all is quiart on our lines I am on camp gard to knight
> "Nov. 16: Newtown I am on gard to day releved to knight it [is] quit plesant to day all is quiart
> "Nov. 17: in Newtown Camp near Opquan All is quiart to day John Goss and I air stockading our tents to day with hatits [hatchets] and one spaid
> "Nov. 18: Newtown Camp near Opquan we finished our [work] this morning it is rainry to day I reseved a letter from Edwin A Smith [B. B.'s son] to day
> "Nov. 19: Newtown Camp near Opquan rainy this morning Cleard off in the middle of the day plesant I am on camp gard to knight
> "Nov. 20: Newtown it is wet and rainy all is quiart in our front I was releved from gard at dark to knight it is muddy
> "Nov. 21: New town Camp near Opquan all is quiart to day it is vary wet an rainy we had one compny drill from 10 to 11 AM it is gitting vary muddy
> "Nov. 22: Newtown Camp near Opquan all is quiart I have roat two letters one to B. one to my wife two compny drills I drilled the requits
> "Nov. 23: Newtown all is quiart to day it is fair and cold the ground is frozen dresperaid ordors Corps bage army of the Cumberland Camp Rusill [Russell] the band com to the regment

A gladsome sight to the Blue Coats was the arrival of a long train of Wagons loaded down with poultry and table luxuries contributions from Friends for a Thanksgiving feast. James E. Taylor Sketch. Courtesy of the Western Reserve Historical Society.

> "Nov. 24: Camp Rusell I went on camp gard last nit at dark I shall be releved at 5 PM for this thankgivin Turkeys chickins ducks an geas for this army a drespraid"

Thanksgiving was cold and quiet—except for the poultry, Lewis noted the occasion without sentiment. In fact, twenty-five wagons, "under heavy escort," carrying 43,814 pounds of poultry, had rolled into Winchester on Tuesday evening, November 22. A gift of the Thanksgiving Committee of New York to Sheridan's army, an additional six thousand pounds had been dropped off at Harpers Ferry and Martinsburg. Sheridan magnaminously ordered that the gifts "be distributed only among the enlisted men, and by Wednesday night . . . the distribution was fully and fairly made." There was a benefit to the late-November cold: "Thanks to the very cold weather of Tuesday and Wednesday, we found the turkeys in first rate condition." Agents of the Thanksgiving Committee rode the lines and surveyed the impact of the 24 1/2 tons of poultry:

The want of proper appliances compelled most of the men to broil or stew their turkeys, but every one seemed fully satisfied, and appreciated the significance of this sympathetic thank-offering from the loyal North. One soldier said to me, "It isn't the turkey, but the idea that we care for," and he thus struck the keynote of the whole festival. Could the donors of this Thanksgiving gift have been with us on this ride, they would have felt satisfied that, whether as a token of grateful appreciation of past valor or as the inspiration of future effort in the good cause, it had not been made in vain.[36]

"Nov. 25: Camp Rusell all is quiart it is fair an plesant Co drill at 10. AM. battalon drill at 3. P.M. drespraid at 4 1/2 PM

"Nov. 26: Camp Rusill all is quiart to day it is plesant a little rainy this after noon we had drespraid and drills to day

"Nov. 27: Camp Rusill we had a generill inspection and a bridgad drespêraid Frank Fellowes Herman Blood James Parit come to the regment to day[37]

"Nov. 28: Camp Rusill all is quiart to day fair an plesant to Co drills and dresperaid I am on Camp gard to knight

"Nov. 29: Camp Rusill It is vary plesant I was on camp gard today releved at 6. AM a battalon drill this forenoon and dresperaid at 4 PM

"Nov. 30: Camp Rusill Plesant and fair battalion drill monthly inspection dresperaid I reseved a letter from home mailed the 17 an a pair of mitens and feattings

"Dec. 1: Camp Rusill it is vary plesant two company drills an dresperaids the part of the Six Corp left to day

"Dec. 2: Camp Rusill Fair an plesant all is quiart two Co drill I drilled the recruits one co on dresperaid to day I am on Camp gard to knight

"Dec. 3: Camp Rusill it is squally I am on Camp gard to day two Coprills air aporntid. H. Gilman T. Fenton one drill C. A. Coffiren"[38]

It may be recalled that 1st Sgt. James H. Gilman had been busted, reduced to ranks, on November 7, 1863. Subsequently, he served honorably. He was wounded on September 19 at Opequon, but, the wound not being severe, he recovered. Promoted to corporal on November 15, 1864, he mustered out with the regiment on July 8, 1865. He did not return to Sandwich, but moved to Grand Detour, on the Rock River, about eighty miles due west of Chicago in northern Illinois. Grand Detour was home to the Vermont blacksmith John Deere and the first steel plow in 1837.

Among those mentioned below is Pvt. Benjamin Estes, a farmer who died of consumption in 1866 after returning home to Sandwich. Ransom D. Buzzell, an eighteen-year-old recruit and a carpenter from Lake Village (Lakeport), New Hampshire, enlisted with his sixteen-year-old brother, Ebenezer M. Buzzell, in Company K on January 5, 1864. Ransom, hit by a ball, sustained a scalp wound at Fisher's Hill on September 22, 1864, and Eben was similarly struck in the head three days before at Opequon. Both survived. Warren A. Glidden was a Pembroke farmer, age nineteen, when he enlisted on August 15, 1862. Both he and Henry H. Moulton, another Company K Sandwich farmer, survived the war.

"Dec. 4: Camp Rusill it is vary plesant Sunday inspection Bridgade drespraid Some fits today
"Dec. 5: Camp Rusill All is quiart it is plesant one Battalon drill one Co drill and a dresperaid We had a first Liu in our Camp A. Hassa 2 brig
"Dec. 6: Camp Rusill all quiart fair an plesant two Co drills drespraid Benjamin Esters come to the regment Sunday the 4
"Dec. 7: Camp Rusill all is quiart in front one battalon drill one Co drill drespraid I drilled the recruits one our
"Dec. 8: Camp Rusill Fair and cold I am on picket to day all is quiart and coldist day we have had this fall a dresperaid
"Dec. 9: Camp Rusill I was on picket untill 4 PM it was a vary cold knight Ransom Buzzell, Henry Moulton come to the regment last knight.
"Dec. 10: Camp Rusill all is quiart we had a snow stowm last knight thare was about eight inches I reseved two letters one from Lucy and one from wife
"Dec. 11: Camp Rusill it is plesant to day I roat two letters one to Lucy one to my wife Henery Moulton come into the tent with Goss an I
"Dec. 12: Camp Rusill it is cold an windy the snow flys like fog James H Gilman come to the Co. last nite and Worin Glidden come today"

In December 1864, Gen. George Henry Thomas (1816–1870) defeated Confederate Gen. John Bell Hood's (1831–1878) army in a two-day battle outside of Nashville. For this major victory over the Confederate Army of the Cumberland, Thomas was promoted to major general and received the thanks of Congress. General Thomas and his army were the first of Sherman's men to enter Atlanta.

"Dec. 13: Camp Rusill all is quiart it is coald and windy it has bin cloudy all day I reseved a ltter from my wife to day

"Dec. 14: Camp Rusill it coald and windy all is quiart to day Capt Tolman is Promotid to Major of our Regment and took Comand to knight[39]

"Dec. 15: Camp Rusill Cloudy and coald all is quiart Capt. O. H. [Marston] returned to his Compny and took Comand of his Compny cold out wind[40]

"Dec. 16: Camp Rusill All is quiart thar was 30 guns fiard from our batter[ie]s to day for a chear over Gin Tomas victry am on camp gard to nit dresperaid 1500 prisners 17 guns

"Dec. 17: Camp Rusill all is quiart thar was a surlute of 30 guns fiard heare to day over Gin Thormas is victtry 60 guns an 5000 prisners taken I came of from gard to nit dresperaid"

Confederate President Jefferson Davis's demise from poison, referred to below, was rumor.

"Dec. 18: Camp Rusill Va all is quiart we had a Sunday inspection to day it dull and misty I helped Henery Moulton an Gorge Haddock bild them a tent[41]

"Dec. 19: Camp Rusill dull wether the 8 Corps left hear to day [for West Virginia] and I took down one of thair tents and have bin agarding it

"Dec. 20: Camp Rusill Va it fair and coald I gut my stockadin along to the regment I gardid it till noon the[y] halled it dresperaid henry gilman come to day

"Dec. 21: Camp Rusill Va it snows this morning we heard that Jef Davas was ded pois[on]ing himself Gen Grant telegraf to Gen Shirden yesterday he was ded

"Dec. 22: Camp Rusill it is vary coald an windy I am on picket to day thare is about two or three inches snow"

The remnants of Early's army were now out of the valley: "On the 22d a cavalry reconnaisance brought back the news . . . Our work was done but we did not know it."[42] There was other good news: the capture of Savannah on the morning of December 21, 1864. General Sherman notified President Lincoln of the victory as a Christmas present. Despite the cold, this Christmas had substantially more promise than any of the previous four.

If Friday, December 23, 1864, was the "coaldist nit" for Lewis, the folks back home were no better off. Wednesday's snowstorm had been followed by a "cold snap," high northerly winds and temperatures that were eighteen below at Concord Depot, on Friday morning. Stages were shut down and the previous day's "Owl train"—the "down express," or night run, from Montreal to Boston—was fourteen hours late rolling into Concord. The Friday down train had not even reached White River Junction, Vermont, and the telegraph reported that "hands were busy at Northfield, Vt., sawing wood to raise steam—not a very easy task, considering the extreme temperature."[43]

Lewis was "laid up with the sick" headache. In classic migraine, nausea and vomiting typically follow the onset of a severe one-sided (unilateral) headache. The misery of the headache is thus compounded by the "sickness." The previous mention (twice) of Lewis's mother's having "the headache" suggests the commonly accepted familial relationship.[44] Without any details, it is difficult to identify Lewis's "nuritys." Neuritis is generally an inflammation of a nerve, resulting in pain, numbness or a tingling sensation, or muscle weakness (or all), usually in an extremity.

"Dec. 23: Camp Rusill it is faire and coald I gest come in from picket to knight it was the coaldist nit I ever was on duty John Atward [of Sandwich] an Em[er]son come to the regment last nit[45]

"Dec. 24: Camp Rusill Va all is quiart it is faire and plesant H. Gileman J. Goss J. Parot and I have bin pooting up a tent for winter to day

"Dec. 25: Camp Rusill Va All is quiart and it is vary plesant to day it is Crismas day and I have bin in my tent all day a writing one to my wife

"Dec. 26: Camp Rusill Va it is foggy and misty I am laid up with the sick hedach thair was a surluit of 50 guns fiard by our batrs over the capture of Survaner [Savannah]

"Dec. 27: Camp Rusill Va it is vary plesant I am laidup with the nuritys [neuritis] John [Goss] an Henry [Moulton] air finishing our tent to day

"Dec. 28: Camp Rusill it is plesant and we air amooving into our tent this morning I am deatail to go on picket to knight

"Dec. 29: Camp Rusill I come in from picket to nite it stormed all nite an we have gut ordors to move to morrow morning

"Dec. 30: Camp 3 ms from Winchester we brock camp at 8. A.M. and gut heare at 2. P.M. it was 9 ms that we march it was vary muddy

> "Dec. 31: Camp at the depot it ha s bin vary stormy last nite an to day snow we was misterd for four months pay I reseved two letter one Lucy one wife"

Lewis had been fortunate in the battles in the Shenandoah—no bayonet, bullet, or shell fragment had had his name on it. In addition, good health had finally favored him. In the New Year and in January's cold, his luck would last. Instead of joining Union forces to be ground up by Lee's Confederates at Richmond in the coming months, another voyage awaited him and the Fourteenth.

~ Fifteen ~

The New Year 1865

Ordered to Georgia and War's End
January 1 to July 27, 1865

> *. . . thay air a releveing som of the troops I wish my turn wood come thay cant releve me to quick if thay try to sute me I am tyard of this plase*
>
> —Lewis Q. Smith, May 24, 1865

THE NEW YEAR OF 1865 OPENED WITHOUT SIGNIFICANT military news. The weather was nominally cold with freezing or subfreezing temperatures reported at least as far south as New York. The ice crop in northern New England, which was shipped to California, India, and even Australia, was already of "sufficient thickness for the market"—a foot or more thick. Sleighing in the vicinity of Boston was "superb" with no drifts or bare ground and an "icy foundation." The moonlit nights of the first week of January were expected to "be well improved by sleighing parties."[1] Sleigh riding was a singular American recreation (and mode of travel) and a very popular one: "Was there ever seen a person riding in a sleigh that looked unhappy? The eyes of the ladies fairly sparkle with delight as they step into one . . ."[2] Sleighs ran so quietly (and undoubtedly smoothly) that the law required bells on the horses; their jingling warned of a sleigh's otherwise "noiseless approach" and prevented accidents.[3]

Much farther to the south, Savannah had fallen to General Sherman's forces. The flooding of surrounding rice fields by Confederates had made attack of the city untenable—a siege was the result. On December 13, 1864, Union forces took Fort McAllister, lying on the Great Ogeechee River about a dozen miles south of Savannah, and established a vital supply link with the Union navy. Sherman's men quickly began moving the fort's heavy guns to within range of the city, demanding its surrender on December 17, 1864.[4]

Confederate Lt. Gen. William J. Hardee (1815–1873) refused to capitulate. Instead, he led his army out of the city, crossed the Savannah River on a makeshift pontoon bridge, and escaped in the early hours of December 21. As a result, there was little damage to Savannah. Union troops captured an estimated "five hundred thousand bushels" of rice, siege guns, gunboats, and whiskey, which was promptly "locked up, and the stills were all seized . . ." Residents of the city were taken by surprise "and were totally unprepared for such a result . . . very few of them succeeded in getting away."[5] Despite the surfeit of rice, the city was short of food and northern cities, including Boston, New York, and Philadelphia, responded. The crisis eased as supplies were donated and shipped south, arriving by the third week of January.

If the mood that characterized much of the North in early 1863 had been down and gloomy, it was equally so in the South by January 1865. A woman traveling north from Richmond represented that "affairs in that city" were "more gloomy than ever. Declarations that the rebel cause is hopeless are openly made among the people." It was also noted: "The rebel House of Representatives made enquiry of Jeff Davis if passports have been granted young men who do not wish to be in on the death of the Confederacy on their arrival at fighting age."[6] Despite steadily increasing desertions, significant Confederate forces remained in the field, and the war was not yet over.

With manpower in the South exhausted—the Confederate Congress still debated using blacks in its struggle—alternatives were becoming few to nil. In the North, in January 1865, despite optimism, the problem of *quality* recruits remained:

> One hundred sailors were selected at Portsmouth, N.H., to be sent to Baltimore . . . in the steamer *De Soto*. Upon being searched, most of them were found to be dressed in citizen's clothing under their outer dress, and were armed—with the intention, probably, of making their escape upon a convenient opportunity. Many of them are desperate characters. They were sent into the hold of the U.S. ship *Vandalia* and the hatches fastened down.[7]

After Saturday, December 31, Lewis's few remaining diary entries were written on the blank MEMORANDA pages with the dates penned in.

> "Sunday, Jan 1, 1865: Gin. Grovors. Hedquaters Near Spevenson depot I was deataild last nite in charge of 10 men to go to Gin. Grovers. hedquatars as his hedquaters gard and I have bin fixing up bunks to day
> "Monday 2: Grovers hedquaters we have bin a cleaning up to day
> "3: it is fair and coald I am on duty all of the time I reseved a letter from my wife to day I went to the regment to day
> "Jen 4: Grovers hedquartars it is coald and squaly the win blows and the snow flys thair is 18 men from 9 Coneta—[Connecticut?] with us heare on duty
> "Jen 5: it is vary coald our duty is vary lite one [h]our out 26 I am on duty all of the tim we draw rasho[n] heare to day to the hedquarters"

In late November 1864, the Nineteenth Corps had anticipated orders to join Grant's army. However, the Second Division of the Nineteenth, which included the Fourteenth, left on January 6, 1865, for Georgia. "Its final experiences" of the war would be "less thrilling and imposing than those of the veterans who confronted Lee at Five Forks and Appomattox," but they would have "a share in the culminating event,—the capture of the arch-traitor, the petticoat hero, the starver of our Union boys, the still unreconstructed, rabid Rebel, Jefferson Davis."[8] For Cpl. Lewis Smith and the Fourteenth, snow and sleighing would be part of a distant landscape. They were now destined for duty in Savannah.

> "Jen 6: Grover hedquarters we gut ordors last nit at dark to be redy to moove this morning at 9 o clock so we did and went to the cars and loaded our stuff and startid at 2 O C
> "Jen 7: Boltemoar we arived hear at 8 this morning we air still at the Gin yet we road all nit it rain all nit we sufferd vary badly
> "Jen 8: Boltmore we air awaiting for transport it vary coald I sent a box bundle in Scinners box
> "Jen 9: Boltimore we air still heare I am on six ours and off six we have ordors to be redy to moove at 8 O C to morrow morning I reseave a letter number 3
> "Jen 10: Boltomore we air all redy to moove at a minit worning it rains vary hard it rain all nite the first Bridgaid left at 10 for the boat and went aboard
> "Jen 11: Boltmore we air heare yet the hedquaters the first Bridgad is gon the 2 Bridgaid left to day I drawed raihions for this Squad to day

"Jen. 12: Boltemor we air still heare we air quartard in a bildin that Gin Washington bilt it is a brick house it has bin built 130 years
"Jen. 13: Boltamore we air heare all pack redy to move"

Smith's last diary entry is January 13, and he likely left on that date. Boarding the steamer *Ariel*, the Fourteenth sailed for Savannah, where they arrived on January 17—almost as Sherman's army was departing from that city. Savannah lies on the right, or south bank, of the Savannah River about eighteen miles from the sea. Fort Pulaski, situated on Cockspur Island at the mouth of the river, had guarded the ocean approaches. Built to withstand ordinary cannon fire, its seven-and-half-foot-thick *brick* walls crumbled to shells fired from rifled guns on nearby Tybee Island. In a notable military lesson, Fort McAllister's much smaller *earthworks* had withstood similar fire and had to be taken by infantry, not artillery. Fort Pulaski fell early in the war, on December 12, 1862, effectively closing Savannah to trade.

The city was (and is) known as the Forest City due to its large number of shade trees, both tropical and semitropical, and live oaks draped with Spanish moss. One of Sherman's men regarded Savannah as "the finest City I have seen in the Confederacy, and laid out in the best shape, with a great many Parks and Squares and Water works, and everything in good order."[9] The city, designed by its founder, James Edward Oglethorpe, who arrived in 1733, was a sharp contrast to the rather chaotic streets and thoroughfares of Boston. One of Savannah's colonial traditions is that powder stolen from a British magazine on May 11, 1775, was sent to Boston and used at the battle of Bunker Hill on June 17, 1775.[10]

Officially, the Fourteenth relieved the One Hundred Second Regiment New York Veteran Volunteers on January 19.[11] One member of the One Hundred Thirty-seventh New York Volunteers grumbled at the arrival of his fellow Yankees: "The 2d Division of the 19th Corps has arrived here from the Shenandoah Valley to relieve us, which we don't like much, as we think we are entitled to do the garrison duty after capturing the city." The writer described Savannah's citizens as "very sociable and <u>kind</u> to <u>us</u> and determined that our Division shall stay here."[12]

Initially camped in the middle of Savannah and assigned provost duty, the Fourteenth moved to a railroad yard on the west side of the city in late February. At the time, Savannah was filled with rebel deserters, Union sympathizers hiding from southern conscription, and thousands of black

View of Savannah, Looking East from the Cupola of the Exchange. Bay Street is to the right. Note the tents in the distant center. Author's Collection.

refugees. Military authority and control were essential during this period of instability, and two provost courts were quickly established to serve justice and to mete out punishments—to soldiers as well as citizens.

One such case was that of "Special Police vs. James Dobson." Company K's Private Dobson, a Scot and a substitute, served with the Fourteenth from July 1864 to July 1865. He was charged "with forcibly taking away a horse and wagon, the property of a negro." The sentence read that "he be placed in confinement five days."[13] On occasion, the maintenance of law and order was swift and severe, as in the death of a member of the "12th Me. Vols." Pvt. John King had been arrested for "drunkenness, and profane and indecent language in the street." While attempting to escape from the guardhouse, the "sentinel on the beat halted him twice, and then shot him through the neck, killing him almost instantly."[14]

One event of significance that could not have been missed by anyone in the Fourteenth was "a bombardment combined with a great conflagration" that occurred on January 27. A fire broke out just before midnight "at the

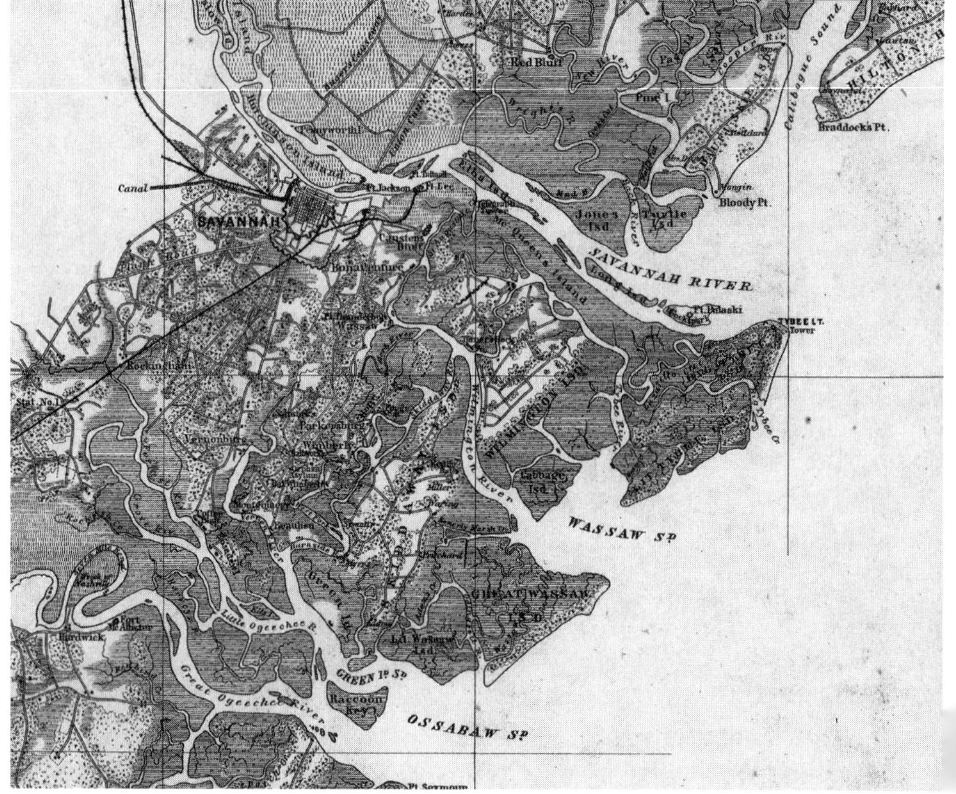

Civil War Map of Savannah and Environs. Note Hilton Head Island on the upper right, Fort Pulaski at the mouth of the Savannah River, and Fort McAllister on the Great Ogeechee River on the lower left. Adapted from Library of Congress Map

west-end of the city, not far from the Central Railroad buildings." Aided by a cold wind, the fire spread and touched off a nearby rebel naval magazine said by some to contain fifty tons of powder and three thousand shells. As the fire expanded, shell fragments rained "thick and fast all over the city . . ." General Grover quickly organized "the soldiers into a working force" and the fire was controlled in a matter of hours.

On the following day, one witness described the destruction as "a wilderness of chimneys" spread over five acres, mostly "small wooden tenements . . . There were many narrow escapes" from shell fragments, but very few were killed or wounded.[15] Whether the fire was the result of an incendiary, as reported by the *Savannah Daily Herald,* or not is unclear.[16] Chimney fires had occurred in the city with sufficient frequency to urge chimney sweeps to "shoulder their scrapers and brushes" and "rush to the rescue of our people."[17]

The city's other newspaper, the *Savannah Daily Republican* (Sherman had ordered that there be only two), also supported the fire's incendiary origin: "some fiend had placed a keg of powder at the side of the Arsenal . . . to blow up the city, as the Arsenal contains over thirty tons of powder . . . A single spark would easily have carried out the hellish designs of the wretches as the top of the keg was entirely open."[18] The two newspapers, the *Republican* and the *Herald*, clearly had Northern sympathies; the military governor was not about to have it otherwise. In fact, the *Herald's* publisher was Samuel W. Mason, the son of prominent Larkin Dodge Mason of Tamworth, New Hampshire, and undoubtedly a kin of Company K's Capt. Octavius C. Mason from next-door Sandwich.[19] Samuel Mason was also the reason for the *Herald*'s content of New Hampshire news.

April 1865 was crowded with significant events: principally, the fall of Richmond, Lee's surrender, and Lincoln's assassination. The news of the April 3 evacuation of Richmond reached the Fourteenth rather quickly: "The report came through rebel sources by way of Augusta."[20] The news of Lee's surrender on April 9 was recorded in the *Savannah Daily Herald* on April 16.[21] Word of Lincoln's assassination on April 14 and his death the following morning arrived on April 18, and was recognized by salutes fired from gunboats on the Savannah River.

The first surviving letter is from Libby, dated April 15, 1865:

> *Dear Lewis I set down to right a few lines to let you no how we all are all wel hear at home Susan Hackett little baby died this morning at 10 i see her last night her sufring great it has got through with all of that and gone to rest John Clark is a failing Father has ben up hear and a went a fishin and got to trouts and Parker come up hear to day and cared him home Frank and Lucy has bin up hear and went home yesterday Frank is a goin after George [Wiggin] as soon as he can get a pass from Washington this is from your wife Mary E Smith*
>
> *Burleigh has bin to North to day to preach staid to susan last night he is goin home this week it is bad The news to us to hear our*

(12)

Sandwich Apr 15

we hear to day they hav
got the man that shot the
president and the sectary son is ded
he was stabed

Dear Lewis i set
down to right a few lines to
let you no how we all are
all wel hear at home Susan
Hackett little baby died
this morning at 10 i see
her last night her sufring
great it has got through
with all of that and gone
to rest A John Clark is
a failing Father has ben up
hear and as went a fishing
and got too trouts and
Parker Come up hear to day
and cared him home
Frank and Lucy has bin
up hear and went home
yesterday Frank is a goin after
George as soon as he Can get
a pass from Washington

Libby Smith's letter of April 15, 1865. Sandwich Historical Society.

> *Presidint was killed and sectary [Seward] was stabd perhats their wil not be eny more fighting i hope not do not wery eny thing about us for we have enought to make us comfortable we have enough to eat and to weir Jacob was up hear to day [every]thing is a faling hear Cloth that has bin seling for 50 cents is goin for 25 cents I dont think of eny thing only George Gurdy is goin to move his wife over to Parkers house to live this summer he is goin to work for Unkil John*
>
> *we hear to day they have got the man that shot the president and the sectary son is ded he was stabed*

Only a few letters of Lewis's exist from this period. One, written in late April, clearly reflects on Southern morale. William Combs also commented on the situation: "the rebs come in every day they are glad to get in to get something to eat they are done plaid out as the darkeys say they are dog ond tired of it [the war]."[22] Combs had been transferred to Fort Pulaski, within whose walls Yankee soldiers played baseball. And, in contrast to the plight of the Confederates, Combs wrote: "we have all the oysters and fish we want we live well here have soft bread and potatoes and meat beens onions pickls and pea storage."[23]

Lewis's comment (below) about "rebel prisners . . . coming in heare every day" was not overstated. On April 25, the steamer *Wilmington* arrived at Savannah and its cargo of Confederate parolees expressed appreciation for the captain's "kindness and courtesy."[24] The *General Sedgwick* docked the same day with 890 paroled prisoners, also from Lee's Army of Northern Virginia, as were more than five hundred aboard the U.S. transport *Kingfisher*. The men of the latter vessel similarly acknowledged their gratitude:

> . . . to return their sincere thanks to Capt. Rector, his officers and crew, for extreme kindness and unceasing attentions to make comfortable all his passengers. To the colored stewardess of the *Kingfisher* we return our thanks for her kindness to our sick; and her Samaritan conduct will ever remain a bright oasis in our past.[25]

Lewis was not alone in anticipating the war's end. William Combs was philosophic about home: "take care of yourself as well as you can for six months more and then if God spars my life I will bee with you never to go to war again this from your treu husband."[26]

> *Savannah City Apr 28 1865 My ever dear wife*
>
> *I agan seat to write a few lines in answer to yours I reseve this morning one daitid the 3 the other the 9 I was glad to see a leter from you if I cant see you but should like to see much better I was glad to heare that you wor all well as for my helth has gut to be vary good agan hoping this may find you all in good helth and prosparity. I am in hop that we shall be able to come home soon the war is about to a close and it cant be agrait while befor this will be woand up and peas onse more restoard you must have herd of all the perseedings so it will be uselis for me to say eny thing about it every thing is quiart hear in Savannah thare is rebel prisners from Lee army coming in heare every day thay talk as though thay was sick a fighting and I ges thay air and not to blaime for thay gut northing to eat or waire and thay look like it this is only thare one storry I cant think of much to write to nite fore I am vary tyard I have bin to work all day a fixing up a tent and mooved into it we had to moove down into the middle of the City and I felt sorry to leave whair we was for it was a vary plesant plase whair we have bin a stoping Wel Libby I am in hops that we shall git paid off in a few days for we have sind the pay roals yester day and you must feal pleas to think thare is some sinse of your giting some mony I will send you some as soon as I git it so keep up good curidg and not blame me for I am not to blame I am a goin to send you a box to morrow with some cloth in it a over coat dress coat pair of pants two woling blanket you can take the blankets and do what you pleas with them and the pants you can wair an coat if you like when you air a farming I will try and do better next time my love to you all I will close by biding you good nite from your Husban Lewis Q Smith to his wife Mary E Smith*

On May 6, 1865, the Fourteenth broke camp and, with several other regiments, marched west into the "splendid hard-pine" forest bound for Augusta, which lay about 140 miles northwest and upriver from Savannah. Arriving there on May 14, they occupied a former shoe factory for barracks. Sergeant Buffum found the scene "semi-tropical and of transcendent beauty."[27] On the afternoon of their arrival, the men were issued forty extra rounds of ammunition and the officers loaded their pistols. Tension rose as the regiment marched to the main avenue leading from the depot to the steamboat landing. After clearing the street of people, including many surrendered Confederate cavalrymen, the troops awaited the outcome.

From the depot came several coaches packed with Union cavalrymen brandishing carbines. Six more coaches followed the first two and bore Mr. and Mrs. Jefferson Davis; Mr. and Mrs. Alexander H. Stephens, the vice president of the Confederacy (who would be confined at Boston Harbor's Fort Warren), and wife; Capt. Henry Wirz, superintendent of Andersonville prison, who was executed in November 1865; and other Southerners. More armed cavalrymen brought up the rear. On a veranda overlooking the scene, Augusta's elite wept as Davis stood from the carriage and tipped his hat. The men of the Fourteenth, outnumbered fifty to one, were there to prevent an escape or rescue attempt of the captured Confederate president. No attempt evolved; instead, the dispirited men in gray, most unpaid for their last year or two of service, jeered Davis. Many fingers relaxed from their triggers as the captives were borne from the landing by a federal transport.

The following letters of Libby's are brief and dated May 17 and May 27, no year identified. They are very likely from 1865, due to several references to Lewis's coming home, which appeared to be imminent that spring. Libby's admonition "dont you inlist again" was appropriate for May 1865, since Lewis's enlistment would expire in several months. Among the many Smiths in Sandwich was Lewis Smith, who lived not far from the Lewis Q. Smith farm in Sandwich.[28]

> *Sandwich May 17 [1865] Dear Lewis*
>
> *i seat myself to right a line to let you no we are all wel i hope this wil find you the same Lucy and Frank was up hear sunday Aunt Dolly is little more cumtable Mother has gone down to see her to day i received your letter dated the 4 Hannah Hakett got your letter last night they told father that you and Mastin [Marston] and Henrye Gilman was left their a lone and the others was coming home that to bad i think i hope they wil let you come soon father is getting long wel he has got the ground most all ploud the Lewis Smith and Saml plan[te]d it the ground has ben very wet he has got some Oats soed and he is goin to soe his Wheat to morow he was goin to soe it to day but it come up a hale shower i of much news to right when you get home i can tell you all i will close this is from your wife Mary E Smith*

Sandwich May 27 Dear Lewis

i seat myself to right a line to let you no we are all wel and i hope this wil find you the same last fri (blot) i was glad to hear [from] you again i hope i shall soon see you once more i am goin to say one thing to dont you inlist again it you i want not your money i dont sel my husban i kneed you hear more then your k[n]eeded eny where els your boys wants a good Marster and you are the one for them Father has got his corn planted Burleigh and Edy was [up] yesterday and helped him our things is all doing wel your box has come all safe father has ben [up] to see me i caried (blot) –ome last Thursday (blot) -her wife has got so she (blot) go but her leg is –ard up about 3 inches Sarah Gurdy is happy as a clam be a good boy i hope you wil soon get home i dont think of eny thing els to right so good day this is from your wife Mary E Smith

It is obvious from the correspondence that Lewis was part of a small force that remained in Savannah and did not undergo the long, hot march to Augusta. As entertaining as providing escort for the captured president and vice president of the Confederacy might have been, it was a few hours of amusement for two weeks of marching. Lewis's luck had held. Lt. Col. Oliver Marston noted orders to begin the return march from Augusta on May 30 at "6 a.m." and added: "Don't flatter yourself that we are on the way home for I don't believe it."[29] Also on the return march, Capt. O. C. Mason observed the hot climate's benevolent effect: "see corn silked to day [June 4] as we came along the road."[30]

Savannah Ga May 24 year 1865 My ever dear wife

I agane seat my self to write you a few lines to inform you of my helth whitch is vary good hoping this may find you all the same thare I have not hern from the regment but onse then it was in orgustea [Augusta] doin northing and I dont see what thay air a keeping them for thare was one regment of reglars come heare last Sunday [May 21] and thay air a releveing som of the troops I wish my turn wood come thay cant releve me to quick if thay try to sute me I am tyard of this plase

My ever dear wife I have gest reseved your dear and welcom letter of the 19 I was glad to heare from you onse more to heare from all I am vary glad you air gitting along so well I hop the time is not far distan whitch I can bee with you agan I reseved a letter from Hanah hacket to day I shall answer it soon she was mistaken about my saying the regment goin home it had gon to Augusta thay wore thair the last I heard from them I have not eny news to write it is vary worm hear you can tell farther I have seen corn all silk out heare ask him if that dont beet him

Wel Libby I am in hops that we will bee releve heare for the hedquater gard has bin on a drink to day a raising the oald hary and some of them air in the lockup but I can say one thing the boys from my regment air all strait and I feal thankful for it Henry and Daneil Gilman A. Wallise H. Sinkler[31] *air all four air heare a doin northing in good bisness As I have no news to rit I will close tell farther to try and rase a Coalt this year if he can from the best horse he can find tell to git his and yours out to a good pastur if he can eny way try and keep up good curidg as you can and try and git a long the best you can untill I git home I do not expect to git paid of untill my time is out or I git out of this remember my love to yourself and others your frends in a speshel maner I will close with a thousan cissis to you rite often from your husban Lewis Q Smith to my wife Mary E Smith*

On the final day of May, the regiment, amid rumors of imminent departure for home, began the march to Savannah. As the men neared the city on June 7, they were met by a staff officer with orders relieving them from the brigade "in order to be mustered out of service"—upon completion of their "muster-out rolls."[32] Weeks of delay were inevitable as the men anxiously awaited orders to depart. While the Fourteenth waited, other regiments were already passing through Concord, New Hampshire, en route home. One, the Eleventh, witnessed Gov. Frederick Smyth's (1819–1899) inaugural there on June 5, 1865.[33]

None too surprisingly, in March the Republicans had continued to be victorious in the Granite State: "Vote of the Fourteenth Regiment 198 Union to 12 Democratic."[34] "Many towns" made "considerable Union gains over the vote of last year," and the Republicans "have elected all the Councillors, nine of twelve Senators, and a majority of about one hundred in the House."[35] Governor Smyth's majority was the largest received by any candidate for governor "for twenty-four years."[36]

On July 6, "to the joy of all" the orders came. On the following morning, a "pleasant" one, the order "all hands up" rang through the camp. A "general destruction fol[l]owed our removal from camp," and at six in the morning the regiment was finally aboard the U.S. steam transport *Constitution*, steaming down the Savannah River.[37] The *Savannah Daily Herald* acknowledged: "Their departure will be regretted by many warm friends of the regiment."[38] The following day, July 8, was the Fourteenth's official date of discharge from the army. Stopping briefly at Hilton Head two days later, the steamer passed Cape Hatteras uneventfully on July 13.

Under clear skies and fair weather, the transport entered Boston Harbor on the morning of July 18. Their arrival was noted: "The members of the regiment were treated with a substantial collation at Faneuil Hall by the City Government before taking the cars for their homes."[39] The men, numbering 521, detrained in Concord at about midnight. From the station, they were escorted by the Brigade Band to a number of hotels "where supper awaited them." After dining, they re-formed and "the regiment marched to camp, where they passed the night."[40] Given a week's leave, they returned to Concord on July 26, signed their payrolls, and were paid off and discharged the following day.

Four hundred and forty-two original members (or forty-five percent of those enlisted at Concord three years before) returned home. The Fourteenth Regiment New Hampshire Volunteers, which mustered in with bugle and drum roll, now ceased to exist, without ceremony or fanfare. Unlike the long transition from farmers to soldiers, the return to farming must have been almost immediate.

Ironically, after four long years of war and devastation, some measure of normalcy had already returned farther south. As commerce resumed, 270 tons of New England ice arrived at Savannah via schooner for use by troops under the care of "the Medical Department and Hospital . . ."[41] Yankee soldiers challenged the citizens of Savannah "from whatever State he may come, from whatever army he may have belonged to, or may now belong to . . ." to a "friendly contest" on the Fourth of July—the "exhilarating manly exercise of Base Ball."[42] Although reconstruction would be measured in decades, not years, a similitude of peace also appeared in Virginia's great valley:

> The Army of the Shenandoah is virtually abandoned. There are no troops in the Valley but one year men. The guerillas have totally disappeared, and

Fourteenth NHV Regimental Battle Flag. Courtesy of New Hampshire Historical Society

> the people are diligently employed in raising crops. In a few days there will probably be no troops in the Valley, except at Winchester.[43]

Although unceremoniously mustered out, a little recognition of three years of duty was better than none at all. Battle flags, "covered over with the names of the battles . . . fought in so gallantly, and torn into fragments with rebel shot and shell," were relinquished to the New Hampshire adjutant general's office and council chamber where they could be viewed by the public from nine to four o'clock daily.[44] The Fourteenth's regimental colors had been inscribed: Opequan, Fisher's Hill, and Cedar Creek.[45] On May 30, 1865, the War Department announced:

> General's Order No. 101
>
> Retention of Arms by Soldiers on being honorably discharged from service.
>
> Upon an honorable muster-out and discharge from the service of the United States, all volunteer soldiers, desiring to do so, are hereby authorized to retain their arms and accoutrements, on paying therefor their value to the Ordinance Department.[46]

Cpl. George W. Nye, of Company C and Roxbury, New Hampshire, was one who elected to take his Springfield home. His balance of ten months and twenty-five days' back pay, clothing allowance, and state bounty totaled $294.57. From this amount, he recorded: "I was deducted $6.00 for my Springfield rifle & equipments." It was Nye's last diary entry.[47]

By late June, Congress had acted to establish preferential hiring for veterans. In New Hampshire, an impecunious *appeal* went out to employers: "Give them something to do, and your reward will be in Heaven."[48] However, the state had provided $2,775,000 in bounties, and $1,837,000 in state aid to families of volunteers, and another $2,206,000 by assuming town and city war debt. It was estimated that the direct monetary cost of the war to New Hampshire, population 326,073 in 1860, was "from eight to ten million dollars"—taking "no account of the loss of lives, and lacerations of hearts and homes, that can never be computed."[49] The legislature authorized towns and cities to raise funds for monuments honoring their deceased veterans and subsequently provided relief for indigent disabled sailors and soldiers. Later, about 1890, the state established the New Hampshire Soldiers' Home at Tilton, "an enchanting retreat." Veterans were not forgotten.

Years later, Francis Buffum went back to the battlefields of the Shenandoah, but it is unlikely that Cpl. Lewis Q. Smith ever did. Returning to his family and to Sandwich alive was his fondest dream, and that was most likely closure enough. Lewis farmed on the homestead until his death in 1913—more than half a century after leaving for the war. Sergeant Jenks, whose dreams ended with the shot that struck his head, wrote a few months before his death: "Oh what a horrid thing war is, and for all that, how eager some are to be engaged in it."[50]

Gen. Franklin Pierce, who had witnessed and fought in the war with Mexico, recorded his thoughts at that time:

> Perhaps a peace can be conquered by our present system of operations and policy. If so, we have made a grand leap in civilization, we will astonish the world—nay more, we will make wars to *cease,* a desideratum to every philanthropic heart, of all others, the most desirable because if we can conquer a peace in this way we can conquer it better without arms than with them . . . that in this 19th Century *war* to be effectual must be *war* not a mission of civilization and humanity . . . I hate war in all its aspects, I deem it unworthy of the age in which I live & of the Govt. in which I have borne some part . . .[51]

Dr. Child, reflecting on the hanging of three deserters, concluded: "But such events are continually transpiring in all wars. A nation going to war takes a step toward barbarism—even if they are in the right."[52] If barbarism was measured by the tally of dead and wounded, the Civil War could be regarded as the most barbarous of all American wars.

Finally, Francis Buffum honored the men of Company K, and was, perhaps, more gracious than in his mention of the Fourteenth's other companies:

> With the exception of a few mechanics, Company K was composed of those who follow the plough. Situated in the very heart of the Commonwealth, the peaceful farming community which sent forth these sturdy young men to the aid of their country was well fitted to produce those capable of bearing the privation, fatigue, and danger of soldier-life. Such men, born and bred on the farms of New England, and inured to toil which calls forth and develops powers of strength and endurance, were of great value in the Rebellion, and carried with them to the front a fixedness of purpose as unchangeable and resistless as their own granite rocks. The men of Company K, sober, steady, little given to boisterousness and insubordination, were not wanting in the more conspicuous traits of unflinching bravery, and loyal devotion to country.[53]

Epilogue
Lewis Q. Smith, Post–Civil War

I hop we shall have the privelige of meating and spending meny long and happy day in safty to gether the time seams long to me I think it dos to you thare is a day a comine when I shall be free from this an the war hoop an bludy steal will be no more shant we be glad yes we shall

—Lewis Q. Smith, January 23, 1864

BORN ON JANUARY 20, 1832, IN SANDWICH, THERE IS NO known record of Lewis Quimby Smith's (or that of his siblings') childhood or adolescence. However, it is very likely that Lewis's rearing was not much different from that of his own children. Both Lewis and his progeny were raised on a farm that changed little in means and methods over most of the nineteenth century, as the government agricultural censuses from 1850 through 1880 both illustrate and confirm. Lewis, as would have his children, attended School No. 12, a single-room schoolhouse less than a mile away.[1]

This small structure, about eighteen by twenty-three feet in dimensions, served two to three dozen students annually from 1824 to 1888. There, a basic level of education was realized, and, indeed, Lewis's (and Libby's) letters reflect ordinary writing skills. In contrast are the writing capabilities of brother B. B. Smith, who spent two years at the Biblical School, in Whitestown, New York, and of sister Lucy J. Wiggin. Lucy became, at least briefly, a teacher[2] and later homeschooled both her daughter and Lewis's son, Johnny. From the Smith family correspondence, one can extrapolate to Lewis's youth and his later decades—farm life (and death), the seasons, and the people of Sandwich and the rest of New Hampshire are well described.

One event that caught Lewis's attention as a young man was the California Gold Rush. In a few pre–Civil War letters, mostly exchanged between

Lewis and Lucy, there is contemplation of going west to California and the gold fields. For a few years, Lewis was absent from Sandwich and appears to have tried his hand in the Massachusetts cities of Lawrence and Methuen. During this period of wanderlust, he seldom wrote home. That he may have even been estranged from home is evident in a somewhat enigmatic letter from "brother" Jonathan P. Chase:

> I found the folks at home in good spirits when I told them you would go west with Lucy Jane for thay could [not?] bare the thought of your goin to the gold mines and I think you had beter stay away for a good many reasons.[3]

On December 17, 1853, Lucy Jane was not yet married when she wrote to Lewis from Sandwich. She mentioned several Sandwich people who had sold out and were moving west, and she corroborated Jonathan Chase's statement: "we will go next summer wont we I am bound to go what say you to it."[4] At this time, Lewis was clearly not the correspondent that he would be a decade later. On October 15, 1854, Lucy again wrote to him:

> Having recently learned . . . that you still live, and are in Lawrence, I thought I would again write you, and see if I could not break this spell of silence that has long bound you. It is now about two months since I have received one word from you. I got ready to go West at the time we talked and waited till the last of September for you to come home but neither you nor a letter came, so I concluded you had relinquished the intention of going this fall so I engaged to teach school this fall and Winter and go West in the Spring.[5]

Almost immediately after accepting the teaching opportunity, Lucy received an offer "out West." As she had no one to accompany her, she remained at home that winter. However, Lewis did not just disappoint his sister; he turned the tables on her: "As I [Lucy] hear that instead of my getting married and going to leave you, you have gone and left me . . . Now I want to know why you have not told me of this before . . . I feared you had gone to California."[6] In fact, Lewis had married, and, although Lucy did not yet know the bride's identity (not yet announced), she had corresponded with her—Mary Elizabeth Paine, Lewis's wife for the next fifty-eight years.[7] Almost a year before, Lewis had received a letter signed: "This is from your true love and friend Mary E. Paine."[8]

There are several other suggestions that Lewis had remained remote and absent from home. In February 1856, brother B. B. wrote from India: "How glad we were to hear that Lewis had gone home. Hope he will not stay away so long another time." In the same letter, he added: "Lucy informed us of Lewis's marriage, and we hope that as he is now married he can afford to write us and be kind of social . . . We feel anxious to know where Lewis is going to settle."[9]

It is fair to say that Lewis's wandering was over and life with family at the foot of Sandwich's Mount Israel was beginning. The event that brought Lewis home to Sandwich may have been the birth of his first child. In September 1856, B. B. wrote: "We wish Lewis much joy with his little son."[10] If Lewis appeared to have been distant, then perhaps the demands of farming and family were now the reason. In an April 1859 letter, also from India, "sister" Dorcas castigated Lewis:

> She [Lucy] wrote in her last letter that she had not had any letter from you for a long time. I dont know but you ought to have a bit of a scolding for your neglect of your friends, but I had rather not scold on paper, could I see you however I do not know but you would have a little talking to, in order to stir up your ideas, and pen too.[11]

Except for his absence during the Civil War, Lewis and his family, including his parents and his children, would work the farm continuously. B. B. Smith commented half a decade before Lewis's marriage: "There is no place so near to any one as the home of his childhood, or this is the case with me."[12] B. B. wrote it, but Lewis ultimately lived it.

By 1860, the year of Abraham Lincoln's election, the Smiths had three sons: John, Frank, and Hiram, four, three, and two years old, respectively. Little Lucy M., still a baby, was only five months old. Their world, Sandwich, was typical of the majority of rural towns in New Hampshire. In that year, Sandwich's population stood at 2,227. Its numbers had peaked in 1830 at 2,744; fallen to 2,625 in 1840, to 2,577 in 1850, and to 1,077 in 1900; and bottomed at 615 in 1950. The mid-nineteenth century and the decade of the Civil War displayed a flattening of growth in the state as well. From a population of 284,574 in 1840 and 317,976 in 1850, the numbers increased to 326,073 in 1860 and dropped to 318,300 in 1870 before recovering to 346,991 by 1880.

Sandwich's rural character was further defined by the occupations reported in 1860: farmer and farm laborer were the leading occupations and numbered 446 with about three dozen day laborers. Shoemakers totaled fifty-one, with one bootmaker and one harnessmaker. Eleven blacksmiths, seven carpenters, two cabinetmakers, three tinmen, four millers, three teamsters, a stone cutter, and a stage driver complemented the farmers and shoemakers. In the slightly more densely populated localities of North Sandwich, Center Sandwich, and Sandwich Lower Corner (or "Corner"), one finds fewer farmers. These small villages supported nine traders, three painters, "three gentlemen," a taverner, two clerks, a butcher, three physicians, and five clergymen.

At the end of Lewis's two-year, eleven-month, and thirteen-day career in the Union Army, he returned home, where he remained until his death almost five decades later.[13] Lewis joined the Moulton S. Webster Post of the Grand Army of the Republic, No. 68, at Center Sandwich. The post boasted more than fifty members by the late 1880s and included Benjamin F. Fellows, John W. Goss, John Atwood, Alfred Wallace, James M. Parrott, Samuel F. Vittum, Edward W. Burnham, Lemuel F. Vittum (all of Company K), and William A. Heard, Quartermaster of the Fourteenth.[14] The record

Smith Homestead, Courtesy of Dottie Burrows. Collection of Robert Burrows.

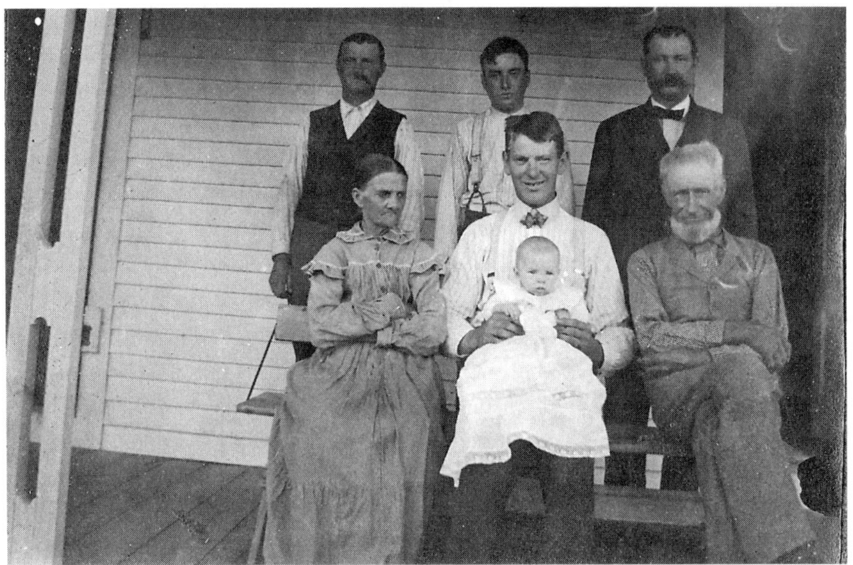

Mary Elizabeth (Paine) Smith, John J. Weed (holding Leslie Weed), and Lewis Quimby Smith On the Porch of the Smith Homestead, About 1907. Author's family.

also reflects the membership of Lewis's sons, Lewis E., Leslie, and Demerit, as sons of veterans in the W. P. Ham Camp, No. 13, of Sandwich.[15]

As a library member, Lewis was one of the signers of the articles of incorporation of the Sandwich Library Association when that institution became an incorporated body on May 10, 1882. The library dated from the Sandwich and Moultonborough Social Library of 1800 and the Sandwich Social Library of 1810.[16]

In 1867, Lewis and Libby acquired the farm and continued to work the property just as John and Eliza had with Lewis and his siblings.[17] In 1850, the cash value of the Smith farm was eight hundred dollars; that of implements and "machinery" was thirty dollars. Obviously, at that time, most farmwork was performed with manual labor and teams of animals rather than machines. While many farms of similar size as that of the Smith's—forty improved acres and twenty unimproved—had one or two horses, John and Eliza Smith worked with a pair of oxen.

For domestic animals, the elder Smiths had a pair of milk cows, two steers, ten sheep, a pig, and undoubtedly some fowl.[18] Annual production of food grains and feed amounted to ten bushels of wheat, forty bushels of Indian corn, ten bushels of oats, fifty bushels of potatoes, and three bushels of peas and beans. The Smiths' small farm also made 150 pounds of butter, twelve tons of hay, twenty-six pounds of wool, and four hundred pounds of maple sugar. Sugar was certainly a cash crop and the Smiths may have sold hay and butter as well.

That agriculture was already declining by the mid-1850s is beyond doubt, a decline that was acknowledged at the time:

> The result of the late census (1850) showed that from 1840 to 1850 the whole tendency of the population had been agricultural pursuits to manufacturing and mechanical pursuits . . . almost without exception, the towns of the State, even the most fertile, which had remained purely agricultural, had diminished in population . . . where a small factory village had sprung up, or where a locality had become a small center of some mechanical pursuit, the population had either remained nearly stationary or increased a little . . . in the next ten years it is quite certain that the manufacturing towns will continue to increase, until manufacturing and mechanical pursuits will become the leading interests.[19]

Another challenge to New Hampshire farming towns' poor soils, harsh climate, and short growing season was the superior agriculture and open lands of the West, then Ohio, Indiana, Illinois, and Missouri. The migration west had already begun by mid-century, and, despite the decline, Sandwich and the farming communities of Sanbornton, Weare, Chester, Hopkinton, Goffstown, and Deerfield remained among the twenty most populous towns of the state until 1850.[20] The Sandwich pre–Civil War population of 2,227 lived in an area of about ninety-five square miles. Sandwich's population of about two dozen souls per square mile was about two thirds of New Hampshire's average density of three dozen per square mile.

In 1860, Sandwich's 485 families occupied about 452 dwellings, largely small farms. Some, like Lewis and his family, lived with parents; extended families were not uncommon at the time. Twenty-one dwellings in Sandwich stood unoccupied, vacancies that were rare a decade or two before. One North Sandwich house, on Wing Road, had nineteen inhabitants—the "Poor House"—home to paupers, and one blind, one insane, and one idiot. The Poor House remained in use until 1869, when the Carroll County

Commissioners bought two 260-acre parcels and established the County Farm in Ossipee.[21]

"Sister" Hepsa L. Paine reflected the transition from farm subsistence to wage earner as well as anyone. In March 1870, she wrote: "Julia and I am hear to work in the mill . . . I am making good pay I run eight looms make 45 dollars a month."[22] Her pay in 1870 was almost triple Lewis's pay as a soldier five years before. On the other side of the family, Frank Wiggin still worked as a Meredith harnessmaker a decade and a half after B. B. Smith expressed concern that Frank would work himself to death. Ten years later, by 1880, Frank and Lucy had moved and were living in Plymouth, New Hampshire.

By 1870, Lewis and Libby had increased their holdings to eighty-five improved acres with twenty-five remaining as woodlot. The farm's value remained at eight hundred dollars and his implements at fifty dollars. Lewis had four working oxen, two horses, seven sheep, and a milk cow. Farm products were essentially the same as his father produced twenty years before. Maple sugar brought about twelve cents per pound in the mid-1850s and was annually subject to the vicissitudes of supply and demand, variable spring weather, and growing production of cane sugar in the South, Cuba, and the Carribean. Lewis's 1870 production of sugar was five hundred pounds.

The 1870 census taker found two more children at home—Leslie A. and Demerit E., ages three and one, were both born after Lewis's return from the war. Lewis and Libby's last child, Leonard A. Smith, was born about 1872.

Ten years after his mustering out, the Smiths' dear friend and neighbor Asa Magoon died, on January 2, 1875, possibly the result of the gunshot wound sustained at Cedar Creek. Others soon followed Asa. Jeremiah Smith died in January 1880 of wounds received at Opequon, a "fractured shoulder." John Bennett and Benjamin Estes both died of consumption, the latter a year after his discharge. A few other Sandwich men of Company K died of unknown causes or at unknown times when Francis Buffum closed out his table of "Deaths Since Discharge" in 1882.

Among the elders of the Smith-Paine family, Libby's father, Amos M. Paine, died on April 25, 1868, at age eighty-six. He was followed by John Smith, age eighty-three, on November 28, 1876, and wife, Eliza W., on

June 14, 1880, almost eighty-six. John and Eliza lie in the North Sandwich Cemetery, next to the Chase family. Jonathan was buried in 1892 at age seventy-two, and his second wife, Sally M., at age sixty-three, in 1882. Irene Chase, who died at age eighteen after Christmas 1862, lies there as does her mother, Mary W. Chase, Jonathan's first wife.

By the end of the century, the hill farmers of New Hampshire continued in decline. The self-contained and mostly self-sufficient farm that produced its own dairy products, wheat, wool for clothing, lard and ashes for soap, wood for heat, apples for cider, both sweet and hard, would become extinct. Today, there are almost no farmers left in Carroll County and one can count those left in Sandwich not on the fingers of one's hands but practically on the ears of one's head. Open fields and grazing livestock are long gone and with them views of the mountains that lay just over the shoulder. Stone walls, laboriously constructed, now serve little purpose except as boundary markers and monuments to the past, while the ever contentious and dominating forest gradually dismantles them.

In late 1913, two important events occurred in Sandwich, one of which attracted universal attention and one that initially did not. In the first instance, on November 14, a fire that quickly spread from a nearby blacksmith shop to Sandwich Town Hall resulted in the loss of both structures. Insured for fifteen hundred dollars, the estimated replacement cost for the town hall was seventy-five hundred dollars—also, the town had "no insurance upon contents." Salvaged from the fire were the Civil War Memorial Tablet, now displayed in Sandwich's Wentworth Library, a few settees, and the town clerk's chest. Lost was a new piano. The fire, though total, did not approach the loss of records in William Weed's fire about a half century earlier:

> The town records were in danger of being destroyed on account of the warping of the safe, but upon opening it, it was found that none of the records were lost and only the covers of the books were scorched.[23]

Two issues later, on December 4, the *Sandwich Reporter,* in its regular, front-page column, "News About Town," noted: "Lewis Smith is on the sick list." Perhaps of somewhat more concern, on page four was found this item: "North Sandwich, Mrs. J. J. Weed is helping care for her grandfather, L. Q. Smith, who has been on the sick list for the past week."[24] Lewis died at home ten days later. His obituary is reproduced here:

> *Another life-long resident of Sandwich, in the person of Lewis Q. Smith has been called to his reward. His illness was la grippe, from which he suffered for several weeks. The end came Sunday, Dec. 14.*
>
> *Mr. Smith was the son of Eliphalet and the grandson of Jacob, one of the early settlers of Sandwich, where the three generations have lived. Mr. Smith was born Jan. 20, 1832. He was married 58 years to Elizabeth Paine of Moultonboro. To them were born nine children, seven of whom are now living: John and Leslie of Boston, Hiram of Woodsville, Lewis, Demerett, Leonard and Mrs. J. Alphonso Smith of Sandwich. There are nine grandchildren and four great grandchildren.*
>
> *Mr. Smith was a soldier and served three years in Co. K, 14th N.H. regiment. His father served in the war of 1812 and his grandfather in the Revolutionary war. He was a good farmer, neat and thrifty in all his work. For 23 years he had charge of the Sandwich Notch Road as agent for both town and state and the substantial work he did there will live as a monument of his good judgement and hard work. As a citizen he was one of the best, as a veteran he was loyal and true, as a father he was loved and respected by all his children.*
>
> *The funeral was held at his home, Wednesday, Dec. 17, Rev. Coller in charge of the service. The seven children were in attendance and the Sandwich Veterans were present as bearers. Interment was in the Free Baptist cemetery.*[25]

Lewis Quimby Smith family burials. Jonathan Taylor photograph.

A week after Lewis's death, Mrs. J. J. Weed, Lewis's granddaughter Lucy M. (Smith) Weed, returned to her home in North Sandwich. Two years later, also over the Christmas holidays, the Smith family again sustained a loss. On December 23, 1915, at age eighty-four, Mary Elizabeth Smith died at home, having been sick a mere five hours—"in her usual health up to the time of her death." In her passing, she was "a woman endeared by all who knew her . . . a devoted mother and the beautiful floral tributes showed the esteem and devotion that her children and friends had for her."[26]

In addition to the legacy of the children and grandchildren left by Lewis and Libby are the many family letters, somehow collected and preserved, for later-day readers. It is a singular gift not only to the town and state but also to any student of mid-nineteenth-century rural living and New Hampshire's Civil War soldiers.

Endnotes

Chapter 1 Prologue to War

1. "High Wind," *Winnipesaukee* (Laconia) *Gazette (WG),* January 4, 1862, 2.
2. *Laconia Democrat (LD),* January 10, 1862, 2.
3. *WG,* January 4, 1862, 2.
4. "Fire in Sandwich—Court Records Burnt," *WG,* January 11, 1862, 2, and *LD,* January 17, 1862, 3.
5. "Small Pox," *LD,* February 7, 1862, 2.
6. "Small Pox in Laconia," *WG,* January 4, 1862, 2.
7. "New England Manufacturing Interests," *WG,* January 18, 1862, 1.
8. "Domestic Manufactures," *WG,* January 4, 1862, 2.
9. "Perished in Sandwich," *LD,* March 14, 1862, 2. In today's terminology, hypothermia.
10. *LD,* March 28, 1862, 2.
11. James D. Richardson, *A Compilation of the Messages and Papers of the Presidents 1789–1897,* 10 vols. (Washington, D.C.: Government Printing Office, 1897), vol. 6, 1861–1869, 114–15.
12. Allen Johnson and Dumas Malone, *Dictionary of American Biography,* 21 vols. (New York: Charles Scribner's Sons, 1937), vol. 2, 227–28.
13. Richardson, 115.
14. Ibid., 115–16.
15. Ibid., 120.
16. "State of New Hampshire," *WG,* August 16, 1862, 2: Ages of those enrolled by State of New Hampshire, Executive Dept. General Order No. 12, which followed the War Department order. With the Enrollment Act of March 1863, those enrolled were from age twenty to forty-five. For enlistments, the ages were eighteen to forty-five. See Eugene C. Murdock, *One Million Men: The Civil War Draft in the North* (Madison: State Historical Society of Wisconsin, 1971), 27 and 142.
17. Richardson, 121.
18. Ibid.

19. "Circular from the War Department," *Boston Daily Evening Transcript* (*BET*), August 11, 1862, 3.
20. "Arrest for Evasion of the Draft," *BET,* August 9, 1862, 4, and "Arrest of Skedaddlers," August 11, 1862, 1. *Skeedaddle* or *skedaddle* was Civil War slang for running away or a hurried retreat.
21. "Conjugal Dilemmas," *BET,* August 11, 1862, 3.
22. "Arrest for Discouraging Enlistments in New Hampshire," *BET,* August 30, 1862, 3.
23. Richardson, 121.
24. Even by 1900, when New Hampshire's population stood at 411,588, those foreign born were 88,107, or about twenty-one percent. However, two thirds of the 88,107 were native to neighboring Canada. *Encyclopaedia Britannica, 11th edition*, 28 vols. (Cambridge, England: University Press, 1911), vol. 19, 493.
25. Letters of Sgt. John Henry Jenks, Milne Special Collections and Archives Department (MSCAD), University of New Hampshire Library, Durham, New Hampshire, letter of July 30, 1863, Camp Adirondack, Washington.
26. Letters of Capt. Oliver H. Marston, Rauner Special Collections Library (RSCL), Dartmouth College Library, Hanover, New Hampshire, letter to wife Sarah, September 20, 1862, Camp Colby, Concord, N.H.
27. Marston, letter of September 20, 1862, RSCL. See also Merrill, *History of Carroll County,*163. Hoit died on December 17, 1892, at almost eighty-two years of age.
28. Marston, letter of October 2 and 3, 1862, Camp Colby, Concord, RSCL.
29. Marston, letter of October 10, 1862, Concord, RSCL.
30. Francis H. Buffum, *A Memorial of the Great Rebellion: Being a History of the Fourteenth Regiment New-Hampshire Volunteers, Covering Its Three Years of Service, with Original Sketches of Army Life* (Boston: Franklin Press; Rand, Avery, & Company, 1882), 283.
31. Jenks, letter of October 3, 1862, Concord, MSCAD.
32. Letters of Sgt. Elbridge Smith, Historical Society of Cheshire County (HSCC), Keene, N.H., letter to his mother, October 13, 1862, Camp Cheshire, Concord.
33. Jenks, letter of October 3, 1862, Concord, MSCAD.
34. Letters of William H. H. Bennett, Company K, Fourteenth Regiment NHV, Sandwich Historical Society Collection (SHSC), Sandwich, N.H., letter to "Friend Henry" of December 12, 1862, Maryland.
35. Buffum, 61.

36. *The War of the Rebellion: A Compilation of the Official Records of the Union and Confederate Armies* (U.S. War Department: Government Printing Office, 1889), Series 1, vol. 25 (part 2), 32 and 184 (hereafter, ORA).
37. To this day, an area of Sandwich and a road near Lewis's farm retain the name Smithville.
38. B. F. Hubbard, *The History of Stanstead County, Province of Quebec* (Montreal: Lovell Printing & Publishing Company, 1874), 240. Asa and Riley Magoon's grandfather Jonathan Magoon emigrated from Exeter, N.H., to Magoon Point, Quebec, on Lake Memphremagog, in 1796. His son, Jonathan Jr., was born in Exeter and was the father of Riley, Levi, and Asa and their eight siblings.
39. Georgia Drew Merrill, *History of Carroll County* (Somersworth: New Hampshire Publishing Company, 1971), 162–63. Moulton S. Webster is not found as a Sandwich resident in the census of 1860 and it is likely that he was in Massachusetts during this period.

Chapter 2 Duty in Maryland: Guarding the Potomac and the Northwestern Approaches to Washington City

1. Jenks, letter of January 25, 1863, Poolesville, Md., MSCAD.
2. Maj. Alexander Gardner, Adjutant, Fourteenth Regiment NHV, RSCL, Hanover, N.H., letter to Maj. Samuel A. Duncan, November 2, 1862, near Seneca, Maryland.
3. Meredith, N.H., Town Records, Personal Communication of Ann Wallace, Meredith, N.H. By 1870, Lizzie Ann is not living with Charles E. Moulton, and he is listed as divorced in 1880.
4. Merrill, 692. This statement originally appeared in the *Sandwich Reporter,* December 13, 1883, 3.
5. "Matters in General," *LD,* February 22, 1867, 3.
6. Selah Hibbard Barrett, ed., *Memoirs of Eminent Preachers in the Freewill Baptist Denomination* (Rutland, Ohio: Selah Hibbard Barrett, 1874), 299–304. Smith served in Balasore from 1852 to 1861 and from 1869 until his death.
7. Capt. A. W. Bartlett, *History of the Twelfth Regiment New Hampshire Volunteers in the War of the Rebellion* (Concord: Ira C. Evans, Printer, 1897), 8 and 23.
8. "Cider Drinking," *Belknap Gazette and Carroll County Advertiser,* October 3, 1843, 1.
9. "Temperance in Sandwich," *BG and CCA,* August 1, 1843, 2.
10. Buffum, 81.
11. Ibid., 83.

12. The only other Gilman in the Fourteenth was Sandwich's Daniel R. Gilman, who was reduced in rank, at his own request, on November 6, 1862. There is no "Henry Gilman" found in any N.H. regiment.
13. Letters of Pvt. Christopher Hoyt, Co. I, Fourteenth Regiment NHV, New Hampshire Historical Society (NHHS), Concord, letter of October 29, 1862, Seneke [Seneca] Md.
14. Richardson, 149.
15. Jenks, letter of January 25, 1863, Poolesville, Md., MSCAD.
16. Buffum, 77.
17. Lucy Jane Wiggin, letter of December 12, 1858, M.Ville (Meredith Village), SHSC.
18. William H. H. Bennett, letter to "Friend Henry" of October 29, 1862, Maryland, SHSC.
19. This letter is a transcription of the original. SHSC.
20. It is unclear who George Dexter is. He may have been George Dexter Quimby of Sandwich, Company K, who died of typhoid fever at Offutt's Cross-Roads, Maryland, on December 14, 1862. Only two George Dexters served from New Hampshire: one from the Second Regiment enlisted in November 1863 and deserted in early March 1864; the second, from the Eleventh Regiment, was wounded at Fredericksburg and died two days later on December 15, 1862.
21. "The New Hampshire Troops," *BET,* May 8, 1861, 2.
22. "The Militia System," *New Hampshire Democrat (NHD),* November 1, 1849, 2.
23. "Militia," *NHD,* January 18, 1861, 2. See also April 26, 1861, 1.
24. "The State Arsenals," *WG,* October 10, 1857, 1.
25. Buffum, 70.
26. "Rifle Regiments, To the Editor of the Transcript," *BET,* May 17, 1861, 3.
27. *LD,* August 15, 1862, 1.
28. "News Items," *LD,* October 9, 1863, 2.
29. Hoyt, letter of November 6, 1863, Washington, D.C., NHHS.
30. Jenks, letter of July 30, 1863, Camp Adirondack, Washington, D.C., MSCAD.
31. Letters of Cpl. Henry M. Sanborn, Company H, Fourteenth Regiment NHV, NHHS, letter to Dear Sister, Thursday [February or March] 12, 1863, Poolesville, Md.

Chapter 3 Death and Darkness at Home

1. Bennett, letter of December 12, 1862, Maryland, SHSC.
2. Buffum, 90.

3. Ibid.
4. "Baltimore and Ohio Railroad," *WG,* January 18, 1862, 4.
5. Pvt. William Combs Collection, Department of Special Collections, University Libraries of Notre Dame (ULND), Notre Dame, Ind., letter of February 27, 1863, Poolesville, Md.
6. "Soldiers' Views," *Belknap Gazette (BG),* April 4, 1863, 1. By 1863, the ownership of the *Belknap Gazette and Carroll County Advertiser* had changed, and the newspaper became the *Belknap Gazette.*
7. Ibid.
8. Abraham Lincoln, ed. Arthur Brooks Lapsley, *The Writings of Abraham Lincoln,* 8 vols. (New York: G. P. Putnam's Sons, 1923), vol. 6, 1862–1863, letter of January 5, 1863, 233–34.
9. Moulton H. Marston of North Sandwich, age fifty-three, "Gentleman" 1860 census. He was a Democratic candidate for councilor in March 1862, and a Sandwich delegate to the January 7, 1864, Democracy Senatorial Convention, Sixth District, held in Moultonboro. The other Sandwich delegates were John Burleigh, Albert Hackett, and J. D. Quimby. *LD,* January 22, 1864, 2.
10. Merrill, 720.
11. Augustus D. Ayling, Adjutant General, *Revised Register of the Soldiers and Sailors of New Hampshire in the War of the Rebellion 1861–1866* (Concord: Ira C. Evans, 1895), 646. In 1860, Benjamin Woodman of New Hampton, N.H., (post office Meredith Village) had six children, the oldest being John Woodman, age fourteen. See the 1860 census for New Hampton, Belknap County. No other New Hampshire Woodmans fit John O. Woodman's age and circumstances.
12. Ayling, 621. The abbreviations used are Disch. Disab. for "discharged disability."
13. Generally, those volunteers under the age of eighteen needed parental permission to enlist.
14. "Died," *WG,* October 15, 1859, 3.
15. Cemetery Committee of the Moultonborough Historical Society, ed., *Cemetery Records of Moultonborough, New Hampshire* (Moultonborough: Harvest Press, 1988), 10.
16. Reid Mitchell, *The Vacant Chair: The Northern Soldier Leaves Home* (New York: Oxford University Press, 1993), 50.
17. Remarque, 40.

18. Stephen E. Ambrose, ed., *A Wisconsin Boy in Dixie: Civil War Letters of James K. Newton* (Madison: University of Wisconsin Press, 1961), 72. Newton was promoted to lieutenant in July 1865.
19. For a discussion of commutation and the Civil War draft(s), see James W. Geary, *We Need Men: The Union Draft in the Civil War* (De Kalb: Northern Illinois University Press, 1991).
20. William Marvel, "A Poor Man's Fight: Civil War Enlistment Patterns in Conway, New Hampshire," *Historical New Hampshire,* 1988, vol. 43, no. 1, 21–40.
21. 2nd Lt. William H. Bryant, Company D, Fourteenth Regiment NHV, letter to Maj. Samuel A. Duncan, November 6, 1862, Camp, RSCL.
22. Jenks, letter of August 16, 1863, Camp Adirondack, Washington, MSCAD.
23. Elbridge Smith, letter to his mother, February 11, 1863, Poolesville, Md., HSCC.
24. Sheila M. Cumberworth and Daniel V. Biles, *An Enduring Love: The Civil War Diaries of Benjamin Franklin Pierce (Fourteenth New Hampshire Volunteer Infantry) and His Wife Harriet Jane Goodwin Pierce* (Gettysburg, Pa.: Thomas Publications, 1995), 95.
25. Jenks, letter of January 25, 1863, Poolesville, Md., MSCAD.
26. Combs, letter of February 27, 1863, Poolesville, Md., ULND.
27. Merrill C. Sawyer, *Letters from a Civil War Surgeon,* Dr. William Child, of the Fifth New Hampshire Volunteers (Solon, Maine: Polar Bear & Co., 2001), letter of January 26, 1863, 87.
28. Buffum, 93.
29. Dearborn, his wife Elizabeth, and their son Bradbury were prewar neighbors of William E. S. Foss.
30. B. B. Smith, letter to John and Eliza Smith, Jellasore, India, February 1, 1856, SHSC.
31. Lucy J. Smith, letter to Lewis Q. Smith, Sandwich, October 15, 1854, SHSC.
32. Ibid., letter to Lewis Q. Smith, Sandwich, September 28, no year, probably 1854, SHSC.
33. Buffum, 146.
34. Maj. Alexander Gardner, letter to Maj. S. A. Duncan of October 15, 1863, Washington, D.C., RSCL.
35. Sawyer, 83–85.

Chapter 4 Gloom Continues: Duty on the Potomac and Winter Camp at Poolesville, Maryland

1. Roy P. Basler, ed., *The Collected Works of Abraham Lincoln,* 8 vols. (New Brunswick, N.J.: Rutgers University Press, 1953), vol. 6, 164.
2. T. Harry Williams, *Lincoln and His Generals* (New York: Alfred A. Knopf, 1952), 7.
3. "The Value of Confederate Currency," *BET,* October 14, 1864, 2.
4. Hoyt, letter of January 8, 1863, to Dear Brother and Sister, Poolesville, Md., NHHS.
5. Combs, letter of November 23, 1862, Poolesville, Md., ULND.
6. Buffum, 91.
7. Jenks, letter of March 10, 1863, Poolesville, Md., MSCAD.
8. *Twenty-Eighth Annual Excursion of the Sandwich Historical Society, August 21, 1947,* 48, and *Eighteenth "Excursion," August 26, 1937,* 9. Gould, a Sandwich shoe manufacturer and a Republican, was elected state representative in March 1863.
9. Sandwich Historical Society (SHS), *Sandwich, New Hampshire 1763–1990* (Portsmouth: Peter E. Randall, 1995), 99–100. See "The Case of William M. Weed and the Families and Dependents of Volunteers in the Army," not signed, 44 pages, SHSC. Ezra Gould's records of disbursements, required by state law, were meticulous and supported by vouchers, unlike those of Weed.
10. "15th Regiment," *LD,* October 17, 1862, 2.
11. *LD,* November, 7, 1862, 2.
12. Ibid., July 4, 1862, 2.
13. The total value of Sandwich real estate in 1870, other than that of Adams, was about seventy-five dollars short of $622,000—Adams owned one third the value of Sandwich! "He purchased farms with reckless abandon . . ." SHSB, #6, 1926.
14. Jenks, letter of August 16, 1863, Camp Adirondack, Washington, MSCAD. William H. Thayer (1822–1897) served as the Fourteenth's surgeon. He graduated from Harvard College in 1841 and Harvard Medical in 1844. See Granville P. Conn, *History of the New Hampshire Surgeons in the War of Rebellion* (Concord: Ira C. Evans Co., 1906), 173–78.
15. John R. Barden, ed., *Letters to the Home Circle: the North Carolina Service of Pvt. Henry A. Clapp* (Raleigh: Division of Archives and History, North Carolina Department of Cultural Resources, 1998), 93.
16. The term *gravel* generally referred to aggregations of urinary crystals, but was also popularly used to indicate pain or difficulty with passing urine.

17. Tom Okie, "Coming Back to the Land: 240 Years of Human Activity at Mead Base," *Eighty-third Annual Excursion of the Sandwich Historical Society,* Sandwich Historical Society, August 11, 2002 (Tilton, N.H.: Sant Bani Press, 2002), 14.
18. Warren Dearborn died on February 3, 1863, at age sixty-one and was buried at Center Sandwich's Grove (Methodist) Cemetery. Mr. Straw may have been seventy-three-year-old Samuel Straw, possibly the father of Oceanus Straw.
19. Mary Eliza (Smith) Magoon, Asa's wife, is listed in the 1870 census, age forty-two. Their son Levi L. was nineteen, and daughter Hattie, fifteen. Daughter Orrila E. died November 9, 1865, at age six. Riley Magoon, thirty-five, and wife Lydia (Smith) Magoon, thirty-six, are listed in the 1850 census and were neighbors of the Smiths. Their children were Charles W., Albert E., and Emma E., ages nine, six, and two.
20. "Accident and Miraculous Escape," *NHD,* May 22, 1851, 3.
21. The *Laconia Democrat* noted that "most of the cotton mills in New England announce that they have 'stopped for the present.' " *LD,* August 16, 1861, 2.
22. Ephraim Douglass Adams, *Great Britain and the American Civil War,* 2 vols. (New York: Russell & Russell, 1924), vol. 1, 92. See also vol. 2, 1–32, "King Cotton."
23. *WG,* August 30, 1862, 3.
24. Geary, 192–93.
25. "Whether Negroes Will Fight," *BG,* June 25, 1864, 2.
26. Sandwich Lower Corner lies about halfway from the village of Center Sandwich to Moultonborough. The village of North Sandwich ("the North") was known for a time as Skinner's Corner.
27. *Writings of Abraham Lincoln,* 269–70.
28. *LD,* May 1, 1863, 2.
29. *BG,* June 11, 1864, 3.
30. Eugene C. Murdock, *One Million Men: The Civil War Draft in the North* (Madison: State Historical Society of Wisconsin, 1971), 25.

Chapter 5 Politics, Smallpox, Sapping, and Spring

1. Mitchell, 122.
2. Combs, letter of November 23, 1862, Poolesville, Md., ULND.
3. "Vote of the 14th Regiment," *LD,* March 6, 1863, 2.
4. "The Election—Popular Reaction," *LD,* March 27, 1863, 2. *Note:* Page 2 of this issue is (incorrectly) dated April 3.

5. There was a second Daniel S. Bedee, from Laconia, who was a private in the Twelfth. See Bartlett, "Roster of the Twelfth Regiment," 6. Ayling and Bartlett and the censuses for Sandwich of 1850 and 1860 use *Bedee.* There are no *Bedees* in the Sandwich cemetery records, only *Beedes.* The censuses of 1840, 1870, and 1880 for Sandwich use *Beede.*
6. Bartlett, 651.
7. Ibid., 296.
8. Sawyer, 339–44 and 369.
9. "Sixth Senatorial Convention," *LD,* January 22, 1864, 2. Moulton H. Marston also attended.
10. Dan P., Albert D., and Major J. Nelson, ages twenty-three, twenty-two, and twenty-one, enlisted in the Twelfth, Company D, and were probably Hiram Nelson's nephews. Dan was killed May 3, 1863, at Chancellorsville, where both Albert and Major were wounded. Albert died of disease on February 10, 1865, in Bristol. Ayling, 634.
11. Richardson, 163.
12. John L. Smith was the son of John M. and Charlotte Smith; Marcellus and Herbert were the sons of James M. and Lydia Smith.
13. "Died," *BG,* April 4, 1863, 3.
14. He appears in the 1860 and 1870 censuses as a Sandwich resident. Dr. Sweat's obituary is found in the *Concord Monitor* of January 24, 1884, 3.
15. "News Items," *LD,* May 9, 1862, 2.
16. Ibid., *LD,* May 29, 1863, 3.
17. "Maple Sugar," *LD,* May 27, 1864, 3.
18. *WG,* August 2, 1862, 1.
19. "News Items," *LD,* May 29, 1863, 3.
20. Ayling, 982.
21. W. Springer Menge and J. August Shimrak, eds., *The Civil War Notebook of Daniel Chisholm* (Ballantine Books: New York, 1990), 106.
22. B. B. Smith, letter of July 27, 1858, to Eliza W. Smith (My Dearest Mother), from Balasore, India, SHSC.
23. "Small Pox," *NHD,* January 12, 1854, 2.
24. Ayling, 417.
25. Buffum, 93.
26. Ibid., 98.

Chapter 6 Washington City: Duty in the Union Capital

1. Buffum, 99.
2. Ibid., 104.

3. Ibid., 102.
4. "News Items," *LD*, April 3, 1863, 1.
5. Buffum, 115.
6. Jenks, letter of June 11, 1863, Washington, MSCAD.
7. Sanborn, letter to Sister Selura, May 4, 1863, NHHS.
8. Buffum, 109.
9. "General Hooker in Washington," *BET*, May 15, 1863, 2, and "From Washington," May 18, 1863, 2.
10. "Washington Rumors" *BET*, May 15, 1863, 4. "From Washington," 3, "it is said there is serious disagreement between Generals Halleck and Hooker and is positively said that Hooker's new movement was countermanded by Gen. Halleck."
11. Hoyt, letter of May 17, 1863, Washington, NHHS.
12. Buffum, 50–51.
13. Ibid., 119.
14. Geary, 81.
15. John Currier was the Methodist minister on the Sandwich circuit from 1863 to 1864. (Merrill, 683). There is no listing for Mrs. Currier in Harriet Vittum Lighton, *Sandwich, N.H., Cemeteries* (Reprinted by Higginson Book Co. from 1930 original), nor are the Curriers found in Sandwich in the 1860 census.

Chapter 7 Rebel Invasion of New Hampshire and Union Successes

1. "Rebel Invasion of New Hampshire," *BET*, July 6, 1863, 2.
2. "Fourth of July," *LD*, July 10, 1863, 2.
3. "Rebel Invasion of New Hampshire," *BET*, July 6, 1863, 2.
4. "Democratic Convention in New Hampshire," *BET*, July 6, 1863, 4.
5. "The Copperhead Ex-President," *BET*, July 7, 1863, 2.
6. "Sympathy with Vallandingham," *BET*, July 11, 1863, 2. (Italics original).
7. "The Fourth," *LD*, July 3, 1863, 2.
8. "The Opposition," *LD*, July 3, 1863, 1.
9. "The Platform of the Democracy of New Hampshire," *LD*, July 17, 1863, 2.
10. "What Is It," *BET*, July 11, 1863, 2. Isaac Hill (1789–1851) founded the *New Hampshire Patriot*, a Concord newspaper. He served as a U.S. senator and as New Hampshire's governor for several terms in the 1830s.
11. Roy Franklin Nichols, *Franklin Pierce: Young Hickory of the Granite Hills* (Philadelphia: University of Pennsylvania Press, 1969), 523.
12. Ibid., preface to the first edition, ix.

13. Ibid., 523.
14. Henry Steele Commager, ed., *The Blue and the Gray* (New York: The Fairfax Press, 1982), 714.
15. "Draft Riot at Portsmouth, N.H. Promptly Put Down," *BET,* Friday, July 17, 1863, 2.
16. "White Mountain Items," *BET,* July 22, 1863, 2.
17. "News Items," *LD,* August 21, 1863, 2.
18. Sarah A. Quimby, who died on July 17, 1863, at age thirty, was North Sandwich carpenter Albert W. Quimby's first wife. Buried at Skinner's Corner (North Sandwich) Cemetery, she left behind at least six children. 1860 census, Sandwich, 75, and *Sandwich, N.H., Cemeteries*, 123.
19. Hoyt, letter of July 27, 1863, Dear Brother & Sister, Washington, D.C., NHHS.
20. J. A. Gilmore, letter to Hon. Edwin M. Stanton, Concord, July 14, 1863, *The Conscription* (Concord: Fogg, Hadley and Company, 1863), 8. This printing lay before the public all the correspondence, by both letter and telegram, from July through September 1863, with the War Department.
21. Gilmore, 21–22.
22. Richardson, 185.
23. Geary, 16.
24. *Compact Edition of the Oxford English Dictionary* (New York: Oxford University Press, 1971), 697
25. Cpl. Caleb G. Bean was born in Sandwich and his enlistment in Company G, Second Regiment NHV, at age thirty-seven, was credited to Portsmouth. Sgt. William P. Ham, of Company L, Twelfth Regiment NHV, was born in Farmington, a resident of Sandwich in 1850, and lived in Center Harbor, N.H., at the time of his enlistment. Wounded on June 3, 1864 at Cold Harbor, Virginia, he died on June 15, 1864. Following his death, his wife, Louisa M. Ham, moved from Meredith to Sandwich, where she died a few years later. Jed Dinsmore was most likely Conway-born Jeremiah S. Dinsmore, who enlisted from New Hampton (or Meredith) in the Twelfth.
26. On July 30, Sergeant Jenks wrote that "the 2nd, 5th and 12th have been called in from the front and are now in the city, ready to go, when wanted . . ." Jenks, letter of July 30, 1863, MSCAD.

Chapter 8 More Guard Duty in the Capital

1. Buffum, 107.
2. "Forts and Fortresses," *BET*, May 8, 1861, 2.
3. Buffum, 124.

4. Ibid., 124–25.
5. Ibid., 116.
6. "News Items," *LD,* September 11, 1863, 2.
7. Combs, letter of February 27, 1863, Poolesville, Md., ULND.
8 Jenks, letter of February 9, 1864, Harpers Ferry, MSCAD.
9. Sawyer, 271.
10. Combs, letter of March 2, 1865, Savannah, Ga., ULND. Combs is not listed in the wounded in Buffum's tabulation and was probably hospitalized for illness.
11. Sawyer, letter of November 15, 1863, 183.
12. Ambrose, 74. Newton was particularly distressed by pervasive gambling.
13. Both John A. (1829–1910) and B. Ellen Marston were members of the Second Freewill Baptist Church of Sandwich. They are listed in the 1860 census, ages thirty and thirty-one, respectively, with no children. John A. Marston's burial is in the Baptist (or Rural) Cemetery in Sandwich and a B. Ellen Marston is also buried there. Her dates are 1829–1861, *Sandwich, NH, Cemeteries*, p. 28. The year of death, 1861, is in conflict with the year of Libby's letter, 1863.
14. Margaret Leech, *Reveille in Washington 1860–1865* (New York: Grosset & Dunlap, 1941), 261.
15. "News Items," *LD,* January 15, 1864, 3.
16. Just to the east of the Old Capitol, now the site of the Supreme Court building, lay a row of private residences utilized as the Carroll prison. The Library of Congress, constructed with Concord, New Hampshire, granite, now occupies the place of Carroll prison.
17. Jenks, letter of November 8, 1863, Camp Adirondack, Washington, MSCAD.
18. Jenks, letter of November 21, 1863, Camp Adirondack, Washington, MSCAD.
19. *LD,* October 23, 1863, 3.
20. "News Items," *LD,* January 15, 1864, 3.
21. "Diphtheria," *LD,* February 12, 1864, 2.
22. Sanborn, letter to Dear Sister, October 25, 1863, NHHS.
23. George C. Bean, a farm laborer, was a neighbor of Lewis and Libby. Born in Sandwich and a resident of Orford, George was indeed drafted and served in Company A, Seventh Regiment NHV. He mustered out on July 20, 1865. Ayling, 357. There is no Joseph Clark or Lucinda Bryant found in Sandwich or Moultonborough in the 1860 census.
24. Jenks, letter of October 8, 1863, Camp Adirondack, Washington.

25. Letters of Lt. John W. Sturtevant, Company G, Fourteenth Regiment NHV, HSCC, Keene, N.H., letter of Capt. Solon A. Carter to Sturtevant, October 10, 1864, Chapin's Farm, Before Richmond.
26. "News Items," *LD,* April 17, 1863, 2.
27. SHS, 50.
28. *First* "Excursion," August 21, 1920, 2. Also, *Sixteenth* "Excursion," 10.
29. ORA, Series 1, vol. 25, part 2 (Correspondence), 491–92.
30. George W. Adams, *Doctors in Blue* (New York: Henry Schuman, Inc., 1952), 199.
31. Marston, letter to Sarah of September 30, 1863, Washington, D.C., RSCL.
32. Marston, letter to Sarah of October 11, 1863, Washington, D.C., RSCL.
33. Marston, letter to Sarah of September 30, 1863, Washington, D.C., RSCL.

Chapter 9 The Holidays and Year's End

1. Geary, 84.
2. Buffum, 123.
3. Ambrose, 47.
4. Jenks, letter of November 8, 1863, Camp Adirondack, Washington, MSCAD.
5. "Substitute Desertions," *Concord Monitor (CM),* January 4, 1865, 2.
6. James W. Hart, born in New Hampshire and a sash and blind maker, is listed as a resident of Lowell, Massachusett, in the 1860 census.
7. "Side Arms," *BET,* May 21, 1861, 2.
8. Amas Paine and Joe Clark are not identified. Although Amos ("Amas") Paine may be the son of "Father" Amos Paine, he is not found in the 1850 or 1860 census. Of the half dozen Joseph Clarks that served in all units from New Hampshire, none was born in or was from Meredith. Both Joseph Clark, age twenty-one, and Joseph S. Clark, age twenty-two, lived in Meredith Village in 1860.
9. The only Jonathan Bean in Carroll County in 1860 lived in Tuftonboro. There were more than several Bean families in Sandwich—the Bean Road runs from Center Sandwich through a corner of Moultonborough to Center Harbor.
10. Buffum, 138.
11. Jenks, letter of September 6, 1863, Washington, MSCAD.
12. SHS, 99.
13. Merrill, 73–74.
14. Geary, 109–10.
15. "News Items," *LD,* May 4, 1866, 2.
16. "News Items," *LD,* December 21, 1866, 2.

17. Smith appears to mention Company I twice. There was no Company J in the Fourteenth and no other letter resembles I. The company breakdown totals twenty-two—or twenty-one if the first reference to Company I is dropped.
18. Combs, letter of March 2, 1865, Savannah, Ga., ULND.
19. Buffum, 243.
20. Buffum, 137.
21. Letters of Cpl. Daniel C. Currier, Company I, Fourteenth Regiment, NHV, MSCAD, Durham, N.H., letter of December 2, 1863, Navy Yard Bridge, Washington, D.C.
22. Sturtevant, letter of December 27, 1863, to Friends at Home, Washington D.C., RSCL.
23. Buffum, 41.
24. "One of the Riot Cases," *BET,* December 24, 1863, 3.
25. "The Weather," *BET,* December 26, 1863, 2 and "The Skating," December 24, 1863, 2.
26. Hoyt, letters of May 17 and December 31, 1863, NHHS.
27. "A Salute of 100 Guns," *BET,* January 1, 1864, 2.
28. "Pocket Diaries for 1864," *BET,* January 1, 1864, 2.

Chapter 10 Washington and Harpers Ferry

1. Buffum, 138.
2. Robert Underwood Johnson and Clarence Clough Buel, eds., *Battles and Leaders of the Civil War,* 4 vols. (New York: Thomas Yoseloff, Inc., 1956), vol. 4, 522.
3. Combs, letter of January 6, 1864, Camp Adirondack, ULND.
4. Ibid.
5. ORA, Series 1, vol. 33, 487, 1891.
6. Diary of Capt. George W. Nye, Company C, Fourteenth Regiment NHV, entry for February 2, 1864, RSCL, Dartmouth College Library, Hanover, N.H.
7. "Seizure of Jeff. Davis's Library," *BET,* July 27, 1863, 2, and "Capture of Jefferson Davis's Library," July 28, 1863, 1.
8. *Sandwich, N.H., Cemeteries,* 127.
9. Now Lake Waukewan, Meredith, New Hampshire. The lake's outlet supplied waterpower to mills at the shore of Lake Winnepesauke just to the east.
10. George Nye diary, entry for February 7, 1864, RSCL.
11. ORA, Series 1, vol. 33, 1891, 557.
12. Sanborn, letter of February 25, 1864, NHHS.

13. See the U.S. Geological Survey's Geographic Names Information System (GNIS).
14. James Marcellus Smith, letter of February 16, 1864, Harpers Ferry, SHSC transcription.
15. George Nye diary, entry for February 17, 1864, RSCL.
16. Ibid., entry for February 22, 1864, RSCL.
17. Sanborn, letter of February 25, 1864, NHHS.
18. Buffum, 157-58. The lead line or sounding line was used at sea to determine water depth and bottom characteristics.

Chapter 11 Battle with Ballots and Duty at the Crescent City

1. Buffum, 147.
2. Ibid., 149.
3. "The New Hampshire Election," *BET,* March 8, 1864, 2.
4. Richard H. Sewell, *John P. Hale and the Politics of Abolition* (Cambridge: Harvard University Press, 1965), 214-17.
5. *BET,* March 8, 1864, 2.
6. *BET,* March 9, 1864, 2.
7. Ibid., 3.
8. Geary, 153–54.
9. Buffum, 151.
10. "Bushwhacker Murders," *BET,* October 14, 1864, 2.
11. Sturtevant, letter of March 23, 1864, Park Barracks, N.Y., RSCL.
12. Marston, letter of March 20, 1864, to Sarah, New York, NHHS.
13. Sturtevant, letter of March 23, 1864, Park Barracks, N.Y., RSCL.
14. George Nye diary, entry of May 16, 1864, RSCL.
15. Hoyt, letter of April 20, 1864, NHHS.
16. Buffum, who sailed on the *Daniel Webster,* makes no mention of a return to Fortress Monroe—only the stops at Port Royal and Key West. Buffum, 161. Sgt. A. H. Tyrell of Company B was also aboard the *Daniel Webster* and, on April 7, 1864, noted just the stops at Port Royal and Key West.
17. Letters of Sgt. Albert H. Tyrell, U.S. Army Military History Institute (USAMHI), Carlisle, Pa., letter to his brother, J. R. Tyrrell, April 7, 1864, On board the Steamer *Daniel Webster*, Key West, Fla.
18. Jenks, letter of May 22, 1864, Camp Parapet, Louisiana, MSCAD.
19. Buffum, 161.
20. A. H. Tyrrell, letter of April 29, 1864, Camp Parapet, La., USAMHI.

21. The tabulation of promotions in Buffum (table III) gives the date as May 1, 1864. The difference in dates may reflect the time involved in processing the promotion.
22. "Smuggling Liquor," *New Orleans Times (NOT),* April 29, 1864, 5.
23. "Mortuary Report," *NOT,* April 28, 1864, 5.
24. *WG,* December 24, 1859, 3.
25. "The City," *Daily Picayune* (New Orleans), May 22, 1864, 3.
26. ORA, series 1, vol. 34 (part 4), 17, Special Orders No. 135, Headquarters, Department of the Gulf, New Orleans, La.
27. "Whether Negroes Will Fight," *BG,* June 25, 1864, 2.
28. G. Parker Lyon, *The New Hampshire Annual Register for the Year 1865* (Concord: G. Parker Lyon, 1865), 132.
29. *Sandwich, N.H., Cemeteries,* 28.
30. Ayling, 148.

Chapter 12 Searching for the Enemy, Affair at Bayou Grosstete, and Return to Washington

1. Judy Riffel, ed., *A History of Pointe Coupee Parish and Its Families* (Dallas: VAAPR, Inc., 1983), 48.
2. Jenks, letter of June 9, 1864, Morganza, La., MSCAD.
3. George Nye diary, entry for June 7, 1864, RSCL.
4. Buffum, 166.
5. Jenks, letter of June 9, 1864, Morganza, La., MSCAD.
6. Buffum, 400 and 411.
7. Ibid., 442.
8. Ibid., 379 and 407.
9. Ibid., 165.
10. Military usage of the word *affair* is defined as "vaguely, and with intentional indefiniteness of any proceeding which it is not wished to name or characterize closely . . ." *Compact Edition of the Oxford English Dictionary* (New York: Oxford University Press, 1971), 38.
11. ORA, Series 1, vol. 34 (part 1), 1033.
12. "Letter from the 15th New Hampshire Regiment," *LD,* January 30, 1863, 2. Signed "Blossom," Camp Mansfield, Carrollton, La., dated January 1, 1863.
13. Letter to Mrs. Marston written by "B. F. Fellows for Capt. O. H. Marston," St James Hospital, N. O., July 8, 1864. RSCL.
14. Octavius C. Mason was a furniture dealer from Sandwich and was promoted to first sergeant of Company K on June 23, 1864, to second lieutenant in January 1865, and to captain on June 7, 1865. Pvt. Warren J. Brown, a

Sandwich farmer, was promoted to corporal on June 17, 1864, but "reduced to ranks" on May 1, 1865.

15. Wentworth S. Cowan, a farmer from Wentworth, New Hampshire, was a recruit who enlisted on August 11, 1863. Pvt. Hazen O. Baker, a joiner from Pembroke, New Hampshire, was shot in the head and neck at Opequon on September 19, 1864. He died the same day and was buried at the National Cemetery at Winchester, Virginia.
16. Samuel S. Smith also made corporal, on June 25, 1864, and, although wounded almost three months later at the battle of Opequon, would join Mason and Brown in surviving the war.
17. Henry Druker, a Pembroke farmer, transferred to the U.S. Navy on June 30, 1864. After the war, Druker settled in Amherst, New Hampshire, where he died of heart disease in 1882.
18. Jenks, letter of June 9, 1864, Morganza, La., MSCAD.
19. Tyrrell, letter of July 8, 1864, Algiers, opposite New Orleans, La., USAMHI.
20. Hoyt, letter of June 2, 1864, NHHS. Alum is usually aluminum potassium sulfate used as a clarifier and purifier.
21. De B. R. Keim, "The Mississippi River and Its Peculiarities," *Continental Monthly* (New York/Boston, J. R. Gilmore: 1864), vol. 5, issue 6, June 1864, 638.
22. "Local Intelligence," *NOT,* July 5, 1864, 5.
23. *NOT,* July 14, 1864, 4.
24. "While Bathing," *NOT,* July 15, 1864, 5.
25. Buffum, 182–83.

Chapter 13 Battles of Third Winchester (or Opequon Creek) and Fisher's Hill

1. Buffum, 189.
2. This letter is from a transcription. SHSC.
3. "War News," *LD,* August 19, 1864, 3.
4. Buffum, 197.
5. *Battles and Leaders,* vol. 4, 531–32.
6. Buffum, 200.
7. Philip H. Sheridan, *Personal Memoirs of P. H. Sheridan General United States Army,* 2 vols. (New York: Jenkins & McCowan, 1888), vol. 1, 499–500.
8. "The New Hampshire Deserters," *CM,* August 23, 1864, 2.
9. "Serious Trouble with New Hampshire Troops," *BET,* August 22, 1864, 4.
10. Hoyt, letter to Dear brother and sister, August 25, 1864, Halltown, Va, NHHS.

11. Ibid.
12. Sometimes spelled "Opequan," especially in Sergeant Buffum's history of the Fourteenth. It is spelled "Opequon" in Sheridan's memoirs, which is the usage in this work, except when "Opequan" appears in quotes.
13. Buffum, 200.
14. "The Constitutionality of Greenbacks," *BET,* May 12, 1863, 2.
15. Sturtevant, letter of April 28, 1865, Savannah, Georgia, RSCL.
16. Buffum, 428.
17. J. R. Tyrrell, letter of March 28, 1865, Nashville, USAMHI.
18. Buffum, 210. See Elliott W. Hoffman, "General Theodore Ripley and Ultimate Revenge," *Historical New Hampshire,* vol. 46, no. 3, 155–75, 1991.
19. Sheridan, vol. 1, 154.
20. Ibid., vol. 2, 6.
21. Ibid., 2–4.
22. Buffum, 205.
23. George Nye diary, entry for September 19, 1864, RSCL.
24. Buffum, 212.
25. J. W. De Forest, "Sheridan's Battle of Winchester," *Harper's New Monthly Magazine* (New York: Harper & Bros, January 1865), vol. 30, issue 176, 196.
26. De Forest, 199.
27. Buffum, 224.
28. De Forest, 200.
29. "Glorious Victory," *CM,* September 20, 1864, 3.
30. Buffum, 229.
31. Ibid., 230.
32. "Movements in Shenandoah Valley," *BET,* September 27, 1864, 2.
33. *Report of Surg. James T. Ghiselin, U.S. Army, Medical Director, Middle Military Division, of Operations August 27–December 31*, ORA, Series 1, vol. 43, 140. Obviously, the very severe "cases" were too injured to transport and were the most likely to die—on the field or in a field hospital rather than in overtaxed ambulances or wagons. The very slightly wounded could be quickly treated and even returned to duty.
34. *Report of Surg. Ghiselin,* 141. A young surgeon, Ferdinand V. Hayden (1829–1887), who would later make his mark surveying much of the mountain West, became physician in charge.
35. Adams, 110.
36. Buffum, 230.
37. Ibid., 238.
38. Ibid., 249.

39. *Battles and Leaders,* vol. 4, 511.
40. "Glorious Victory," *CM,* September 24, 1864, 2.
41. Buffum, 255.
42. Lewis Q. Smith, letter to, "My Dear Wife," August 23, 1864, SHSC.
43. "Reports from Various Union Generals," *BET,* October 10, 1864, 3.
44. Ibid., October 10, 1864, 3.
45. James Marcellus Smith, letter of August 30, 1864, SHSC.
46. Henry Kyd Douglas, *I Rode with Stonewall* (St. Simon's, Ga.: Mockingbird Books, Inc., 1989), 297.
47. There is no Dr. Faire listed either in Ayling or in *History of the New Hampshire Surgeons in the War of the Rebellion* by Granville P. Conn, (Concord, N.H.: Ira C. Evans Co., 1906). Dr. William H. Thayer joined the Army from Keene, New Hampshire, and served as Surgeon to the Fourteenth. Drs. Marshall Perkins and Franklin Weeks, from Marlow and Chester, New Hampshire, respectively, were mustered as assistant surgeons. Dr. Aaron R. Gleason was not mustered and served as a contract assistant surgeon. See Conn, 173–80.
48. Thomas A. Lewis, *The Guns of Cedar Creek* (New York: Harper & Row, 1988), 112.
49. *Battles and Leaders,* vol. 4, 512.

Chapter 14 Battle of Cedar Creek: Eve of Near Defeat and Final Victory

1. James E. Taylor, *With Sheridan up the Shenandoah Valley in 1864* (Dayton, Ohio: Morningside House, Inc., 1989), 4.
2. *Battles and Leaders,* vol. 4, 515.
3. Winchester August 17, Halltown August 26, Berryville September 3, Lock's Ford September 13, Opequan September 19, Fisher's Hill September 22, Tom's Brook October 9, Strasburg October 13, Cedar Creek October 19. From Granville P. Conn, *History of the New Hampshire Surgeons in the War of Rebellion* (Concord: Ira C. Evans Co., 1906), "Abstract of the History of the Fourteenth New Hampshire Volunteer Infantry," 172–73.
4. Lewis, 140.
5. *BG,* September 26, 1863, 2.
6. D. Eldredge, *The Third New Hampshire and All about It* (Boston: E. B. Stillings and Company, 1893), 972.
7. Buffum, 276.
8. Ibid., 278.
9. Ibid., 278.

10. Ibid., 279.
11. Ibid., 285.
12. Ibid., 291.
13. Jenks, letter of July 12, 1863, Camp Adirondack, Washington, MSCAD.
14. Adams, 75.
15. Ibid., 97.
16. James Marcellus Smith, letter of October 22, 1864, transcription, SHSC.
17. Buffum, 295. Account of the battle by Lt. M. M. Holmes of Company H.
18. *Battles and Leaders*, vol. 4, 529.
19. Douglas, 305.
20. "White Mountain Items," *BET,* October 24, 1864, 2.
21. *Report of Surg. Ghiselin,* 145.
22. Sawyer, letter of October 5, 1862, 45.
23. Sawyer, letter of October 7, 1862, 45.
24. Eldredge, 889-907. Some soldiers received multiple wounds. Thus, the total number of wounds, not the total men wounded, was 609.
25. Frank Moore, *The Civil War in Song and Story* (New York: Peter Fenelon Collier, 1882, reprinted), 349–50.
26. LQS, entry for November 8, 1864. Buffum reported the New Hampshire soldiers' vote: 2,066 for Lincoln and 690 for McClellan. See Buffum, 313.
27. "The Granite State Looking Well," *BET,* November 8, 1864, 2.
28. Ulysses S. Grant, *Personal Memoirs of U. S. Grant,* 2 vols. (New York: Charles L. Webster & Company, 1886), vol. 2, 332.
29. "Sheridan Breaks through the Platform," *BET,* October 3, 1864, 2.
30. "Early was on our front in full force, while both sides did considerable manoeuvering without bringing on more than a skirmish conflict," Buffum, 313.
31. Richardson, 242.
32. Letter of December 19, 1864, Camp 143 NYV, Near Savannah, Ga., "Divine" to Capt. J. H. Everett, Collection of J. H. Everett Papers, MS-241, Item No. 1, Georgia Historical Society, Savannah.
33. ORA, Series I, vol. 43 (part 2), 638.
34. *DAB,* vol. 16, 241.
35. ORA, Series I, vol. 43 (part 2), 638. Lewis's reference to the Army of the Cumberland is enigmatic.
36. "The Thanksgiving Dinner," *BET,* November 30, 1864, 2.
37. The abovementioned men are Pvt. Benjamin F. Fellows, a Sandwich farmer, Pvt. Herman Blood, a Pembroke farmer, and Sgt. James M. Parrott, also a Sandwich farmer. All survived the war.

38. Pvt. Charles N. Cofran, a Pembroke farmer, was discharged with the regiment on July 8, 1865.
39. Sgt. Flavel L. Tolman, a farmer from Rindge, N.H., enlisted in Company G on August 13, 1862. He was promoted to captain and then to major on December 6, 1864.
40. Capt. Oliver H. Marston, a Sandwich pail maker, became a lieutenant-colonel in March 1865. He was apparently wounded by a gunshot to the left arm at Cedar Creek and survived. The record is contradictory. It is stated in Buffum, p. 424, that he was wounded at Cedar Creek. However, the date is given as September 19, 1864. There is no mention of a wound in Ayling.
41. Recruit George H. Haddock, a Canadian boatman from Plainfield, N.H., enlisted at age nineteen, on Sept. 6, 1864. He apparently deserted on June 21, 1865, at Savannah. Buffum, 401 and Ayling, 709.
42. Buffum, 313.
43. *CM,* December 23, 1864, 2.
44. Eliza Smith had headaches severe enough to note *in writing* on two occasions: May 14 and December 16, 1863. Lucy Jane Wiggin wrote of a headache "so I can hardly see" on February 1, 1864.
45. James Emerson, a laborer, came to Company K from Chatham, New Hampshire, as a recruit. Despite being hit by a shell in the left leg and a gunshot wound to the thigh at Opequon, he survived.

Chapter 15 The New Year 1865: Ordered to Georgia and War's End

1. "The Ice Crop" and "The Sleighing," *BET,* January 3, 1865, 2.
2. "Sleigh-Riding," *BG and CCA,* February 6, 1844, 1.
3. Alfred Bunn, *Old England and New England, in a Series of Views Taken on the Spot* (Philadelphia: A. Hart, 1853), 27.
4. Charles C. Jones Jr., *The Seige of Savannah in December 1864, and the Confederate Operations in Georgia and the Third Military District of South Carolina During General Sherman's March from Atlanta to the Sea* (Albany: Joel Munsell, 1874), 143–44. Heavy guns were also moved from Port Royal and from ships of the Union navy.
5. "Savannah," *BET,* January 3, 1865, 2.
6. "Gloomy Condition of Richmond, Jeff Davis Questioned," *BET,* January 2, 1865, 4.
7. "Items of Interest," *Savannah Daily Reublican (SDR),* January 20, 1865, 1.
8. Buffum, 316.

9. Lt. William A. Scofield to "Father," Savannah, January 22, 1865, M-S 1042, Item 1, Georgia Historical Society (GHS), Savannah.
10. *Encyclopaedia Britannica,* 11th edition, 29 vols. (Cambridge, England: University Press, 1911), vol. 24, 240.
11. ORA, Series 1, vol. 47 (part 1), 760.
12. Scofield, letter of January 22, 1865, GHS, Savannah.
13. "Second Provost Court," *Savannah Daily Herald (SDH),* April 8, 1865, 2. Ayling, 704, "Dobson, James. Co. K; substitute; b. Scotland; age 28; cred. Gilford; enl. July 29, '64; must. in July 29, '64, as Priv., must. out July 8, '65; originally assigned to 11 N.H.V., but failed to join that regt."
14. "Prisoner Shot While Attempting to Escape from a Guard-House," *SDH,* April 29, 1865, 1.
15. "Savannah Fire," Carleton's letter to the (Boston) *Journal, CM,* February 7, 1865, 2.
16. "Great Conflagration," *SDH,* January 28, 1865, 2.
17. "Chimney Sweeps," *SDR,* January 27, 1865, 2.
18. "A Diabolical Attempt to Blow Up the City," *SDR,* January 28, 1865, 2.
19. Capt. Octavius C. Mason diary, entry for February 8, 1865, NHHS. Captain Mason called on the *Herald* office but Samuel Mason was not in. Samuel had published the *Palmetto Herald* at Port Royal, South Carolina, until the end of 1864, when he occupied the offices of Savannah's *Daily News* (or *Morning News*) and began the *Savannah Daily Herald.*
20. A. H. Tyrrell, letter of April 9, 1865, Savannah, USAMHI.
21. "Most Glorious News of the War," *SDH,* April 16, 1865, 1.
22. Combs, letter of March 2, 1865, camp at the depot, Savannah, ULND.
23. Combs, letter of March 24, 1865, camp at Fort Polasca [Pulaski], Ga., ULND.
24. "A Card, Transport Steamer Wilmington," *SDH,* April 26, 1865, 2.
25. "Another Arrival of Paroled Prisoners," *SDH,* April 28, 1865, 2.
26. Combs, letter of March 24, 1865, camp at Fort Polasca [Pulaski], Ga., ULND.
27. Buffum, 340.
28. The 1860 census lists Lewis Smith, age fifty-seven, a farmer.
29. Marston, letter to My Dear Sarah, May 29, 1865, Augusta, Ga., RSCL.
30. O. C. Mason diary, entry for June 4, 1865, NHHS.
31. Henry and Daniel Gilman and Alfred Wallace, Sandwich farmers, would be discharged with Lewis in a matter of weeks. Sandwich's William H. H. Sinclair died of epilepsy in Savannah on May 30, 1865, about five weeks

short of his discharge. His body was transported for burial at the National Cemetery at Beaufort, S.C.

32. Buffum, 357.
33. "Letter from New Hampshire," *SDH,* June 22, 1865, 1.
34. "The New Hampshire Election, Vote of the Fourteenth Regiment," *SDH,* March 15, 1865, 2.
35. "New Hampshire Election. The Republican Party Victorious," *SDR,* March 21, 1865, 1.
36. Major Otis F. R. Waite, *New Hampshire in the Great Rebellion* (Claremont, N.H.: Tracy, Chase & Company, 1870), 587.
37. Author unknown, Fourteenth Regiment NHV, MS 170, pocket diary in the Milne Special Collections and Archives Division, University Library, University of New Hampshire, Durham.
38. "Homeward Bound," *SDH,* July 7, 1865, 3.
39. "Arrival of New Hampshire Troops," *BET,* July 18, 1865, 2.
40. "Arrival of the 14th Regiment," *CM,* July 19, 1865, 2.
41. "Ice for U.S. Troops," *SDR,* June 9, 1865, 3.
42. "A Game of Base Ball for July 4th," *SDR,* June 28, 1865, 3.
43. "Affairs Shenandoah Valley—Presentation to Booth's Captor," *BET,* July 20, 1865, 4.
44. "Appeal for Veteran Soldiers," *CM,* June 23, 1865, 2 and "Battle Flags," *CM,* July 20, 1865, 2.
45. ORA, Series 1, vol. 43 (part 2), 740. General Orders No. 26, Headquarters, Second Division., Nineteenth Army Corps. Camp Russell, Va., December 4, 1864.
46. "Important to Soldiers," *CM,* June 23, 1865, 2.
47. George Nye diary, entry for July 26, 1865, RSCL.
48. "Appeal for Veteran Soldiers," *CM,* June 23, 1865, 2.
49. Col. Daniel Hall, an address entitled "The Civic Record of New Hampshire in the Civil War," *Proceedings of the New Hampshire Historical Society* (Concord: Published by the Society, 1906), vol. 4, June, 1899 to June, 1905, 395–414.
50. Jenks, letter of June 22, 1864, Morganza, La., MSCAD.
51. Nichols, 156.
52. Sawyer, letter of November 13, 1864, 300.
53. Buffum, 33–34.

Epilogue: Lewis Q. Smith, Post–Civil War

1. Joan Cook, *Exposed, Unbanked, Weatherbeaten, Knowledge Box: The Schools of Sandwich, New Hampshire 1802–1950* (Portsmouth: Peter E. Randall, 2004), 109.
2. Lucy taught about two dozen students for the summer term of 1852 (and quite likely later) in Sandwich's School No. 6, located at Chick's Corner. "We think good order and fair progress characterized this school." *Annual Report of the Selectmen of the Town of Sandwich, 1853,*16 (For the year ending February 1853.)
3. Letter from J. P. Chase to brother Lewis, Farmington, July 9, no year, SHSC.
4. Letter from Lucy J. Smith to LQS, December 17, 1853, SHSC.
5. Ibid., October 15, 1854, SHSC.
6. Ibid., October 15, 1854, SHSC.
7. "Obituary," *Sandwich Reporter,* December 25, 1913, 1.
8. Letter from Mary E. Paine to LQS November 9, 1853. Transcription, SHSC.
9. Letter from B. B. Smith to John and Eliza Smith, February 1, 1856, SHSC.
10. Letter from B. B. Smith to Eliza Smith, September 3, 1856, SHSC.
11. Letter from Dorcas Smith to My dear brother Lewis, April 19, 1859, SHSC.
12. Letter from B. B. Smith to Eliza Smith, Whitestown, N.Y., January 31, 1849, SHSC.
13. 1890 Special Census, Civil War Veterans and Widows. New Hampshire State Library, Concord.
14. Merrill, 179.
15. Ibid., 183.
16. Ibid., 693.
17. See Okie, 14–16.
18. New Hampshire Agricultural Census for 1850, "Production of Agriculture in the Town of Sandwich in the County of Carroll State of New Hampshire during the Year ending June 1, 1850. New Hampshire State Library.
19. *WG,* December 8, 1855, 2.
20. *NHD,* October 4, 1849, 1.
21. *LD,* May 21, 1869, 2.
22. Hepsa L. Paine, letter of March 6, 1870, SHSC.
23. *Sandwich Reporter,* November 20, 1913, 1.
24. *Sandwich Reporter,* December 4, 1913, 1 and 4.
25. *Sandwich Reporter,* December 25, 1913, 1. The obituary omitted Lewis's father, John Smith. Lewis was the grandson of Eliphalet and the great-grandson of Jacob Smith.
26. *Sandwich Reporter,* January 6, 1916, 1.

Bibliography

Newspapers

Belknap Gazette and Carroll County Advertiser (after 1863, the *Belknap Gazette*)
Boston Daily Evening Transcript
Concord Daily Monitor
Daily Picayune (New Orleans)
New Hampshire Democrat (after mid-1861, the *Laconia Democrat*)
New Orleans Times
Sandwich Reporter
Savannah Daily Herald
Savannah Republican
Winnipesaukee (Laconia) *Gazette*

Letters and Diaries

Author unknown, Fourteenth Regiment NHV, MS 170, January to July, 1865, pocket diary in the Milne Special Collections and Archives Division, University Library, University of New Hampshire, Durham.

John R. Barden, ed., *Letters to the Home Circle: the North Carolina Service of Pvt. Henry A. Clapp* (Raleigh: Division of Archives and History, North Carolina Department of Cultural Resources, 1998).

Pvt. William H. H. Bennett, letters (4), Company K, Fourteenth Regiment NHV, Sandwich Historical Society Collection, Sandwich, New Hampshire.

Pvt. William Combs Collection, letters (9), Company C, Fourteenth Regiment NHV, Department of Special Collections, University Libraries of Notre Dame, University of Notre Dame, Notre Dame, Indiana.

Cpl. Daniel C. Currier Collection, letters (several dozen), Company I, Fourteenth Regiment NHV, Milne Special Collections and Archives, University Library, University of New Hampshire, Durham.

J. H. Everett Papers, MS-241, Georgia Historical Society, Savannah.

Maj. Alexander Gardner, Adjutant, Fourteenth Regiment NHV, letters (7) to Major Samuel A. Duncan, Rauner Special Collections Library, Dartmouth College Library, Hanover, New Hampshire.

Pvt. Christopher Hoyt, letters (18), Company I, Fourteenth Regiment NHV, New Hampshire Historical Society, Concord.

Sgt. John Henry Jenks Collection, letters (12 prewar, 28 1862–1864), Company C, Fourteenth Regiment NHV, Milne Special Collections and Archives, University Library, University of New Hampshire, Durham.

Lt. Col. Oliver H. Marston, letters (10), Company K, Fourteenth Regiment NHV, Rauner Special Collections Library, Dartmouth College Library, Hanover, New Hampshire.

Capt. Octavius C. Mason, diary, Company K, Fourteenth Regiment NHV, New Hampshire Historical Society, Concord.

Capt. George W. Nye, diary and letters (5), Company C, Fourteenth Regiment NHV, Rauner Special Collections Library, Dartmouth College Library, Hanover, New Hampshire.

Cpl. Henry M. Sanborn, letters (11), Company H, Fourteenth Regiment NHV, New Hampshire Historical Society, Concord.

Sgt. Elbridge Smith, letters (11), Company A, Fourteenth Regiment NHV, Historical Society of Cheshire County, Keene, New Hampshire.

Cpl. Lewis Quimby Smith, 1864 pocket diary and letters (69), Sandwich Historical Society, Sandwich, New Hampshire.

Capt. John W. Sturtevant, letters (5), Company G, Fourteenth Regiment NHV, Rauner Special Collections Library, Dartmouth College Library, Hanover, New Hampshire.

Capt. John W. Sturtevant, letters (5), Company G, Fourteenth Regiment NHV, Manuscript Group 43, John and Clifford Sturtevant Papers, Historical Society of Cheshire County, Keene, New Hampshire.

Sgt. Albert H. Tyrell, letters (5), Company B, Fourteenth Regiment NHV, letters to his brother, J. R. Tyrrell, U. S. Army Military History Institute, Carlisle, Pennsylvania.

Books

Adams, Ephraim Douglass. *Great Britain and the American Civil War,* 2 vols. (New York: Russell & Russell, 1924).

Adams, George W. *Doctors in Blue* (New York: Henry Schuman, Inc., 1952).

Alcott, Louisa May. (Bessie Z. Jones, ed.) *Hospital Sketches* (Cambridge, Mass: Belknap Press of Harvard University Press, 1960).

Ayling, Augustus D. Adjutant General. *Revised Register of the Soldiers and Sailors of New Hampshire in the War of the Rebellion 1861–1866* (Concord: Ira C. Evans, 1895).

Barden, John R., ed. *Letters to the Home Circle: the North Carolina Service of Pvt. Henry A. Clapp* (Raleigh: Division of Archives and History, North Carolina Department of Cultural Resources, 1998).

Barrett, Selah Hibbard, ed. *Memoirs of Eminent Preachers in the Freewill Baptist Denomination* (Rutland, Ohio: Selah Hibbard Barrett, 1874).

Bartlett, Capt. A. W. *History of the Twelfth Regiment New Hampshire Volunteers in the War of the Rebellion* (Concord: Ira C. Evans, Printer, 1897).

Basler, Roy P., ed. *The Collected Works of Abraham Lincoln,* 8 vols. (New Brunswick, N.J.: Rutgers University Press, 1953).

Battle Flags of the New Hampshire Regiments (Concord: Kimball & Sons, 1866).

Bowman, John S., ed. *The Civil War Almanac* (New York: World Almanac Publications, 1983).

Brooks, Stewart. *Civil War Medicine* (Springfield, Ill.: Charles C. Thomas, 1966).

Buffum, Francis H. *A Memorial of the Great Rebellion: Being a History of the Fourteenth Regiment New-Hampshire Volunteers, Covering Its Three Years of Service, with Original Sketches of Army Life* (Boston: Franklin Press, Rand Avery, & Company, 1882).

Bunn, Alfred. *Old England and New England: A Series of Views Taken on the Spot* (Philadelphia: A. Hart, 1853).

Cemetery Committee of the Moultonborough Historical Society, ed., *The Cemetery Records of Moultonborough, New Hampshire* (Moultonborough, N.H.: Harvest Press, 1988).

Compact Edition of the Oxford English Dictionary, 2 vols. (New York: Oxford University Press, 1971).

Conn, Granville P. *History of the New Hampshire Surgeons in the War of Rebellion* (Concord: Ira C. Evans Co., 1906).

Cook, Joan. *Exposed, Unbanked, Weatherbeaten, Knowledge Box: The Schools of Sandwich, New Hampshire, 1802–1950* (Portsmouth: Peter E. Randall, 2004).

Cumberworth, Sheila M. and Daniel V. Biles. *An Enduring Love: The Civil War Diaries of Benjamin Franklin Pierce (Fourteenth New Hampshire Vol. Inf.) and His Wife Harriet Jane Goodwin Pierce* (Gettysburg: Thomas Publications, 1995).

Douglas, Henry Kyd. *I Rode with Stonewall* (St. Simon's, Ga.: Mockingbird Books, Inc., 1989).

Eldredge, D. *The Third New Hampshire and All about It* (Boston: E. B. Stillings and Company, 1893).

Encyclopaedia Britannica, 11th edition, 29 vols. (Cambridge, England: University Press, 1911).

Geary, James W. *We Need Men: The Union Draft in the Civil War* (DeKalb: Northern Illinois University Press, 1991).

Grant, Ulysses S. *Personal Memoirs of U. S. Grant,* 2 vols. (New York: Charles L. Webster & Company, 1886).

Hawthorne, Nathaniel. *The Life of Franklin Pierce* (with additions), (Portsmouth, New Hampshire: Peter E. Randall, 2000).

Hubbard, B. F. *The History of Stanstead County, Province of Quebec* (Montreal: Lovell Printing and Publishing Company, 1874).

Johnson, Allen and Dumas Malone. *Dictionary of American Biography,* 20 vols. (New York: Charles Scribner's Sons, 1937).

Johnson, Robert Underwood and Clarence Clough Buel, eds. *Battles and Leaders of the Civil War,* 4 vols. (New York: Thomas Yoseloff, Inc., 1956).

Jones, Charles C. Jr. *The Seige of Savannah in December, 1864, and the Confederate Operations in Georgia and the Third Military District of South Carolina During General Sherman's March from Atlanta to the Sea* (Albany: Joel Munsell, 1874).

Lewis, Thomas A. *The Guns of Cedar Creek* (New York: Harper & Row, 1988).

Lighton, Harriet Vittum. *Sandwich, N.H., Cemeteries* (reprinted by Higginson Book Co. from 1930 original).

Lincoln, Abraham. Arthur Brooks Lapsley, ed. *The Writings of Abraham Lincoln,* 8 vols. (New York: G. P. Putnam's Sons, 1923).

Lyon, G. Parker. *The New Hampshire Annual Register for the Year 1865* (Concord: G. Parker Lyon, 1865).

Merrill, Georgia Drew. *History of Carroll County* (Somersworth: New Hampshire Publishing Company, 1971).

Miller, William J. *Mapping for Stonewall* (Washington, D.C.: Elliott & Clark Publishing, 1993).

Mitchell, Reid. *The Vacant Chair: the Northern Soldier Leaves Home* (New York: Oxford University Press, 1993).

Moat, Louis Shepheard, ed. *Frank Leslie's Illustrated Famous Leaders and Battle Scenes of the Civil War* (New York: Mrs. Frank Leslie, 1896).

Moore, Frank. *The Civil War in Song and Story* (New York: Peter Fenelon Collier, 1882), reprinted.

Murdock, Eugene C. *One Million Men: The Civil War Draft in the North* (Madison: State Historical Society of Wisconsin, 1971).

Nichols, Roy Franklin. *Franklin Pierce: Young Hickory of the Granite Hills* (Philadelphia: University of Pennsylvania Press, 1969).

Richardson, James D. *A Compilation of the Messages and Papers of the Presidents 1789–1897,* 10 vols. (Washington: Government Printing Office, 1897).

Riffel, Judy. ed. *A History of Pointe Coupee Parish and Its Families* (Dallas: VAAPR, Inc., 1983).

Sawyer, Merrill C. *Letters from a Civil War Surgeon: Dr. William Child of the Fifth New Hampshire Volunteers* (Solon, Maine: Polar Bear & Co., 2001).

Sewell, Richard H. *John P. Hale and the Politics of Abolition* (Cambridge: Harvard University Press, 1965).

Sheridan, Philip H. *Personal Memoirs of P. H. Sheridan, General United States Army,* 2 vols. (New York: Jenkins & McCowan, 1888).

Taylor, James E. *With Sheridan up the Shenandoah Valley in 1864* (Dayton, Ohio: Morningside House, Inc., 1989).

Vandiver, Frank E. *Jubal's Raid: General Early's Famous Attack on Washington in 1864* (New York: McGraw-Hill, 1960).

Waite, Maj. Otis F. R. *New Hampshire in the Great Rebellion* (Claremont, N.H.: Tracy, Chase & Company, 1870).

The War of the Rebellion: A Compilation of the Official Records of the Union and Confederate Armies (U.S. War Department: Government Printing Office, 1889).

Williams, T. Harry. *Lincoln and His Generals* (New York: Alfred A. Knopf, 1952).

Wilson, Rufus Rockwell. *Washington: The Capital City,* 2 vols. (Philadelphia & London: J. B. Lippincott Company, 1901).

Articles

De Forest, J. W. "Sheridan's Battle of Winchester," *Harper's New Monthly Magazine* (New York: Harper & Bros, January, 1865), vol. 30, issue 176.

Geier, Clarence, Warren Hofstra, and Joseph Whitehorne. "The Sheridan Military Field Hospital Complex at Shawnee Springs," *Winchester-Frederick County Historical Society Journal* (Stephens City, Va.: Commercial Press, Inc.), vol. 7, 1993, 1–32.

Governor J. A. Gilmore Correspondence with Hon. Edwin M. Stanton, U.S. War Department, July–September 1863, *The Conscription* (Concord, N.H.: Fogg, Hadley and Company, 1863).

Daniel Hall, an address on "The Civic Record of New Hampshire in the Civil War," *Proceedings of the New Hampshire Historical Society* (Concord: published by the society, 1906), vol. 4, June 1899 to June 1905, 395–414.

Hoffman, Elliott W. "General Theodore Ripley and Ultimate Revenge," *Historical New Hampshire,* vol. 46, no. 3, 1991, 155–175.

Keim, De B. R. "The Mississippi River and Its Peculiarities," *Continental Monthly* (New York/Boston: J. R. Gilmore, 1864), vol. 5, issue 6, June 1864.

Marvel, William. "A Poor Man's Fight: Civil War Enlistment Patterns in Conway, New Hampshire," *Historical New Hampshire,* vol. 43, no. 1, 21–40.

Okie, Tom. "Coming Back to the Land: 240 Years of Human Activity at Mead Base," *Eighty-third Annual Excursion of the Sandwich Historical Society,* Sandwich Historical Society (Tilton, N.H.: Sant Bani Press, 2002).

Squires, J. Duane. "The Contribution of New Hampshire's Governors to the Civil War 1861–1865." A paper presented before the National Assembly of the U.S. Civil War Centennial Commission held in Boston, on 22 May 1963. Mimeographed and distributed by the New Hampshire Civil War Centennial Commission, Cleon E. Heald, Executive Director, Keene.

Index

A. Williams Co., 166
abolition, 61. *See also* slaves
absentee balloting, 183
Adams, Issac, 62
Adams Express Company, 88
Adams Press, 62
African Americans, 61
    as soldiers, 68, 71, 196, 266
    See also slaves
Alabama, CSS (raider), 59, 147, 209, 211
alcohol. *See* liquor
All Quiet on the Western Front (Remarque), 50, x
alum, 309
Ambrose, Oliver L., 85
Ambulance Corps Act (1864), 252
ambulance system, 251–252
Amendatory Act (1864), 158
ammunition, 10. *See also* arsenals; weapons
Amoskeag Company, 36
amputations, 254–255. *See also* casualties
Anaconda Plan, 11
Anacostia River, 139–140
Anderson, Robert, 135
Antietam, battle of, 10, 173
apple cider, 23–24, 295
applebee, 54
Aquia Creek, 212–213
Ariel (steamer), 268
Armed Liberty, 165
Army of the Potomac, 59, 148–149
Army of the Shenandoah, 216, 240, 258, 278–279
arsenals, 36, 269–271
Association Test, 158
Atocha, Judge, 191
Atwood, Augusta A. Batchelder, 163
Atwood, Harrison, 112
Atwood, Harrison II, 163–164, 233, 234*p*
Atwood, John, 111–112, 286
Atwood, Mary and Philip, 112
Augusta, Georgia, 274–278

Baker, Edward, 41
Baker, Hazen O., 309
Ball's Bluff, 41, 41*p*
Baltimore, Maryland, 10, 39–40
Baltimore and Ohio Railroad, 39, 172, 177, 233
Banks, Nathaniel P., 187, 202
baseball, 6, 273, 278
Batchelder, Nathaniel, 6
Battery Wagner, 125
battle flags, 279, 279*p*
Bayou Grossetête, 204–205
Bean, Caleb G., 129, 303
Bean, George C., 142, 304
Bean, Jonathan, 305
Beauregard, P.G.T., 138
Beede, Dan, 79, 80, 83, 301
Beede, Capt. Edwin, 79, 79*p*
Beede, Parker, 88
Belle Grove House, 248*p*
Bennett, John, 289
Bennett, William H.H., 32, 294

Berry, Nathaniel S., 4, 6, 20
Birge, Henry W., 199, 223, 247
Black Cherries, 148
blockades, 11, 59, 119
Blood, Herman, 312
Booth, John Wilkes, 144
Boston, 224, 275, 278
Boston Daily Evening Transcript (newspaper), 117–119, 166
bounties, 50, 152–153, 280
Boyd, Belle, 138–139, 138*p*
bread riot, 60
Briant, Lucinda, 142
Brierfield, 173
Broom, Asa, 133
brothels, 134, 137, 138
Brown, Warren J., 308–309
Bryant, Lucinda, 304
Buerling, Henry, 211
Buffum, Francis H., ix, 25, 54, 56, 96–97, 111, 151, 158, 181, 203, 222, 225, 230, 241, 246, 274, 280, 281, 289
Bull Run, battles of, 138, 147, 173
Bulletin, vii
Burleigh, John, 297
Burnham, Edward W., 286
Burnside, Ambrose, 51–52, 54, 59, 68, 69, 71
Buzzell, Ebenezer M., 261
Buzzell, Ransom D., 261

Camp Adirondack, 95
Camp Belknap, 74
Camp Fever, 188
Camp Parapet, 185, 188, 196
Camp Russell, 258–264
Canby, Edward R.S., 196
canes, 173
Capitol Building, 164–165, 165*p*
Carroll County Court, 1
Carroll Prison, 138, 304
Carrollton, Louisiana, 185, 186, 188, 190, 202*m*
Carter, Solon A., 143, 305
casualties, 310, 312
  of the Fourteenth Regiment, 231–233, 233*p*, 234*p*, 235, 249–251, 250*p*, 309, 313, 314–315
  See also amputations
Cedar Creek, battle of, 8, 219–220, 228–229, 241, 242*m*, 243–252, 248*p*, 249*p*, 279
  casualties of, 253–254
censorship, 147
Center Sandwich, N.H., 286, 300
Central Guard House, 110, 110*m*, 132, 138, 139
Chain Bridge, 212, 213
Chancellorsville, Virginia, 102, 121
Charleston, South Carolina, 60
Chase, Irene A., 34, 40, 41, 43, 43*p*, 106, 290
Chase, James E., 52
Chase, Jonathan P., 14, 34, 84, 284, 290
Chase, Lemuel, 141
Chase, Lucy J., 34
Chase, Marietta, 34, 107
Chase, Mary W. Smith, 14, 34, 290
Chase, Sally M. Smith, 14, 15, 34, 107, 108, 114, 290
Chase, Sarah E., 34, 82
Chesapeake and Ohio Canal, 39, 233
Child, William, 54, 56–57, 79, 134, 254, 281
Christmas, 163, 165, 262–263
The Civil War in Song and Story (Moore), 254–255
Civil War Memorial Tablet, 290
Clapp, Henry A., 62–63
Clark, John, 67, 123
Clark, Joseph, 142, 304, 305
Clinton (transport), 196

clothing, 244. *See also* supplies
Cockspur Island, 268
Cofran, Charles N., 313
Cold Harbor, battle of, 121
Columbia, South Carolina, 125, 134–135
Combs, William, 41, 53–54, 61, 77, 134, 161, 168, 273, 304
commutation, 50, 298
Concord, New Hampshire, 116, 117, 129
Concord Monitor (newspaper), 224
Congress, U.S., 280
Conscription Act, 59, 74, 75, 79
conscripts, 151
Constitution (steamer), 278
Continental (steamer), 211–212
Copperheads, 45, 69, 71, 75, 118, 159, 173, 256
Corps badge, 258
Cotton, Eli N., 92
cotton mills, 66–67, 300
Cowan, Wentworth S., 309
Crawford, Thomas, 165
Crook, George, 210, 230, 235, 243, 247
currency, 60, 226–227. *See also* money
Currier, Daniel C., 306
Currier, John, 302
Curtis, Samuel R., 46
Custer, George, 230–231, 243

Dahlgren, John, 135
Daily Picayune (newspaper), 195
Dale, Ebenezer, 108, 108*p,* 109, 163
Daniel Webster (steamer), 187, 307
Davis, Jefferson, 173, 262, 267, 275
De Soto (steamer), 266
Dearborn, Bradbury, 298
Dearborn, Elizabeth, 298
Dearborn, John, 54, 298
Dearborn, Warren, 300
Democrat Party, 45, 46, 81
  convention of, 117
  election of 1864, 77–79, 181–183, 256, 277
  military and, 77–78
deserters, 82, 95, 152–153, 183, 266, 268, 281, 313
Dexter, George, 296
diaries, 166
Dickinson, Anna E., 122
Dinsmore, Jed, 129, 132
Dinsmore, Jeremiah, 133, 303
Dinsmore, Sarah Jane, 124
Dinsmore Pond, 137
diseases, 39, 50–51, 85, 188
  cancer, 170
  consumption, 170, 289
  diphtheria, 141–142, 198
  in the Fourteenth Regiment, 13, 50-51, 95, 107, 142
  malaria, 62, 125
  in New Orleans, 195
  in Sandwich, 1, 87, 92, 136, 141–142, 198
  smallpox, 1, 7, 87–88, 89, 92, 106
  tuberculosis, 170
  typhoid, 13, 23, 95, 149
  varioloid, 87
Dobson, James, 269, 314
Douglas, Henry Kyd, 252
draft, military, 4–7, 75, 124–125, 151, 294
draft riots, 122, 123, 124, 166
Druker, Henry, 309
Du Pont, Samuel Francis, 134–135
Duncan, S.A., 298
Dustin, Ezekiel E., 52

Early, Jubal A., 11, 40, 167, 168, 172, 210, 219–220, 222, 228, 230, 233, 234, 236, 241, 247, 252, 256, 262
East Weare, N.H., 15*m*

Eastman, Ira A., 78
Eighth Army Corps, 229–231
Eighth Regiment, NHV, 93
Eighty-Third Annual Excursion of the Sandwich Historical Society, vii
election of 1864, 77–79, 181–183, 255–257, 277, 312
Emancipation Proclamation, 45
Emerson, James, 313
Emory, William H., 196, 205, 223
employment
  veterans and, 280
  women and, 92, 113
Enrollment Act (1863), 7, 75, 79, 293
Estes, Benjamin, 261, 289

farming, 64–65, 106, 109, 132, 137, 192, 228, 280, 283, 285, 287–288, 289, 290
Farragut, David Glasgow, 188
Fellows, Benjamin F., 206–207, 286, 308, 312
Fellows, Christopher, 89
Fifteenth Regiment, NHV, 62, 205
Fifth Regiment, NHV, 56–57, 129, 152
financial aid, 61–62, 280
fires
  in Sandwich, 1, 158, 290
  in Savannah, 269–271
First Manassas, battle of, 138, 147
Fisher's Hill, battle of, 235–236, 253–254, 261, 279
Fisk, Jesse A., 204
flags, 279, 279*p*
Florida, CSS (raider), 59
food, 95–96, 148–149. *See also* supplies; wagon trains
Ford's Theatre, 79
Forest City. *See* Savannah, Georgia
Fort Adams, 202*m,* 205
Fort Banks, 188
Fort Delaware, 131
Fort Massachusetts, 116
Fort McAllister, 265, 268, 270*m*
Fort Pulaski, 268, 270*m,* 273
Fort Star, 188
Fort Stevens, 116, 210
Fort Sumter, 126, 135, 141
Fort Wagner, 141
Fort Warren, 275
Fortress Monroe, 131, 211–212, 307
Foss, Lizzie, 47, 48
Foss, William E.S., 47, 48, 298
Fourteenth Regiment, NHV, 74
  at Camp Adirondack, 95
  at Camp Russell, 258–264
  casualties of the, 231–233, 233*p,* 234*p,* 235, 249–251, 250*p,* 309, 313, 314–315
  at Cedar Creek, 243–252, 247–252
  Company C, 7, 54, 179–180
  Company E, 185, 187, 211
  Company F, ix, 25, 211
  Company G, 185, 187, 211
  Company H, 142, 231
  Company I, 52, 187, 203, 306
  Company K, 6, 7, 8, 9, 13, 61, 74, 85, 88, 91, 183, 185, 187, 203, 211–212, 216, 231, 233, 243, 255, 261, 269, 271, 281, 286, 313
  desertions in the, 95, 183
  discharge of, 278–281
  discipline of, 181
  disease in the, 13, 50–51, 95, 142
  draft riots and, 124
  flag of the, 279, 279*p*
  at Fort Adams, 205
  at Fort Stevens, 116
  furloughs for the, 151–152, 181
  in Georgia, 267–278, 274–278

guard and provost duty of, 95–116, 119–120, 131–132, 137–138, 150, 152, 168, 183
in Harpers Ferry, 168, 171–172, 175
Jefferson Davis and, 275
join with Nineteenth Army Corps, 199
letterhead of, 30*p,* 31
lice and the, 36–37
in Maryland, 30*p,* 31–34
medical care in the, 311
in Morganza, 201–205, 202*m,* 203*p,* 209
in New Orleans, 180, 187–188, 190, 209–211
in New York, 184–185
officers in, 56–57
at Opequon Creek, 229–231
at Poolesville, Maryland, 60–61, 60*p,* 84
recruiting by the, 151–152
in Shenandoah Valley, 213, 219–222, 221*m,* 236–237
voting by the, 78, 255–257, 277, 312
in Washington, 11, 26, 95–116, 110*m,* 132–150, 154, 158, 164–165, 166, 168, 179–180
winter camp of, 94
Fourth of July, 117–119, 131
Fourth Regiment, NHV, 182, 183
Frederick Junction, Maryland, 215–216, 216*p*
Fredericksburg, Virginia, 59, 68, 82, 173
Freewill Baptist Church, 18
French, George N., 74, 75
furloughs, 83, 151–152, 163, 173, 174, 181, 182

Gamble, H.R., 46
gambling, 304
Gardner, Alexander, 56, 295, 298
General Lyon (steamer), 211
General Orders, 257–258
General Sedgwick (ship), 273
Gettysburg, battle of, 116, 121, 125, 129
Gilman, Daniel R., 296, 314
Gilman, Henry, 25, 126, 148, 149, 162, 296, 314
Gilman, James H., 25, 260
Gilmore, John A., 181–182, 183, 303
Gilmore, Joseph Albree, 78, 124–125
Gleason, Aaron R., 311
Glidden, Warren A., 261
Goddess of Liberty, 165
Gold Rush, 283–284
Gordon, John B., 241, 243
Goss, John W., 286
Gould, Ezra, 61, 78, 299
Grant, Ulysses S., 237, 256
gravel, 299
Great Western Railroad, 209
greenbacks, 227. *See also* currency; money
Greenhow, Rose O'Neal, 138
ground itch, 37
Grover, Cuvier, 199, 223, 270
guerillas, 208*p*

Hackett, Albert F., 14, 53, 80, 81, 83, 86, 87, 88, 297
Hackett, Augustus M., 81
Hackett, Burleigh B., 81
Hackett, Hannah E., 81, 107
Hackett, Susan A. Smith, 14, 15, 53, 81, 107, 271
Haddock, George H., 313
Hale, John P., 182
Halleck, Henry W., 102, 171, 175, 302
Ham, Louisa M., 303
Ham, William P., 129, 303

hangings, 219*p,* 281
Hardee, William J., 266
Harper, Robert, 175
Harpers Ferry, 168, 171–172, 175, 175*p,* 176*p,* 177, 216, 244–245, 244*p*
Harris, Mark, 148
Harris Powders, 148
Hart, James, 154, 305
Hayden, Ferdinand V., 310
headaches, 263, 313
health
  of Lewis Q. Smith, 13, 23, 50-51, 62, 63, 72, 77, 84-85, 91, 98, 149, 150, 203, 263
  in Sandwich, 107
  of Smith family, 169–170, 173, 174
  See also diseases
Heard, William A., 25, 286
Hill, Isaac, 119, 302
Hoit, Calvin, 8
Hood, John Bell, 261
Hooker, Joseph, 54, 59, 60, 102, 145, 149, 302
hookworm, 37
horses, 114
hospitals, 51, 132–133, 231–233, 232*p,* 251–252. *See also* medicine
Hotchkiss, Jedediah, 241, 243
Hoyt, Christopher, 104–105, 187, 225, 296
hunker, 45–46
Hupp's Hill, 238
Hutchins, Lucy M. Smith, vii–viii

Invalid Corps, 152, 154
ironclads, 134–135

Jackson, Mississippi, 173
Jackson, Thomas Stonewall, 168
Jenks, Almina, 250
Jenks, John Henry, 7, 9, 27, 51, 53–54, 61, 62, 83, 97, 134, 139, 141, 143, 151, 158, 181, 203, 207, 215, 250–251, 251*p,* 280
Jewett, A.B., 10
Johnson, Andrew, 71
Johnson's Island, 131

Kearsage, USS (ship), 209, 211
Kershaw, Joseph B., 220, 222, 225, 228
Kiah Pond, 64
King, John, 269
Kingfisher (ship), 273

Laconia Democrat (newspaper), 78, 141, 142
Ladd, N.G., 92
Lake Village, N.H., ix, 15*m,* 73–74
Lake Waukewan, 306
Lake Winnepesauke, 306
Lakeport, N.H., ix, 73–74
Lancaster, N.H., 36
Lander, Frederick W., 41
Leach, William S., 81–82, 82*p*
lead line, 307
Lee, Robert E., 40, 116, 125, 147, 271
Legal Tender Act (1862), 226–227
Letterman, Jonathan, 149
Levi Smith Cemetery, 173
Lewis, Enoch, 198
Lewis, Freeman, 198
Liberty (transport), 185
Library of Congress, 304
lice, 36–37
Lincoln, Abraham, 46
  African American soldiers and, 71
  assassination of, 79, 271
  battle strategy of, 59–60
  call for more troops, 4–5
  capture of Savannah, 262
  changes in the military, 57
  deserters and, 82, 152

draft and, 125
election of 1864, 77-79, 183, 256
Emancipation Proclamation, 45
General Orders, 257–258
in New Hampshire, 122
soldiers' pay and, 27
Vallandigham and, 71
Lincoln, Mary Todd, 122
liquor, 24–25, 96, 97–98, 128, 134, 144, 191, 295
Little North Mountain, 234, 235
Louisiana Belle (steamboat), 208*p*
Lyon, Nathaniel, 211

Magoon, Albert, 68, 69, 300
Magoon, Asa, 11, 22, 23, 69, 83, 88, 149, 173, 174, 243, 289, 295
Magoon, Charles W., 300
Magoon, Eliza, 66, 89
Magoon, Emma E., 300
Magoon, Hattie, 300
Magoon, Jonathan, 295
Magoon, Levi, 295, 300
Magoon, Lydia Smith, 300
Magoon, Mary Eliza Smith, 11, 23, 300
Magoon, Orrila E., 300
Magoon, Riley, 41, 68, 109, 295, 300
mail service, 89
Maine Aroostock War, 62
Mallon, Mary, 149
Malone, Patrick, 166
Manchester, N.H., ix, 66
maple sugaring. *See* sapping
Marston, B. Ellen, 136, 304
Marston, John, 136, 304
Marston, Moulton H., 46, 297
Marston, Oliver H., 6, 8, 8*p,* 136, 150, 185, 206–207, 245, 247, 276, 313
Maryland, 30*p,* 31–34
Mason, Larkin Dodge, 271
Mason, Nathan, 78
Mason, Octavius C., 276, 308, 314
Mason, Samuel W., 271, 314
Massanutten Mountain, 241, 242*m*
McCall, Richard, 205
McClellan, George B., 183, 257
Mead Base, vii
Meade, George, 102, 125, 147
medicine, 148, 169–170. *See also* hospitals; vaccinations
Meredith Village, N.H., ix, 15*m*
Middle Military Division, 216. *See also* Army of the Shenandoah
military police, 96–97, 269
militias, 36
Mint, U.S., 128
Mississippi River, 199, 202*m,* 207, 211
blockades of, 11
Port Hudson, 126, 127
Mitchell, Reid, 50
money, 127, 128, 226–227, 244, 280. *See also* payroll issues
Monocacy Junction, Maryland, 210, 215–216, 216*p*
Moore, Frank, 254–255
morale, 54, 111, 148, 161, 188, 273
Morganza, Louisiana, 201–205, 202*m,* 203*p,* 209
Morris Island, 125
Mosby, John S., 218
mosquitos, 188, 189
Moulton, Charles E. Ned, 14, 16, 295
Moulton, Ed, 101
Moulton, Henry H., 52, 261
Moulton, Lizzie Ann Smith, 14, 15, 15*m,* 16
Moulton S. Webster Post, 286
Moultonborough, N.H., ix, 15*m,* 25, 81, 88, 141
Mount Israel, vii
mud march, 59, 68, 129
musicians, 47, 61, 85, 178, 251
muskets, 154

Navy, U.S., 125, 134–135, 309
Navy Yard Bridge, 139, 140*p,* 144, 165
Nelson, Albert D., 301
Nelson, Dan P., 301
Nelson, Hiram, 82, 83, 301
Nelson, Major J., 301
neuritis, 263
New Hampshire
  agricultural census, 316
  congressional elections, 181–182
  draft in, 124–125
  draft riots, 122, 123
  elections in, 256, 299
  enlistments from, 293, 294
  governorship in, 77–78, 181, 277
  hiring veterans in, 280
  lakes in, 306
  population of, 280, 294
  presidential election, 182–183
  rebel invasion of, 117–119
New Hampshire Patriot (newspaper), 302
New Hampshire Soldiers' Home, 280
New Hampshire Volunteers. *See* Eighth Regiment; Fifteenth Regiment; Fifth Regiment; Fourteenth Regiment; Fourth Regiment; Second Regiment; Seventh Regiment; Sixth Regiment; Tenth Regiment; Third Regiment; Thirteenth Regiment; Twelfth Regiment
New Jersey Volunteers, 96
New Orleans, 180, 185–188, 202*m*
  diseases in, 195
  Fourteenth Regiment in, 180, 187–188, 190, 209–211
  railroad in, 190
New Orleans Times (newspaper), 211
New Year's Day, 166
New York, 122, 123, 184–185
New York Evening Post (newspaper), 119
New York Volunteers, 95
Newton, James K., 50, 134, 151, 298
Nineteenth Army Corps, 199, 202, 210, 229–231, 230*p*
  at Cedar Creek, 243–252
  Corps badge, 258
  in Georgia, 267–278
  revue of, 204
North Sandwich, N.H., 6, 286, 300
Nye, George W., 178, 280

Offutt's Cross-Roads, 27
Oglethorpe, James Edward, 268
Okie, Tom, vii
Old Capitol Prison, 100, 100*p,* 110, 110*m,* 132, 138, 139, 304
Opequan. *See* Opequon Creek, battle of
Opequon Creek, battle of, 108, 123, 225, 227, 229–231, 230*p,* 253-254, 279

Page, Doctor, 85
Page, Henry P., 203–204, 204*p*
Paine, Amos M., 48, 49, 112, 115, 289, 305
Paine, Demerit, 49
Paine, Harriet Varney, 115
Paine, Hepsa, 49, 66, 67–68, 114–116, 123–124, 289
Paine, Hepsis Lee, 48
Paine, Julia M., 49, 67
Paine, Lucy, 49
Paine, Parker, 49
Paine, Sarah, 49
Paine, Sarah J., 49
pairing bees, 54
Parrott, James M., 286, 312
payroll issues, 27, 50, 60, 61–62, 72–73, 226–227, 280

Peace Democrats, 81, 256
Pearl, James W., 91, 143
Perkins, Marshall, 51, 311
Pierce, Benjamin Franklin, 52
Pierce, Franklin, 117–119, 173, 280–281
pistols, 154. *See also* weapons
Plummer, Henry, 144, 157
Point Lookout, Maryland, 129
Poolesville, Maryland, 27, 37, 41, 60–61, 60*p,* 84
population
    of New Hampshire, 280, 294
    of Sandwich, 7, 285, 288
Port Hudson, 126, 127
Port Royal, South Carolina, 187
Porter, David D., 188, 211
Portsmouth, N.H., 36, 122
Portsmouth Grove Hospital, 132–133
Potomac River, 26, 39–40, 41*p,* 59, 139–140, 140*p,* 175*p,* 176*p,* 212, 213
Prescott, John M., 5
presidential elections, 181–183, 255–257
printing press, 62
prisoners of war, 131–132, 273
promotions, 308–309, 313
prostitution, 134, 137, 138
provost courts, 269, 314

Quaker Meetinghouse, 158
Quimby, Albert W. and Sarah A., 303
Quimby, George Dexter, 296
Quimby, J.D., 297
Quimby, William F., 74
quinine, 62–63

railroads, 39–40, 131, 172, 177, 190, 209, 233
Rappahannock River, 60, 147
Read, T. Buchanan, 252
Red River, 202
refugee camp, 188
Remarque, Erich Maria, x, 50
Republican Party, 81
    election of 1864, 78, 181–183, 256, 277
Revolutionary War, 3
Richmond, Virginia, 271
Ricker, Joseph L., 49
Ricker, Rachel H., 49, 67
rifles, 36, 39, 100, 154, 280. *See also* weapons
rings, 53
Ripley, Theodore, 8, 227–228, 228*p,* 247
road agents, 109
Russell, David Allen, 258

Sanborn, Henry, 37
Sandusky, Ohio, 131
Sandwich, N.H., vii, 74
    Bean Road, 305
    census of, 92, 314
    County Farm, 289
    description of, 286
    diseases in, 1, 87, 92, 107, 136, 141–142, 198
    financial aid for military families, 61–62, 280
    fires in, 1, 158, 290
    maps of, 2*m,* 15*m*
    poor house, 288–289
    population of, 7, 285, 288
    real estate in, 299
    Sandwich Notch Road, 3, 108, 109
    sapping in, 88
    schools in, 108, 109, 137, 283, 316
    Town Hall, 6
    town meetings, 77
    Wing Road, 288–289
Sandwich Historical Society, viii, 85

Sandwich Library Association, 287
Sandwich Lower Corner, 286, 300
Sandwich Reporter (newspaper), 290
Sanitary Commission, U.S., 148
sapping, 88–89, 289
Savannah, Georgia, 262, 265–278, 269*p,* 270*m*
Savannah Daily Herald (newspaper), 271, 278
Savannah Daily Republican (newspaper), 271
Savannah River, 268, 270*m*
Sawtelle, Benjamin F., 91
Sawtelle, Frank, 194, 195
Sawtelle, Judith H., 195
schools, 108, 109, 137, 283, 316
Scott, Winfield, 11
Second Freewill Baptist Church, 304
Second Regiment, NHV, 129, 303
Selective Service System, 75
Semmes, Raphael, 209
Seventh Regiment, NHV, 45, 304
Seymour, Horatio, 122
sheep, 168–169
Shenandoah Valley, 11, 167, 175*p,* 219–222, 221*m,* 242*m*
  Fourteenth Regiment in, 213, 219–222, 221*m,* 236–237
  gaps, 234
  See also Cedar Creek, battle of
Sheridan, Philip Henry, vii, 11, 216, 219–220, 221–223, 229–231, 232*p,* 233, 235–236, 237–240, 256
  appointment to major-general, 257
  at Cedar Creek, 241, 243–252, 248*p,* 249, 249*p*
Sheridan Field Hospital, 233
"Sheridan's Ride" (Read), 252
Sherman, William Tecumsah, 135, 262, 265–266, 271
shillings. *See* silver
Sickles, Daniel E., 204
Signal Knob, 241
silver, 128
Sinclair, William H.H., 314–315
Sixth Army Corps, 210, 229–231, 243, 249
Sixth Regiment, NHV, 47, 173, 174
Skinner, Benjamin C., 140, 141
Skinner's Corner, 300, 303
slaves, 61, 116, 188
  emancipation of, 45
  See also African Americans
Slitton, Phinias, 115
Smith, Benjamin Burleigh, 14, 15, 18–20, 22–23, 54, 84–85, 92, 107, 283, 285, 289
Smith, Betsey Moulton, 173
Smith, Charlotte, 301
Smith, Demerit, 287, 289
Smith, Dorcas Folsom, 14, 18, 92, 285
Smith, Dorothy, 3, 14
Smith, Edwin Augustus, 18
Smith, Elbridge, 294
Smith, Eliphalet, 3, 14, 113, 316
Smith, Elizabeth "Eliza" Webster, 3, 11, 14, 16, 27, 29, 31, 39, 40, 287, 289–290, 313
  letters from Lewis, 33–34
  letters to Lewis, 43–44
Smith, Frank B., 11, 20, 285
Smith, Hepsa A., 11, 17
Smith, Herbert H., 25, 85, 301
Smith, Hiram G., 11, 285
Smith, Jacob, 3, 14, 15, 316
Smith, James Marcellus, 85, 178, 251–252, 301
Smith, Jeremiah S., 123, 124, 136, 141, 146, 289
Smith, John, 3, 11, 14, 20, 23, 27, 109, 208–209, 287, 289–290, 316
Smith, John B., 11, 283, 285
Smith, John L., 61, 85, 86, 92, 301

Smith, John M., 301
Smith, Joseph E., 3
Smith, Leonard A., 289
Smith, Leslie, 287, 289
Smith, Levi, 11, 101, 173
Smith, Levi H., 88
Smith, Lewis E., 11, 17, 89, 153, 287
Smith, Lewis, 113
Smith, Lewis Quimby, *3p,* 167, 265, *287p,* 314
  at Camp Russell, 258–264
  at Cedar Creek, 243-252
  Corps badge, 258
  correspondents by location, 15*m*
  death of, 290–291, *291p,* 316
  diary of, 184–186, *185p,* 187, 188, 189–190, 192, 195, 197, 199, 202, 203, 204, 207, 210–211, 212, 217, 218–219, 220, 222, 224, 225, 227, 229, 235, 236, 237, 238–239, 243, *246p,* 247, 253, 255, 256–257, 258–259, 260, 261, 262, 263–264, 266–268
  discharge of, 275, 276, 277, 278
  early life of, 3
  education of, 283
  family of, 11, 14, 53, 285, 287, *287p,* 289
  farming and, 280, 283, 285, 287–288, 289
  food and, 95–96
  on furlough, 183
  gifts from, 171
  Gold Rush and, 283–284
  guard duty and, 139–141, 144–148
  at Harpers Ferry, 177–179
  health of, 13, 23, 50–51, 62, 63, 72, 77, 84–85, 91, 98, 149, 150, 203, 263
  infant son and, 153
  letters from BB, 18–20, 22–23, 84
  letters from Mother, 43–44
  letters from sister Hepsa, 114–116, 123–124
  letters from sister Lizzie, 16, 74–75, 81–83
  letters from sister Lucy, 20–22, 34–36, 41–43, 47–48, 53–56, 69, *70p,* 71–72, 80–81, 106–108, 125–127, 173–175
  letters from wife Libby, 17–18, 25–26, 44–45, 64, 65–66, 68–69, 78–79, 87, 88–89, 93–94, 100–102, 103–104, 105–106, 113–114, 121, 122–123, 127–128, 133–134, 136, 137–138, 141–143, 179, 192, 198–199, 271–273, 275–276
  letters to BB, 32–33
  letters to Father, 208–209
  letters to Mother, 33–34
  letters to sister Lucy, 32–33, 48–50, 84–85, 149–150
  letters to wife Libby, 23, 40, 52, 53, 63, 64–65, 73, 86, 90–91, 97–100, 102–103, 105, 110–111, 112–113, 114, 120–121, 128–129, 135–136, 140–141, 143–148, 153–158, 159–163, 168–173, 177–178, 179, 184–185, 186–187, 188–189, 190–191, 192–194, 196–197, 205–206, 217–218, 223, 226, 239–240, 245–246, 250–251, 274, 276–277
  as library member, 287
  marriage of, 284
  in Massachusetts, 284
  money and, 192
  morale of, 83, 111, 172-173
  in New Orleans, 180, 185–188, 209–211

in New York, 184–185
in Shenandoah Valley, 236–237
volunteers for military service, 5
in Washington, 97–116, 132–150, 154
Smith, Lizzie Ann, 73–75, 81-83
Smith, Lucy M., vii, 17
Smith, Lydia, 301
Smith, Marcellus, 238, 301
Smith, Mary Elizabeth Libby Paine, vii, 48–49, 287*p*
death of, 291–292
family of, 11, 49, 289
farming and, 64–65, 106, 109, 137, 192, 287, 289
health of, 93–94
letters from Lewis, 23, 40, 52, 53, 63, 64–65, 73, 86, 90–91, 97–100, 102–103, 105, 110–111, 112–113, 114, 120–121, 128–129, 135–136, 140–141, 143–148, 153–158, 159–163, 168–173, 177–178, 179, 184–185, 186–187, 188–189, 190–191, 192–194, 196–197, 205–206, 217–218, 223, 226, 239–240, 245–246, 250–251, 274, 276–277
letters to Lewis, 17–18, 25–26, 44–45, 64, 65–66, 68–69, 78–79, 87, 88–89, 93–94, 100–102, 103–104, 105–106, 113–114, 121, 122–123, 127–128, 133–134, 136, 137–138, 141–143, 179, 192, 198–199, 271–273, 275–276
marriage of, 284
money and, 192
politics and, 77–79, 89, 104
sapping and, 88–89
Smith, Mercy, 14
Smith, Samuel S., 52, 92, 113, 309
Smith, Sarah, 14, 15
Smithville, New Hampshire, 295
Smyth, Frederick, 159–160, 277
Snell, Jason D., 8
sounding line, 307
spies, 138–139, 138*p,* 228–229, 229*p*
Springfield rifles, 36, 39, 100, 280. *See also* weapons
Stanton, Edwin M., 5, 57, 124, 183, 235, 303
Star Redoubt, 188
Stephens, Alexander H., 275
stockading, 31–32, 37
Straw, Oceanus, 233, 233*p,* 300
Straw, Samuel, 300
Stuart, J.E.B., 116
Sturtevant, John W., 165, 165*p,* 185, 228, 305
Sumter, CSS (ship), 209
supplies, 244–245, 244*p. See also* clothing; food; wagon trains; water
Supreme Court, U.S., 304
surgeons, 51
Susquehanna River, 132
sutlers, 245, 252
Sweat, Thomas J., 88, 301

Tacony, CSS (raider), 147
Tanner, Edward E., 87–88, 89
Tanner, Henry H., 88, 126
Tanner, Joshua, 88
Tanner, Sarah, 88
Taylor, James E., 241, 248*p*
temperance movement, 24–25, 295. *See also* liquor
Tenth Regiment, NHV, 182
tents, 178, 178*p,* 203*p*
textile mills, 1, 3, 67, 92
Thanksgiving, 159–160, 232*p,* 259–260, 259*p*
Thayer, William H., 51, 299, 311

Third Regiment, NHV, 182, 183, 198, 254
Third Winchester, battle of, 108, 229–231, 230*p,* 253–254
Thirteenth Regiment, NHV, 182, 183
Thomas, George Henry, 261
Thompsonianism, 148
Tilton, Albert, 1
Tilton, N.H., 280
Tip-Top House, 122
Tolman, Flavel L., 313
Tom's Brook, 238
town meetings, 77
Townsend, E.D., 257
troop misconduct, 224, 268–269
Twelfth Regiment, NHV, 20, 46, 47, 68–69, 73–74, 79, 82, 121, 129, 132, 301, 303
Tybee Island, 268
Tyrrell, Albert H., 187, 189, 207, 228, 307
Tyrrell, J.R., 307

The Vacant Chair: The Northern Soldier Leaves Home (Mitchell), 50
vaccinations, 92, 94. *See also* medicine
Vallandigham, Clement, 69, 71, 118
Vandalia (ship), 266
Varney, Russell T., 160
Vermont Volunteers, 96
veterans, 280
Veterans Reserve Corps, 132
Vicksburg, Mississippi, 59, 118, 119, 173
Virginia, 28*m,* 116
Vittum, Lemuel F., 286
Vittum, Samuel F., 286

wagon trains, 236*p,* 238. *See also* supplies
Wallace, Alfred, 286, 314
Wallace, James, 52
Wallace, Lew, 210
War Department, 124, 147
Washington, D.C., 10, 210
    Capitol Building, 164–165, 165*p*
    Carroll Prison, 304
    Central Guard House, 110, 110*m,* 132, 138, 139
    duty stations, 110*m*
    Ferry Landing, 104*p*
    Fourteenth Regiment NHV in, 11, 26, 95–116, 110*m,* 132–150, 154, 158, 164–165, 166, 168, 179–180
    military police in, 96–97
    Navy Yard Bridge, 139, 140*p,* 144, 165
    Old Capitol Prison, 100, 100*p,* 110, 110*m,* 132, 138, 139, 304
    Seventh Street Wharf, 110
    trains to, 39–40
Washington's Birthday, 179
water, drinking, 207
Watson, Elmira, 198
Watson, Oliver, 198, 199
Watson's Hotel, 81
Waud, Alfred R., 152*p,* 216*p,* 236*p,* 249*p*
weapons, 154. *See also* muskets; pistols; rifles
Webster, Jacob, 3
Webster, James Y., 90, 91, 101
Webster, Moulton S., 8, 8*p,* 11, 90, 144, 164, 197, 233, 233*p,* 295
Webster, Samuel W., 11
Weed, Chester A., vii
Weed, Cleveland, vii
Weed, J.J., 290, 291
Weed, John J., vi*p,* vii, 287*p*
Weed, Larkin, D., vii
Weed, Leslie, vi*p,* vii, 287

Weed, Lucy M. Smith, vi*p,* vii–viii, 291
Weed, William M., 1, 6, 61–62, 62*p,* 113, 290, 299
Weeks, Franklin C., 51, 311
Welles, Gideon, 182
Wentworth Library, 290
West Virginia, 116, 167, 172, 175*p,* 176*p*
Whipple, Thomas J., 20
White, Elat, 198, 199
Wiggin, Benjamin F., 106
Wiggin, Eddie, 46
Wiggin, Edward F., 106
Wiggin, Frank, 54, 155, 198, 289
Wiggin, George W., 46–47, 48, 173, 174, 271
Wiggin, John M., 155, 156
Wiggin, Joseph Frank, 14, 15, 20
Wiggin, Lucy Jane Smith, 11, 13, 14, 15, 39, 40, 46, 155, 283, 284, 289, 313, 316
  Copperheads and, 69, 71
  furloughs and, 83
  health of, 198
  letter to Mother, 27, 29, 31
  letters from Lewis, 32–33, 48–50, 84–85, 149–150
  letters to Lewis, 20–22, 34–36, 41–43, 47–48, 53–56, 69, 70*p,* 71–72, 80–81, 106–108, 125–127, 173–175
  politics and, 79, 80–81
Wiggin, Nellie, 46
Wiggin, Polly F., 155, 156
Wilmington (steamer), 273
Wilson, Robert, 143, 143*p,* 165–166, 199, 227
Winchester National Cemetery, 233, 234*p,* 250, 251
Wirz, Henry, 275
women
  in camps, 141, 166
  employment of, 92, 113
  as spies, 138–139, 138*p,* 228–229, 229*p*
Woodman, Ben, 46, 297
Woodman, John O., 46, 46*p,* 48, 297
Woodstock Races, 238
woolen mills, 1, 3, 67
W.P. Ham Camp, 287
Wright, Rebecca, 228–229, 229*p*

Yazoo River, 127
Young America movement, 223–224

About the Author

ALAN FRASER HOUSTON graduated from Amherst College and Boston University School of Medicine. He served in the United States Navy as a flight surgeon from 1970 to 1972. He and his family settled in Sandwich, New Hampshire, near the family homestead, where they lived for over two decades before moving to Durango, Colorado. Both he and his wife, Jourdan, are life members of the Sandwich Historical Society.

Dr. Houston is the author of historical articles that have appeared in *California History: the Magazine of the California Historical Society*, the *Pioneer: the Journal of the Society of California Pioneers*, *Montana: the Magazine of Western History*, and the *Annual Excursions of the Sandwich Historical Society.* Fraser has also been researching the career of Rear Adm. Cadwalader Ringgold (1802-1867), the last of the old Navy. Fraser and Jourdan have two daughters: Clancey, who lives with her husband and two sons in Shanghai; and Sloan, who is in her senior year at Sweet Briar College in Virginia.